TROUBLESHOOTING YOUR LAN

Susan Sasser

Mary Ralston

Robert McLaughlin

Line Art by
Lora McLaughlin
(unless otherwise noted)

Photos by
Robert McLaughlin
(unless otherwise noted)

First Printing

ISBN 1-55828-168-1

Printed in the United States of America

10 9 8 7 6 5 4 3 2 1

MIS:Press books are available at special discounts for bulk purchases for sales promotions, premiums, fund-raising, or educational use. Special editions or book excerpts can also be created to specification.

For details contact: Special Sales Director
MIS:Press
a subsidiary of Henry Holt and Company, Inc.
115 West 18th Street
New York, New York 10011

Trademarks

Acknowledgements

We would like to thank the following people for their ideas and criticisms of this book as we wrote it: Cynthia Johanson, Phil Raidt, Clark Miller, Lora McLaughlin, Emil Paska, and Ian Levit.

This book would have been impossible without the assistance of Toshiba, Novell, Frye Utilities, Allyson Almieda, Computer System Products Incorporated, Brightwork Development, Kelly Christiansen of Novell, Novell Corporation, Intel, Microtest, Viteq, Cheyenne Utilities, SCO, and FTC.

Lora McLaughlin produced all her line art and flowcharts in DrawPerfect on a 286 Clone PC.

Many thanks to our friends and family who supported us throughout the editing, writing, and panicking process: Katherine Hancock Ragsdale, Ryan McKisson, John Sasser, Vic the Wonder Dog, the Drs. Cambareri, Butler, Meister and staff, the BMT Unit of Georgetown University Hospital, Mitchell Koff, Bernoulli, Katherine, Andy, Robin, Leslie Ralston, and GTE Spacenet.

TABLE OF CONTENTS

Introduction 1

How to Use This Book 1
What is a LAN? Definitions, Explanations, and Alibis 3

PART I — The Chapters 5-72

1 Getting a LAN Up and Running 7
2 The Politics of LANs 17
3 Designing a LAN 21
4 Nuts and Bolts Survival Tips for LAN Administrators 27
5 Choosing and Using Network Utilities 35
6 Survival Tips for Users 41
7 The Seven-Layer OSI Network Model 47
8 Installing LAN Cards and Drivers 57
9 WYSIWIMP: What You See Is What Might Print 63
10 E-Mail: The Most Popular Application 71

PART II — The Data Sheets 73-162

File Servers, Workstations, and the Network Operating System 75

A Novell NetWare 386 File Server 75
The Workstation 82
The Network Operating System—Novell NetWare 386 84
NetWare Loadable Modules 92
(UPS) Uninterruptible Power Supply 93
Print Server 97
Tape Backup Units 101

Network Cards and Cables 103

Network Interface Card 103
Network-To-Parallel-Port Adapters for Laptops 116
Ethernet on Coax Cable 117
Ethernet on Unshielded Twisted-Pair (UTP) — 10Base-T Ethernet 125
Fiber Optic Inter Repeater Link (FOIRL) 132
ARCNET on Coax and/or Twisted-Pair Cable 133
Token Ring Twisted-Pair Cable 141
Fiber Optic Cable 144
Wireless Network Card 145

Interconnection Devices 149

Interconnection Devices in the ISO 7-Layer Network Scheme 150
Repeaters 151
IEEE MAC-Layer Bridges 153
A Novell NetWare Router or Bridge 155
Routers 157
Gateways 158
3270 Cards and 3270 Gateways 159
Communications Servers 160

PART III — The Troubleshooting Flowcharts 163-194

Appendices 197

A: Novell NetWare Online HELP 197
B: COMCHECK — A Netware Communications-Testing Utility 199
C: List of Suppliers 201

Glossary 205

Index 217

INTRODUCTION

How To Use This Book

This book is divided into three major sections: Chapters, Data Sheets, and Troubleshooting Flowcharts. Our first book, *Fix Your Own PC*, uses the same format. We assume you have access to that manual or a similar PC repair guide. LAN problems are often traceable to broken-PC problems.

The Chapters provide introductions to topics and our opinionated advice on LANs, their installation, operation, and maintenance. We hope you'll find these interesting, but it's not necessary to read them before you start troubleshooting.

The Data Sheets provide the down and dirty details of LAN hardware, wiring, installation, and repair.

The Troubleshooting Flowcharts give you a quick way to discover what is wrong with the LAN and how to fix it.

We don't expect that you will read this book cover to cover. We hope you will be able to find what you need, quickly solve your problem, and get on with life.

Why We Wrote This Book

We wrote this book, as we wrote *Fix Your Own PC*, to keep you from falling into the hands of the fake gurus and electronic charlatans who profit whenever a necessary piece of your business equipment seems to be an indecipherable Black Box. If you thought PC repair provided expensive lessons in humankind's ability to be gulled by sleazoids, wait until your first LAN mistake. Figure on spending about ten times as much for that lesson.

We hope to save you a few of those dollars and several bits of your sanity. You may not want to do your LAN troubleshooting yourself (although we'll tell you how to prevent many problems and solve a fair number by yourself), but you'll be in a better position to tell whether the $135-an-hour "consultant" is doing you a service or doing you in.

Why Novell NetWare 386

We chose to concentrate on Novell, a decision which pre-dated their generous provision of hardware and software to set up and run our test

LAN, because NetWare is popular, sturdy, and mysterious enough to sell books. We also chose it because the majority of PC-based LANs use Novell software. Novell has the largest market share because it responds to customer concerns and it has a good track record for maintaining and improving its products. It makes a good product and has been rewarded by a loyal (though occasionally apoplectic) customer base. Part of the apoplexy is because Novell, like IBM, tends to invent its own language.

We specifically focus on NetWare 386, because 80386 computers are so cheap these days. Mail order 386s can even be ordered with NetWare already installed. Moreover, most offices over ten people will quickly outgrow NetWare 2.2 (the 286 version).

The price structure for NetWare products changes fairly rapidly, but it is currently as low as $1899 for the 20-user version of NetWare 3.11, and $3799 for the 100-user version. Where Novell NetWare was once considered impossibly pricey for small businesses, it is now a relative bargain.

Prices for Novell's 286 products are even lower ($499 for a 5-user version of NetWare 2.2), though we almost always recommend NetWare 3.11 if you intend to grow. Businesses usually underestimate LAN growth.

LANs Have Been Around for a Long Time, but They Still Seem Mysterious

In the spring of 1987, when we were all working for one of the original clone chains, our whimsical boss ran an ad for a rock-bottom LAN. For $5000, you got a PC XT file server with a 30-meg RLL drive, 2 two-floppy PC workstations, and the cards and cables to hook these things together. There were a few problems with this architecture, since Novell didn't support RLL drives at the time, but the owner suggested we hand off potential customers for this putative LAN to the staff network guru, who would sell the customer what he really needed.

The day after the LAN ad ran in the *Washington Post* Business section, a big gregarious guy sauntered into the headquarters store asking to see the bargain LAN. We asked the usual questions: What did he want to do with the LAN, how many stations did he want to network, etc. "Oh, just what I've got now, three stations." He had a four-year-old Commodore LAN in his insurance office. We never found out what he used for wiring—probably waxed string tied to tomato cans bolted to the rear of the machines. Commodores could be linked for file transfer, after a fashion, and the customer liked his network just fine. He just wanted to see what else was out there.

That same customer probably has a Novell LAN now, with remote dial-in, multi-printer queues, an X.25 board and networked FAX. Maybe not. He may just have applied a new coat of wax to the string between the Commodores.

LANs seem far more mysterious than the dependable old PC, which was once just as unfathomable. Now that people have finally become comfortable with their desktop PCs, the machines all sprout cable out their rear slots and hook up together. We hope to take some of the mystery out of networks for you, whether you're the purchaser, administrator, or user.

Our approach is practical and hands-on. We don't quote many current prices, because they change too fast. A quick look through the computer magazines or newspaper business section will bring you up to date on any product we mention. We discuss products that we use and like, but we don't aim to review every product in a given category. As former service manager, engineering tech, and store manager, we tend to adopt reliable solutions and stick with them. You'll see a good many references to WordPerfect, PCTools, and QAPlus/fe because we use these products. There are other good ones too, ones that you may like better.

Don't be intimidated by your LAN. If you have enjoyed tinkering with PCs, you'll enjoy tinkering with the LAN. Don't singe your eyebrows, but have fun with it.

What We Expect You To Know

Because we are going to jump into LAN installation immediately in the first chapters, you need a good background in PCs. We expect you to know:

- basics of PC operation
- PC card installation
- hardware basics (IRQ's, memory address, etc.)

If you don't have this background, refer to the Data Sheets in the back of this book, especially the section on Network Interface Cards, and/or a good PC repair manual whenever you get stuck. Novell's red **Concepts** manual, which comes with your network software, should be useful too.

What Is a LAN? Definitions, Explanations, and Alibis

A LAN is a number of PCs (or Macintoshes) interconnected to communicate and share resources, such as disk storage, printers, and modems.

Elementary? You knew all that? You'd be amazed how often the innocent think that a LAN provides processing horsepower for the user applications. Not so. The user program runs just where it used to, on your workstation. If word processing runs at glacial speed on the wheezy XT, connecting it to a LAN just uses up some RAM and lets it use a group printer, a process that takes longer than using a local printer.

A few client-server database applications use the file server as a SQL server, notably Novell's BTRIEVE. These databases are searched and sorted on the server rather than at the workstation. Since writing software that shares the file server with NetWare is no trivial task, most database servers require a dedicated machine.

But 99 percent of PC networks are not running distributed applications or SQL databases. The program and files live on the file server, but the processing happens on the workstations. We wouldn't take the time to point all this out, except that we've met so-called network consultants who don't know this.

You can skip this chapter, and any others, if you know networks and want to proceed straight to the Data Sheets and Troubleshooting Flowcharts to solve immediate problems. Network neophytes are invited to browse through this explanation of LAN parts and pieces and how they work together.

Let us define some LAN terms.

File Server. The machine the network software runs on. It's where the files that are stored on the network physically live. This PC is usually a 386 or 486 with at least one large hard drive (300 MB is the standard for medium-sized networks; you could get by with a 130 MB drive with a small network). This machine is used only as a file server and runs no user application software, unless you are using a "nondedicated" network operating system (which we do not recommend). The file server may contain just one network interface card (NIC) or multiple cards, and it's connected to the workstations either by a direct wire bus (Ethernet), through a hub (ARCNET), or a concentrator (10Base-T, 10Base-F, and 1Base5).

Workstation. Also called a node. This is the user PC which runs everyday applications. This machine can be an XT on up; some networks have more powerful workstations than file servers, if the user application would benefit (mathematical analysis and CAD applications, especially).

Print Server. A PC dedicated to printing, or a specialized device (a small box) which performs only print server duties. It handles the printer, feeding it print jobs from print queues stored on a file server. This computer (an XT will do) is not available for user programs. A separate print server computer is optional in your network, since the file server can do double duty, running print server software along with the NetWare operating system software. In Chapter 9 we compare the five ways to set up network printing.

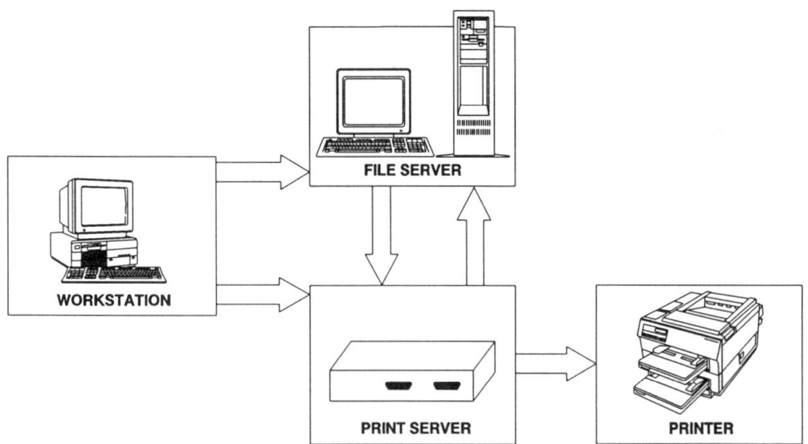

File server, workstation, print server, and printer.

Network Interface Card (NIC). The card you stick in your machine to make the physical connection to the network. A socket at the back of the card provides connection to whatever network wiring you use. Many network cards use idiot lights on the back of the card to show if it is working properly.

The Wire. We still call it "the wire," but it's a coax cable, twisted-pair wire, or fiber optic cabling. The wire connects the file server, any other servers, and the workstations together. See the Data Sheets for details on all the various combinations of wire medium and wiring geometry (also called topology).

Network Software. In the beginning there was XNS (Xerox Network System), the grandfather of all PC network sofware, and even of the OSI model. GCom, 3Com, Corvus, IBM's PC LAN (now Microsoft's LAN Manager), and Novell were all descendants. The strongest survivor right now is Novell NetWare.

Peer-to-Peer Architecture. In this particular network architecture, any one computer can make a request of any other computer. There is no dedicated file server, nor any machine dedicated to only one task. Although peer-to-peer is usually considered suitable only for small networks, the largest network in the world is peer-to-peer: Internet, a world-wide network of UNIX computers. NetWare Lite and LANTASTIC are peer-to-peer network software.

Client-Server Architecture. In this network architecture, client machines make requests of other machines called servers. The work flow is from many points to a central point. In practice, many UNIX networks have a dual flavor: a machine can be both a client and a server. In the PC world, though, client-server usually means the plain-vanilla architecture in which workstations request services and files from a file server. Novell NetWare (but not NetWare Lite) is client-server, with PC and Mac clients requesting services from the NetWare file server(s) and print server(s).

Part I
The Chapters

CHAPTER 1

Getting a LAN Up and Running

Novell assumes a professional LAN consultant or certified engineer is installing NetWare 3.x, not an end user or even the average small-network supervisor. And yet, with PC repair experience and no network experience, I (Sue) did it. I'll tell you the story. Please remember, as you read, this chapter is not a guide to installation—see your Novell **Installation** manual for that. Read this chapter for the tale of a real-life LAN complete with booby traps.

You might as well know, up front, that I'd never used a network before I installed my first one. Honestly, I had never typed the fatal phrase "Login SUPERVISOR." In fact, I'd never even typed the word "Login" as an ordinary user.

Since both Mary and Bob are network veterans, I was clearly the right guinea pig to oversee NetWare 3.10 installation on our test LAN. We would be installing Ethernet cards and thin coax cable—again, totally new to me.

The Scene

A large room containing a defunct ARCNET network (it never worked) in an ordinary office building set in ordinary suburban sprawl. This office building was, we eventually discovered, serviced by one of the most erratic electric utility companies in the Mid Atlantic (names have been omitted to protect the guilty). A pile of crisp red boxes, and a dog pound collection of old PC clones.

The Players

Me. Two guys who have never installed a network either, but think they know a lot. Another guy who knows he knows nothing.

Sunday Morning

We open the Novell carton. There are lots of red three-ring binders with obscure names. **Print Server**—what's that? **BTRIEVE**? Ah, **Novell NetWare 386 Installation**! OK, let's go.

<My first error. You should find the ***Supplements*** *manual as well as the* ***Installation*** *manual.* ***Supplements*** *is hardware supplements—the nitty-gritty card and cable installation information for Ethernet, ARCNET, Token Ring, 3COM Etherlink, and the IBM PC Network. The IBM PC Network is not, as you might guess, merely a network running on IBM PCs or PC clones. Nope, it is altogether different — a proprietary IBM network system with its own cabling rules and proprietary adapters. So this IBM PC Network section is irrelevant to those of us using ordinary Ethernet network cards and cabling.>*

I start flipping through **Installation**, but it is not very helpful. It is very explicit about dedicated power lines and uninterruptible power supplies, then it skips to installing memory, hard disks and hard disk interface boards in the file server. After that, it appears to cover only software installation. A little hardware installation pamphlet which shows network card switch settings comes with the network boards (Novell's NE1000 and NE2000 Ethernet boards for 8-bit and 16-bit computers). But there's no explicit start-to-finish hardware directions integrated with the software installation directions. Therefore, we run into a problem. Should we put the network cards into the workstations first—yeah, probably. How about putting a network card in the server? Yeah, that sounds right too; they seem to be expecting a network card in the server here on page 147. How about cabling everything up? Well, maybe not. They never said to attach the cables, so it must come later.

I don't really know where to start. Before he left, Bob gave us all a firm handshake and the advice, "Get the workstations and file server running okay with DOS, then install the cards, then install NetWare." I guess we'll start with the computers.

My three assistants have been working with the computers and the ARCNET network that never really worked (no criticism of ARCNET intended, it was bad cards and software misinstallation, not ARCNET itself, that killed the old network). I hand two of them workstation configuration sheets and tell them to pop the covers off the computers, pull out the old ARCNET cards, test that the machines boot DOS, and install our NE1000 and NE2000 cards. The third guy can do the clone 386 file server—which unfortunately has only a 5-1/4" disk drive. We better add a 3-1/2" drive as the A: drive so the file server can read the NetWare 3-1/2" diskettes.

<Big mistake. They were over-eager and anxious lest they miss anything. Though they collectively had enough skill to fix the miscellaneous bad drives in the workstations and transplant a working 3-1/2" disk drive from one of the workstations to the file server, this one lacked a screw-driver, that one a DOS boot disk (or even a blank disk to make a new one), the third didn't have a clue about PC repair so he wanted to watch the others to see how it was done (but he did know where to find a blank diskette). In addition, they wanted to go ahead and do something *instead of wasting time reading the manuals. We compromised—I read the manuals and held them back, they kept starting off in one direction or another half-cocked, but stopped when I insisted. I decided to work alone next time.>*

Two hours later we have a working 386 computer with 2 Meg of memory and a 3-1/2" floppy drive, plus four workstations that boot DOS, format diskettes and copy files. All ARCNET cards have been removed. It's time to fill out the file server and workstation configuration worksheets and install the Ethernet cards.

I figure the network cards all need to be set to the same configuration so they can communicate with each other.

<Don't laugh, it's an easy mistake to make, especially since Novell ***Installation*** *says "Set the same configuration option on like network boards for all your workstations. This reduces the number of master workstation diskettes you have to make," page 163.>*

We are having a heck of a time coming up with a configuration option (a combination of base I/O address and interrupt number) that will work fine with all four of the workstations and the file server. One workstation has both a serial port and a modem (we want to keep both). That eliminates the default configuration of 300h base I/O address and IRQ3 because the modem is a second COM port and already uses IRQ3.

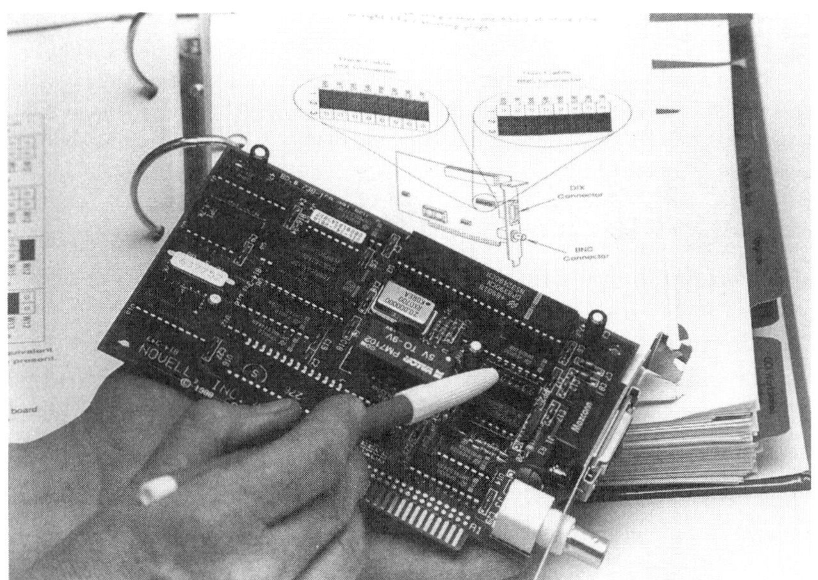

Figure 1.1 *Carefully check the jumper settings against those found in* Supplements.

Finally, we decide to standardize on base I/O address 360h and Interrupt 5 (IRQ5). None of our computers have a second parallel printer port, the normal IRQ5 user. This works fine for the four NE2000 network boards installed in the 286 and 386 computers, but the NE1000 board for our XT workstation is a problem. A footnote in the NE1000 installation chart says IRQ5 is not available in a PC XT or equivalent when hard disk controller is present. In exasperation, we decide to yank the hard disk out of the XT and stick with our original plan.

<Major misunderstanding here! The configuration options do not have to be the same in all the workstations. The base I/O address is an inside-the-computer address, not a network-card-on-the-network-cable address. Therefore, we can set each workstation to a different configuration option, or all to the same option — it has absolutely nothing to do with the cards communicating with each other! An appropriate configuration option allows the card to talk to the computer it's in, without interfering with the other hardware already installed in this computer. So I tortured us all for no reason.>

Finally, we've got all five Ethernet boards installed, the File Server Worksheet started, and four Workstation Configuration Worksheets started. The worksheets have a lot more empty fields than filled-in ones, but I guess everything is going okay.

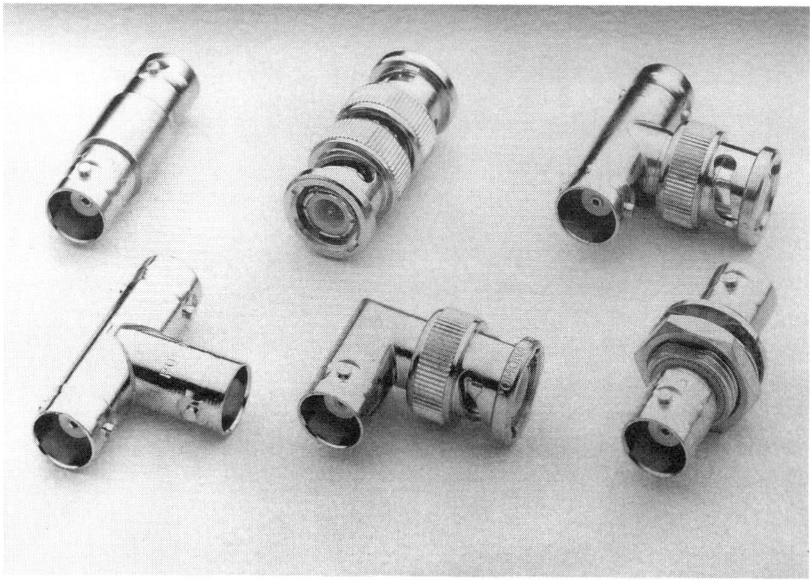

Figure 1.2 *Typical Ethernet T fittings. Photo courtesy of Specialized Products.*

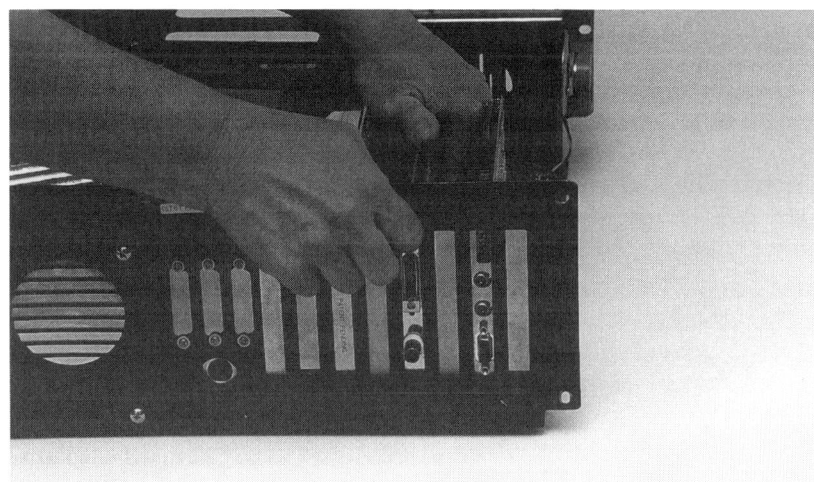

Figure 1.3 *Installing an Ethernet card.*

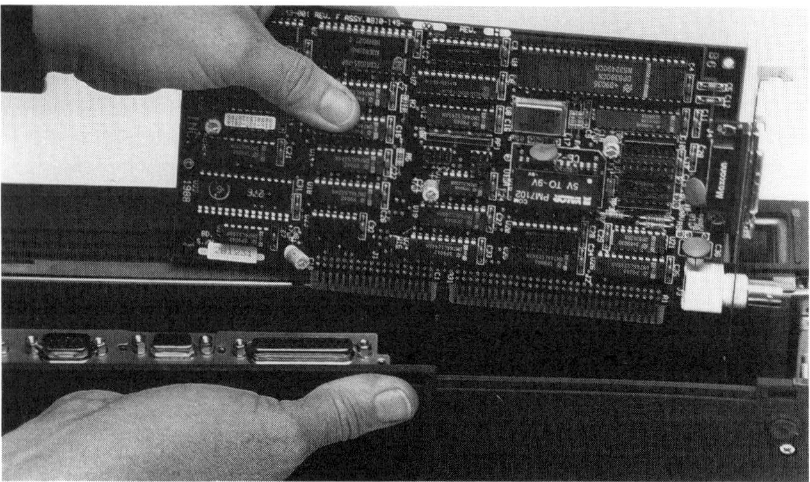

Figure 1.4 *Installing an Ethernet card in a Toshiba 5200 portable.*

Lunchtime

Pizza all around. I try to feel relaxed about blowing an entire morning getting the computers working and the cards installed. At least we're ready to start installing the software itself this afternoon.

Back to the Installation Manual

This is fairly intimidating. In *Where to begin*, before we even get to the numbered pages, they're throwing trick questions at me like "Choose between DOS Workstation Installation and DOS ODI Workstation Installation," page xii. Don't panic. Start at the first direction: "Read *Site Preparation* to ensure your working environment, power requirements, and working diskettes are ready."

Site and Equipment Preparation says I need dedicated power lines and power conditioning equipment. Surely not. I can't believe that all networks use dedicated power lines (that means a separate electrical circuit with its own breaker for the network outlets). We haven't acquired a UPS, an Uninterruptible Power Supply, either (our "power conditioning equipment"). They also want us to treat the carpeting against static electricity and connect one megohm resistors to each computer to bleed off static electricity. Are these guys for real? This cannot be true; it must be the standard boilerplate to cover Novell in case anything goes wrong, like my periodontist who tells me to floss my teeth three times a day, then blames me for not following his advice when I have gum trouble. You ever try finding a place to floss three times a day? Perhaps in the bathroom at McDonald's? I decide to ignore the warnings.

> *<An error? I don't know. Our test network worked fine for the first month without a UPS, and fine after that with it. On the other hand, when I moved our test LAN to another office I had to load the software on a different server. The new office had window air conditioners on the LAN power lines and the electric company was doing rolling brownouts in the summer heat. Despite the UPS, we got lots of ABEND errors (which are often power-quality errors). I managed to blow up the SYSCON file on*

our original NetWare disks when the file server ABENDed and apparently had disk drive convulsions while I was in the middle of installing NetWare. On the other hand, what fool was using the original NetWare diskettes instead of working copies?>

The last directive: Make working copies of the NetWare diskettes. So we did.

<We used working copies for this installation, then lost track of them in the move to the new office.>

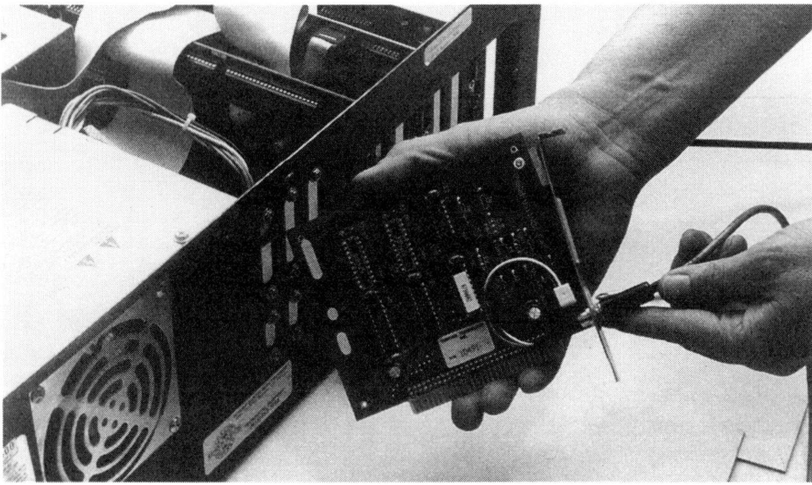

Figure 1.5 *Installing the UPS card into the file server.*

At the end of *Site Preparation*, the *Where To Go From Here* chart on page 5 of the **Installation** manual says: "If you need to ... Complete a first-time file server installation... see *File Server Installation* on page 111."

<Major error. The next line in the chart is "If you need to ... Install cabling before installing the file server software ... see the installation supplements or the documentation that comes with your network board(s)." I did indeed need to install cabling, but I jumped instead to File Server Installation. *This will cause suffering later when I combine it with a second misinterpretation.>*

File Server Installation asks us to calculate the memory we need for the file server. We have an 80 MB (megabyte) hard disk and intend to make only one NetWare volume, so the calculation looks like this:

Memory Needed for DOS volume = (.23 X 80) / block size
Total memory needed = Memory for DOS volume + 2 megabytes

We only have 2 megabytes in the file server, we're clearly low on memory. The manual says "NetWare 386 supports 386-based hardware with a recommended minimum configuration of 4MB of RAM." I decide to give it a try with 2 megabytes anyway.

The NetWare installation is uneventful, though stressful, as we gradually work and guess our way through the instructions and questions like: "Do we want to Mirror disks? How big should the Hot Fix Area be? Do you think our hard disk controller uses Port 1F0 and Interrupt E?"

We'll be booting our server from its own hard disk, so we prepare a 5 megabyte DOS hard disk partition with FDISK and FORMAT. This will hold the boot files and SERVER.EXE, "the DOS executable file that establishes the NetWare operating system." I remember what Bob says, that we should be certain we have completely removed the old files from the server (unless we're doing an upgrade of the Netware Operating System software, and doing it as per Novell instructions). Since we're replacing NetWare 286 running on ARCNET with NetWare 386 on an Ethernet network, we'd better reformat the hard disk (low level) and repartition it to remove all alien bits. We don't want any old ARCNET or 286 files around. It takes 20 minutes extra, but we "Format Disk Drive."

We copy SERVER.EXE, the LAN card driver for our NE2000 Ethernet card, our hard disk driver, and VREPAIR.EXE to the DOS partition. Okay, the DOS partition is all set.

Next we run SERVER.EXE, name the file server, and give it an internal network number (you make these up). We load the hard disk driver and the INSTALL utility. Using INSTALL, we create NetWare volumes on the hard disk, mount them, and copy the SYSTEM and PUBLIC files to the NetWare partition of hard disk.

> <*It was midafternoon of the first day. I didn't know it at the time, but I had everything in place for a functioning server. The SERVER file was running (that makes a NetWare server), the ISADISK hard disk driver was loaded (the server could talk to its own hard disk), the NetWare volumes were mounted and full of NetWare files. We had not loaded the LAN card driver (we couldn't talk to the network cable yet), and we needed to load a heck of a lot of NLMs (NetWare Loadable Modules) before the file server would* do anything *but the basics were all in place. Unfortunately, we took a series of wrong turns next, and it would take almost 24 hours to return to this exact point again.*>

We are about 90 percent through the installation process (though we didn't know it) and it's time to load the NMAGENT module. One of my helpers is certain this is the Network Management module, the module that lets the file server talk to the workstations.

> <*It isn't. In fact, there is no Network Management module in NetWare 3.10. NMAGENT, as the* **Installation** *manual clearly states, "enables other LAN drivers to load." The name is probably a contraction for NetWare Module AGENT rather than a dyslexic adaptation of MaNAGEmeNT.*>

We probably should be cabled up when we load NMAGENT, and it doesn't seem wise to connect network cables with the power on. We shut off the file server to cable up, we then hook up all the Ethernet cables, including the T connectors and terminating resistors. See Figures 1.6 through 1.8. But we can't restart where we left off.

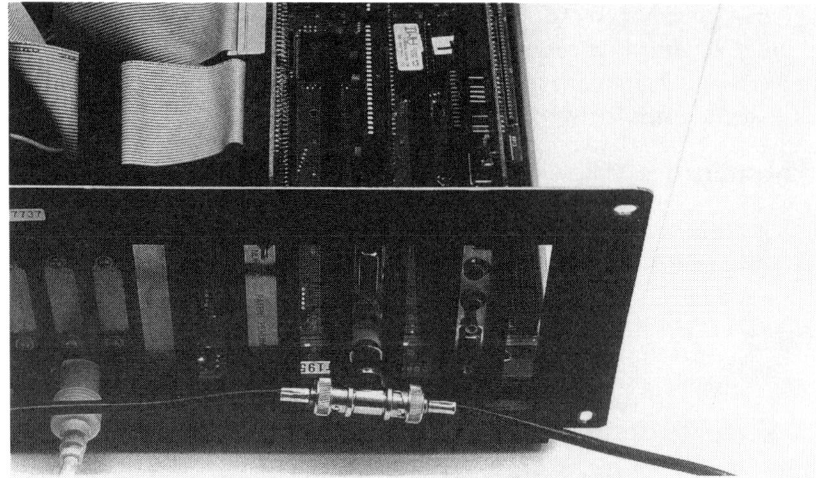

Figure 1.6 *Thin Ethernet cable and T connector at a typical workstation.*

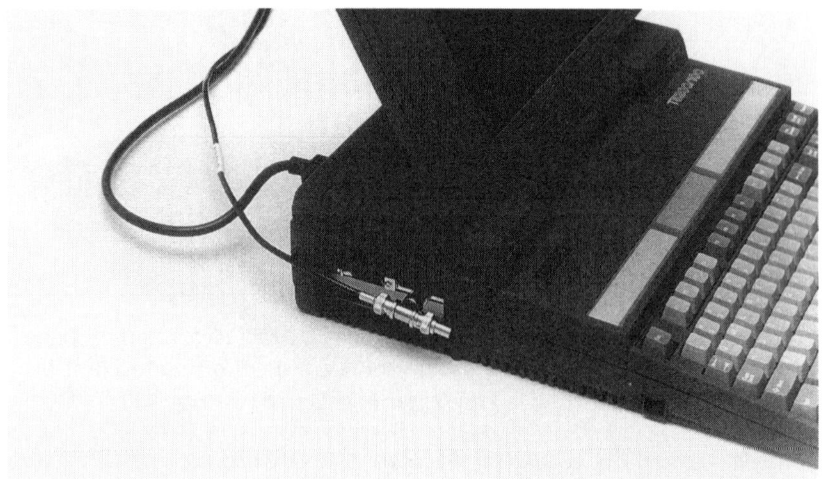

Figure 1.7 *One end of an Ethernet cable run must have a plain terminating resistor.*

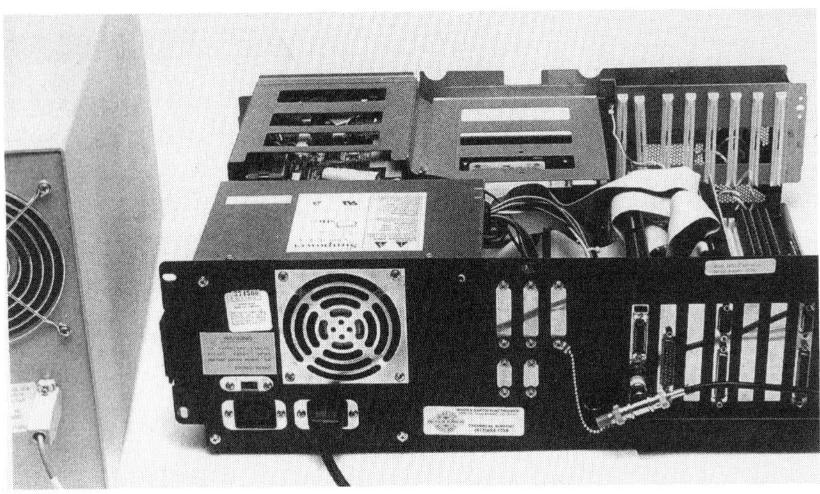

Figure 1.8 *The other end of an Ethernet cable run must have a terminating resistor with grounding cap. Note the short chain from cable to computer case.*

I call Bob, who confirms my worst fear — we have to start over from the beginning. When installing NetWare 386 program files, we can't stop half way through. Even if it appears to be the end of a section and time to load an entirely different module, you won't be able to continue where you left off.

> *<This is not exactly true. You can stop half way through, but you'll have to reload the disk driver and INSTALL, and use INSTALL to mount the NetWare volume(s), etc., being careful not to miss a single detail. Then you can proceed again. The trouble is, you have to really, really know how NetWare 3.1 works to get back to the right place without going through all the steps as per the* ***Installation*** *manual. And I didn't know NetWare 3.1 at all then — witness my willingness to believe the wild tale about "NMAGENT, the Network Management module that lets the file server talk to all the workstations.">*

We start over from the beginning (that means low level format of file server drive, set up a DOS partition, copy files to the DOS partition, etc. — the whole ugly story).

Finally, back to the place where we were two hours ago. Time to load NMAGENT. The file server chokes at the same place, but gives a different error. This time we have an "Insufficient Returnable Memory to load file" error. The lesson: They weren't kidding about the memory-needed calculations on page 113 of the **Installation** manual. We do the calculations again, with more respect this time.

Memory Needed for DOS volume = (.23 X 80)/block size
= 18MB/block size

Total memory needed = Memory for DOS volume + 2 megabytes

The file server is an old 386. It will only hold 4 MB of memory on the mainboard. If 2 MB goes to NetWare, we've got to pick a really big block size to get the additional memory needed for the DOS volume below 2 MB. We can choose from 4K (the default), 8K, 16K, 32K, or 64K blocks. A bigger block size will waste more of the hard disk if we have a lot of little files, but can't be helped. 16K gets us an acceptable number:

Memory Needed for DOS volume = (.23 X 80)/16 = 1.15 MB of RAM

We get two more SIMM memory modules for the file server from the computer warehouse store down the street, increasing the memory to 4 megabytes.

Unfortunately, when we install the extra memory in the file server we get a CMOS setup error. Bad memory settings, it says. We try to write the correct memory numbers in the CMOS, but the computer will not set the memory right. It has 4 Megs of RAM, but thinks it's got 5. Reluctantly, we decide this computer is hopeless as our file server.

We have a second 386—maybe it will work. We'll come back tomorrow and give it a try.

Monday Morning

The other 386 computer, one we originally planned to use as a workstation, works fine. The CMOS setup goes fine. Okay, we'll start from the beginning again and reload the NetWare software. It's a new hard disk (100 megabytes this time), so we'll low level format it and do everything step-by-step. Since it's our third time through we're getting pretty slick (though we forget to mount the NetWare volume because we're so slick we don't follow the written directions anymore). Still, a minor problem, and easily fixed (just mount it!) when we finally figure out what is wrong.

Everything loads okay now. We come to NMAGENT, and breeze right through. The Novell manual tells us to:

Load NMAGENT.

Load LAN card driver(s). (Now the server can talk to its LAN card, but card can't talk to its network cable yet.).

Bind (connect) the IPX protocol to the LAN driver (now the file server's LAN card can talk to the cable).

Give the network a unique number (you make it up).

We check the NetWare boot files, STARTUP.NCF and AUTOEXEC.NCF, for errors or additions and we're done.

The file server boots. Using a newly-created NetWare workstation diskette, we can test it. It's up to me. What do I do? One of my helpers says "Type IPX" and I do. "Type NET4" and I do. "Type LOGIN" and I do. Name? They want a name—whose name? He tells me to "LOGIN SUPERVISOR" and damn if the blasted thing doesn't work!

It works! It works! It can't do a bloody thing but log me in, but I'm delighted.

We need an application program. WordPerfect (the five-user network version) installs fairly easily. Though an ordinary non-network copy of WordPerfect seems to work fine when we run it from WordPerfect files stored on a workstation's local hard drive (in other words, running the program like it was on a standalone computer), I can't get the network version to kick over at first. When I finally get the MAP commands and the trustee rights worked out (so the user can find and access the word processor files stored on the file server) the network version works great too. The instructions in the Novell manuals for MAP and trustee rights are clear, but it still requires a lot of trial and error because Novell's examples don't exactly match my situation.

Now that we've got word processing, we need a network printer. We'll run the LaserJet directly off the file server because this test LAN is small, it's all in one room. Besides, we don't have enough workstations to waste one as a dedicated print server. Therefore, we need to load PSERVER.NLM (the print server NetWare Loadable Module that runs on the file server).

The printer won't work. Though we try and try, setting up print server and print queues, then trashing those queues and setting up others, it just won't work. We get the error "Printer port requested by printer 0, print 0, is already in use. Printer not initialized." According to the Novell manual, this error means: "Another printer is using the port requested by the specified printer." That's silly. There is no other printer using this port. And there's only one printer port in the file server. We check the server with QAPlus/fe—no interrrupt conflicts (the network card is using IRQ5, the LPT2 interrupt, and our printer port at LPT1 is using IRQ7).

Maybe the network hates the LaserJet. Nope, exactly the same trouble when I substitute an old Epson for the LaserJet.

Finally, we decide to try setting up the XT workstation as a dedicated print server, running the PSERVER.EXE program. It works fine. We can print, once we issue the necessary CAPTURE commands, to either the Epson or the LaserJet. It's hard to remember the exact CAPTURE command, complete with queue name and timeout switches, etc. — I must have mistyped it six times before I finally got it exactly right. I better put CAPTURE into the system login script. It will load whenever anybody logs in to the network and will automatically redirect all printer traffic from their workstation's LPT1 port to the print queue attached to the dedicated print server and the LaserJet.

To my surprise, putting CAPTURE in the login script is a tricky problem. Can't put it at the top, I get a "Bad command or file name" error message. I move it down in the script so CAPTURE runs after I've mapped a search drive to the PUBLIC directory, where the CAPTURE file is stored. It still chokes. Finally I realize that CAPTURE is an EXE file, and not part of the normal login script language. You can use a DOS EXE file in the login script, but only if it's prefaced with a # symbol. So the script line #CAPTURE works, (if you're careful to put # CAPTURE after the MAP commands).

I'm still puzzled, though, by my inability to drive the LaserJet printer off a file-server-based print server. PSERVER.NLM should have worked. When I call Novell, the technician has never heard of the problem, and is unable to replicate it himself on his server. Nevertheless, he thinks the problem is caused by the network card. He wants us to reconfigure the card so it uses IRQ3, which is not a parallel port interrupt, instead of IRQ5.

Bob, Mary, and I consult, decide the Novell guy must be crazy and his suggestion couldn't possibly work, then do what he suggested. It works.

> *<When the print server software sees something using IRQ5 (the interrupt that would normally be used by a second parallel printer port, LPT2), it apparently assumes a printer is hooked up to LPT2 on the file server. PSERVER's phantom "printer" doesn't respond appropriately at all — I should guess it wouldn't, it's a network card, not a printer. Therefore, the PSERVER.NLM program bombs out.>*

Postscript

It took three more weeks to set up reasonable network security, with MAP commands, login scripts, trustee rights to various directories, and appropriate user rights. I set up, then scrapped, two different directory tree designs — aggravating the new network users mightily. Since it was an experimental network, we allowed multiple SUPERVISOR-EQUIVALENT users — which aggravated me mightily. Do not do these things, to yourself or to your users. If you insist on setting up your network security yourself, plan on wasting some time following blind alleys. Don't let anyone start using the network for real work until you've smoothed out the rough spots.

Admittedly, I'm a hardware person and not particularly adept or patient with software. Nevertheless, I suspect my experience may be typical — it took two days to get the hardware working, and twenty days to get the NetWare software configured so it met our work needs.

Then again, I'd never seen or worked on a network — and I didn't have this book to help me. Believe me, if I can do it, no matter how painful it was, so can you. And, for the majority of you who are already overburdened with your regular duties, you will have a better idea what you need to contract out and what you can do in-house.

CHAPTER 2
The Politics of LANs

When the LAN was put in, did your job double? Or, when your company didn't fill vacant positions, did you inherit a network? Maybe you're in a bifurcated situation—two or more departments share one network, but no one manager has responsibility or funds to spend on the LAN.

Small offices cannot afford to hire a person solely to take care of the network, but certain tasks have to be done by someone, and done consistently. It's not uncommon for the best secretary in an office to be handed the responsibility for the network, sometimes in addition to her usual job. This may sound like a nightmare situation to professional LAN managers and CNEs, but it happens out there in the messy real world. It can actually be fun, if you get it organized right.

In this chapter, we share some tips on handling the political difficulties inherent in LANs and LAN jobs. Chapter 4 looks at some ways to handle the system administrator chores, Chapter 5 looks at useful network utility programs, and Chapter 6 provides tips for users to understand and control their network environment.

Is LAN Administration a Good Career Path?

Organizationally speaking, the network systems administrator is only visible when things go wrong. The administrator is identified with the machinery, which gets attention when it doesn't work, not when it does. Getting only negative attention is not a profitable career path, since most of us try to move up by gaining favorable attention. What's more, the systems administrator has to impose restrictions and limitations, like passwords, access, and hard disk storage space. And the network has to be brought down occasionally for repair and upgrade (during working hours if the administrator isn't paid to come in on Sundays). It takes a fair amount of self-promotion and in-house PR to create your own favorable notice. These are not usually the primary talents of computer folk and over-worked secretaries.

However, if you like running networks, and have a knack for them, systems administrators in large firms who have a CNE (Certified Novell Engineer) certificate and several years experience make about $70,000 a year, running 1000-user LANs with 8 or 10 people reporting to them. At the other end of the scale is the junior Paradox programmer who also minds the network, and does it all for $18,000 year. It all depends on the value the organization places on the job, as well as the size of the company and the size of its networks.

How to Handle Orphan LANs

Orphan LANs cross department boundaries. Because they have no corporate parent, they must beg for resources from both. Corporate budgeting policies can worsen matters: an accounting distinction between operating and capital budgets can create hardware-heavy networks (capital budget) with no overtime authorized for backups and upgrades (operating budget).

Whatever your situation, here are some tips that may save your sanity and/or your job. Authority and financing for the LAN must 1) come from the Big Boss or 2) come from a committee of LAN-consumers that crosses all of the departmental lines crossed by the LAN.

Option 1. Report to the Big Boss

If you administer a network that crosses domains (two departments), you may find that neither department has the responsibility for maintaining or upgrading the LAN. Neither your boss nor the other manager wants to commit money from her budget. You'll have to go about this in a style that fits your organization, whether that's in-your-face tactics or smooth politics, but you want to end up reporting to whoever both managers work for.

Find out what mission-critical applications are running on your orphaned LANs. "Mission-critical" just means "makes money." Keep a record of what happens when important applications and users aren't happy. Armed with a Disaster Log, your manager and his peers might well decide that LAN expenditures should come out of the Big Boss's pocket, not theirs. We won't tell you how to pull the strings in your company to get the Big Boss's ear, but that's the main aim here.

Option 2. Report to a Committee

You can instead campaign for a committee to take charge of the LAN. This solution works well in government agencies where networks cross a number of fiefdoms. All the relevant department managers should be represented, by someone who has the power to commit some dollars.

The only alternative to these solutions, in the long run, is to get another job. You'll only be visible when something goes wrong, you'll have no authority to prevent disasters, and that's no way to keep your present job or get a better one in the same company.

Should you Administer a LAN Part Time?

It all depends on the size and the purpose of the LAN, of course. Big federal agency networks require one full-time LAN support person for every 20 users. A network with all non-technical users will need more training time (a network full of technical users will have its own problems!). Twenty users is a convenient dividing line between part-time and full-time LAN administration.

Your software applications also affect the amount of administrative time needed to oversee a LAN. A word processing and E-Mail LAN will reach a fairly large size before it needs a full-time person to manage it. A heavily-used database application LAN will ordinarily be managed by the chief database programmer. She will need an assistant when LAN management starts cutting into her programming time.

Power Peacocks and Their Toys

The OSI seven-layer network model should include an eighth layer: the Political Layer. The politics and organization of a company can transform a so-so LAN into a useful tool, or a technically great network into a nuisance or a potential disaster. How an office LAN works depends on the politics of the office—a well-run company has solid networks that help people get their work done. A volatile company with difficult departmental relations will have troublesome equipment as well as troublesome people.

Some of the equipment trouble is directly traceable to the policy of awarding senior people higher budgets for computers than the people who use them all day. The Executroid boasts a rarely-used Mac II and a color Laserwriter on his credenza, while the department receptionist, who also word processes stacks of letters all day, struggles with her creaky XT with a monochrome monitor.

Many LAN troubles may be traced to a clash between the MIS department and the rest of the corporate world. An otherwise engineering-hip company can be saddled with an MIS department that wants to control all corporate computing but doesn't have a clue about the LANs. This kind of internal politicking leads enterprising and desperate managers to subvert mainframe rules and security. Consider a manager who needs to analyze mainframe data, but can't get an application out of the MIS department in less than 24 months. If company policy allows any senior manager an SNA port into the mainframe system by request, nothing prevents a resourceful manager from hooking up his department network to the port and sucking in the data he needs for processing by his network. If he then ties in modems so his programmers can work off-site, mainframe security is destroyed.

Too many MIS departments are run by people who came up the ranks on the non-programming side. They know the bureaucracy, but they don't know present-day computing, where the real action is out on the desktops, not in the Ops rooms with the raised floors. As *PC Magazine* quipped recently, "What's a mainfame? The biggest PC peripheral you can buy."

What is a Good LAN?

The real issues are organizational and political. A bad LAN crashes at 4 p.m. every other day because the wiring doesn't get fixed, is managed by a distracted systems administrator who has too many bosses, loses your files, and has the printer attached to a dedicated machine in a locked room down a long hall. The workstations are awarded by seniority instead of need and half-repaired when they break. The file server's disk drive is always full. The software is two versions outdated. The operating systems on the workstations haven't been upgraded since DOS 3.1. The users end up running local copies of their applications, saving to their own hard disks, and losing their files when these local hard disks crash.

The very worst LANs are caused by incompetent consultants. A possibly apocryphal story concerns a dBase IV application that took a year to write, and then was put up on a 1000-user network, immediately crashing it. There is no possible way a 1000-user database application can run on a PC network without using a database server.

A good LAN stays up, has backups for the files you accidentally delete and need two months later, is fixed promptly when it has problems, has sensible upgrades to software, a trained systems administrator who has the boss's ear, and prints no more slowly than any LAN. This system can be any size, from four stations to a thousand. It's been our pleasure to use these networks, and we hope we remember to thank the administrators who make it happen. It's like thanking running water, think of life without it.

A good LAN administrator asks the users what they prefer in monitors, keyboards, chairs, and the other equipment that can make a real difference in workplace health. Some jurisdictions have regulations about CRT emissions. Others mandate operator rest breaks.

Ergonomic concerns are real. An 8-hour day on a terminal can cripple hands, eyes, and backs. Forty percent of the classified advertising staff of a Washington, D.C., newspaper suffers from repetitive stress injury (RSI), the umbrella term for carpal tunnel syndrome and similar maladies. This is no joke. If left untreated, these injuries can prevent you from driving a car, holding a book or a fork, or lifting your grandchild. The hands, elbows, shoulders, and/or wrists just don't work anymore. Full-time data entry employees, primarily women, are rated by the number of keystrokes or lines they produce a day, so they are effectively chained to the keyboard and terminal, under stress. Good system administrators and good LAN consultants take the time to find out what equipment is the best for the users. In most cases, users know what designs are comfortable and efficient. If people at your workplace are already experiencing RSI symptoms, early diagnosis and treatment can be critical in preventing further damage.

Three Real Reasons for a LAN and One Excuse

How do you know if you need a LAN? There are four reasons for organizations to have LANs:

1) there is a real need to share information
2) information must be kept secure
3) we have money left in the computer budget and we better blow it on something (the happy result of zero-based budgeting)
4) status

The first reason, a real need to share information, kicks in when you buy a piece of software that requires a LAN, such as some accounting packages. Or management may believe that electronic mail and group schedulers will improve productivity. In a well-run office, that's probably true. In a crazy one, it's an electronic KYA exercise.

Many offices that do government contracting need to keep information secure. The CIA is not the only agency that needs secure computers. The Department of Agriculture has a very secure LAN in the crop prediction office. A secure LAN puts the server(s) and concentrators in a room with limited access, and has few if any workstations with diskette drives. This limits the possibility that information can leave the LAN. We talk more about security in Chapter 4.

Zero-based budgeting, which rewards a department head for using up his budget before the end of the fiscal year, accounts for many of the LAN installations in the D.C. area. The Federal agencies start calling for quotes in July to get the money spent before October 1. In November, corporations using a January 1 fiscal year swamp the dealers with orders. Zero-based budgeting is not a good reason to install a LAN, though it keeps many consultants employed. Once the equipment is stacked up, it takes a good consultant some time to figure out how to put it all together. If the missing necessities (like bridges and repeaters) weren't in the budget, there's an obvious problem. Remedy: Do some planning first.

Status needs are realistic. If you have a computer consulting company, your clients expect to see a LAN. The absence of a network looks peculiar. If you have a law office, and all the other legal beagles have a LAN, you need one, too. The same goes for any other business where appearances count. It's a valid business reason, and worth the money. Status accounts for 40 percent of the LAN sales in the D.C. area.

Having considered the political issues surrounding LANs, we move in Chapter 3 to the practical problems you'll encounter when you try to design a network for people.

CHAPTER 3

Designing a LAN

The major difficulty with setting up a LAN of any size is not the physical installation, but the preliminary planning. What sort of LAN will fit your current needs without making future growth impossible? How can you plan for easy expansion? How do you pick the wiring, topology, software, and hardware?

This isn't easy, especially when you remember that computer stuff has a habit of growing expotentially. Planning is a process that forces you to figure out what you need now, and predict what you will need in the future. You're not just solving today's problem, but next year's, or the year after that.

The answer is frequently found by analyzing what the organization actually does, and what the employees do, on a daily basis. Every organization is different, so the best way to show you what the planning process involves and what the results are is to give some examples.

Scenario One

YOYOTEL is a telecommunications software engineering company whose motto is "It's Not Us, It's The Network." The accounting department has an accounts receivable clerk, an accounts payable clerk, a payroll clerk, and a general ledger person. They have two or three standalone Joe's Garage generic 286s and one copy of a software package like Peachtree, managed by shuffling diskettes around among them. Each computer has a cheap dot-matrix printer attached. This is a typical accounting department in a small company with less than $10 million a year in sales. It's big enough to require three or four people, and has grown by at least one staff position a year for three years.

Physically, the accounting staff may be all jammed in together in one room. Accounting departments traditionally get the least desirable space in the company, possibly because they were the first non-marketing (or "back office") people the owner is forced to hire.

The LAN solution most often proposed for this department is to turn the A/P clerk's machine into a non-dedicated file server (perhaps Novell 2.2, running non-dedicated), take away all but one of the printers presently in the department, and run the network version of Peachtree.

This is an appealingly low-cost solution, but it's a bad one:

The Accounts Payable clerk will become far less productive. She is usually one of the busiest people in the department, but using her machine as a file server will markedly slow her inputting. A non-dedicated file server is only available as a workstation part of the time, since the rest of the time it's doing file server computations. The company does not understand why her productivity drops, so the A/P clerk often ends up getting fired.

Since you've taken all the printers away except for one, it's a lot harder for the staff to print out transactions and double-check them. The overall productivity of the office goes down.

Better Solutions

Consider a peer-to-peer program like NetWare Lite. This will be adequate for only a year before the department outgrows it, but if you just want to put up a network and see how it works, a peer-to-peer is an easy temporary solution. You could probably wire it up yourself, too. This will slow down all of the computers in the department, but no one person's computer will suffer disproportionately.

Novell NetWare 2.2 is a better solution, because it will allow for growth and future interconnection with other LANs. Use a dedicated 386SX for the server (these are less than $1000, at current street price). We rarely suggest a non-dedicated file server, and then only on a PC that is rarely used.

If you think at some future date you're going to wire up the whole company, or connect this network to another network in the company, you might as well buy NetWare 3.11. You will outgrow NetWare 2.2. A business with $7 million in sales can grow to $20 million in another two years, requiring a doubling of the accounting staff. At this point, the Guy in the Suit replaces Heidi the Comptroller. He moves into a corner office, and expects a network with the first class security features available in 3.11.

Do not remove the "extra" printers. Leave them on the network as local printers for the workstations.

If the accounting department is responsible for confidential letters regarding financial status, it's a good idea to get a laser printer in this department to print the reports and letters the banks require. You really don't want them spooled to the public laser printer for everybody to read.

Wire this network with 10Base-T. It is quick, not particularly expensive, and is easy to hook up. It requires a concentrator box at about $400. 10Base-T is much easier to handle and much more forgiving than coax. On paper, coax sounds great, but you should see what happens when someone who doesn't know what they're doing fools around with one end of it: the other end catches fire.

For backup, designate one person to back up the daily changes to floppy disks. A complete backup is necessary only once a month.

Scenario Two

Our next business is funded by three retired military officers, and has two guys and a receptionist pumping out proposals. Right now, all they want to do is share a good printer.

There are cheap ways to go about this, but since the company is probably growing rapidly, the best solution is Novell 3.11, running the big fancy printer off the full-bore 386 dedicated file server. This may sound ridiculously expensive for two or three people doing proposals, but the chances are that this company will have three times that many front office people within 18 months. This LAN will also service the contract programmers who will create the software code they peddled in the successful proposals. The most efficient solution for the fastest-growing LAN in the company is a powerful network operating system—NetWare 3.11.

If the proposal writers have laptops, you should consider putting in something like a LANPort so they can dial into the LAN from off-site. These guys have so much at stake getting this company going that they are apt to be re-jiggering proposals at 2 a.m. the night before the due date. Arrange things so they can dial in from home.

Back up this file server for the first several months by having each user back up his own daily changes to floppy disks. This solution won't last long, but there is no systems administrator for this LAN yet.

Scenario Three

This plan links the two previous LANs. There are now 20 people in the front office and five or six in the back office. The two LANs need to communicate, because the front office people need financial attachments to the $2 million proposals they're putting out. They need to prove they can do the job, which they really didn't have to do with their initial $20,000 proposals. Somebody in the accounting department spends most of her time producing these pieces of paper to prove financial status, and another person spends her time checking the bids to see if they make sense.

SneakerNet won't work anymore. It's time to connect the two LANs. It would be nice if both LANs were running 3.11, but most startup companies won't put the money out for three back office people to run a dedicated file server and expensive software. It's hard enough to persuade them to run 2.2 on a dedicated 386SX.

We don't just extend the 3.11 network to include Accounting, because most of the front office people (marketing, word processing, software development) should not have access to the financial information. Some of the front office people will have logins to the accounting network, and all the financial people have a login to the word processing server. They need it to offload printing, which is slowing up their server.

We can connect Accounting's Novell 2.2 and the 3.11 through a NetWare router. Two 3.11 servers would be totally transparent to each other, including passwords, bindery, and utilities. Two related but dissimilar servers are generally compatible, but there will be subtle and annoying differences. Nevertheless, we can connect the two.

Back up this system daily on a tape drive in Accounting's file server. From there, they can back up either or both file servers. They'll need at least a 200 meg tape capacity for this configuration.

Eventually, YOYOTEL becomes a $25 million a year company with interconnected UNIX systems running XWindows, TCP/IP, and Lord knows what else, but we leave them now to consider two more scenarios.

Scenario Four

Petersen's Feed and Grain in Sycamore, Nebraska, wants to stick a PC in the shed next to the weighing station, another in the front office where Lyle sells agricultural and lawn chemicals, and a third in the back office where Lyle's wife Nancy keeps the books and runs some custom linear programs to analyze the commodities markets. They may eventually connect some more PCs to do data acquisition by measuring weight in the grain bins and silos. For now, they want three machines, each with a printer, but only one laser printer.

Use ARCNET to wire this one up, using outdoor-rated coax. If you must run wire outside, it's dangerous to do anything else, since the outdoor run can get iced over or blown down and run over by the grain trucks. ARCNET is forgiving; the still-connected stations will work fine, even if the cable to the shed has been severed. We need an active hub for this configuration because the cable out to the weighing platform and shed will be a long run. Passive hubs only work with short runs.

The two old PCs the Petersens likely own can go to the Point of Sale position and out in the shed. We'd put a 486 in the back office for Nancy to run her linear programs and financial analysis on. The software from Cornell University will run nicely on it. The 486 is a workstation on this network, because Nancy is running fancy mathematical analysis. Remember, the workstation runs the applications, not the server. Our network software is Novell 3.11 in a clone 386SX.

Back up this machine on a tape drive in the 486, not the file server, because the 486 holds so much of the total network data.

Scenario Five — High School Computer Lab

Typically, this is 10-20 machines in one room, with two or three printers. These machines are heavily used. ARCNET is ideal. We need a durable solution; some kid is going to unscrew the coax connector from the back of his workstation and stick it in his ear. A passive hub goes on each work table to serve three machines, and an active hub drives the passive hubs. Off one of the passive hubs is the server and the teacher's workstation. This lab could support 21 student workstations, plus the server and the teacher's station. For a file server, Novell 2.2 would be fine. There's no compelling reason (security, redundancy, etc.) to use 3.11.

The hardware: a 386SX for the server, 286 clone PCs with one 3-1/2" floppy drive in each (no hard drives here for the students to crash). Even if the school is teaching programming, there's no reason for more horsepower. Basically, this lab is replacing the old roomful of Selectrics where the kids used to learn typing.

The teacher's station should be a 386SX with a decent-sized hard drive (80 Meg) so she can play with the machine and enjoy it. With VGA monitors, the workstations shouldn't cost more than $700 apiece. It's a good idea to have more machines than students, to allow for machines down for repair. We'd also buy extra keyboards, and good ones at that. This is also the typing class, and it's dismal to learn on a cheap keyboard. We'd put mice, gameports, and joysticks on all the machines, and buy extras of these. Educational software resembles computer games and uses the same equipment.

The students make their own diskette backups, but the teacher/administrator should make up one full initial backup and then back up weekly changes.

Can You Do it Yourself?

If you have no knowledge of PC anatomy, have never installed a device driver, and have never had your hands on a LAN before, the money spent for an honest consultant is worth it. A good consultant should be able to pick out the machines, pick the right kind of wiring, put up the file server and show you how he did it, and show you the cards and how they were installed. If you know these items, you can do much of your own troubleshooting. A good consultant should build in a price for this sort of training from the beginning and not charge you ad hoc extras for showing you what's going on. As part of the package, he'll set up administration and deal with print queues and all those issues. Some training is required for the users so they know how to logon, how files are organized, and how to print. This kind of training should be specified in your RFPs (Request For Proposal) for your network.

How do you tell an honest consultant from a dishonest consultant? First of all, when you get ten people to bid on a job, one bid will be ridiculously low and one will be ridiculously high. Throw those out. The remaining bids for a small LAN will be grouped closely together in price and solutions.

Check the reputations of the remaining consultants. A good consultant has satisfied customers. A bad consultant has mystified customers.

Compare what the consultant tells you with what you know. If it is radically different, then there is a problem. Watch out for the consultant who wants to charge you extra for "a special OSI chip." This is from the there's-one-born-every-minute school of consultancy. A recent advertisement in *InfoWorld* claimed a premium price for an Ethernet card because it was compatible with "NetWare 2.2, 3.11, TCP/IP, UDP/IP, SNMP, and is OSI-compliant." All the named protocols run on any Ethernet card at all, whether premium-priced or not. And OSI does not test hardware, so there's no such thing as an OSI-compliant card.

If you want your 24 new workstations to burn in for 72 hours, you are probably going to have to do it yourself or pay somebody to help you.

This sort of preparation is no longer a normal standard of the trade. Your consultant should be responsible for determining new machines' health, though, and/or making sure the computers work.

The systems integrator or consultant who sells you NetWare will be designated a Platinum or Gold dealer or an Authorized Reseller. Platinum and Gold dealers have purchased medallions, have a certain number of CNEs (Certified NetWare Engineers) on staff, and are required to purchase a certain amount of product. This arrangement is common between manufacturers and dealers. The Platinum and Gold dealers are also distributors who can sell Novell products to Authorized Resellers, who are not required to have CNEs on staff and who get support from the dealers above them, not from Novell. The criteria for these designations change fairly often, but the chances are you'll be dealing with an Authorized Reseller if you contemplate a small LAN. Support could become an issue: all the more reason to check references. This isn't the realm of the 800-number, free lifetime support that made WordPerfect famous. A new NetWare user is entitled to just one hardware and one installation question before they're referred to Novell's 900 number for paid support. This is an improvement from earlier years, when Novell wouldn't talk to anybody at all. See the tips in Chapter 4 for advice on obtaining support through NetWire and user groups.

"Novell Certified" hardware is a different issue. Hardware components like computers and NIC cards are tested by Novell and certified as compatible with NetWare. This is expensive for a manufacturer, so there are many non-certified components that work with NetWare—but get a guarantee in writing from your systems integrator if he assures you this hardware will work fine with the network. Because so many clone and mail order computers are now certified, we would buy a Novell Certified machine for a file server. Support could again become an issue: Novell asks "Is the hardware certified?" If not, it declines to pursue the matter.

If you want to purchase your own hardware, be sure to discuss the deal with your systems integrator. He or she may be just as glad to avoid the hardware headaches, but she may need to adjust her other charges because she isn't making any profit on the machines. You may be able to sit down and discuss this frankly. In any event, make sure you pay your systems integrator enough. Too low a price may mean she won't be in business next year.

Should You Take a Course?

Most Novell authorized courses are very good. The network supervisor should take at least the Supervisor and Troubleshooting courses. Without the courses, or major prior experience with NetWare, it is not possible to understand its subtleties or what all those utilities do. It is also a good place to hear the war stories about what goes on with LANs and to make some useful contacts.

What is Involved if You Put up the LAN Yourself

It involves some hard work and at least one lost weekend. Actually, quite a lot of hard work. Chapter 1, *Getting a LAN Up and Running*, gives you the basics, including some things Mother Novell Never Told You.

If you want to install the LAN yourself, and you have already done your planning, be prepared to lose a week of your job life. You also will be putting out fires for the first month the LAN is up. But it can be done. Sue tried an unaided installation to see what would happen if you attempted it. The installation took three tries (one time out for file server woes) but the LAN worked. Eventually, it even printed properly. So it's not a sacred mystery of the universe that ordinary mortals cannot comprehend. Few things are, we've found.

These are the steps:

1. **Plan the physical layout and do the wiring.** The layout of a LAN depends on the physical plan of the site. The workstations are already set

up in certain offices and the file server needs to go in a secure or out-of-the-way location. There may already be wiring in the building.

Decide what type of wiring you are going to use. For the most part, 10Base-T is the simplest way to wire up a LAN. The concentrators can be placed in the same room as the server(s) and other shared devices, in the telephone wiring closet, or even out in the work area among the computers.

CheaperNet (thin coax cable) is acceptable for a small LAN that you don't expect to expand. However, it can become a real pain when problems occur, because it is very difficult to isolate problems on a bus (one long wire with taps for the workstations).

FOIRL (Fiber Optic Inter Repeater Link) and Thick Ethernet are generally only backbone options. There is no reason to use them to connect individual workstations.

Pick the kind of wire that meets your requirements. We don't mean just the physical wire, but the whole physical medium, including cards, cables, and topology. Do you have strange security requirements? Do you have survivability issues like they have at the grain elevator or school computer lab? Is there something about your business that makes ARCNET or Token Ring a better choice? If coax is your choice, do you have a ceiling run where you must use teflon-shielded cable?

If these questions don't make sense to you, it's a good idea to take a course or hire somebody to help you make the choice. And even if you reason that 10Base-T is what you need, you're not necessarily qualified to run the wire. You're not necessarily disqualified, either. We've seen amateurs bring down coax from an attic TV antenna, leaving polygonal holes all over the house. The TV worked, but you may not be prepared to live with those aesthetics in your office.

2. **Prepare the hardware.** Install network cards in all the machines, after determining the right interrupts and setting jumpers. Connect the cables. Prepare the file server by burning it in for several days to make sure everything stays working. (Novell says it's a good idea to turn on the machines to make sure they work. We'd do a whole lot more than that.)

3. **Install the server software.** You will have to do this two or three times to get it right, taking about two working days. Even though NetWare 2.2 manuals tell you to put the diskette in the A: drive and type Install, installation is not a trivial undertaking. Installing NetWare 3.x is harder. But neither resembles a NetWare 2.15 horror story.

4. **Generate the shells for the workstations and install them.** This done, the workstations should be able to communicate with the server.

5. **Last (and this will take the most time), create all the users and set up their security and trustee rights.** Prepare a document to hand out to the users that tells them how to use USER-BAS.ICS, a printable ASCII file in NetWare's PUBLIC directory. It is a good foundation for the customized document you will need to create for your specific LAN.

Now you can see why your consultant is worth the price, and why planning ahead is essential. Planning has little to do with deciding where to put the cable drops. An electrician can do this. The art of planning is knowing what the employees of the company do, how much the company might grow, and what it will need next year. Most businesses underestimate their needs. They also forget to allow for LAN Lust—everybody wants to get on the network. The least expensive solution, therefore, is often the more expensive network software and file server—because it won't have to be replaced next year.

CHAPTER 4

Nuts and Bolts Survival Tips for LAN Administrators

This book provides separate Data Sheets for the file server, workstations, cables, cards, and other hardware. Check the appropriate Data Sheet for maintenance and troubleshooting hints. If you have a problem right now, but don't know which particular part is bad, use the Troubleshooting Flowcharts in Part 3. This chapter gives you practical tips for day-to-day network administration.

Protecting the Hardware

If your area, like ours, has unreliable electrical service, we strongly recommend an Uninterruptible Power Supply for the file server. Your building may have conditioned power that protects you to some extent, but a UPS is still a sanity saver. The new office buildings in Tysons Corner, Virginia, have their own generators which kick in during power glitches during our Jakarta-like summers. The change-over causes a noticeable drop-then-surge in power as the generators kick in, and that momentary loss of power is bad news for file servers. Again, see the Data Sheets for details.

You need to keep a record of the hardware and software configuration of each PC on your network. In addition to keeping the information in your notebook, tape a 3 x 5 card noting that machine's configuration inside the case of each PC. The Novell **Installation** manual provides sample configuration sheets. Your notebook should record problems on each machine, as well. Chapter 5, *Choosing and Using Network Utilities*, provides more detail on configuration management utilities.

Keep your file server turned on all the time. It's easier on the hardware, and performance statistics are zeroed out each time you turn the server off.

Backing Up Data

There is more to backing up data than putting in a tape drive. You have to persuade your users that the system is backed up, and that the backup works. Otherwise, they don't trust the LAN and won't use it. Or, worse, they keep all their data files on their local hard disks and then forget to back them up.

The simplest backup method is to use a tape drive with timed software, preferably a tape drive that runs off the server. This way, the backup can take place during off-hours. Another method, but much more expensive in terms of hardware, is to have a second hard drive and controller in the server that "mirrors" the information on the first. This is the best way to go if continuous, online data is essential to operate your business.

If you, like most of us, will be using tapes, systemize your tape backup cycle. A typical business does a complete backup of all files once a week and an incremental backup every day. Label the tape cartridges for the day of the week and Weekly, and date them. Cycle the weekly tapes through the month (Week 1, Week 2, etc.). Keep the last weekly backup as the monthly backup. Keep these monthly backup tapes for at least one year.

It is useful to have a tape drive that can back up the whole file server at once. Be aware that high capacity tape cartridges are not cheap. And you will need 20-30 of them. Add it up: one for each day of the week, one for each week of the month, one for each month of the year, plus offsite archive tapes.

NBACKUP, the NetWare 286 and 386 utility, stores network files on any DOS read-and-write device, and can back up the network while it's up. The bad news is, it lacks selection features, lacks the ability to back up multiple volumes, and it won't let you back up to a server-mounted tape drive (it backs up through a workstation). Like DOS BACKUP, it's a program that no one uses.

Third party backup utilities (like PCTools Deluxe 7.1, Cheyenne ARCServe, and Palindrome) allow you to select only the subdirectories you choose, back up from the file server, and do unattended back ups at night. See Chapter 5 for specific recommendations.

If you're using a tape backup program that will choke when interrupted by messages on the monitor screen, use CASTOFF to reject any BROADCAST messages. Because such messages prevent screen updates until the user has acknowledged the message with CTRL-ENTER, the tape program will be suspended until the operator presses CTRL-ENTER. You could come back the next morning and find only one hour of a four-hour tape backup has been done.

Back up the MAIL directory daily, even if not using a mail program. Many third party programs know that MAIL exists and store user-related information in this directory. NetWare stores individual users' printer configuration files there.

Creating a Directory Structure

Create NetWare directories with care. A multi-user file server needs explicit user rights, and security protection attributes are attached to each directory. If you don't set up a structure, users will have trouble finding their own files again, others will be able to read private files, and the file server will fill up with junk files that you, as the administrator, are afraid to delete. Establish a set of rules, enforce them, and inform users of any changes. The simplest set of rules does the following:

- **Isolate data from programs.** This way, you know which directories have to be backed up daily. Some network managers refuse to back up user data that is not stored in the right place; some even delete user data that shows up in the wrong place. They only have to do it once.
- **Segregate directories by user.** If there are many users, segregate by workgroup, then user. The MAP command will make this transparent to the user. In other words, the user who only needs word processing will not even see the accounting files and programs.
- **Create consistent directories for each user.** This will make maintenance and troubleshooting easier. For example, put all of Tim's data files (text, spreadsheets, etc.) arranged in subdirectories under HOME\TIM, as in HOME\TIM\WP, HOME\TIM\EXCEL, and HOME\TIM\MISC. The executable programs live over in PUBLIC\APPS. To Tim, the data file directories look like J:, K:, and L:. He doesn't (and maybe shouldn't) know the actual directory structure.

- **Most software comes with explicit installation instructions specifying the required directory names. Follow those instructions or the software will not work.**
- **Stick to eight-character NetWare directory names.** NetWare directory names can be 14 characters long, which sounds handy. But what if your backup program only allows DOS-length 8-character directory names? Backup chokes.

DOS Directories for Mixed-Salad Networks

DOS directories are usually subdirectories under the PUBLIC directory. Not all versions of MS-DOS 3.3 are the same (e.g., Toshiba DOS 3.3, MSDOS 3.3, Compaq DOS 3.3). You need a separate DOS directory for each DOS 3.3 version, as well as for your DOS 4's and 5's. Mixing the versions can cause "Bad COMMAND.COM" errors when the user goes back to pick up COMMAND.COM as they exit an application or log off the network. One solution: Write the COMSPEC command in the user's login script so the user's computer looks for COMMAND.COM on the C: drive.

Novell suggests putting the command **COMSPEC=S2:COMMAND.COM** in the system or user login script. This tells the computer to look for COMMAND.COM on the second search drive on the network—a good idea if you must be sure all your users are running the same version of DOS. On the other hand, this could be a problem if the user logs off the network and can no longer get to the network drive where COMMAND.COM is loaded.

Applications Directories

Some Novell documentation suggests creating a master applications directory called APPS or APPL with a subdirectory for each application program on the network. You might choose to hang this APPS directory off the PUBLIC directory. This is efficient because the kind of security you need in an application-program directory is already set up for PUBLIC, and the subdirectories will inherit security from the parent PUBLIC directory.

We didn't do this in our test LAN. The NetWare 3.1 documentation suggested setting up a separate directory off the root (off the volume name SYS:) for each individual application program. Our experience suggests that it would have been smarter to set up an APPS directory.

No matter which system you choose, the application directories should contain only program files, not data files or user-created documents.

Place files that need to be backed up daily in directory trees together, and files that do not change from week to week together in separate directory trees. For example, the PUBLIC NetWare utilities and DOS files will only need to be backed up when you upgrade NetWare or DOS to a new version. Data files in the individual user directories, by comparison, need to be backed up daily if you want to maintain user confidence in the LAN. So put all the user subdirectories together in a HOME, USER, or PERSONAL directory to make backup quick.

Because NetWare 3.x allows workgroup managers, it may make sense to follow the above recommendations, but in workgroup modules. Some manuals advise creating a separate directory for a department like Accounting, with its own program and data files. We think it is better to give Accounting a separate file server if your budget can handle it.

Sanity Savers and Quick Tips

If you're having trouble getting an application to run: Are the trustee rights set right? Is the PATH set correctly? Is a user saving her application configuration files into a public directory on the network server so now her software configuration is everyone's default?

With all these search drives MAPped into the path, you can run into trouble if you try to access a popular file name—like INSTALL, or MEMO.

NetWare will search until it finds the first INSTALL or MEMO file. That may not be the one you want. For example, we started to fire up our copy of QAPlus/fe without really paying attention to the directions. We typed INSTALL, and ended up in the Norton Utilities install program because QAPlus doesn't have a file named INSTALL on the program diskette. Our MAP command sent us through one directory after another until it finally found a file called INSTALL on the C: drive.

In a multi-server environment, MAP commands can be tricky. Be explicit with the MAP commands — define the server explicitly. You will need to do ATTACH commands before mapping to the various servers. For example, to ATTACH to a second file server named SALES and MAP the directory MARY to your J: drive, type

ATTACH SALES <enter>

Enter your username and password. Then type

MAP J: = SALES/SYS: HOME/ MARY

If you want to be in the MARY directory on the file server named SALES, say so. Don't leave it to chance, especially in a login script.

Some administrators create an AUTOEXEC.BAT file for a user's workstation that automatically connects it to the network, prompts the user to login, then continues with other commands. When setting up batch files for users, remember that they only get one chance to login—if they enter the wrong login name or password, they are dumped back out. This could be a problem if LOGIN is in the middle of the AUTOEXEC file, because AUTOEXEC would continue on and the user would think everything was fine, until he tried to use the network. At best the user would have to reboot the workstation (and give the right LOGIN response), at worst the administrator would get a trouble call. The solution is to create a loop in the AUTOEXEC.BAT file that checks to see if the user has successfully logged onto the network. Use the DOS **If Exist** command, for example, to look for a file on the file server, or use **If Errorlevel** to be sure the login proceeded without error. Don't let your user out of the loop until he or she has logged on to the server.

Quick Check List for Installing an Application

- Make sure it is NetWare compatible software.
- Create an application program-file directory.
- Per the application installation instructions, install the program to that program-file directory on your network hard drive.
- Set up a search mapping to this directory for all users who need to use this application. This is most easily done by setting up a group that uses this application, then adding the appropriate users to the group. Give them at least Read, Open, and File Scan rights in this program-file directory.
- Ask your users to start all applications from their home directory (or whatever subdirectory tree they have set up under their home directory). We presume the software will automatically save all data files to the directory the user was in when she started the application. Consider using the Novell MENU utility to set up a little customized menu for your system (or different menus for different classes of users), that will automatically start each application from the user's home directory.
- If this application uses special environment variables, set these up in the login script.

How to Delete Files to Make Space

The LAN administrator has to ensure that there is enough disk storage space at all times. This is not an easy task. The sister of one of the authors created a logo for her company that took up 80 Kb by itself. Because it was used in all the company's material, she estimated it took up over 10 Meg of hard disk space.

The simplest way to ensure that enough space exists on the network is archive all files older than 90 days. Software is on the market that does this. This policy will also force users to understand that their files take up limited resources. Reminder: Network print queues are subdirectories of the SYSTEM directory. The user needs space there to be able to print and can get a wide variety of errors from the applications when jobs won't print because there is no space on the server.

Security/Insecurity

Security on a LAN must be enforced, no matter the size of the LAN. It is too easy for a semi-smart user to kill the LAN.

Security is best enforced with NetWare's trustee assignments and rights features. Whole directories can be hidden from users who do not need to know they exist. Many applications also keep their own list of authorized users. Consult your Novell **Concepts** manual for details.

Never allow multiple users to be SUPERVISOR, no matter how tempting this might be in a small office. There should never be more than one SUPERVISOR on the network. It is important, however, that at least two people know the SUPERVISOR password. And if you intend to fire the current supervisor, change the SUPERVISOR password **before** you fire him.

You will have temporary users from time to time. Don't let them use the GUEST username. Instead, set up a TEMP user, and give them exactly the rights you want to give them, no more. On some networks, this may mean copying the rights of GUEST, but on most it's likely to be more restrictive.

If you want better password control than is available under NetWare, you can purchase third party software or hardware (like a user-card to operate the PC) to increase security. Remember, though, if the file server is not physically secure, all this stuff is useless. For real deep security, put the server in a locked room and check out whoever enters or leaves the room. This network would probably have diskless workstations so no diskette copies could be made.

Want to know who uses the network and how much? Set up accounting in SYSCON, and "charge" for service requests. This is probably more accurate than accounting by time on the network (Yes, he was logged in from 9 to 5, but was he doing anything?) and more accurate than judging by disk storage used.

Use Menus

The easiest way to make networks work for the greatest number of users is to use menus. NetWare's MENU command allows you to create individually-tailored menus. If the menus are driven by the groups that the user belongs to, the menu system can be customized and can provide some additional security by allowing the user to see only the applications and utilities he has rights to. You might write a system login script that exits directly to a menu. Consult your Novell **Utilities** manual for details.

Getting Help

Some alliances are starting up (between, for example, Novell, Compaq and WordPerfect) in which the vendors are trying to set up cooperative support for their products. This can cut down on the infuriating situation when the hardware, network, and software folks all point at each other as the culprit when you have a problem. At least Novell says this is the trend.

Whatever problem you have with your network, someone else has probably experienced it. Here's how to arm and educate yourself:

- **If you haven't been to a Novell-sponsored school, get the company to send you.** Take at least the Systems Administrator course. You may also find the Service and Support courses helpful. LAN consulting firms often teach these courses for a third of the cost of the Novell schools. Ask around to find the best ones, which are often the Novell schools.
- **Get the company to send you to a good PC diagnosis and repair course.** These take as little as two or three days and should include

a comprehensive manual and troubleshooting chart. Keeping the computers in good standalone health is most of the administrator's job. In a pinch, buy our previous book, *Fix Your Own PC*, or a similar repair guide.

- **Join a Novell Users Group.** In the D.C. area, CANU—the Capitol Area Novell Users group—is quite active. It publishes a monthly newsletter and holds well-attended meetings.
- **Join a PC Users Group.** Again, in the D.C. area, the Capitol PC Users Group is one of the oldest and largest in the country. CPCUG runs its own members-only BBS with an active LAN Interest Group. The current dues are $35 a year, and well worth it.
- **Join CompuServe and monitor the Novell forums.** There are now five of them: Novell A, Novell B, Novell C, and Novell 2.x and 3.x. Collectively, these forums are known as NetWire. Here's where you can get downloads of patches, bug fixes, new versions of shells, menus, PSERVER and other NLMs. NetWire promises a 24-hour turnaround on problem reports. This may not be nearly fast enough, but it can help. Novell also uploads product announcements, price lists, education listings, and an interesting listing of FYI trouble reports and fixes.
- **If you think CompuServe and NetWire will be useful to you, get a copy of Tapcis, a share-ware program** (but not cheap, it's $79 for the software and printed manual). This is a batch front-end to CompuServe that automates logon, forum navigation, downloads, and message retrieval. Tapcis can be a frustrating program to learn, but the effort is worth it. The forthcoming new version is allegedly more user-friendly. Call or write Support Group, Inc., Lake Technology Park, McHenry, MD 21541 (800-872-4768).
- **Read the Novell Systems Administrator manual thoroughly.** You must become familiar with all those red books. The most pertinent information is in **Concepts** (2.2 and 3.11), **System Administrator** (3.11), **Quick Access Guide** (2.2 and 3.11), **Using the Network** (2.2), and **Utilities** (3.11). The **Installation** manual is worth reading even if someone else installed your system.
- **Aftermarket books.** This book assumes you have the Novell books at hand and can navigate through them, so we don't repeat their contents. Our opinionated stance in the Chapters might not suit your needs, so check out other books. Look for books that concentrate on NetWare 386; many are primarily 286 with just an appendix of differences.

Running Local and/or Network Versions of Software

If you use more than three copies of a software package, the network version makes sense from a financial standpoint. Three copies of WordPerfect is $650, while the LAN version with support for five users is $700. The network version knows about the network and operates more efficiently on it. WP, for example, has "underflow" and "overflow" temporary files. Network versions of WordPerfect use your initials to keep track of your personal temporary files.

Any time you want the network to share files between users you should use the network version. Network versions of software should provide file locking mechanisms that prevent two users from changing the same file at the same time. This is very important when a group of people are putting together a document.

The greatest difficulty with networked software, especially word processing software, is version control. There are several software packages that handle version control and some word processors have version control built in. The easiest way to handle version control is a cover sheet at the beginning of the document that records changes to the document. By examining this you can tell if you are working on a current document and if anybody has changed it since you last worked on it. If multiple people are working on a document simultaneously, consider ForComment, a document review package that keeps the document and associated correction/comments in order. It allows multiple editors, without allowing document overwrites and corruption.

Fellow Clone Warrior Phil Raidt shares these tips about databases and other single-user versus multi-user programs: You need a network version of a database so you don't get "deadly embrace" problems when multiple users are trying to open a number of files. Imagine that two users need the same files. Each for some reason grabs one, then waits to open the other one—but of course the other one is not going to get free because the other user is waiting for your file. The result is stalemate. Network versions know how to deal with a "deadly embrace" situation.

If you insist on using single-user software, at least put each user in her own individual directory with her own copy of the software. If just one person uses that software, no copyright or license laws are violated. If more than one person uses it, buy the appropriate number of copies. It's not only tacky to do otherwise, it's illegal.

CHAPTER 5

Choosing and Using Network Utilities

The NetWare Operating System utilities, though impressive, do not provide all the information you will need to keep a network running smoothly. Enter third-party network management packages. We examine six categories of utilities in this chapter: configuration management utilities, user support tools, software audit utilities, file server backup programs, performance/troubleshooting packages, and support tools for supervisors. Here, as throughout this book, we have not made an exhaustive survey of the many utilities in each category. Instead, we mention an example or two of programs that we like, that do the job. This chapter is a starting point and gives qualitative guidance, it is not an attempt to replicate (less effectively) the comprehensive product-category surveys that *PC Magazine* and *Byte* do so well.

Configuration Management

Managing your system's configurations requires you to keep up-to-date information about each file server, workstation, and router/bridge or special purpose server on the network.

For **workstations** you need information about:

- Hardware—the workstation computer's CPU, manufacturer and BIOS ROM; network boards installed and their switch settings (interrupts used, base I/O address and memory address, DMA, network node address); hard and floppy disks installed; hard disk controller(s) installed; video card and monitor; amount of memory and its configuration as DOS, expanded, or extended memory; workstation boots from hard disk, floppy disk, or network with remote boot PROM.
- Software — DOS version running on this workstation; IPX or ODI driver version(s) and NETx version running on this workstation; text of AUTOEXEC.BAT, CONFIG.SYS, and SHELL.CFG files; other files needed to connect to network; network address for each LAN board installed in the workstation.

For **file servers** you need information about:

- Hardware—the file server computer's CPU; the computer manufacturer; network boards installed and their switch settings (interrupts used, base I/O address and memory address, DMA, network node address); internal C: drive (make/model, storage capacity, DOS partition size, NetWare partition size); other hard disks installed (make/model, capacity, heads and cylinders, drive mirroring setup); floppy drives installed; video card and monitor; amount of memory and its configuration as base DOS memory or extended memory.

- Software—NetWare version running on this file server; IPX version; text of AUTOEXEC.BAT, STARTUP.NCF, and AUTOEXEC.NCF files; internal network number for this server; external network number(s) for the network(s) connected to LAN cards inside this server.

Tools to Help You Do the Job

A looseleaf notebook with a hand-penciled configuration worksheet on each piece of network equipment works fine, if you are self-disciplined and dealing with a fairly small network. Use QAPlus/fe on each workstation or file server to print a report for each unit. If you staple the QAPlus report to the Novell File Server Configuration sheet or the Novell Workstation Configuration sheet for each machine, you have got a very complete record. With this kind of small network you can give each machine a nickname (Bluebird, Old Crow, Buzzard, Catbird, and Eagle perhaps?). This sounds hokey, but it really helps your users (and you) keep the machines straight. "Buzzard is losing my WordPerfect files today, just like Eagle did last week." You need the configuration data sheets because you'll be looking for similarities between Buzzard and Eagle (the same outdated IPX version?) — or maybe it's trouble with the user, not the workstation. Has anybody else complained about lost files (especially lost WordPerfect files) on either Buzzard or Eagle? Look in your network log book to find out.

Alternatively, buy a configuration management utility, like LAN Directory from Frye Utilities. LAN Directory collects most of these statistics automatically from each workstation, plus many more, and you can add your own custom data fields (for example, a repair and error log history on each machine). If you have more than ten workstations, you really need LAN Directory. The larger the network, the more configuration changes per week you're trying to keep track of — an automatic program is worth it.

User Support Tools

You must be able to answer user questions as quickly and efficiently as possible. Unfortunately, your office may be in a separate building or on a different floor, far from the user who needs help.

Tools to Help You Do the Job

Remote control software (you remotely operate a user's workstation while she watches the screen) and remote monitoring software (on a duplicate monitor screen in your own office, you watch a user manipulate her computer) can be very handy, especially if you, the system administrator, are physically separated from users you must support. LANSight from LANSystems does all this, as well as letting you run programs on unused workstations.

Set up LANSight so you can only look at users' work with their permission. When misused, these programs arouse privacy concerns. Users, quite properly, don't want Big Brother watching their computer screen. Show some sensitivity, and try to avoid making your corporation a defendant in the court battles that will erupt over these issues in the next few years.

Software Audit

Corporations buy most network software on a number-of-users basis, not on a per-site basis. To conform to your agreement with the software vendor, you must ensure that no more than the number of licensed users are running the software program at one time. Government contractors, for example, are regularly audited by the federal government to ensure compliance with software copyright laws.

Tools to Help You Do the Job

Software metering utilities, such as SiteLock from Brightwork Development, allow only the authorized number of users to run the program in question. Additional users will be queued and notified when a copy of the software is free. One warning here: Windows users can check out a copy of the software merely by clicking on the icon for the software, whether they're actively running the program or not. If they suspend but don't exit, they still have a copy of the software checked out.

File Server Backup

The network administrator must protect against catastrophic file server failure with a complete backup of all network hard disk data and must archive unused data files, removing them from the (possibly crowded) file server hard disk.

File server backup can be done in several ways. The quickest, simplest, and most expensive is disk mirroring (a second hard disk, on line, which is an exact duplicate of your primary network hard disk). DAT tape is the most common backup medium, but it only provides a way to reconstruct a trashed hard disk after a crash, it doesn't provide an online substitute for the ailing disk the way disk mirroring does. WORM (Write Once Read Many) optical disk drives are becoming a popular backup medium, even though they are more expensive than tape. WORM disks are permanent while tape deteriorates and may not be readable after five years, unless someone occasionally reads the tape. Therefore, WORM drives are ideal for legal archives or other long term data storage. Like tape, WORM disks don't replace your trashed hard disk—they merely let you reconstruct the contents once a replacement disk drive is up and running.

Tools to Help You Do the Job

Because there are two parts to this job—making copies of your data and archiving little-used data files—it makes sense to pick a product that will do both parts at once. Palindrome's Network Archivist is a great example. The Archivist automates a lot of the tape-organizing work and performs scheduled backups as per your custom backup scripts. Network Archivist keeps a history of every file in your network, so it knows which tapes the file is on (each file is always on at least three tapes to provide redundant backup in case of tape failure). The Archivist will also recommend files for archiving, based on when the files were last changed.

You can do all the good things in the paragraph above manually with PCTools CPBACKUP—one of the best, general-purpose backup programs because it is network-aware. You will have to organize your tape rotation yourself, however. Like most DOS backup programs (as compared to dedicated NetWare backup utilities), CPBACKUP records the data files on the server, but it does not back up the NetWare bindery file or any other files open while CPBACKUP is running. Therefore, use the Novell NBACKUP utility to make a copy of the bindery files so you are covered in case of server crash.

ARCserve from Cheyenne Software, like Palindrome, will back up your entire server, whether the files are DOS, Macintosh, or NetWare bindery and other operating system files. ARCserve requires more operator skill than Palindrome, since you must plan your own tape rotation and keep file histories yourself. Like all dedicated network backup software, ARCserve backs up both the file and the special NetWare attribute bits associated with the file (e.g., Delete Inhibit, Read Only, System, and Transactional attributes). An ordinary DOS backup program, like CPBACKUP, will not save these bits!

Performance and Troubleshooting Packages

You can save yourself a lot of pain and trouble if you can recognize impending network trouble before the entire network collapses. If you hope to recognize a developing problem you need to know what is normal on your network, so you can pick up subtle changes. Some of the utilities below help you to establish baselines for your network, and these are as important for troubleshooting as are the more overtly "diagnostic" utilities.

Tools to Help You Do the Job

Performance packages are useful, because they allow you to judge how the network is doing. Remember, though, that the benchmarks from two different packages do not provide useful comparisons. A performance rating using package A is useful when you compare it with the same performance rating from last week. If the network performance has dropped, you better figure out why.

Frye Utilities for Networks, for example, provides a great baseline diagnostic report. Both TDX from Thomas-Conrad and Monitrix from Cheyenne Software will also collect the baseline network performance statistics you need to compare this week's performance with last week's. Frye Utilities for Networks is superior in one major respect—it gives you some guidance, based on rules of thumb, about what those statistics mean. For example, Frye suggests that a high "Duplicate packets received" percentage indicates you may need a faster workstation at this particular node. You can get the same data from TDX or Monitrix, but not the clear-English recommendation.

If you have isolated a problem to a particular workstation or to a particular set of workstations, the classic "diagnostic" packages really shine. As we've said before, we really like QAPlus/fe for PC troubleshooting — and your network workstation PCs must function perfectly as standalone PCs, or you're wasting your time looking for obscure network problems. TDX provides excellent point-to-point testing. TDX is very specific about the particular network layer where the trouble is occurring (e.g., Is it scrambled Ethernet frames or malformed IPX packets?). You have to know a lot about networks before TDX is useful, but it is very good if you do. The Frye Utilities are useful to expert and novice alike.

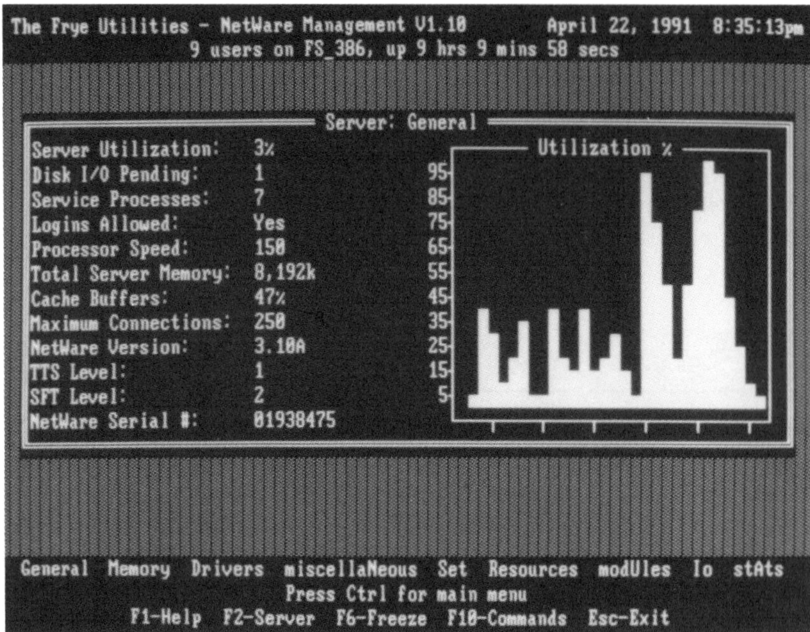

Figure 5.1 Frye's NetWare Management shows utilization statistics for your network. Photo courtesy of Frye Computer Systems, Inc.

Support Tools for Supervisors

Supervisors must maintain control of the network and respond promptly to emergencies, whether on-site or off.

Tools to Help You Do the Job

Supervisor-notification tools are a new wrinkle in network management. Frye's NetWare Early Warning System (NEWS) monitors the server (Is it up, does it have sufficient empty disk space, too many cache read errors or lost packets, etc.?). You can set the warning trigger levels yourself or stick with the program defaults. NEWS will page you, call you on the phone, or send a message to your network workstation monitor screen. (Pagers and voice cards are, of course, extra-cost items).

Alternatively, NEWS will automatically run a batch file you have written to cover this contingency. Imagine, for example, that your file server hard disk is getting too full—NEWS notes that the Volume threshold has been passed (the disk is over 90 percent full). Your batch file script could respond by backing up a particular low-use directory to tape, then deleting the files in that directory from the server, freeing up space.

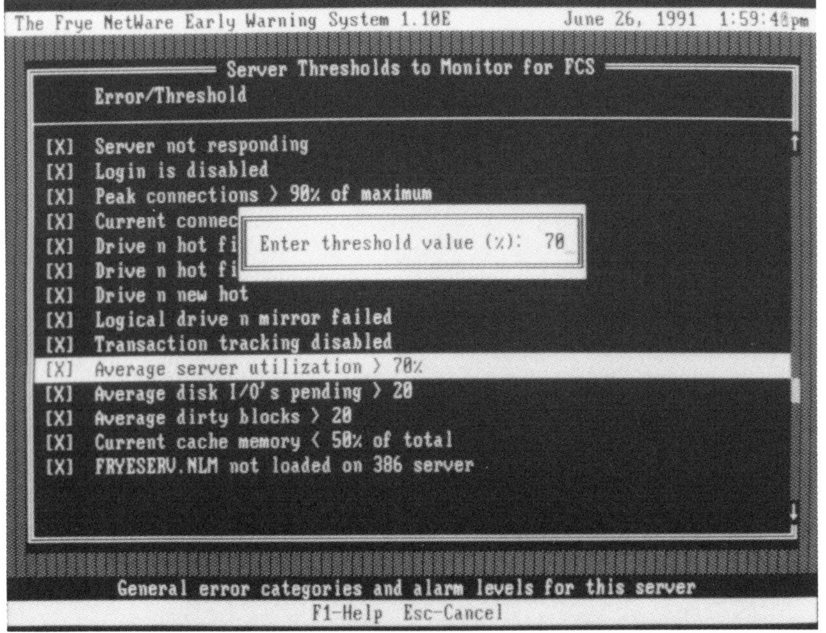

Figure 5.2 *NEWS allows you to set thresholds before you are warned of an impending problem. Photo courtesy of Frye Computer Systems, Inc.*

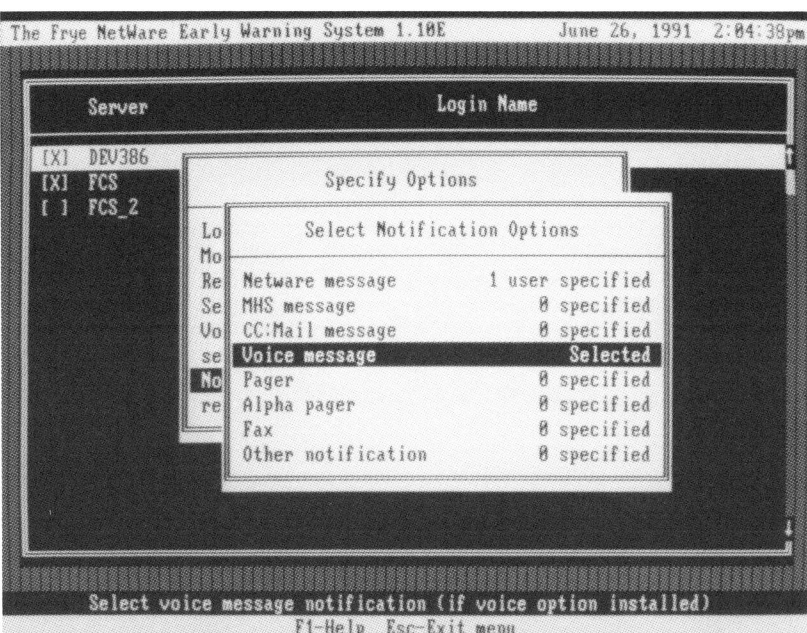

Figure 5.3 *Setting NEWS notification options. Photo courtesy of Frye Computer Systems, Inc.*

CHAPTER 6

Survival Tips for Users

So, the network is up, the users are trained, the administrator keeps things humming, and print jobs roll off the laser without a hitch. Is everything wonderful in LANland? What if you're the new kid in the office and somehow the administrator misses the fact that you have absolutely never seen a LAN before? You've got a Deadline from Hell coming up, of course, and it'll be three weeks before the company schedules another LAN class.

However experienced you are with standalone PCs, you'll need some LAN survival tips to make it through the first week on a LAN of any complexity.

HELP is Really There—Just Type it

NetWare provides extensive Help functions, available to users and administrators alike.

- Type HELP (not case sensitive) at the command line when you're logged in to the network to access the Help database. Turn to Appendix A in this book for tips on using Novell's online Help index.
- In menued NetWare utilities such as SYSCON, press F1 for help with that specific utility. Be aware that your user rights may not be sufficient to perform all the possible functions in that utility.

There IS a Users Guide

The Novell System **Administration** manual for 3.10 contains a *User Basics* section. This is the last tabbed section in that manual. It is a separate booklet in 2.2 and 3.11. Your system administrator can copy and distribute this freely, but she may have run out of copies, or doesn't know you're new to networks, or just forgot. It happens. Ask the administrator for a copy, and read it. It's well-written and almost complete. The most pertinent NetWare error messages are listed with solutions in Novell's *User Basics*.

For tips on how network printing works and how to get it to work for you, see Chapter 9. Specifically, be sure to read the section on Novell's CAPTURE command and about setting the Time Out value to a greater value.

Here are some more trail marks in the network wilderness:

Handy Network Commands

WHOAMI tells you about yourself as a network user. It tells you what file servers you are attached to and your name on each of them, the security equivalences you have, any groups you are a member of, plus your effective rights on each file server. You may be ANDY on one machine and GUEST on another, for instance. Your rights are likely different, depending on who you are to that machine. A program problem may be due to GUEST not being able to save a file to ANDY's home directory, for example. Or you may not have attached to the server you thought. This happens frequently on a multi-server network.

NDIR is similar to the DOS dir command, but far more detailed. Very handy. **NDIR SYS:*.* SUB** shows every subdirectory and every file on the volume. It displays a deluge of detail. If you choose continuous display rather than leafing through the list a page at a time, be prepared to hit Control-S to stop the screen from scrolling by so fast you can't read anything. Hitting Control-Q resumes scrolling. Control-S will stop it again.

NDIR is powerful. For example, if you think it would be handy to view all the hidden files on the SYS: volume of this file server (only the ones in the directories you are authorized to look at, of course), type

NDIR SYS: SUB H <enter>

To find a lost file on the volume SYS, type

NDIR SYS: the_file_name SUB<enter>

Substitute your actual volume name and lost-file name in the appropriate spots when you try it on your server. The NDIR utility will search all those directories you have rights to on this volume, looking for the file name you specified. Get all the details about NDIR from your red Novell **Utilities** manual, or type

NDIR HELP <enter>

to pull up a detailed help menu. Or type

NDIR <enter>

alone and highlight the options you want (for example, current directory only versus all directories on this volume). NDIR uses the * wildcard as flexibly as you always thought DOS should: ***CON*** finds files named PCONSOLE.EXE and CONTRACT and TACONITE.LTR. So it's easy to find that lost file even if you only remember a few letters of the name.

Type **RIGHTS** to check your rights in your default directory. Type **WHOAMI /R** to see your effective rights in other directories, both on this and other servers. Insufficient rights in the application program-file directory or in your working data file directory is one of the major reasons why applications choke.

LISTDIR SYS: /A /S shows the directory structure of the entire SYS: volume with the date and time each directory was created, all the subdirectories and the rights you have in each directory.

Use **RENDIR** to rename your personal subdirectories when you need to.

Use **SLIST** to check what file servers are up and running on the network. This is helpful if you get an error like "Server <servername> not found" or "Unable to attach to server <servername>." You don't know if the server is down for maintenance, if you misspelled the server name, or if there is no such server on the network.

SALVAGE is the NetWare undelete utility. Menu-driven, SALVAGE can recover both deleted files and files from deleted directories.

Type **MAP** to view your present drive mappings. This is helpful if the mapping got messed up and you need to figure out what is mapped to where. Novell refers to the drives mapped by the MAP command as "drive pointers." DOS drive pointers (A: or C:) point to physical drives, but Novell uses drive pointers to signify logical locations in the directory tree, not physical drives.

Also use **MAP** to set up new drive pointers. In other words, you can MAP to create a handy shortcut (for example, "drive K:" to instantly navigate to your word processing file for the new proposal) instead of typing a long path name every time.

When you don't want to overwrite your old mappings, use the MAP commands that are equivalent to using the Insert mode in a word processor rather than the Overtype mode. **MAP NEXT** maps the next available drive letter to a particular path. If you want to set up another search drive (the network equivalent of a PATH command) use **MAP INS S16:** to map the next available search drive letter to the path you need. Because regular MAP commands overwrite the PATH command stored in the AUTOEXEC.BAT file on your workstation boot disk, use **MAP INS** if you want to continue to work with the local applications on your workstation's hard disk. By the way, don't MAP drive C: to a network drive or you won't be able to get back to your local hard disk.

Type **FILER** to access a great multi-purpose file and directory maintenance utility. It is menu driven, so fire it up and poke around among your files and directories. Use FILER to move, copy, or delete files and directories. You can change a directory's ownership, prune and graft/copy directories with their subdirectories and files intact, even manipulate file or directory security rights. For example, if you want your co-author to copy files from your working directory, better give her Read and File Scan rights to those files. Use FILER to give your co- author these rights, and while you're in there, check who else has rights to read or write to your working files.

SESSION, another menu-driven utility, will help you to map drives and to attach to another file server if you've forgotten the command syntax. SESSION also displays the users attached to the file server, and the user groups defined on this file server—allowing you to view info about users and groups, and send short messages to other users. One warning: Any changes you make with SESSION are temporary—if you reboot, all your beautiful new drive mappings disappear.

SYSCON stands for SYStem CONfiguration. To change your password type SYSCON, arrow key to User Information, then to your name, then to Change Password, pressing Enter at each step. SYSCON is the system administrator's Rosetta stone. A good supervisor or workgroup manager can and does view everything with SYSCON. It's not as powerful in the hands of a humble civilian, but SYSCON is still a useful user tool. It tells you your restrictions and rights on the network. It gives you access to your individual login script—handy if you want to permanently save drive mappings, or set a path or an environment variable for a program (e.g., **WP=F:wp51\setup** tells WordPerfect where to look for user setup files). You can tailor your user login script to individualize your network. Read all about login scripts in *User Basics* or Appendix A of the Novell NetWare **Installation** manual. The first will help you get the script correct; the second will show you how to dazzle your co-workers.

CHKVOL allows you to check your allotted space on this file server volume. To keep the file server from filling up, the administrator may have limited the amount of space you can use to store files on the server. Keep tabs on your remaining capacity, if you don't want to be stuck with a big file you can't save for lack of storage space.

Do not use the DOS CD (change directory) command to jump from branch to branch in the file tree while you're on the network. If you do, you might lose your old mappings and find yourself unable to either navigate or use the MAP command to create new signposts. It's probably safe to use CD to navigate up and down your own personal subdirectories, but if your administrator set things up so all your files are saved in an area called "H:\FILES\YOURNAME, you could still find yourself lost. So don't use CD; use the drive letter (H:), mapped to the directory where you want to go.

What Novell Doesn't Tell You

Even though your private file space is "yours" and can be kept from being accidentally overwritten, deleted, or otherwise trashed, it's not as private as you might think. Your network space is not the place for love letters, your pitiful pleas to the IRS, or job applications. Usually, no one will look, but anyone with SUPERVISOR or SUPERVISOR-equivalent rights can look at your files. What's more, electronic files are not considered your personal locked space and are not subject to wiretap laws, as are the telephone and telegraph. This means that no search warrant is required to read E-Mail or examine "personal" files on a network. Search warrants are probably not your concern, but your private correspondence undoubtedly is.

Seriously, if you're working on confidential company matters, like staff or budget cuts, you need to encrypt your files. WordPerfect and Lotus 1-2-3 provide for encryption with a separate password. Just don't forget the password; it can never be retrieved.

Despite the ability to encrypt secret files, we'd be inclined to use a plain old typewriter and keep only one copy. Network printers are not secure, except possibly at midnight. Even then, you could forget about sending that last print job—and there it is at 8 a.m. for somebody else to read.

Network files are not secure if more than one person, or the wrong person, has SUPERVISOR rights. For example, a gargantuan New York bank was planning to lay off a dozen network gurus, when one of them, with otherwise legitimate SUPERVISOR rights, browsed through Business Planning's supposedly locked text files. He found his and his buddies' names on the cut list, and took action. The memorandum was repeatedly corrupted. ("Must be a virus," Planning probably mumbled.) They kept their jobs.

Although Novell 386 encrypts passwords stored on the file server, the sorry truth is that many applications will not run with passwords encrypted on the wire. In addition, network passwords for many E-Mail applications, like WordPerfect Office, are in ordinary text files that the SUPERVISOR or equivalent can read.

Accidentally pressing Return when the wrong set of recipients is highlighted can send your embarrassing E-Mail message to **everyone**. That can mean everybody in the company. Mary worked at a company where the receptionist sent a frank appraisal of her Saturday night date to a secretary friend two floors up. The message was rated R-17 and was both graphic and ungrammatical. When it showed up on every screen in the building, an apology was immediately posted, but the chatty friends were both gone within a month.

The Novell SYSCON utility allows you to change your password with SETPASS. Change it fairly often and don't use easily guessed or sequential passwords like NANCY01, NANCY02, etc. Sabotage does happen. Some workgroups all know each other's passwords and use them freely, a necessity in a desktop publishing environment, for example, where one writer's sudden illness or emergency could keep deadline files locked up. It's a good idea to keep your own backups of anything important on floppies. If you save your files to your own C: drive, be sure to back up this drive. Every hard drive eventually crashes. Every single one of them.

Keeping Your Machine Healthy

Your system administrator has charge of the LAN, but if she's doing her other job, too, she won't have time to do more than call a tech when your machine goes down. You might be machineless for several crucial days if there are no spares. To lessen the likelihood of PC withdrawal, keep a log of weird symptoms and sudden lockups. The repair tech may be able to trace the problem faster with these clues from you.

Keep track of software glitches, too. No program is totally free of bugs, even those on the market for years. You may have accidentally uncovered one of the remaining bugs, when you try an unforeseen combination of keystrokes. If you're using WordPerfect, Microsoft Word, or other popular software, call their 800 help number and report the problem. They may have a workaround. If a version reissue is out that fixes a bug, have your network administrator order the disks ($15 or so).

If your monitor is blank, the cause is usually a loose video cable. Attach it, if you're sure you know where it goes. Some network cable connectors look just like video connectors.

If you can't make contact with the file server (the shell tried to make connection, but no file server answered), the network may have been knocked loose at the back of your machine or at the wall. Turn off your computer, reattach the cable, and try again. The reason for turning off your computer is not safety, this time: the network card may not reset unless you do.

Most people use a mix of network and local software, since not all software is network compatible. If you really rely on the programs or data files that are stored on your local hard disk, take care of your local hard drive. Run a disk health check program and unfragmenter regularly. Don't attempt to test or repair a network hard disk or your systems administrator will, quite rightly, invent ingenious tortures for your benefit.

CHAPTER 7

The Seven-Layer OSI Network Model

We wrote (and trashed) a scholarly discussion of the OSI system—too boring, too confusing, too irrelevant. But your life as a network administrator will be much easier if you understand the OSI layers, especially when dealing with bridges, routers, and gateways. So we decided to tell the story again, this time using mechanical analogies to illustrate how a network job travels through the layers.

Once upon a time, not so long ago ... Jo at Olde Fraud S&L was running a local copy of WordPerfect on her workstation. She wanted to retrieve a copy of the document PLEABARG.AIN from the file server's hard disk. This is the story of PLEABARG.AIN's travels through the network to find a home in Jo's workstation.

We start in the middle, with the file server sending PLEABARG.AIN across the network cable in small pieces. The pieces travel (in our analogy) inside boxes on a conveyor belt (the network cable). This conveyor belt runs past Jo's workstation, past the file server, and past all the other stations on the network. The file server tosses standard-sized boxes on the belt, some addressed to the network card in Jo's workstation, some to other stations. The conveyor belt is Layer 1, the OSI Physical Layer.

The automatic box-snatcher (Layer 2, the Link Layer) at Jo's workstation is alertly reading the address on each box as it flies past. It snatches boxes addressed to this station and inspects the box for damage. The box is return-receipt requested, so the automatic box-snatcher must reply "Box received" or "Box damaged, please send a replacement." Good boxes are handed to Layer 3 (the Network Layer). Meanwhile, Layer 2 at the file server has a stack of return-receipt stubs (to remind it who it sent a box to). If Layer 2 at the file server hears nothing about one of its transmissions, it will assume the box fell off the conveyor belt and got so horribly mangled that it's useless, so the file server sends a replacement box and waits again for a reply.

Layer 3, OSI's Network Layer, unpacks the box. We think it's pretty bogus to name one of the layers the Network Layer—after all, aren't we talking about seven network layers? Nevertheless, they named the third one the Network Layer, so we'll capitalize it to help you keep the terminology straight. When the Network Layer unpacks the box it might find one or many individually addressed envelopes inside. Each envelope will be marked with the process (the conversation) they are part of,

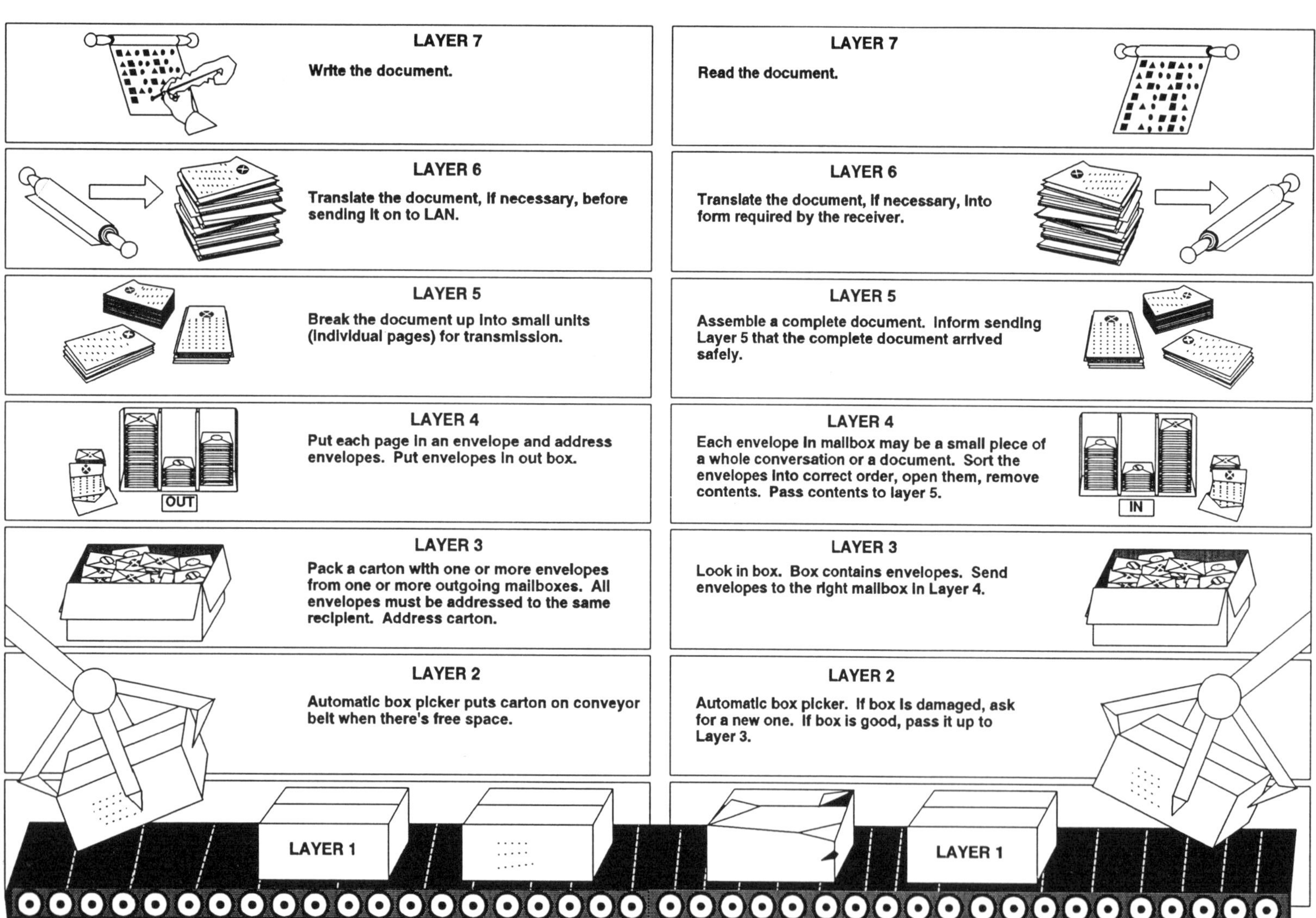

Figure 7.1 7-Layer OSI stack.

and with a number much like the mover's 1/7 (that means Box 1 of 7). Our file PLEABARG.AIN comes in seven envelopes marked A 1/7, A 2/7, A 3/7, etc. Maybe all seven envelopes will be in this box, but more likely not. There may also be envelopes for a second conversation between the file server and this workstation (perhaps someone on the network needs to use Jo's printer—the one she set up as a remote printer with RPRINTER). The Network Layer tosses all envelopes destined for conversation A (in this particular case, the WordPerfect file retrieval process) into Mailbox A. Envelopes for other conversations go into Mailboxes B (RPRINTER stuff), C, etc., as per the instructions on the outside of the envelope.

Layer 4, OSI's Transport Layer, inspects the envelopes in Bin A. Each envelope must be intact (contents still inside) and undamaged. Bin A may have many envelopes in it—in our example we've been talking about a seven-part message. Transport sorts the envelopes in numerical order. If 3/7 is missing, it waits only a short time before sending a message to its Transport counterpart on the file server asking for a replacement envelope. Often, the last envelope will have a checksum (a mathematical way to check if all the data bits arrived safely). When the Transport Layer can be sure it has received the entire message, in order and without error, it hands the envelopes to Layer 5.

In LANs, Layer 5 (the OSI Session Layer) does very little unless you're dealing with fancy distributed processing tasks. Other networks, for example X.25, work the Session Layer pretty hard. Our LAN Session Layer will take the sorted pile of envelopes from Transport, open the envelopes, collate the sheets of paper inside, and staple the pile. Then it's on to the Presentation Layer.

Presentation, OSI's 6th Layer, may do a lot or a little depending on the state of the reassembled message handed to it by Session and the demands of the Application Layer above it. If the message is the way Layer 7 wants it, Presentation just passes it along. On the other hand, the message may be from an Apple to an IBM—and these guys record their information quite differently, as Hebrew reads from right to left and English left to right—and this would require a file translation.

Layer 7, OSI's Application Layer, reads the message. The message is, of course, the text of our WordPerfect document PLEABARG.AIN.

Jo works on the letter at her own workstation, using either a local copy of WordPerfect (one that is stored on her workstation's hard disk) or a network copy (WordPerfect stored on the file server). In either case, much of the WordPerfect program has been loaded into the workstation RAM, and this program in the workstation's RAM is doing most of the document manipulation. Eventually, though, Jo will need to store a file on the file server hard disk. Here's what happens when she does.

Jo tells WordPerfect to save her document to a network drive. Drive H: is mapped to Jo's personal directory of WordPerfect files on the server, so Jo tells the program to "Save document," and "Document to be saved: H:LETTER1.DOC." This is called "making a request."

The network shell running on Jo's workstation intercepts the request and discovers that it is a network request, not a local request. It then packages the request so the file server will understand and obey. A Novell NetWare workstation uses the NETx.COM requester shell with NetWare Core Protocol (NCP). A UNIX workstation uses a requestor from the alphabet-soup of UNIX utilities (NFS or RPC). In either case, the workstation requester functions in Layers 5, 6, and 7 of the OSI model (the Application, Presentation, and Session Layers).

Once the request is constructed, the requester hands it off to the lower layers for transport across the wires. Transport puts pieces of the file into packets and addresses the packets to the file server. The Network Layer packs one or more packets into a carton (a frame) addressed to the file server's network address. The Link Layer tosses the frames onto the wire, and the Physical Layer (the wire) carries the frame along until the file server's Link Layer snatches it off the wire.

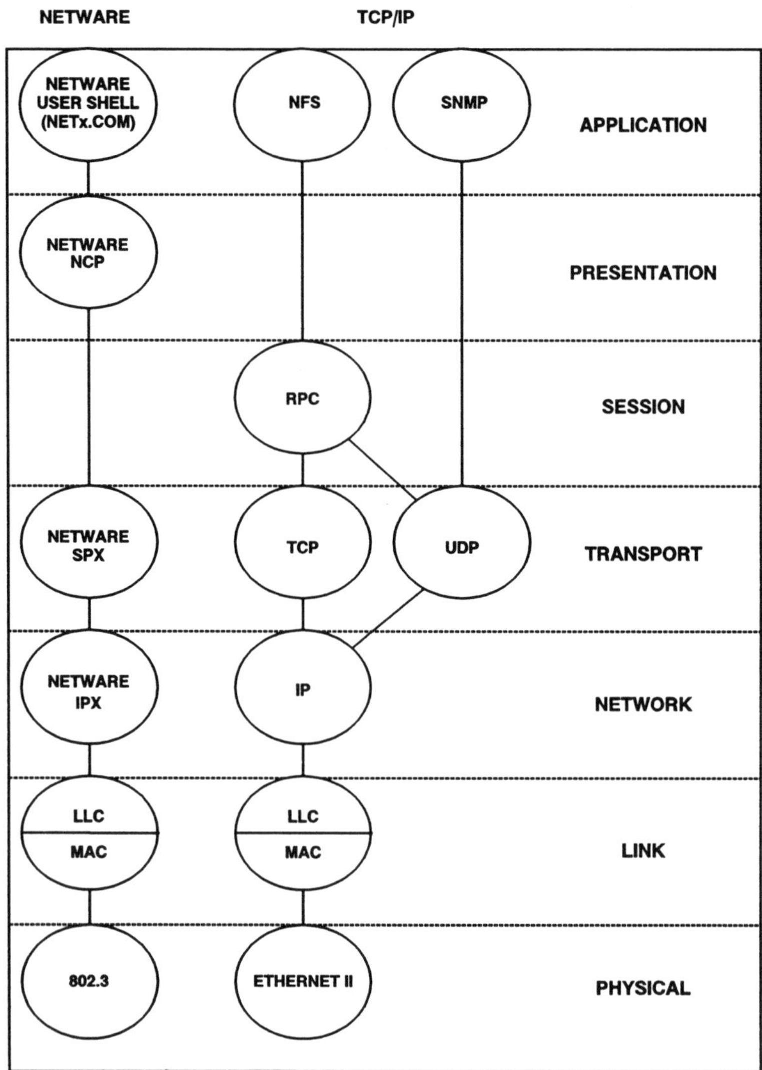

Figure 7.2 TCP/IP and NetWare family tree.

Fun With OSI Layers

Whenever two devices on a LAN talk to each other they must use a common language. Getting different computers to talk to each other is like playing the "How are we related?" game. It's easy for brothers and sisters to see how they connect (same mother or father). But cousins have to go back two generations to find a common ancestor (e.g., his father's mother was my mother's mother). Two people named McLaughlin can probably find a common ancestor if they are willing to go back three, four, or five generations. If you're willing to go back a thousand generations, all people in the world may have a common ancestor. If we want to connect two computers together we work up through the OSI Layers looking for a shared implementation of a particular layer.

Figure 7.3 shows the "family tree" for three networks running Novell NetWare: An ARCNET network, an Ethernet network, and a Token Ring network.

As you can see, Token Ring and Ethernet share the same implementation of Layers 3 through 7 on the OSI model. In fact, they even share the top half of the second layer. Therefore, we need a connecting device that uses the Ethernet-specific factors in Layer 1 (that's the Physical Layer, the card and cables) on one side of the device, but uses the Token Ring-specific factors (Token Ring wiring, etc.) on the other side. In addition, the device (a MAC-Layer bridge) must use the Ethernet version of the MAC-Layer (that's the bottom half of Layer 2) on the Ethernet side. Okay, Ethernet uses CSMA/CD (Carrier Sense Multiple Access with Collision Detect) in the MAC-Layer. On the other hand, the bridge must use Token Ring's token-passing access scheme on the Token Ring side. Once you hit the LLC (Logical Link Control Sublayer—the top of Layer 2), you're home free, because everything else is interchangeable. To use our conveyor-belt-and-box analogy, once the box has been snatched off the conveyor belt, opened up the envelopes inside, and they are all the same (they have all been constructed by the same rules), an Ethernet workstation is as comfortable working with an envelope packed by a Token Ring workstation as another Token Ring station would be.

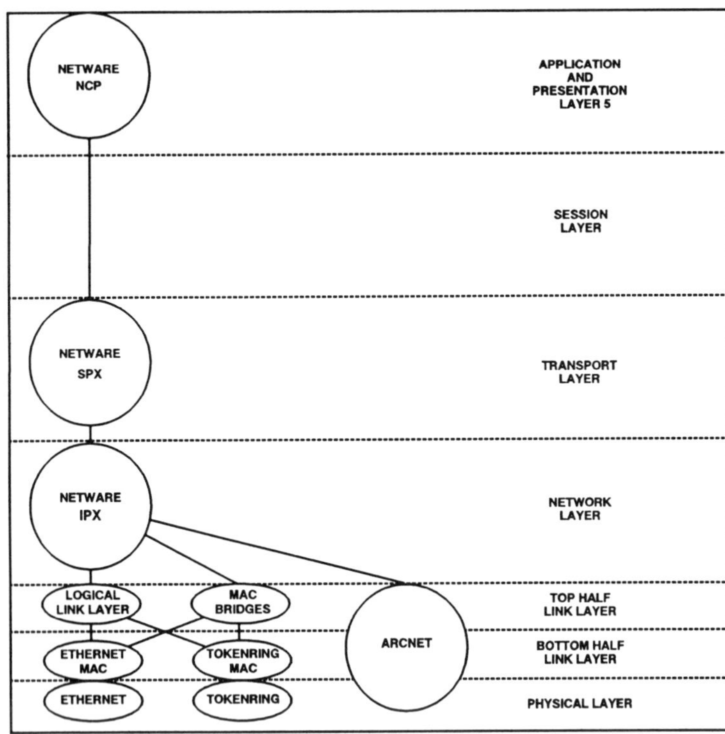

Figure 7.3 *A NetWare family tree (ARCNET, Ethernet, Token Ring).*

When To Bridge, Route, or Throw Open the Gateways

Let's consider some network connections you might wish to make.

We will suggest a simple hardware solution for each example. Remember, though, anything you can do with a simple piece of hardware (one that operates at a low OSI Layer) can usually be done with a more complex piece as well. Repeaters connect two segments of a single LAN together. Bridges, routers, and gateways link multiple LANs, and can do so in very sophisticated ways. We discuss each of these interconnection devices individually in the Data Sheets. It makes sense to think about the problems you need to solve first, though, before we discuss particular hardware solutions.

A segment of an Ethernet LAN to a second segment of an Ethernet LAN, with both segments physically joined (wire-to-wire) at the linking device that we choose.
Use a repeater. We don't have to do any fancy translation here. We don't need to repackage any data; the same boxes will do. The two segments of the LAN (the two conveyor belts in our example) merely need to be connected. We're not dealing with a particularly intelligent device here. The repeater simply passes boxes from one conveyor belt to the other. It does not read addresses or make any decisions. When it sees a box, any Ethernet box, the repeater moves it onto the next conveyor belt.

An Ethernet LAN to another Ethernet LAN, with both LANs physically joined (wire-to-wire) at the linking device that we choose.
Use an IEEE MAC bridge. Why a bridge? Because the frames on both of these networks are constructed to the same exact MAC-Layer protocol. The linking device need not look inside the frames (the boxes on the conveyor) for the data, then repackage it in a different frame format—the original Ethernet frame format will do just fine on both LANs. The bridge does need to differentiate between those frames which should be passed across the bridge and rebroadcast on the far LAN, and the local frames that do not need to cross the bridge to reach their destination. This design puts all the brains in the bridge itself; the bridge keeps a list of which stations are on this side of the bridge and which on that side. In effect, we have a repeater that is smart enough to broadcast a frame only if the other segment needs to hear it.

In box-and-conveyor-belt terms, a frame (a box) is addressed to the recipient, without any additional hints. The bridge has to know if that particular recipient is "on this side" or "on that side" of the bridge—a daunting task in a multi-network, thousand-user environment—so it keeps a list of addresses.

An Ethernet LAN to another Ethernet LAN that is connected to more LANs, again with both LANs physically joined at the linking device. We can use an IEEE MAC bridge with the Spanning Tree Algorithm. When you start connecting multiple LANs together you have to worry about multiple paths between any two stations. Suppose Ethernet card A in accounting sends a frame to card B on the sales LAN. If there are two paths from card A to card B (the frame could go direct, for instance, or take a roundabout route through half the LANs in the company) then card B will get the same frame twice and get confused. Furthermore, the frame will tend to keep circulating endlessly through the LANs because each bridge will pass it over to the next LAN. A Spanning Tree Bridge is capable of recognizing these loops and turning itself off if that's what's necessary to avoid a problem. Again, we have a repeater which is smart enough to broadcast a frame only if the other segment needs to hear it.

A spanning tree bridge works with the standard Ethernet boxes and conveyor belt. The bridge is special, however, because it figures out that it should abstain from connecting conveyor 1 to conveyor 2 if that connection would make a loop. If one of the other conveyor belts breaks down, there is no longer any danger of creating a loop, and the bridge will start connecting conveyor 1 to conveyor 2.

Ethernet networks use the spanning tree technique. Our next example features Token Ring networks.

A Token Ring network to another Token Ring network, both networks physically connected to the linking device.
We can use an IEEE bridge, but it must be the source routing type. (Yes, we are using the word "routing." No, this is not a router, it's another kind of bridge). Source routing bridges are also IEEE MAC-Layer bridges—which is fine, we can use Token Ring frames on each of the Token Ring LANs, so we've found the common ancestor at the MAC level. Source routing puts all the brains in the workstation, not in the bridge. When a workstation sends a frame to a workstation across a bridge, it lists that bridge in the frame's routing field, so the bridge passes it over. Source routing bridges keep no tables of workstation location, they don't need to. They just pass along any frame that contains their bridge number in the routing data field. Again, much like a repeater.

A source routing bridge does not have to do as much work as an Ethernet bridge. In box-and-conveyor-belt terms, any box that needs to be forwarded to the next conveyor belt has the name of the appropriate source routing bridge marked plainly on the outside of the box, "To Jo, care of Bridge 6."

A Token Ring network to an Ethernet network.
Until now we've been discussing "transparent" bridges, the ones that do absolutely nothing to repackage the frame. You'll need a "translating" bridge to hookup the Token Ring to the Ethernet. Again, an IEEE MAC-Layer bridge can handle the problem. Remember that Token Ring and Ethernet are both part of the IEEE's 802 LAN specification, so they are very closely related. Above the bottom half of the second layer, Token Ring and Ethernet are the same. Therefore, a bridge operating at the top half of the second layer can do all of the necessary translation from one frame design to the other. Each network must use the 48-bit address mode (this is the long address form that both Ethernet and Token Ring support) so we will have a common way to address other stations. The bridge keeps a forwarding table of station addresses so it knows whether to send Ethernet frames across to the Token Ring side or not. Any frames coming from the Token Ring side will have the source routing information enclosed (each Token Ring station will have to create a source routing table using long addresses, but that is no problem). The bridge must store the frames coming in from either side. It transmits on the Token Ring network when it gets the token, and follows Ethernet's CSMA/CD access protocol on the Ethernet side.

From the box-and-conveyor perspective, Token Ring conveyors and Token Ring boxes are different from Ethernet conveyor belts and Ethernet boxes. The translating bridge unpacks the Token Ring box, puts the contents in an Ethernet box, and relabels the box using Ethernet addressing conventions.

An Ethernet network in Chicago to an Ethernet network in New York. These two LANs are not physically connected. We'll have to use a pair of "remote bridges." Remote bridges attach to a LAN on one side of the bridge, and to a public or private long-distance data carrier on the other. These bridges operate in pairs.

On the sending LAN, a bridge recognizes that a particular message is destined for the remote LAN. This bridge repackages the Ethernet message inside a package acceptable to the common carrier and hands it off to the carrier. Remote bridges make no attempt to "communicate" with the common carrier. Instead, these bridges employ the carrier as though it were a freight transport company. Properly packaged data should arrive in New York, because that's the carrier's job.

The other bridge, the one in New York, receives the message from the long-distance carrier, removes the carrier's packaging so it looks like an ordinary Ethernet message again, and places it on the remote LAN where the destination workstation is located.

We can choose between a number of common carriers to connect our remote bridges. T-1 dedicated telephone lines are particularly popular in enterprise-wide networks. They are fast and reliable. T-1 and FT-1 (Fractional T-1—which is merely a slice of the full T-1 phone line data-carrying capacity) are point-to-point technologies. For many corporations, this works fine. The head office wants to talk to the branch offices, but branch offices seldom need to directly talk to each other. If you do need a web-like design, which allows any office to talk to any other office, an X.25 public data network is more suitable. Telenet, Tymnet, and most of the long distance phone companies will provide this service. Many writers call X.25 remote bridges "X.25 gateways," not bridges.

If you are using T-1, the Chicago bridge will automatically be connected to its sister bridge in New York. If your organization chooses an X.25 public data network, your gateway must be smart enough to set up the appropriate connection from Chicago to New York, or to New Orleans, or wherever.

T-1 requires a substantial capital investment up front, but the operating cost is less per bit than a public data network. FT-1 costs less per month than T-1, though the bandwidth (the bits/second you can send across the line) is 1/24th of a full T-1 line. Since FT-1 is about 1/20th the cost of a full T-1 line, FT-1 can be a wise choice if you have only moderate traffic between offices. X.25 public data networks charge a lot per bit to transfer data, but you get flexible connections and the up-front cash investment is very small.

From the box-and-belt perspective, imagine that remote bridges connect a conveyor belt to the Roadway Parcel pickup point. Our remote bridge has no control over Roadway Parcel. Presumably the box will get to the sister bridge in New York. Roadway Parcel has its own weird packaging rules, so the bridge snatches a box off the conveyor belt, reboxes it in Roadway Parcel-compliant packaging, and hopes for the best. At the other end, the remote bridge unpacks the Roadway Parcel carton and places the original Ethernet box on the conveyor belt in New York. Because this is a remote connection via common carrier, New York usually sends a return message to Chicago confirming receipt of the package.

An Ethernet network in Chicago to an Ethernet network in New York (Plan 2).
Our last example used a bridge, or X.25 gateway, to connect these two networks. You could use a router instead—a more intelligent (though slower) machine.

A bridge requires that every workstation on every connected network have a unique address. Luckily, there is a universal 48-bit address format which gives each Ethernet or Token Ring network card on the planet its own address. On the other hand, the networks you are connecting may not use this 48-bit universal address format—so you may have to rely on luck and network-supervisor intervention to resolve address conflicts. Routers, by comparison, use the network address to route messages. You must be sure that each network has a unique address, but that's a much easier task, and each workstation on a particular network must have its own address, but again that's a manageable task—and a necessary precondition for working local networks, not just internetworking.

If you're dealing with multiple networks connected through multiple pathways you really should use a router. The router will send the message once, via the best path, even though there are multiple possible pathways. In some cases the router will choose the shortest path, in others, the fastest or the least congested path. These choices are controlled by the routing table, which may be either static (the network administrator specifies which path to use between any two points) or dynamic (the router uses network management software based on SNMP to determine what other network components are up and functioning).

A router performs much like the Roadway Parcel pick-up/drop-off point in the last example, but it is much more flexible. The router snatches boxes destined for the far network, chooses an appropriate common carrier, and reboxes the Ethernet boxes to meet the common carrier's specifications. In some cases, this means repackaging the contents in smaller boxes. In most cases, a quick wrap with brown paper will do the trick.

An Ethernet network to an ARCNET network.
A bridge cannot connect either Ethernet or Token Ring to ARCNET. ARCNET allows up to 252-byte (or 507-byte) data messages inside the ARCNET frame (the data-package on the network wire is called a frame). Ethernet allows up to 1492 bytes of data inside each frame. When an Ethernet workstation tries to send a big frame to an ARCNET workstation the ARCNET station thinks the frame is bad and ignores it. Therefore, we need an intelligent router capable of disassembling the Ethernet frame, extracting the message data, and repackaging the message inside multiple little ARCNET frames.

Our router snatches a box off the Ethernet network, unpacks it, and repacks the contents into a smaller ARCNET box (or maybe a couple of boxes), then sets the ARCNET boxes on the ARCNET conveyor belt. Packages coming in the opposite direction (ARCNET to Ethernet) will have to be repackaged too. ARCNET allows much smaller frames (boxes) than Ethernet, so our repacker will often put a tiny ARCNET box into a huge Ethernet box, then fill the rest of the frame with the electronic equivalent of styrofoam peanuts (with zeros).

An Ethernet or Token Ring network to an IBM mainframe.
We're not talking about a 3270 card in one workstation (a 3270 card would connect that particular workstation, not the whole network, to the IBM mainframe). We want to connect the entire LAN to an IBM mainframe. For this we will need an SNA Gateway on the LAN.

SNA is IBM's wide area network (WAN) scheme. It predates OSI, so it is not strictly compatible on any layer with an OSI Layer. Therefore, our SNA gateway must take a message on the LAN, uncode it layer-by-layer, then re-encode it in the SNA protocol and send the SNA message out on the cable headed toward the mainframe. On the SNA side, the gateway masquerades as a terminal cluster controller or a communications controller. On the LAN side, the gateway looks like any other Ethernet or Token Ring node—this node just happens to be a communications server rather than a file server or a workstation.

Because SNA and OSI share no protocol layers, you can't take any shortcuts. On the Ethernet side of the SNA gateway, a box (frame) enters from the Ethernet wire. The gateway opens the Ethernet box, unpacks the envelopes, and sorts them into appropriate mail boxes. Then the gateway opens the envelopes, removes the contents and collates them, and translates the whole data message into a generic format. The SNA side of the gateway grabs the generic message, translates it into SNA-speak, and packages the message into SNA-style frames for transmission on the SNA conveyor belt using an entirely different box, SNA addressing, and a box-snatcher that follows SNA rules.

Consider a NetWare Router for Local Connections

We have barely scratched the surface of bridges/routers/gateways. Most of you have small LANs—the majority of business LANs are under 20 stations. You are not using cross-country links, nor connecting multiple interlocking networks. For your purposes, a Novell NetWare "bridge" (the original NetWare term, we know it's confusing, but it really **is** a router) or router (NetWare 2.2 or 3.11) will probably do the trick.

NetWare's router (bridge) software is free with your copy of NetWare and it runs on an ordinary XT workstation (or AT if you want to run a print server or a network management VAP on the bridge too). These routers connect ARCNET, Ethernet, and Token Ring networks to each other, and each router may connect up to four networks. Please don't get cheap and try to use a non-dedicated bridge; if the workstation locks up while running an application it will also choke the bridge.

For more info about bridges and routers see *Local Networks* by William Stallings. James Martin's *SNA: IBM's Networking Solution* will help you understand SNA. Wellfleet Communications' *Simplifying LAN/WAN Integration* is a very helpful pamphlet that will help you communicate the technical issues to non-technical management.

CHAPTER 8

Installing LAN Cards and Drivers

It's not hard to install a network interface card. It's just another kind of PC expansion card. If you've ever replaced a video card or installed a modem, you're familiar with the physical skills required. If you haven't, get help with your first card installation. Frankly, getting the cover off the PC is three-fourths of the problem.

Now let's consider the mental work involved. As with most computer cards, you must think through a LAN card installation in advance to avoid common problems. It is important to know the configuration of the machine the card is going into and the configuration of the card. These two configurations must not conflict (that's when your dance partner steps on your foot, or your LAN card steps on your modem's interrupt). So, an important part of LAN management is hardware configuration management.

How to Install Cards and Drivers
(Without Crashing Everything Else)

Know the configuration of the network as a whole.
For example, you might have an ARCNET network equipped with standard ARCNET hubs and cards. You've decided to install three ARCNETplus cards (roughly eight times as fast as original ARCNET) in your file server and your two most heavily-used workstations. The fine print says, though, that you need ARCNETplus-compatible hubs wherever the signal path between these three fast cards crosses a hub. You better know such things before you install the new ARCNETplus cards.

You will need to know:

- Whether the network is ARCNET, Ethernet, or Token Ring—then get a compatible card to install in this workstation.
- If it's Token Ring, the speed of network—either 4 Mbps or 16 Mbps, and all of the cards on the network must be set to use the same speed.

- If it's a Token Ring network equipped with bridges you will need to run the source routing utility on each workstation—see your NetWare **Installation Supplements** manual.
- If it's Ethernet, the frame format the card uses—in most cases this will be the standard 802.3 frame, but you might have a UNIX network running with Ethernet_II frames (some call this Ethernet 2.0).
- The kind of addresses you are using in this network—Ethernet and Token Ring can use 48-bit universal, 48-bit local, or 16-bit local. NetWare only supports the 48-bit universal address or the 48-bit local address (use the ODI driver for local addressing). Most networks use the universal addressing scheme — it's convenient, it's how the card is set by the factory, and it automatically gives you a unique address. On the other hand, a universally addressed card in a locally addressed network could wreak havoc.

Know the configuration of the machine that the card is going into.
Use a diagnostic utility program to get the hardware and software information for your computer. Our favorite, right now, is QAPlus/fe, which is exceptionally complete and accurate. Most comprehensive utility programs, for example PCTools and Norton Utilities, have a system information (hardware/software configuration) module. In addition, Qualitas' ASQ, CheckIt, and WinSleuth (a windows configuration utility) will tell you what cards are installed in the computer, the interrupts they use, the memory addresses and DMAs they're using, etc.

Once you know what's already installed in the computer, you will be able to choose non-conflicting network card settings. For example, many modems are set to COM2. The average Ethernet card comes from the manufacturer set to I/O 360 and IRQ3, causing a conflict with COM2. This is why you need to know the configuration of a machine before you work on it. If you don't know the configuration, you can waste hours of your time.

When you're ready to actually install a network card, turn to the Data Sheets in the back of this book, to the Network Interface Card section—we have extremely detailed card installation instructions there.

Keep a record of the network card settings you used in a particular computer.
If this workstation's IPX and/or boot disk must be replaced, written records give you the data you need to recreate them. Do your best to use the same configuration on all machines. Although complete uniformity is impossible in practice, the more machines using a particular IPX the better. Configuration management utilities are very helpful—see Chapter 5, *Choosing and Using Network Utilities.*

Choosing a Network Card to Install

It is best to use the same brand of card in the entire network. When we have mixed brands we sometimes were plagued with mysterious network crashes which disappeared when we standardized on a particular card. This is not a covert plug for expensive cards—just stick with one brand.

Fast cards should go in your high-use machines: the file server, workstations for graphics users, and workstations for people who have to query a non-network database. A non-network database has no NLM on the server to split the search work between the server and the workstation, so all records must be sent down-wire to the workstation whenever you do a search. Two examples are dBase and Paradox. They're okay for light duty, but use a client-server database for heavy-duty database work on a network.

The Software That Goes With the Cards

The LAN card driver tells the PC how to interact with the physical network card. There are two forms of LAN card drivers:

1. The standard IPX-only driver generated with the WSGEN or SHGEN program. If you will only be using the IPX protocol, this driver will do just fine and will save you about 30K of memory per workstation.

2. The ODI driver for this card, a software file supplied by the card manufacturer or Novell. ODI drivers are software-configurable, a very nice feature. The driver comes from the manufacturer set to popular defaults, but you may easily change the interrupt, DMA, I/O ports, frame format, or protocols supported on this port. When the machine boots, it runs the driver and configures it according to an ASCII list of configuration specifications stored in the NET.CFG file. For complete instructions, see theDOS ODI Workstation section of the Novell manuals. Novell is headed away from the old SHGEN/WSGEN (option 1) toward ODI drivers because they are so flexible. If you want AppleTalk or TCP/IP support, you **must** use the ODI driver. With this driver, a NetWare workstation can support all three protocols (AppleTalk, IPX, and TCP/IP) simultaneously.

Workstation Memory Management Tricks

NetWare's XMSNETx.COM and EMSNETx.COM shells load into extended or expanded memory respectively. They then require only 8K of DOS memory space in the crowded first 640K of memory. Neither shell has been found to cause conflicts with standard software. The card driver, whether IPX or the NetWare ODI driver, is a different matter.

If somebody were smart they'd invent a new Phoenix-compatible BIOS complete with ODI drivers. You'd configure the driver and shell with CMOS, the same way you set the number and type of hard drives in CMOS. Using this BIOS, a workstation would use up no DOS memory to support a LAN card. Since no one has invented this BIOS-with-ODI-driver, we must allocate 80+K of memory to the IPX or ODI driver for each workstation. Even when you log off the network, IPX and NETx remain in the workstation's RAM memory. Why do you care? Because the memory used by IPX and NETx is not available to your DOS programs. "Insufficient memory" errors are annoying.

To get back the memory that IPX or the ODI driver and NETx use, you could reboot your workstation and abstain from loading IPX and NETx. Better to use a memory manager to set your workstation up right in the first place. For the NETx shell, use one of the high loading shells (EMSNETx or XMSNETx). DOS 5, DR DOS 6, or 386MAX will move the standard IPX driver into so-called high memory (HI DOS) on a 286 or 386 computer. ODI drivers are not so easily moved—so don't try it. But maybe you can move other programs out of the first 640K and into high memory.

Here is some background you will need if you're going to move the standard IPX.COM driver or other pesky memory-hogging programs into high memory. Memory is packaged in 64K increments for technical reasons (64K is a round number in hexadecimal, as 100 or 10000 is a round decimal number). The first 64K of memory is the 0-to-0FFFF segment (remember, we're using hexadecimal numbers here). The second 64K segment is 10000-to-1FFFF, the third is the 20000's, etc. In hexadecimal, the tenth segment is A0000-to-AFFFF. The eleventh segment is B0000-to-BFFFF.

There is a second way to write the address BFFFF; some people would instead use this notation: B000:FFFF. Two ways to say the same thing. If you run into documentation using the 0000:FFFF notation, translate that to the 5-digit format like this:

> Take the first part of the number and add a zero on the end. B000 becomes B0000. Add the second part of the number. B0000 plus FFFF equals BFFFF.

A third kind of memory address notation explicitly names the segment and assumes the offset is zero. B0000 (which is also B000:0000) becomes B000 in this third system.

Sorry to torture you with this, but you'll see all three kinds of notation in the literature. Figure 8.1, based on a chart from Qualitas, uses the 4-digit segment notation rather than segment and offset (xxxx:xxxx). We prefer the 5-digit notatation. You need to get used to all three forms. Eventually you will automatically know whether a particular writer is using the 4-digit or 5-digit system from their sentence context.

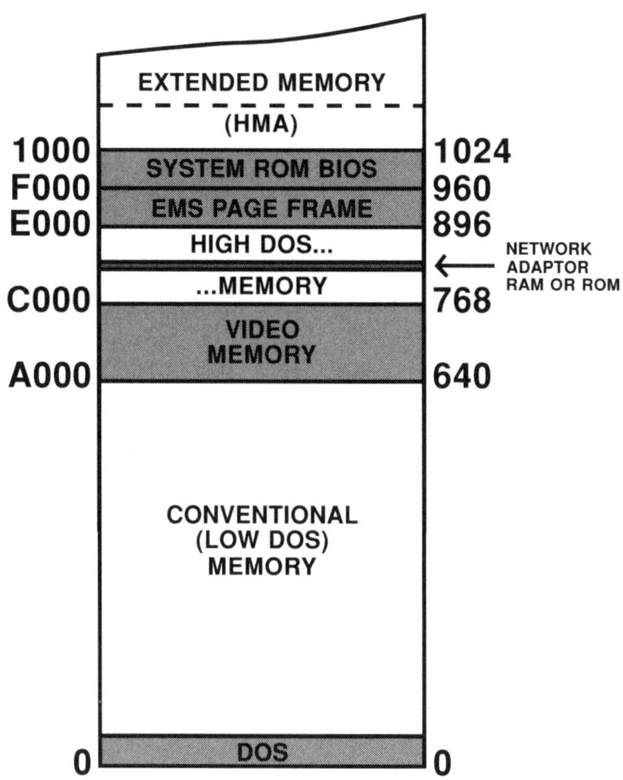

Figure 8.1 *How memory is used in a PC.*

Computer people use four different names for PC memory, depending on the address where the memory exists.

To refresh your memory:

- Conventional (Low DOS) memory is segments 0-9. This is the classic 640K.
- High DOS memory, a term popularized by memory manager utilities, refers to unused portions of segments A-F. Generally, these managers remap extended memory RAM chips so the chips appear to be located in otherwise unused portions of the A, B, C, D, E, and F segments. Doing this can give DOS 728K or more of usable program space. Remember, DOS programs can access only the first 1 meg of memory directly, by name. The first Meg contains segments 0 through F. The more ROMs you have in your computer (sytem ROM BIOS, VGA video card ROM, hard disk controller ROM, network adapter card ROM, etc.) the less extra space available in High DOS memory, but every bit you can squeeze out will help. To use this High DOS memory you will need 386MAX, HIMEM.SYS, or QEMM.
- Expanded memory (EMS) is another technique that allows programs to increase their data space in the magic first megabyte of memory that DOS programs can access by name. Expanded memory, also called bank-switched and LIM memory, uses a small 16K window of memory in the C, D, or E segments to view a much larger collection of memory chips "off line." When you need a particular piece of information in the EMS memory, the EMS memory manager fetches the contents of the off-line memory chips into the window (the EMS page frame) so your program can access the data.
- Extended memory is in segments above the F segment. That means 100000 and up. Only 286, 386, and 486 computers have extended memory, the XTs and XT clones are limited to DOS memory, High DOS memory, and expanded memory.

Memory managers load (map) LAN drivers, and other software, into high memory, often the C0000-to-CFFFF or the D0000-to-DFFFF segments. Such mapping must be done with care or conflicts will arise. If you use a memory manager, note which one and how it is set up on the configuration sheet for this workstation. These memory managers will use one of three methods:

1. They will use expanded memory to store unneeded programs that were formerly loaded into DOS memory. When a program is needed, the manager moves the required piece back into DOS

memory. This is called bank switching. These memory managers may also take extended memory (the physical chips are extended memory) and turn it into expanded memory (it looks like expanded memory to the computer). This is how QEMM works. 386MAX uses a similar technique in one mode of operation. EMSNETx.COM, the NetWare expanded memory shell does this too.

2. They may remap extended memory into unused portions of segments A to F, the High DOS memory we mentioned before. 386MAX also uses this mode of operation.
3. They use extended memory. The manager moves DOS programs into extended memory, then swaps them back into DOS memory space when needed. This is how XMSNETx.COM works.

The best technique for you to use depends on the configuration of your machine and the other programs you're running. Any decent memory manager will have an optimizing utility to help you make these decisions.

Don't Waste Memory

The system login script takes approximately 70K of memory. If you jump out of the login script to a batch file, the computer will keep the login script in memory (tying up that 70K) until you finally EXIT the login script. Therefore, don't put a command like

#WP

(which means go execute the DOS program called WP) in the middle of your login script. If you want the user to exit and immediately execute the WP program, this command is much better:

EXIT "WP"

(which means EXIT from the login script and release the memory, then run the WP program).

CHAPTER 9

WYSIWIMP: What You See Is What Might Print

When the president's secretary hovers around the shared printer, everybody knows that something is up. When users can't run memory-intensive programs (Excel, Lotus 3.0, DrawPerfect), their productivity plummets. When print jobs randomly disappear from the face of the earth, users go crazy. These are symptoms of poor network-printer planning.

First research your printing requirements, then consider the technical aspects. Because network printing technology has advanced substantially in the last three years, you'll be able to do almost anything you want to do. So the real question is "What do I want?" Ask your end-users what they do with their PCs, and what they need to print. Most managers, perhaps appropriately, don't have a clue what their staff actually does. So ask management what their department needs—it's diplomatic and wise to make management happy. But also ask the staff. Ask them what they do, what they like and dislike, and what worked well or poorly the last place they worked. Then design your network printing so both users and management are happy.

Here are some principles of good design:

- Printers should be close to the people using them. Anyone who prints two or three-page letters all day needs her own printer, or one that is only a few steps away.
- Don't put a shared printer next to a person whose work will be constantly interrupted by people who come to pick up their print jobs. People will start calling this printer-sitter to see if their job has printed yet—very disruptive. Better to put it outside the user's cubicle partition.
- People who spend all day printing huge internal documents like database reports and spreadsheets need fast low-quality printers near their desks so they can easily monitor their print jobs.
- If your organization has enough large-document printer traffic, it may make sense to put two laser printers side-by-side and route the laser printer queue to both printers on a first-available-printer basis. That way the small jobs in the print queue will be promptly serviced by the less-busy printer when a 400-page report has the other one tied up for close to an hour.

- A heavy-duty printer can produce 20,000 pages a month or more, can hold a ream or more of raw paper in the input tray, and has an equally large output tray. Lighter-duty laser printers don't hold up when printing multiple reams per day. Buy a printer that matches your print volume.
- If you can, print long jobs during off hours. This will free up network cable space too—these big documents can bog down an overloaded network. You'll need an HP Laserjet IIISi or equivalent heavy-duty printer with the big paper trays if you intend to print enormous jobs unattended.
- If your organization prints a lot of graphics, you'll need a lot of printers and fast computers to feed the graphics files to the printers.For example, an 8-page per minute printer (text) becomes a 10-minute per page printer when composing complex graphics pages. It may make sense to give your graphics users their own dedicated printers to avoid frustrating your text users. Or you may decide to go with one of the very high speed network printers optimized for graphics.
- Consider confidentiality issues. Perhaps the Chief Financial Officer or the accounting department really needs a private printer—or maybe they both do.
- Don't let the political process overly affect your printer placement decisions. A printer right next to the desk is often a sign of status. If you must submit to status considerations, try to provide other, more conveniently located printers for the masses. People with this kind of pull probably require a dedicated printer for confidentiality reasons anyway.
- Predictable printing means happy users. Not speedy printing or beautiful printing, though they'll want that too eventually. By predictable printing we mean the user knows where to find the finished print job and what it's going to look like. To make life predictable, set up a default CAPTURE command in the system login script or the user login scripts. Use the SPOOL command to set up a default print queue for any user who issues his own CAPTURE command but forgets to specify a queue.
- Use the NetWare PRINTCON utility to define preferred print job configuration options for each user. PRINTCON creates a database of pre-defined print job styles. For example, your organization (or an individual user) may want to define a standard spreadsheet format, one which uses compressed printing, an extra-long time-out count, and a special print queue. Then the user can type

  CAPTURE JOB=*jobconfiguration*

  instead of typing (or mistyping) each individual CAPTURE option by hand. One of your users will be particularly skilled at creating print job configurations. When she gets her PRINTCON database set up to her satisfaction, copy the PRINT.DAT file stored in her MAIL directory to each new user's MAIL directory. Be careful not to overwrite an old user's PRINT.DAT file without their permission—you'll destroy all their personalized print job configurations.

Standalone PC Printing Versus Network Printing

An application running in a standalone PC sends a print job to that PC's printer port, where the printer cable carries the print job to the printer. There is no need to queue up multiple user's print jobs, because we only have one user and a single dedicated printer.

Now consider a print job sent from a network workstation and out along the network cable to a distant printer. First, the network workstation is running a network shell which can intercept the print job data stream headed for the printer port and reroute it out onto the network cable. When we issue a CAPTURE command we tell the workstation shell to reroute the print job to a queue.

But which queue? We can explicitly name the queue in the CAPTURE command, e.g., CAPTURE Q=queue1. If no queue is explicitly defined in the CAPTURE command, the print job data stream is automatically sent to the default queue (if the network administrator remembered to set one up with the SPOOL command). If there is no default print queue, CAPTURE chokes with the error message "No default queue name can be found on the server."

The print queues are subdirectories of your file server's SYSTEM directory. Each queue's Print Queue ID, which is listed in PCONSOLE under Print Queue Information, is used for that queue's subdirectory name. Once the print job is in the queue, the print server tracks it and sends it to the queue's printer when that printer is available.

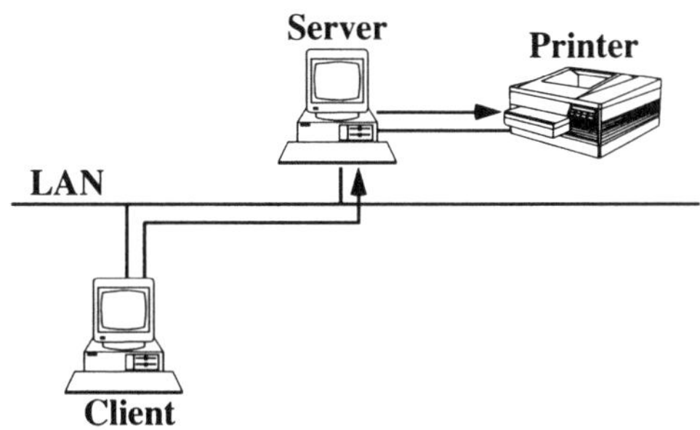

Figure 9.1 File server connect. Diagram courtesy of Hewlett-Packard Company.

Five Ways to Print on a NetWare LAN

In each of the following cases, the printer is connected either directly to the network cable or to a computer/machine which is, in turn, connected to the network cable. That makes sense. We have to move the print jobs out of the print queue on the file server and down the cable to the network printer.

1. Direct file server connection. This technique is cheap, straightforward, and may be suitable for a small office with only a couple of printers. Your file server will probably be locked up, though, or at least sequestered in a low-traffic office. Does that mean the printers must be sequestered with the file server too? Not necessarily, you can run cables out of the file-server room to a printer in a public area. Unfortunately, Centronics parallel printer cables run only 20-30 feet (if you're lucky). Serial printer cables can be run farther, but serial printers are much slower than parallel printers, and even Centronics (parallel) speed is nothing to brag about.

2. Printer attached to a dedicated print server located out in the work area. This is better than connecting directly to the file server. You can put a dedicated print server wherever you wish and run one or more printers off of it. Unfortunately, the dedicated print server looks (and is) just like a workstation. That means people might turn it off and on like an ordinary workstation, disrupting printing and (this is most important) losing one or more print jobs in the process. Losing print jobs drives users crazy—especially the less sophisticated users who can't figure out if the job is really lost, or still waiting in the queue, or it never got to the queue because they blew it when they tried to send the job to the network printer. When space is valuable, many offices don't want to sideline a full-sized computer in productive workspace just to run a couple of printers. Still, the price is right, because any old XT or XT-clone will work fine as a dedicated print server.

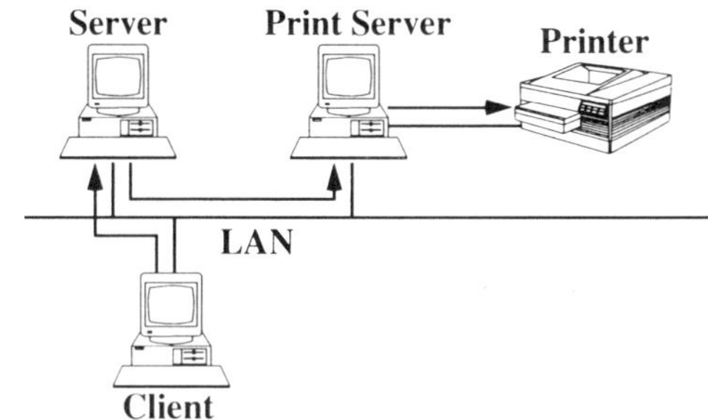

Figure 9.2 Dedicated print server. Diagram courtesy of Hewlett-Packard Company.

3. Printer attached to a specialized print server (e.g. Castelle's LANpress, Intel's NetPort, or Microtest's LANPort). These specialized print servers have all the advantages of a dedicated workstation print server and none of the disadvantages. The print server plugs into the LAN cable wherever

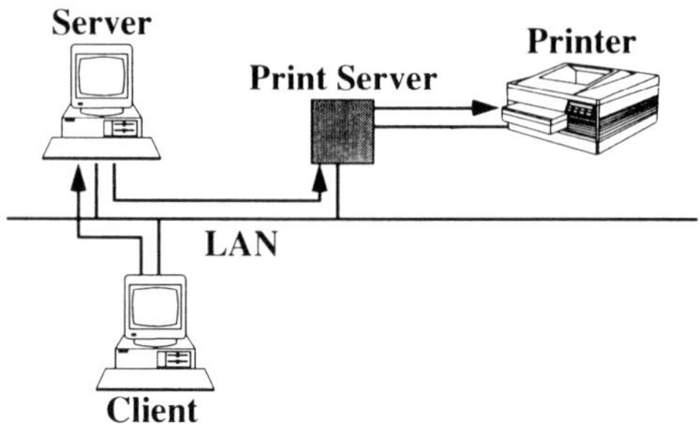

Figure 9.3 Specialized print server. Diagram courtesy of Hewlett-Packard Company.

you wish, drives multiple printers (the numbers vary from manufacturer to manufacturer), and is small enough to mount on the side of your laser printer (see photo, Figure 211). These servers are limited, though, to the speed of the print cable connecting the print server box to the printer. For some of these products, that means Centronics (parallel) printer cable speeds, though others use special high-speed connections between printer and server. We don't attempt to rate particular products here—they are changing fast and you're better off consulting recent computer magazine product reviews when you are ready to buy. We do suggest that you consider using these specialized print servers on any LAN where space, style, and security are a consideration—they are far superior to dedicated workstation print servers on all three counts.

4. A local workstation printer attached to a network workstation running a TSR (Terminate and Stay Resident) program which allows the network to use this printer for network print jobs—this is called (somewhat cryptically) Remote Printing. This sounds like a very attractive alternative, like getting something for nothing. The local workstation printers do double duty as remote network printers, you can put them anywhere in the work area, and it all seems to be free—no additional hardware to buy. We don't recommend remote printing, though, because you pay in network administrator's support headaches for every dollar you save. The remote printer feature uses up precious memory and processing power on the client workstation supporting the remote printer. You're likely to have the workstation's owner angry at you. In addition, any troubles at the workstation (user turns off machine by mistake, user reboots machine in the middle of someone else's print job, user tries to print directly to the printer rather than using the network queues like everybody else) can cause the ultimate network printing sin—losing a print job. And remote printing tends to be substantially slower than printing to a network printer connected directly to a print server or to the network cable.

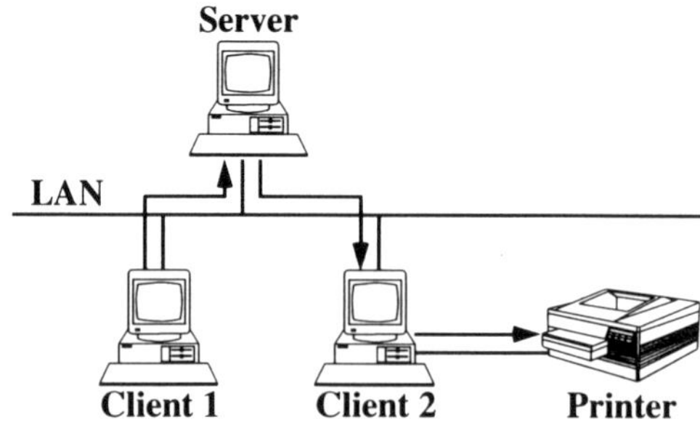

Figure 9.4 Client connect with TSR. Diagram courtesy of Hewlett-Packard Company.

If you want to use Remote Printing, you must run the RPRINTER NetWare utility program on the workstation attached to the printer you are intending to use. RPRINTER allows the print server to take over the workstation's local printer and use it to print network jobs. If you do decide to use this remote printer technique, set NetWare's RPRINTER command up so the workstation can function as a remote printer site whether your user is logged in or not, and tell the workstation's user to leave the computer on 24 hours a day.

Warn users working on stations running the RPRINTER software to route their print jobs to the network print queue with the CAPTURE command like everyone else does. If they don't, choosing instead to print in local mode, the network may insert a few pages of someone else's spreadsheet into the report they are printing. Alternatively, these users may switch their local printer to Private mode with the PSC command before starting a print job.

Type **PSC PS=printserver_name P=printer_number PRI**

Novell's **Print Server** manual gives complete directions for the PSC command. Only authorized print server operators can use the PRIvate switch, so the network supervisor must remember to add the workstation user to the print server operator list.

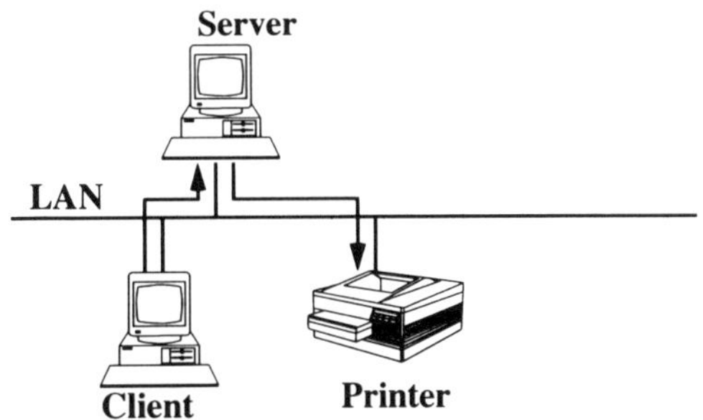

Figure 9.5 *Direct printer connection. Diagram courtesy of Hewlett-Packard Company.*

5. Printer directly connected to the LAN cable with internal network-printer interface (e.g. Castelle's JetPress or HP's LaserJet Network-Printer Interface Cards). These printer interfaces slip inside an HP LaserJet, connecting directly to the LaserJet's high-speed I/O bus. They are fast, really fast. Even older HP LaserJet IIs and IIIs will print substantially faster with one of these network-printer interfaces than they will using any of the four previous techniques. And these interfaces allow you to put the printer anywhere out in the work area along the network cable.

Printing Topology

Your choice of printing topology affects traffic on the network cable and the computational load at the file server. If you run your printers directly off the file server, the print job will travel on the network cable only once—from the workstation to the file server. The print job travels on a separate print cable from file server to printer.

By comparison, when you use a remote printer, a dedicated workstation print server, or a specialized print server, or a network-printer interface inside a LaserJet, the print job travels on the cable twice (once to the queue in the file server, once to the printer). On a network that is already bogging down from cable congestion, this extra traffic may be significant. A couple of suggestions to reduce this traffic: Can you hold any print jobs until off hours? You could also split the long trunk cable into two networks with a bridge (either a bridge in the file server or a dedicated workstation bridge). If you do split the network, split it intelligently, keeping user, printer, and print queue on the same side of the bridge for the majority of your print traffic.

Of course, running the PSERVER.NLM program on your file server adds an additional computation burden to your file server's CPU, but this is no big deal with NetWare 386. It has been designed to gracefully handle multiple tasks.

Setting Up the Print Queues and Print Servers

Our Data Sheet section on print servers covers printing setup. The Novell **Printer** manual also does a good job. Just remember to start simple and do everything step-by-step, and in the order prescribed in the manual.

Using CAPTURE

CAPTURE reroutes printing requests from local printer port(s) to the network print-queue/print-server system. Supervisors who want to specify a number of system-wide printing defaults should put a default CAPTURE command in the system login script to do the following:

- Notify users when their jobs are done.
- Use or eliminate the default user-identification banner at the beginning of each print job.
- Allow printing from an application without exiting that application.
- Other print customizing.

Use the SPOOL command to map SPOOL 0 to a default queue to protect any users who neglect to specify a queue in their print requests. SPOOL is a file server console command, so it is only accessible to Supervisors or other console operators. It makes sense to put the SPOOL command in the AUTOEXEC.NCF file on the file server so it executes each time the file server is booted. AUTOEXEC.NCF, you'll remember, plays the same role on your network file server that AUTOEXEC.BAT does on a workstation.

The SPOOL command also allows us to use applications written for earlier versions of NetWare, which sent print jobs to printer numbers rather than to print queues.

To print without leaving the application, set the Time Out variable with the CAPTURE command to 1-30 seconds. After the TI (Time Out) number of seconds have expired with no additional data sent to the printer, NetWare assumes the print job is complete and sends the captured data to be printed.

> **Warning:** You may need to experiment to determine the right value to use for the CAPTURE TI (Time Out) variable. Consider a workstation running Windows or DesqView which is doing heavy foreground Lotus 1-2-3 work while printing in the background. There might be long pauses in the printing while the foreground calculates. TI=10, a typical value, might be too short, causing the network to truncate your half-finished page and start on a new print job after 10 seconds of silence from your computer.

If an extra sheet of blank paper appears between print jobs, check for an extra FF (Form Feed) in the CAPTURE command. Check for a missing FF if the last page in a print job does not eject from the printer. Laser printers need at least one form feed at the end of a print job because they will not format a page (compute where the black dots should go) or print a page until 1) they get a full page or 2) the print buffer is full. Dot matrix printers will print the half-page, but they won't advance to the top of the next page unless they get a form feed.

It is generally a good idea to set CAPTURE to No Tabs. Text applications seldom give you a problem when CAPTURE is set to byte stream mode (No Tabs) instead of TABS, and TABS can seriously mess up graphics.

A Postscript printer will lock up if you send a Banner at the beginning of the print job (the Banner page is not PostScript). Use the NB (No Banner) CAPTURE command option.

Some Hints to Head Off Printing Angst

Use caution when limiting a user's file server storage space. NetWare print queues are subdirectories of the SYS:SYSTEM directory. NetWare automatically stores a user's print job as a file in the appropriate print queue subdirectory—with the user's name attached as owner, so the print job counts against the user's total authorized file server storage space. Too little space on the volume, or too little space left in a user's space allocation, will cause the print job to choke with a Network Spooler Error. Use VOLINFO periodically, as well, to keep track of the total free space on your file server's hard disk.

Distribute a "cheat sheet" on printing to your users, giving them the details on network printing. Include information such as:

1. What a print queue is.
2. How it works.
3. The name of their print queue(s).
4. How to use PCONSOLE to check their print job status.
5. How to use CAPTURE—give them examples, using your network's queue names, etc.
6. The JOB names that have already been configured for them with PRINTCON, and how to specify a particular print job configuration in their CAPTURE command.

CHAPTER 10

E-Mail: The Most Popular Application

The most popular LAN application is E-Mail, by far. Users are blasé about most network applications, having seen them in their standalone lives, but communications and scheduling are LAN-specific applications that couldn't be done before.

Many users are hooked up to the PC network only for mail, while they do their work entirely on another network. In fact, one 1000-user Federal agency LAN, spanning two buildings and requiring an 11-person staff (one CNE, two technical helpers, and eight support staff), is almost entirely dedicated to E-Mail. Note that, in this context, E-Mail means cc:Mailing a 100-page proposal to 20 different people on the network, not asking Roy to meet you after work for a beer.

This particular network is also connected via a gateway into an IBM mainframe, and from there to NIH's elaborate networks. This is not representative of a typical small business network, but it is quite typical of a modern multi-platform communications environment.

In this kind of environment, picking the right E-Mail software can get interesting. Here is where standards become important: Which one will let you send mail transparently across multiple networks? Right now, probably no one package will, but with add-ons and tweaks and intermediate handling, it's possible.

E-Mail Standards

There are currently two main E-Mail standards: MHS (Message Handling Service) and X.400, the CCITT recommendation for messaging.

Of the two, X.400 is the more important, because it is an international standard and is absolutely required if you will be going that route. The standard defines the international standards for the envelope fields, specifying the order and length of such things as name and address fields. For global E-Mail to become a reality, the standard must be paired with X.500 for directory ("electronic post office") standards.

The problem with X.400 is that it is not really settled. You know for a fact that in four years the standards committee will come out with a different standard, so people in the real world have a hard time implementing X.400, or any standard that is subject to periodic revision. An example is X.25, which is mostly used in its 1980 flavor, despite 1984 and 1988 revisions, because it takes more than four years to deploy one of these things. So you never really catch up. This isn't a great concern to the average user, but it drives the software developers nuts.

If you have some idea of bridging into international public domains, you will need an X.400 gateway. These are not cheap ($5,000), but without one, you won't be able to communicate internationally. You will need an X.400 gateway to MCI Mail if you have substantial traffic on this system. The difference in cost is 50 cents a page without a gate way versus 3 cents a page through the gateway. Even very small companies could profitably install an X.400 gateway if they have substantial international traffic. New York is full of 3-person offices who spend half their day talking to Indonesia. They would save a bundle with an X.400 gateway.

MHS is a Novell standard that came along before X.400. You need a product like this if you want to bridge into other E-Mail domains. An MHS gateway is an accepted way for physically separated dissimilar LANs to pass E-Mail.

MHS is similar to X.400 in its intent, but on a much smaller scale. MHS software deals with queuing messages up for another network and dialing up to send those messages. X.400 doesn't do this, although software that implements X.400 may.

When choosing an E-Mail product, look for something that allows interconnection, if you think you will need it. Some offices may need both MHS and X.400 gateways. The average office may not need to communicate globally right now, but may want to be prepared for it later. We'd be willing to predict a substantial increase in international traffic, once X.400 and X.500 are well-known.

Handy E-Mail Features

Look for products that can send carbons and blind copies, as well as standard messages to one person, or to a group of people. Some can also retract, delete, or edit a message that has already been sent, if it has not yet been opened and read.

The Notify feature is used to tell you when you have mail, when your message to someone else was delivered, and when it was opened.

Products integrated into your word processing package, like WP Office LAN, can use E-Mail to send files to another WP Office user, a slick way to send group work around the network. The recipient can attach notes and corrections and ship it back again, with notification of when it was received and opened.

Other issues to assess are whether the E-Mail product will let you ship text or binary files (graphics or Fax). X.400 lets you bundle anything you want; AT&T Easylink will let you pass binary files and so will SPRINT MAIL, but MCI Mail allows only ASCII. MHS handles only text.

You might think that opens the door to networked Fax, but so far the technology isn't very good. It's easier to photocopy a graphic image and send it through a separate Fax machine. The problem isn't with sending the file, but with translating the fonts without losing legibility.

Try out any E-Mail package you are considering. Some have excellent built-in editors for composing messages, while others are barely functional at best. Other features you might like are group scheduling, personal calendars and reminders, and other integrated-desktop features. CC:Mail (now owned by Lotus) is probably the most popular E-Mail package right now; we've used it and liked it. We've also used and liked WordPerfect Office 3.0. Not everyone is familiar and comfortable with the WP function-key assignments (Help is F3, not F1), but if you are, it's quick to learn. We're critical fans of MCI Mail, whose manual is notoriously confusing. As usual, we're not reviewing and rating the software, simply noting the features you need to look for.

PART II

The Data Sheets

File Servers, Workstations, and the Network Operating System

A Novell NetWare 386 File Server

The file server can be an ordinary personal computer, a specialized high-speed multi-processor computer, or anything in between, as long as it meets the CPU and memory requirements of the network software. The network operating systems we used for our test LAN, Novell NetWare 3.10 and 3.11, require at least a 386 computer with at least 4 Meg of RAM (Random Access Memory). You will need a lot more than 4 Meg of RAM, though, in most situations. The bigger the hard disk, the more RAM you need to track the disk directories and for the cache memory. TCP/IP support and SNMP (the Simple Network Management Protocol) eat memory, too. BTRIEVE and the NetWare SQL server require another 2 Megs of RAM. A properly configured NetWare 3.11 server probably has 16 megs of memory, minimum. Novell sells less expensive versions of NetWare for 286-based file servers, but the way hardware horsepower is dropping in price it makes sense to run these 286 versions of NetWare on 386 file servers, too.

The file server on a NetWare network runs the network operating system software. It communicates packets of data to other devices on the LAN—workstations, other file servers, print servers, communications servers, bridges, routers, and gateways. See the glossary if you need precise definitions of these other devices at this point.

Your file server also provides mass storage for the network, whether on hard disk, CD ROM, or even a mainframe "disk farm." Traditionally, shared programs and data are stored on the file server. So are the shared NetWare utilities (the programs which allow a user to manipulate the network environment), login information for each user, and the Bindery (a NetWare database which associates users with their properties such as passwords, account restrictions, user groups, authorized print servers, etc.). On a well-run network, individual users save their personal data files in an individual work area, a subdirectory on the file server hard disk. When users don't trust the network, because it's always down or because the supervisor doesn't back it up, they start saving all their work to local hard or floppy disks.

Early versions of NetWare and NetWare 2.2 allow non-dedicated file servers (file servers that operate both as NetWare file servers and as DOS workstations). Because file server hardware is dropping in price and because non-dedicated file servers can be a real pain, both to the workstation user and the LAN administrator, these non-dedicated versions of NetWare are disappearing, so we will consider only dedicated file servers in this manual. We concentrate on NetWare 3.x (created for 386 and 486 file servers) because it honors the trend toward modular operating systems, which allow you to add new features or swap hardware without a complete operating system brain transplant.

How a Novell NetWare 386 File Server Works

We are concentrating on the physical file server here — on the hardware. Read this section in conjunction with the *Network Operating System* Data Sheet on page 84, which takes a software-centered approach to the file server.

Novell NetWare will run on almost any brand of PC, but Novell will not give you support unless the server has been certified by Novell Labs. Most name brand computers are Novell-certified (examples are Compaq, Zeos, Dell, Northgate, IBM, Gateway, etc.). When contracting for a LAN, specify a Novell-certified server right on the purchase order. Call Novell before you buy if you have any doubts — they will tell you whether a particular machine is certified. Third-party troubleshooting services generally follow the same rule. When you call, the first question they ask is the brand of computer you're using for your file server. If it's not Novell certified, the computer is the problem, end of call. Please note, we're not saying non-certified computers won't work. We're saying you can't get support.

Take a well-functioning computer equipped with lots of memory, at least one big hard disk, and a floppy drive. Partition the first hard disk into two areas: a DOS partition and a NetWare 3.x partition. The file server will boot from the DOS partition on this first hard disk, exactly like any other DOS computer boots from its C: drive.

If you are paranoid, you can make the server boot from a floppy disk in the A: drive—that way you can lock the boot floppy in a safe when you leave at night. Even so, you'd better lock up the file server, too, to stop a data thief from stealing the hard disk or the entire machine. Many companies are locking file servers in secure rooms, just as they do mainframes.

Once your NetWare 386 file server boots DOS, whether from floppy or hard disk, run the NetWare program SERVER.EXE, which sets up a NetWare file server running the NetWare operating system. Forget DOS now, it's irrelevant—as long as the file server is up and running, NetWare runs the show. By comparison, dedicated file servers running the 286 versions of NetWare (version 2.x) boot directly from the NetWare file server operating system rather than booting DOS first.

The file server communicates with other entities on the network through a network interface card running the IPX communications protocol, Novell's proprietary communications protocol. So the file server speaks IPX to the workstations and the workstations speak IPX to the file server(s).

According to *Novell NetWare Concepts 386*,

> "IPX addresses and routes outgoing data packets across a network. IPX reads the assigned addresses of returning data and directs the data to the proper area within a workstation's or file server's operating system."

IPX, which sends and receives data packets in collaboration with the network interface card driver, works with Ethernet, Token Ring, and ARCNET networks running on any of the standard physical media (coaxial cable, twisted pair, fiber optic, or packet radio).

NetWare 3.11 also supports the TCP/IP protocol (TCP/IP is the INTERNET protocol used by UNIX computers). A NetWare 3.11 server running full tilt IPX support can talk to other NetWare 3.11 servers over an IP (UNIX) network cable (that is called tunneling) and acts like a UNIX server for UNIX workstations while still acting like a NetWare server for your DOS workstations running NetWare.

So "the file server" really has three parts:

- The standalone computer which will become the file server (most often, this is a normal, though high-powered, personal computer).
- The NetWare operating system software which will transform the computer into a file server (SYSCON, SERVER, FILER and other NetWare programs).
- And the network card, cable, and protocols that allow the file server to talk to the rest of the guys on the wire.

Testing Your File Server

First, figure out which aspect of the file server is malfunctioning:

- The PC hardware (memory errors, no video, suspect printer port, etc.).
- The NetWare hard disk (**Warning!** Do not use standard PC repair techniques here.).
- The NetWare operating system software.
- The network card, cable, and communication protocols.
- Or you may not know which is the culprit, just that the file server is very, very slow.

We'll consider each of these possibilities in turn.

PC Hardware

If the file server hardware is faulty, or if you suspect it's faulty, test and repair all parts of it **except the hard disk** like you'd test any other PC. If the video card, keyboard, monitor, memory chips, or printer ports are malfunctioning, we troubleshoot and repair this computer exactly like an ordinary PC. Use *Fix Your Own PC* or any other PC repair book to get the file server hardware working right. Ordinary diagnostics like QAPlus/fe and CheckIt will work fine on the file server if you boot it from a DOS floppy. Just don't mess with the hard disk yet!

NetWare does not use a math co-processor chip, so there is no need to install one in the file server.

NetWare Hard Disks

Hard disks in a NetWare server are a special case, because the NetWare partition uses NetWare rules for storing data, not DOS rules. Therefore, our favorite DOS hard disk utilities (DiskFix in PCTools, SpinRite, Norton's Disk Doctor, Disk Technician, and Mace Utilities) are useless in a NetWare environment. NetWare hard disks require NetWare-compatible utilities.

Ontrack Computer Systems NetUtils for 286 NetWare will perform many of the familiar hard disk maintenance and repair tasks. For example, NetUtils allows you to view and search (and change, watch out!) the hexadecimal or ASCII contents of files on a NetWare 2.x server. It will also scan the server disk, checking the directory and FATs (File Allocation Tables), then comparing the actual data stored on the disk to the directory structure, then looking for cross-linked files and "orphan blocks." If your disk needs repairs, NetUtils will do its best to save as much data as possible. Since this program also can recover files from a NetWare file server that is not able to boot NetWare, you have no excuse for starting repairs without a complete backup of your data. A NetWare 386 version of NetUtils is due out second quarter of '92.

Novell's VREPAIR hard disk repair utility can handle minor hard disk problems without destroying your data. Novell suggests you use VREPAIR if you get disk read or write errors, if a hardware failure has prevented a disk from mounting during server startup, if a power failure has corrupted a volume, if you get a mirroring error message on the file server, or if you get fatal DIR errors. VREPAIR compares the two FATs and the two copies of the directory table on your hard disk, finding and repairing inconsistencies.

If you have turned off your server without issuing the DOWN command first, VREPAIR will fix some of the garbage, and BINDFIX will fix more, but you might have trashed data files too, which can be harder to repair. In most cases, though, the server has had time to write everything stored in the cache buffers to disk (it does this every 3 seconds) so you won't lose much.

For instance, VREPAIR helped with a series of

ABEND "File server not serialized"

errors we were getting on a NetWare 3.10 file server. The NetWare serial number is stored on the first track of the file server hard disk, so "Network not serialized" is just another way for NetWare to say "I can't read the disk."

If you're planning to run VREPAIR, back up your data first (just in case). Then run SERVER (or just leave the file server on if it's up and running). Then dismount the volume you want to VREPAIR. Then LOAD VREPAIR (you should have a copy of VREPAIR on your boot disk, placed there when NetWare was installed). Full directions may be found in the Novell System Administration manual and in the online help (see Appendix A for online help info).

> **Major WARNING!** You must use the right version of VREPAIR with your system. Do not, for example, use the Version 3.1 VREPAIR with a Version 3.0 NetWare file server. When using VREPAIR on your NetWare 286 server you **must** use the customized copy of VREPAIR that you created when you installed NetWare 2.x on your file server. VREPAIR from another system (one with different hard disk or controller, for instance) will trash your data.

If the hard disk will still not mount after running VREPAIR, you can delete the volume (losing all your data) and recreate it with INSTALL. Hope you've backed up your data.

If you're not backed up or your hard disk has really been nuked (fire, flood, earthquake) all your data may not be lost. Get a professional data recovery service like Ontrack Data Recovery to talk you through the data recovery process, or send them the disk. They say they recover data from 95 percent of the "dead" drives sent to them, often by carefully disassembling the drive and replacing a bad bearing or read/write head without destroying your data. They're not cheap, but the cost of replicating your company's data may be much higher. So if you're in deep trouble because your drive has failed mechanically and/or your data is corrupted, give them a call at (800) 752-1333.

NetWare Operating System

Maybe you're having software trouble—trouble with the NetWare Operating System. Look here if your file server won't come up (especially in NetWare 2.x) or comes up but won't run, if workstations hang (especially when running only certain NetWare utilities), or if you're getting error messages that point to the operating system.

If a NetWare utility file is corrupted, the workstation may remain blank, or you may get an error message. When we got a corrupted copy of SYSCON on our file server, the workstations would hang, giving no error message, whenever we tried to run SYSCON. Since other NetWare utilities worked fine, we assumed it was a bad copy of SYSCON and tried to copy the System and Public files from our original NetWare diskettes. Unfortunately, the original diskettes were damaged and the SYSCON file on them was corrupted. Don't do as we did (we worked from the original diskettes)—make copies and install NetWare from the copies! We got a clean version of SYSCON from Novell's tech support bulletin board and copied it to the file server, but we had to beg.

If you're using the wrong version of an NLM (NetWare Loadable Module) or VAP (Value Added Process), the server may hang or a workstation may hang. Or the NLM/VAP may perform almost but not quite right. For example, for a while supervisors were having trouble loading and unloading specific NLMs using the Remote Console utility in NetWare 3.1. Writing and testing a network operating system is an enormous undertaking, so these problems will sometimes get past Quality Control. Novell creates improved versions of the offending utilities and publicizes them through users groups, NetWire (the Novell forum on CompuServe), and technical bulletins.

Novell also issues new versions of the workstation shells (IPX and NETx) fairly regularly, trying to keep up with the new DOS versions and new application software that their users are running. DOS 5.0, for example, provided some challenges, and so did Windows. Keep up to date about version changes; you could spend months trying to run down a bug in the field that the programmers have already corrected and put up on NetWire. The old slogan "If it ain't broke, don't fix it," applies here. Don't upgrade unless you really need the new version. Network bulletin boards are an ideal place to follow the gossip. You'll find the bulletin board users amazingly helpful too if you need to ask a question.

If you're having trouble deleting or modifying a username or changing a user's password and/or security rights, if you get print spooler errors or the login script doesn't come up when a user logs in, maybe the bindery is corrupted. Use BINDFIX; it scans the bindery files, looking for inconsistencies and lost links. Then it rebuilds the bindery files, trying to fix any problems it has found. If BINDFIX fails ("Bindery check **not** successfully completed"), you can restore the old bindery files, run VREPAIR, and then try BINDFIX again. Or try running BINDFIX twice in succession. Back up your data before experimenting, including the bindery files NET$OBJ.SYS, NET$PROP.SYS and NET$VAL.SYS, so you won't be any worse off than you were when you started—even if the utilities go haywire and "fix" your disk so the data looks like it's been through a Cuisinart.

Network Interface Card, Cables, and Communication Protocols

Sometimes the file server is working fine, but we don't know that because it isn't talking to the other guys on the cable. Look for hardware configuration conflicts when the file server comes up and hangs, won't come up at all (NetWare 2.x), or gives you configuration conflict error messages. Look for network card or cable troubles when the file server appears to come up okay, but can't talk to anybody and nobody can talk to it.

Your file server's network card and cable are the same as the other network cards and cables in your system. See page 109 in the Network Interface Card (NIC) section of these Data Sheets. The section titled *How to Test a Network Interface Card* gives specific troubleshooting techniques for your NIC. Because non-dedicated NetWare 2.2 file servers and all NetWare 3.x file servers boot first from DOS, you can use the COMCHECK utility described in Appendix B just as you would use it at a workstation: boot DOS, run IPX (customized with SHGEN or WSGEN for this file server NIC as if the file server were any other workstation), then run COMCHECK.

We have found it handy to make up a file server troubleshooting diskette ahead of time. It should be bootable and contain the files from the *DOS/DOS ODI Workstation Services* diskette called SHGEN-1 (WSGEN if you're using 2.2), and a copy of IPX.COM that matches this file server's network card configuration. If your file server has only a 360K A: drive you won't be able to fit all the files from the DOS/DOS ODI diskette; be sure to include the following files on your troubleshooting floppy if you want to run COMCHECK on the server: IPX.COM , COMCHECK.EXE and COMCHECK.HLP, and all the files with the .DAT or the .OVL extension. When you're done, test it to make sure you understand how it is supposed to work—it's a lot easier to practice your skills on equipment that is working properly.

For cable troubleshooting hints, look in the Data Sheet section covering your network cable media. We have separate sections on Token Ring, Ethernet on Twisted Pair, Ethernet on coax, ARCNET, and fiber optic cable, as well as wireless network designs.

Let's assume that COMCHECK works fine, so your card and cable seem to be functioning, but for some reason the file server can't talk to the cable after you fire it up by loading SERVER (NetWare 3.x) or NET$OS (NetWare 2.x). What operating system feature could be interfering with communication?

NetWare uses the IPX protocol to send data packets across the network. When a file server running NetWare 3.x runs the SERVER program, it loads a Network Card driver module (such as, NE2000.LAN for the NE2000 card) and binds the IPX protocol to that LAN card driver. In NetWare 286 the LAN card driver is permanently bound to IPX as part of the network operating system generation process (the infamous 2.15 NETGEN or 2.2 INSTALL that creates NET$OS). Right now we need only know that these things happen, and check that the right driver got bound to IPX with the right interrupts, I/O address, etc. The Data Sheet section titled *The Network Operating System—Novell NetWare 386* on page 84 has more details if you want to know exactly what happens as the file server fires up.

You can easily check the parameters used with IPX at a workstation—just type IPX/i. To find these parameters on a NetWare 3.x file server, use the INSTALL module on the file server console, first choosing System Options, then Edit AUTOEXEC.NCF File. Look for a LOAD statement like

LOAD NE2000 port=300 int=3 frame=ETHERNET_802.3

Examine it carefully. Do the interrupt and address numbers match the physical jumpers on your file server NIC—the parameters that you know are right because they work fine when you tested this card with COMCHECK? An obvious question, perhaps, but are you loading the right LAN card driver for the card installed in this server? Do you have a BIND statement in this file?

BIND IPX to NE2000 NET=A

binds IPX on our test network, which is running an NE2000 LAN card in the server and named network A. See Figure 200 below, our test LAN AUTOEXEC.NCF file.

```
file server name 386
IPX internal net 11
load CLIB
load cpstart C:\STARTUP.NCF
load NE2000 port = 300 int = 3 frame = Ethernet_802.3
bind IPX to NE2000 net = A
load INSTALL
load MONITOR
load UPS type = STANDALONE port = 240 discharge = 10 recharge = 120
load PSERVER laser
load FRYESERV
```

Figure 200 *AUTOEXEC.NCF file for NetWare 3.1 file server using the IPX protocol and Ethernet 802.3 frames.*

NetWare 286 uses FCONSOLE to show the LAN driver and hardware configuration. From FCONSOLE Available Options, choose LAN Driver Information, select the file server LAN driver that you are interested in, then press enter for the details. Once again, be sure the operating system is sending information to the I/O Base address and the RAM buffer that matches your LAN card's physical switches.

If everything but the interrupt is correct, your file server will talk to the world, but never hear any responses. This produces workstations that hang as they try to load NETx, or on multi-server networks this server shows up on the server list but no one can ATTACH to it to use it.

Network is Mysteriously Slow

If you suspect the file server might be the culprit, the Frye Utilities and Frye's NetWare Early Warning System are ideal here. They analyze your file server's performance, and **most important** they provide expert advice tailored to your system's weak spots. Here, for example, the Frye Utilities NetWare Early Warning System manual discusses the "average Disk I/Os pending" statistic:

> "The number of disk I/Os pending is a measure of the level of disk activity on your file server. A high average number may mean the disk drives on your server are a performance bottleneck. What is a high number depends on the performance of your disks; >20 is a reasonable threshold for a typical server.
>
> **Suggested actions:** If your server is performing poorly, this warning suggests that disk performance, rather than CPU or LAN performance, is the bottleneck.
>
> **Ways of increasing disk performance:** Install more RAM to the file server to make more space available for file caching. Replace the disk drives and/or controllers on your file server with higher performance models. Install additional disk controllers, and divide your disk drives among them. Remove drive mirroring. Convert mirrored (one controller for the pair of drives) to duplexed (separate controllers) drives. Remove users and/or applications from this file server."

If you have more than one NIC in the file server, it may be useful to compare the relative traffic on each of the network cabling systems. Too much traffic on any cabling system tends to cause excessive errors. The MONITOR NLM reports total packets sent, total packets received, and detailed counts of specific send/receive packet errors—for each LAN driver (NIC driver) installed in the server. Look under LAN information on the MONITOR main menu.

Installing a File Server

Because a file server is just another computer, you install individual parts in a file server the same way you would with a standalone computer. Our PC book, *Fix Your Own PC*, can help you here if the procedures are unfamiliar. Remember to back up your data! You should be backing up the network anyway, but be certain the backup is current and useable **before** you grab your screwdriver. We discuss backup (hardware, software, and strategies) in Chapters 4 and 5.

When installing a new server, save yourself some heartaches by testing the server with a DOS batch file for three days before you install NetWare. The batch file should read, write and exercise the CPU. Continuous testing with a troubleshooting program like QAPlus/fe will do the job. If that computer is going to fail, make it fail in pre-installation testing.

If you need to install NetWare 286 on a new hard disk, seriously consider buying Disk Manager-N from Ontrack Computer Systems. It cuts hard disk preparation time dramatically (up to 25 times faster than Novell's COMPSURF utility). In addition, Disk Manager-N gives you the freedom to install drives not supported by your computer's ROM BIOS (called user-definable drives). This can be important because the hard drive with the best price/performance ratio or the optimal data storage size may not be supported by your computer's BIOS.

NetWare 386 doesn't like user-definable hard drives either. We tried to install NetWare 386 on a server set up for a user-definable drive type—NetWare didn't see the drive at all. We finally had to pick a standard drive type (smaller than the actual drive, of course, since it is okay to leave some cylinders or heads unused, but it is not acceptable to tell the computer that there are more tracks or cylinders than really exist). Some hard disk controllers (such as Western Digital's WD1007) allow you to handle this problem in unconventional ways—you'll have to talk to your controller card manufacturer for details.

A money-saving hint: Suppose that one of your mirrored drives has gone bad, and that exact drive size is no longer available or is prohibitively expensive. You need not throw away the working drive and install two new drives to keep using the NetWare mirroring function. Buy a slightly larger drive, then allocate a large Hot Fix area on the new drive to trick NetWare into thinking the new drive is the same size as the drive you are mirroring.

Other than these hard disk hints, we recommend you just go ahead and install NetWare as per the directions in the version you bought.

If you're running NetWare 3.x you really must lock up the file server. An intruder could walk up to the file server, load an NLM in through the A: drive without downing the file server or the network, then do whatever he wished—from his own workstation if the intruder was reasonably clever. This means you need physical security for the file server.

Plan for ventilation. A closet may not be suitable. Got a small air-conditioned room? Periodically inspect the file server for dust buildup, and vacuum out the fan. If the fan gets dusty, maybe the server guts need to be inspected and vacuumed too. By the way, if you're going to lock the file server in a closet, you'll need a remote console utility like Novell's RCONSOLE so you don't have to walk down to the closet for every maintenance task that requires a console utility.

The Workstation

Take an ordinary standalone personal computer, add a network interface card and networking software, and you have a workstation.

The workstation computer must operate properly as a standalone PC. We're not going to reiterate every troubleshooting suggestion from *Fix Your Own PC*, our PC troubleshooting manual, here. Test your workstation with a good hardware diagnostic program. CheckIt and QAPlus/fe are dependable all-purpose hardware diagnostics. If they reveal a problem, fix it. If you need help, consult your favorite PC troubleshooting book.

You must configure a network interface card before installing it in the workstation. We discuss network card operation and configuration at length in the Data Sheet section devoted to Network Interface Cards which starts on page 103.

Each workstation runs its own native operating system. On a Novell NetWare network, the workstation runs two additional software programs:

- IPX.COM, the datagram delivery service which packages data for broadcast on the network cable.
- NETx.COM, the network shell which sorts workstation requests (interrupts) into local (DOS, on the workstation) requests versus network requests.

You must tailor the boot disk for each workstation, because IPX and NETx are customized to reflect the network card configuration and the operating system software installed on that particular workstation. Read all about IPX, NETx, and NetWare in the next Data Sheet, *The Network Operating System—NetWare 386*, beginning on page 84.

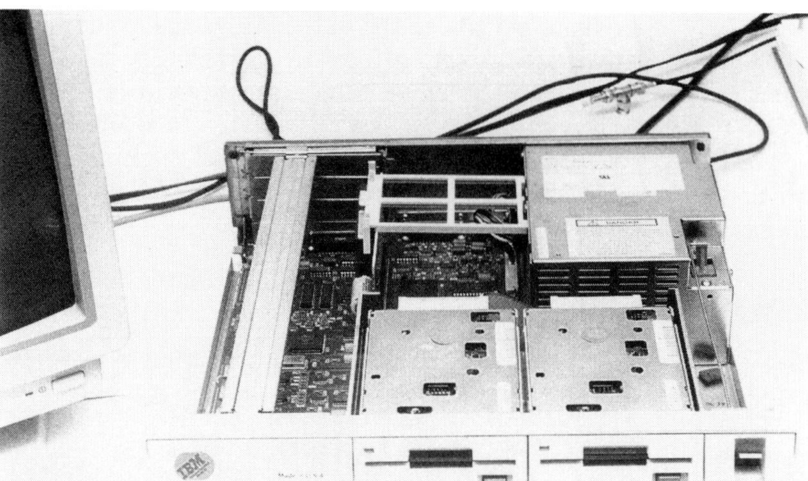

Figure 201 *To install a network card in this PS/2 model 30, first remove the cover. The bus expansion slots are on a separate battery/bus-expansion board, not on the main-board itself. To make space for the card, we must remove a metal slot cover and break off the external plastic slot-cover on the rear of the chassis.*

Figure 202 *We chose an 8-bit NE1000 card for this station.*

Starting a Workstation

1. Turn on the workstation. It automatically checks its own hardware with a POST (Power On Self Test) loaded in its ROM BIOS. It tries to load DOS, typically from a boot diskette or workstation hard

Figure 203 We found it was easiest to stand the PS/2 on its side, then slide the card into the bus connector.

disk, checking for a CONFIG.SYS file and/or an AUTOEXEC.BAT file as it boots up. If you have an AUTOEXEC.BAT file or a network batch file, it may automate the next few steps. Diskless workstations use a special boot PROM that allows the workstation to read the necessary DOS, CONFIG.SYS, AUTOEXEC.BAT, IPX, and NETx files from the file server's hard disk.

2. Load IPX—typically stored on your boot disk. A SHELL.CFG file, if you have one, can set specific parameters for your copy of IPX.
3. Load NETx.COM—typically stored on your boot disk. A SHELL.CFG file, if you have one, can set specific parameters for your copy of NETx.COM.
4. Change to the F: directory—NetWare automatically makes F: the login directory on the network drive when you first attempt to log in to the network.
5. Type LOGIN—this file is stored in the LOGIN directory on the network drive so you can access it before you are actually logged into the network.
6. Type your username and password.
7. The login script executes. This will be the default login script, until the supervisor sets up a system-wide login script and a personal login script associated with your name and password. The login script can do a lot or do a little. At a minimum, it will map network drives. Or it may be a complex batch file, mapping drives, setting up print queues, setting your DOS prompt and the location of your copy of COMMAND.COM, etc. In addition, the login script, like any batch file, can dump you immediately into an application program, pull up a menu, and/or print messages on the user's screen.
8. You're on the network now.

Testing a Workstation

A computer that malfunctions as a standalone computer will malfunction as a workstation. Therefore, when diagnosing a network problem we often test the workstation as a standalone. It's embarrassing and inefficient to rush off looking for subtle network software problems when bad memory chips in the workstation are the real problem.

Right now, QAPlus/fe is our favorite quick diagnostic package because it tells you about your network card (I/O address used, interrupts, DMA, etc.) as well as the standard PC hardware. Whenever you have a problem with a single workstation, it makes sense to run hardware diagnostics.

Remember that a bad or misconfigured network card may crash the standalone computer, as well as failing to make a network cable connection. Therefore, if the workstation is experiencing hardware troubles it makes sense to remove the network card and retest the workstation before you toss the hard disk or mainboard into the wastebasket.

Trying to use an incompatible IPX with a network card chokes the workstation, often with no error message—the workstation boots up and transfers into never-never-land. Keep configuration notes on each workstation. Note the network card installed and its jumper settings, the versions of IPX and NETx that this workstation is using, etc. Sample configuration sheets come with the Novell documentation. Be sure to keep copies of your custom-generated boot disks too—trashed boot disks account for an amazing number of no-network complaints. If you keep a copy for each workstation, you can carry the copy with you when you troubleshoot user complaints.

Your workstation will lock up when you press Shift/Print SCREEN if: 1) you have no local printer and 2) there is no CAPTURE command redirecting the workstation's printer output to the network printers. Head this problem off by putting the line

local printers = zero

in the workstation's SHELL.CFG file when there are no local printers attached to this workstation.

TSRs (Terminate and Stay Resident programs—the ones you can "hot key" into from another program) are notorious. Poorly written TSRs conflict with each other, and they may conflict with the extended or expanded memory versions of the NetWare shell. If your workstation locks up when running XMSNETx or EMSNETx with a TSR, test it with plain NETx and/or no other TSRs loaded. Don't forget to install an XMS version 2.0 driver (such as HIMEM.SYS) on the workstation if you're using the XMSNETx shell.

Installing a Workstation

1. **Run a cable to your work area.** (See the cable installation instructions in these Data Sheets for your cable medium and topology, whether Ethernet on coax, Ethernet on unshielded twisted-pair, ARCNET, Token Ring, fiber optic, or whatever.)
2. **Select an XT or XT clone, an AT or AT clone, a 386/AT, a PS/2, an EISA bus computer, or a Macintosh—network interface cards are available for all these machines.** To your user, the workstation will appear to perform slightly more slowly than it does when running single-user software as a standalone. That's if your network is working well. Bad or overloaded cabling and slow network cards, or a sluggish file server, will slow things down more. So match the workstation speed to the needs of your user.
3. **Install an appropriate network card.** (See the *Network Interface Card* Data Sheet for more information on this).
4. **Create a boot disk for this workstation.** (We give you some hints in the *Network Operating System* Data Sheet which immediately follows. See *On Creating Workstation Boot Disks*, page 91.)
5. **Log in from this workstation as the SUPERVISOR to be sure everything is working well.** Set up the new user as per the instructions in your Novell manual, making sure the user gets adequate security rights and drive mappings to execute the application programs she needs. Log in again from the new workstation as the new user. If all is well, update your network event log, your network cabling diagram, and your user-data lists (workstation configuration, user, software versions on workstation, etc.).
6. **You're done.**

The Network Operating System—Novell NetWare 386

The network operating system is responsible for data transfer between machines on the network. A good network operating system is invisible to the user.

The operating system provides access to network resources without requiring an end user to learn arcane network operating system commands. When we speak of network resources, we're talking about file servers with application programs and data files, printers, mainframe gateways, and shared network modems or FAX machines. The network operating system allows a user to manipulate those resources she is authorized to handle, and protects the organization's security by locking unauthorized users out of private files and refusing them access to unauthorized modems, printers, etc.

We want our users to continue running the application software they know and like, so each user's workstation computer retains its original operating system (whether DOS, UNIX, or Macintosh OS). The workstation computer also runs a network shell which sorts workstation requests (interrupts) into local (on the workstation) requests versus network requests. The shell forwards each request to the appropriate place. You must load this workstation shell before you can access the network login directory and log in to the network.

Networks are designed like layer cakes, or like assembly lines. Each layer (each worker) has a particular job to do, then it passes the product on to the next layer. The bottom layer is the Physical Layer (the network cards and cables). This Physical Layer has to support the next layer (the Data Link Layer)—in other words, the Data Link Layer expects the Physical Layer to do certain jobs and provide certain services. The Data Link Layer, building on the services of the Physical Layer, provides its own particular services to the Network Layer above it. Like a layer cake, each network layer rests on the one below. If the layers below are crumbling, the cake won't stand. We discuss the OSI network model, and each of the seven OSI Layers, in depth in Chapter 7. Figure 204 shows these seven OSI layers again to refresh your memory.

A network operating system is a fairly high layer in the cake. Therefore, the choice of operating system is independent of the lowest layers. An Ethernet Physical Layer works great for Novell NetWare, so does ARCNET and Token Ring. The operating system doesn't care which Physical Layer and Data Link Layer are installed—but they better work right or the operating system will come crashing down.

The converse is also true. The Physical Layer doesn't care what operating system is installed; Ethernet is capable of supporting Banyan Vines or 3COM as easily as it supports Novell NetWare.

Though many network operating systems work well, in this book we limited our discussions to networks running Novell NetWare 3.x (the version of NetWare running on 386 and 486 computers). Our troubleshooting hints focus particularly tightly on the lower layers (the cards and cables) and on network hardware, because 80 percent of network downtime is caused by card and cable failure (mostly cables). Most of this hardware is independent of the operating system, so we could have discussed it in the abstract without specific examples. But in actual networks the interplay between operating system and hardware provides the most challenging troubleshooting problems.

We decided to use Novell NetWare 386 as our operating system because Novell has 60-65 percent of the network operating system market (different sources give different figures), and NetWare 386 reflects Novell's movement toward modular operating systems running on heavy-duty 386 and 486 file servers.

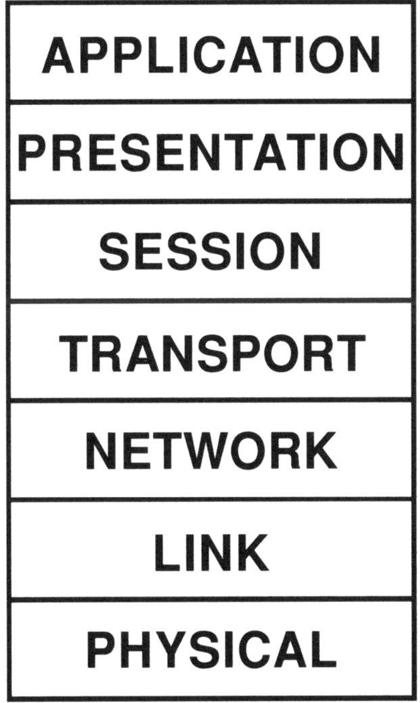

Figure 204 *Traditional diagram of the OSI 7-Layer network protocol reference model. For a peppier version, see Figure 7.1 in Chapter 7.*

Where to Find NetWare 386

The system files and utilities are on the file server. When you install NetWare 386 it sets up a standard directory structure.

- SYS: is the boot volume. It has four subdirectories: PUBLIC, SYSTEM, LOGIN, and MAIL.
- PUBLIC contains NetWare utilities for regular users. Don't dump non-NetWare utilities or programs into the PUBLIC directory, it makes upgrading a hassle. If you wish to use PUBLIC's security rights definitions (which are already in place) to define the security rights for application program files, make subdirectories under PUBLIC for the applications (the subdirectories inherit their parent directory's security rights unless you explicitly redefine those rights for the subdirectory). If you have users who need to access DOS on the file server, Novell recommends putting their DOS subdirectories under PUBLIC as well.
- SYSTEM contains the NetWare operating system files and the high-powered NetWare utilities for the supervisor. Make subdirectories here for potentially dangerous utility programs that should be reserved for the supervisor's eyes only.
- LOGIN contains the log in programs.
- MAIL used to contain the files for Novell's discontinued mail program. The directory is now used by third-party software, because the programmers know that MAIL will exist on every NetWare file server. They find it a convenient place to dump user-specific files. Individual user's login scripts are also stored in MAIL, in each user's subdirectory. So don't delete MAIL, and remember to back it up regularly.

Ordinarily, the workstation's boot disk contains the network shell (NETx.COM, or EMSNETx.COM and XMSNETx.COM which load into expanded and extended memory, respectively) and IPX.COM (the protocol which packages, addresses, and routes data packets on a NetWare network). Diskless workstations with special boot PROMS on the Network Interface Card use copies of the workstation shell and IPX stored on the file server.

How NetWare 386 Works

The network operating system runs on the file server. It controls data storage on file server hard disk(s) and maintains network security by allowing only authorized users to access the network files. The network operating system communicates with the other file servers, the workstations, remote network printers, modems and other network resources via the file server's network card and the network cable.

Each workstation runs its own native operating system. On a Novell NetWare network, the workstation also runs two software programs, IPX.COM (the datagram delivery service which packages data for broadcast on the network cable) and NETx.COM (the network shell). IPX and NETx are customized for each workstation to reflect the network card configuration and the operating system software installed on that particular workstation. Don't expect a neighbor's boot disk to boot your workstation—the two machines may well be using different DOS versions or different network cards. Even if the network cards are the same brand and type, perhaps the installer used interrupt 5 on your neighbor's network card and interrupt 3 on yours. You'll only get onto the network with your neighbor's boot disk if every network card configuration detail is identical. We tell you how to set up a network card's hardware configuration in *How to Install a Network Card* on page 112. That's also a good place to look for explanations of the technical terms used to describe network card hardware configuration: interrupt, I/O port, DMA channel, and memory address. Meanwhile, don't worry if interrupts or DMA channels mean nothing to you. We're concentrating on the operating system software in this section, and taking a broad view first. The details will come.

IPX, the NetWare datagram delivery service, gets you on the cable. It's roughly equivalent to the Network Layer (the third layer) in the OSI Seven-Layer Model. Each workstation's copy of IPX is customized for the hardware in that workstation—the brand of network card installed in this particular workstation as well as the interrupts, I/O port, and memory and/or DMA channels this network card uses. Whenever we change the hardware configuration jumpers on the network card, for example to change the hardware interrupt the card uses, we have to modify the workstation's IPX to match the new hardware settings. Trying to use an incompatible IPX with a network card chokes the workstation, often with no error message at all; the workstation boots up and transfers into never-never-land.

NETx.COM (that means "NET3.COM, NET4.COM, or NET5.COM" or, if you want to use the versions that load into high memory EMSNETx.COM or XMSNETx.COM) provides an interface between DOS and IPX. Choose the version of NETx that matches your DOS. For example, use NET3.COM for the DOS 3's—DOS 3.0, 3.20, 3.3 etc. NETx replaces the DOS interrupt vector tables with NetWare interrupt vector tables. For instance, when DOS asks the hardware to read a file, the network shell intercepts the interrupt and redirects the request through the network card and out along the network cable to the file server (if the file is stored out on the network file server's hard disk). If the file is stored on a local drive (a floppy or hard disk inside this particular workstation), NetWare dumps the problem back on DOS and DOS retrieves the file from the A:, B:, or C: drive, just as it normally does.

File servers use the NetWare operating system. NetWare 2.1x and 3.x require a dedicated file server—a file server that performs only network functions. Though NetWare 2.2 can run in either dedicated or non-dedicated mode, we strongly recommend only dedicated mode unless you only have a two or three-station network. If you are using the simplest versions of NetWare (NetWare ELS and ELS II), where the file server can also double as a workstation running DOS applications, the network operating system functions as a shell.

The file server operating system is customized to reflect the hardware installed, much like the workstation shell. The operating system must know the type of network card installed in this file server, the interrupts, I/O address, memory and DMA addresses chosen for that network card, the number and type of hard disks installed, and whether a UPS (Uninterruptible Power Supply) is installed, and if so, its characteristics.

For NetWare 2.15, network installers custom-tailor an operating system to fit whatever specific hardware is installed in the file server. The process is called NetWare generation. This NETGEN process and the notorious COMPSURF hard drive prep utility are responsible for rumors that NetWare installation is "a 16-hour religious experience." Because NETGEN actually creates an operating system complete with network card parameters, you'll need to regenerate (re-create) the operating system from scratch if major hardware factors change. NetWare 2.2 also uses a custom-generated operating system, but the generation process is less painful than in NetWare 2.15, and it's invoked with the INSTALL command rather than NETGEN.

NetWare 386 has been totally redesigned. The operating system kernel (SERVER.EXE) is generic. Individually loadable modules customize the generic kernel. Hard disk drivers, network card drivers, and server utilities can be loaded and unloaded, even while the server is running. Therefore, a new hard disk or an additional network card can be added to the file server without NetWare 286's lengthy regeneration process. Perhaps more important to the inexperienced installer, errors can be corrected merely by unloading an incorrect hardware driver and loading the correct one.

Though NetWare 386 is easier to install, we still need to properly configure the operating system to match our hardware configuration. We need to accurately tell the operating system the interrupt and I/O ports values and the DMA and memory address values we set on the DIP-switches or jumpers on the network card. Any mistake here will still choke the operating system. But errors in NetWare 386 installation are quickly corrected once we figure out what's wrong.

NetWare Communications Protocols

Novell's NetWare protocols were created before the OSI 7-Layer Model. Therefore, they are not OSI compliant. Nevertheless, we can roughly map NetWare protocol layers to the OSI Layers. The first two Layers are Physical Layers—Ethernet versus Token Ring versus ARCNET. Use whichever one you want. NetWare is happy with them all. The third layer in the OSI scheme is the Network Layer. IPX does this job for NetWare—it is a datagram service much like the U.S. Mail. SPX, NetWare's next protocol layer, is like Return-receipt-requested mail. SPX makes certain that data arrives safely. Not all NetWare communications require the services of SPX, but it is there for those that do. NetWare's NCP (NetWare Core Protocol) runs above SPX. The NCP Layer in a workstation composes directives to the network file server. Because the file server is also running NCP as the top of its protocol stack, it will understand the message from the workstation and respond appropriately (by opening the file that the workstation wants it to open, for instance).

NetWare 3.11 also supports TCP/IP, the protocol stack used by all UNIX computers (and a few others too). A NetWare 3.11 server behaves like an IP router if you install the TCP/IP NLM and connect the server up to an IP network. The server can route between multiple IP networks, or between a NetWare network using the IPX protocol and a UNIX network running TCP/IP. Using the IP tunnel feature, a NetWare server running 3.11 can communicate with a second NetWare 3.11 server across an IP backbone. The tunnel feature sends the NetWare IPX packets across the IP backbone embedded in IP packets. If you're going to use the IP Tunnel, be careful not to give the NetWare server too many peers on the IP network or data transfer will bog down.

A NetWare 3.11 server can also function as a UNIX NFS server. Though NFS (Network File System) was invented by SUN, it is now a defacto UNIX standard and is well understood by UNIX workstations. NFS lets UNIX workstations hook up to your NetWare server.

LAN WorkPlace version 4.0 allows your DOS or Apple workstation to talk to a UNIX server. In addition, LAN WorkPlace allows you to send data across an IP network cable to a NetWare 3.11 server. It's new, it's hot, and Novell intends major improvements over the next few months.

Novell's User Basics Booklet and NetWare On-Line Help

Novell has written an excellent booklet called *User Basics* which explains basic networking concepts and gives an overview of how a NetWare network operates. It's only 50 pages long, clear and simple, and it has some great troubleshooting hints. It also has directions for creating login scripts, mapping drives, managing files and directories (including salvaging deleted files), and printing. It is useful for both novice and intermediate network users.

User Basics is printed in the back of the Novell NetWare 386 **System Administration** manual. Novell encourages system administrators to photocopy this booklet and hand it out to users, so ask your network administrator for a copy. Supervisors: Save time and reduce innocent, ignorant network questions. Hand out the booklet to your users—the troubleshooting hints alone will save everyone a lot of annoyance. Users: If your network administrator doesn't get you a copy of *User Basics*, make your own. The DOS text file of *User Basics* is stored in the PUBLIC directory on the network drive. Almost all users have access to this directory, since it holds the network utilities. Copy the file called USER-BAS.ICS to your local drive, then load it into your favorite word processor and print it.

We also think the on-line NetWare help is wonderful. See Appendix A for instructions. Really, it's great. Use it.

How to Test the NetWare 386 Operating System

If it seems to be working, it probably is. If something goes wrong, try to figure out if hardware or software is to blame. For example, one workstation that won't run any NetWare utilities, plus a second workstation (attached to the same file server) that runs these utilities fine, means bad hardware at the first workstation, or security problems for the user at the first workstation. Get the first workstation's user to log in at the good workstation. If the problem moves with the user, it's a user set-up problem, not a network operating system problem. If the problem does not move with the user, you probably have a bad card or cable at the first workstation—again, not a network operating system problem.

On the other hand, if everyone on the network seems to be up and running, but no one can use SYSCON (the program mysteriously freezes whenever anyone tries to run it), SYSCON has probably been damaged. Recopy it from your master diskettes and try again. Utilities like SiteLock by Brightwork Development protect your files against unauthorized tampering. Many network administrators use an anti-virus, anti-tampering utility on the entire NetWare operating system.

When your network seems to work okay, but one feature chokes, you may have a damaged utility file, or you may have a bug. Consider the workstation shell, NETx.COM. Novell releases new versions of the shell all the time. Sometimes it is because there are bugs in the old shell. More often, though, the shell worked fine until people wanted to do something new. To fully support Windows, for example, you need NetWare shell Version 3.01E, or newer. DOS 5.0 required new shell files, and these new NET5.COM shells all had to be debugged. When NetWare 3.0 first came out, the correct driver file was not on the diskette shipped with Token Ring cards. In situations like these, NetWire (the Novell forum on CompuServe) or a user's group bulletin board can be very helpful. CompuServe often has the right driver or shell file on-line.

It makes sense to standardize on the latest version of NETx and the latest version of IPX, and get everything running. Then, stop changing things. Stick with the shell and IPX versions that work for you until you run into some new application that requires a newer shell.

Upgrading from NetWare 2.x to NetWare 3.x

If you already have a functioning NetWare 286 network you should follow the upgrade directions in the red Novell **Installation** manual. Be sure to **remove** the old 286 partitions on the file server hard disk with DiskManager or the NetWare 286 COMPSURF utility before starting to install 3.x. NetWare 3.x cannot be trusted to write over the old partitions.

The cleanest and easiest way to upgrade from 286 to 386 is to use the transfer method, where you set up a new 386 file server, then move all the data from your old 286 server to the new 386 server across the network. Unfortunately, passwords don't come across to the new file server. Supervisor, here's a tip to avoid entering new passwords for all your users: Go into SYSCON on the 286 server and expire all the passwords before you transfer the files. After the upgrade each user will then have an expired password, so they will need to type in a new one.

Installing the NetWare 386 Operating System

When it's time for you to install NetWare, use your red NetWare **Installation** manual from Novell as your primary guide. The warnings and suggestions below are intended to supplement the Novell **Installation** manual, not supplant or echo it.

If you've never installed a LAN before, you'll enjoy our first chapter, *Getting a LAN Up and Running*. We installed NetWare 3.1 on a no-name 386-clone file server using thin coax and Ethernet. Here are the steps we took.

Network Installation Steps

This is an Ethernet network with Novell NetWare 3.1.

1. **Set up the cards and cables**

   a. Open computers, set Network Interface Card switches, insert cards.

   b. Hook up cables.

   c. Because Ethernet requires it, install cable terminators and ground one of them.

2. **Set up the file server**

   a. Hard disk

      1) Prepare a 4-10 Meg DOS hard disk partition with FDISK and FORMAT.

2) Copy SERVER.EXE, LAN card drivers and disk drivers, and VREPAIR.EXE to DOS partition.

b. The server program

1) Run SERVER.EXE.

2) Give file server a name and internal network number (you make these up). The server now is up and running, but it can't talk to anybody.

c. Disk drivers

1) Load disk drivers. Now the hard disk exists for the server (but not as a NetWare disk).

d. The install utility

1) Load INSTALL.NLM, use it to create a NetWare partition and NetWare volumes on the hard disk.

2) Mount the volumes (now NetWare can find the volumes on the hard disk).

3) Copy the SYSTEM and PUBLIC files to the NetWare partition of hard disk (these are the entire NetWare Operating System—once they're copied, you've got NetWare 3.x).

e. LAN drivers

1) Load LAN card driver(s) (now the server can talk to its LAN card, but the card can't talk to its network cable yet).

2) Bind (connect) the IPX protocol to the LAN driver (now the file server's LAN card can talk to the cable).

3) Give the network a unique number (you make it up).

f. Boot files

1) The install program has created STARTUP.NCF and AUTOEXEC.NCF. Check them for errors or additions.

3. Set Up the Workstations

a. We have already installed the network interface cards and hooked up the cables (if you forgot for some reason, do it now).

b. Make a boot disk for each workstation.

c. Generate workstation shell and copy it to the boot disk.

Okay, you have installed NetWare 386 as per the instructions in your Novell **Installation** manual. What happens when you turn on your file server?

The File Server Comes to Life

1. The file server boots DOS, which is stored on the DOS partition of the network hard drive, or on a file server floppy-drive boot disk (either way works fine).
2. The AUTOEXEC.BAT file runs SERVER.EXE, the file server program that is the kernel of the NetWare 386 operating system. Once you boot from a DOS disk and run SERVER.EXE, you have the server up and running, although it cannot communicate yet with the hard disk(s) or the LAN card(s). We will need to load a disk driver (a software program that allows the operating system kernel to interface with the physical hard disk mounted in the file server) and a LAN driver (software that allows the operating system kernel to interface with the network card installed in this file server). Both disk and LAN drivers are NLMs—they may be loaded and unloaded while the server is up and running.
3. SERVER.EXE executes STARTUP.NCF, which contains commands to load disk drivers for the file server. Disk drivers and the STARTUP.NCF file must be stored on the disk you boot from. Once the disk drivers are loaded, though, the server can find its own hard disk.
4. It then mounts the SYS volume—now NetWare can read the hard disk (at least the SYS volume partition).
5. SERVER.EXE executes AUTOEXEC.NCF, which provides the file server with information to complete the boot process (the file server name, the IPX internal network number, commands to load network card drivers and other NLMs, and mount any additional volumes). AUTOEXEC.NCF is stored on SYS:SYSTEM.
6. You're rolling!

A Network Workstation Comes to Life

For comparison here are the steps that your workstation computer goes through when you turn it on in the morning.

1. Turn on the workstation. It automatically checks its own hardware with a POST (Power On Self Test) loaded in its ROM BIOS. It tries to load DOS, typically from a boot diskette or workstation hard disk, checking for a CONFIG.SYS file and/or an AUTOEXEC.BAT file as it boots up. If you have an AUTOEXEC.BAT file, or a network batch file, it may automate the next few steps. (Diskless workstations use a special boot PROM that allows the workstation to read the necessary DOS, CONFIG.SYS, AUTOEXEC.BAT, IPX, and NETx files from the file server's hard disk.)
2. Load IPX—typically stored on your boot disk. A SHELL.CFG file, if you have one, can set specific parameters for your copy of IPX.
3. Load NETx.COM—typically stored on your boot disk. A SHELL.CFG file, if you have one, can set specific parameters for your copy of NETx.COM.
4. Change to the F: directory—NetWare automatically makes F: the login directory on the network drive when you first attempt to log in to the network.
5. Type LOGIN—this file is stored in the LOGIN directory on the network drive so you can access it before you are actually logged into the network.
6. Type your user name and password.
7. The login script executes (this will be the default login script until the Supervisor sets up a system-wide login script and your personal login script associated with your name and password). The login script can do a lot or a little. At a minimum it will map network drives. It may be a complex batch file, though, mapping drives, setting up print queues, setting your DOS prompt and the location of your copy of COMMAND.COM, etc. In addition, the login script, like any batch file, can dump you immediately into an application program, pull up a menu, and/or print messages on the user's screen.
8. You're rolling!

On Creating Workstation Boot Disks

The Master Workstation Diskette, one that would fit all of the workstations on the LAN, is a LAN fantasy. For such a master disk to work each workstation must have identical LAN adapter cards (the same brand, model and bus type), and all of the cards would have to be set to the exact same interrupt and I/O address. You might be able to locate an interrupt and I/O combination that could be used on every workstation on the network in your dreams, but not in real life.

When Sue installed her first network, she got jammed up with this Master Workstation Diskette concept. She mistakenly thought we had to install all the NICs (Network Interface Cards) with the same interrupt and I/O address — so she looked for a universally available interrupt. Finally she decided on interrupt 5, which interferes with the hard disk controller in XT computers. She removed the hard disk from her single XT workstation (and counted herself lucky she didn't have to do any more cutting and fitting).

Sue was wrong, of course. You don't have to have a Master Workstation Diskette. Just make each NIC work properly in its own computer. Interrupts and I/O addresses allow communication between the NIC and the computer it's installed in, not between NICs on the cable. The NICs take care of communication across the cable, using their individual NIC card node addresses to tell each other apart, not interrupts or I/O addresses.

Keep configuration notes on each workstation. Note the network card installed and its jumper settings, the versions of IPX and NETx that this workstation is using, etc. Sample configuration sheets are included in the Novell documentation. Be sure to keep copies of your custom-generated boot disks too—trashed boot files account for an amazing percentage of user complaints. Configuration management utilties, for example Frye's LAN Directory, inventory both workstation and server hardware and software—they can be a big help.

When generating the workstation shell, use SHGEN for NetWare 3.x (or WSGEN for NetWare 2.2 or 3.11). If you're doing SHGEN on a hard disk, be sure to pay attention to the directions in the Novell manual. SHGEN goes in the parent NETWARE directory. All other files from the diskette go in a subdirectory named SHGEN-1. If none of the standard configurations will work, you can generate a standard shell, then modify it with the JUMPERS shell-editor program.

> **Warning:** A warm boot will not reset the network card. If you change your IPX (for example, if you change the IPX with JUMPERS so it uses a different interrupt) you'll have to cold boot the machine. The IPX that was loaded into memory of the host computer initializes the network card. When you cold boot, the card resets itself so it may be initialized again, this time with the correct values.

NetWare 386 File Servers— A Potential Security Hazard

It is important to lock up your NetWare 386 file server. You can physically lock it up, or you can use the SECURE CONSOLE utility. Physically locking up the file server computer is best.

1. Someone could steal the hard disk out of it. (Do datanappers hold hard disks for ransom? Or do they just copy the contents of the hard disk and reinstall it in the server so you're left with a mysterious power-out failure at the server?)
2. Somebody could use the built-in NetWare operating system debugger to bypass the security system. (SECURE CONSOLE protects against this.)
3. Somebody could load an NLM (NetWare Loadable Module) that does something evil to your network. Novell calls these "Trojan horse loadable modules." (SECURE CONSOLE protects against this.)
4. Somebody could change the file server's date and/or time, so the server thinks it's 10 a.m. at 3 a.m. and allows a daytime employee access to the network. Password expiration, intruder detection, and lockout intervals can also be bypassed if the intruder changes the server's date and time. (SECURE CONSOLE protects against this.)

NetWare Loadable Modules

NLMs (NetWare Loadable Modules) are utility programs that can be loaded or unloaded from file server memory while the server is running. Novell NetWare NLMs provide

- Services (such as the INSTALL, RCONSOLE and MONITOR NLMs)
- Protocols (such as the Novell proprietary IPX/SPX protocol and TCP/IP)
- Name space for long file names (such as Macintosh file names)
- Driver sets (such as hard disk drivers and NIC drivers).

INSTALL is used for NetWare installation and maintenance—for example, INSTALL allows you to format a server hard disk, or create, delete, test, and modify NetWare partitions on a server hard disk.

MONITOR shows how efficiently the network is running—providing info about utilization, cache memory and memory usage, network stations currently connected, both hard drive and volume stats, and NLMs loaded.

RCONSOLE lets the system supervisor remotely access the file server console, so she can perform network management tasks from her own workstation.

The disk driver modules are all named driver_name.DSK, and connect the operating system to the hard disk controller(s) in your file server. Network card drivers are called driver_name.LAN, and connect the operating system to the network board(s) installed in your file server.

Outside developers (often called "third-party" developers) may write their own NLMs to provides services not available in NetWare. For example, Sitelock, from Brightwork Development, provides software metering and virus protection for your file server. The ARCserve NLM, from Cheyenne Software, allows fast, automatic backup and restore to a tape drive, Bernoulli, or optical disk attached to the file server itself. Other third-party NLMs provide printer utilities or collect network statistics for network load diagnosis and/or performance tuning.

Where to find NLMs on your LAN

Go to the file server console (the keyboard attached to your file server), or use RCONSOLE at your workstation (if you prefer troubleshooting the file server remotely from your own station). Run the MONITOR NLM (most likely it is already running; if not, type LOAD MONITOR at the : prompt on the file server console). The System Module Information box in MONITOR lists the modules you have installed on this file server and the module version number (modules get updated periodically, like any other NetWare utility file).

How an NLM Works

NLMs dynamically link to the network operating system. We say "dynamically" because the linkage happens while the operating system is running (it happens on the fly), so you can load or unload (link or unlink) modules without shutting off the file server. "Linking" means connecting the program code in the NLM to the background information and data already available in the main operating system kernel. Like the bionic arms and legs of Robocop, NLMs are linked to the operating system, extending its capabilities.

How to Test an NLM

If an NLM seems wacko (won't load, doesn't work, seems to work wrong), compare the size of the NLM file and its version number with that of the original NLM on your backup disks. Does it appear to be corrupted? If so, recopy it from your backup disks, or reload the entire System and Public file-set from your original NetWare installation disks (if it's a Novell NLM module).

If there's no evidence of file corruption, start checking for hot gossip on the local NetWare user's group bulletin board or NetWire. Some NLMs have bugs when first released, so Novell issues an updated NLM to correct the problem. In general, use the newest version of any particular NLM that you can find. If you still have doubts about the NLM, better call Novell tech support. Third-party NLMs are supported, of course, by the manufacturer, not Novell.

Removing and Installing an NLM

Load NLMs with the

LOAD nlm_utility

command—typed either at the file server console or at your workstation (if you are using RCONSOLE to remotely control the file server console).

Remove NLMs with the

UNLOAD nlm_utility

command—typed either at the file server console or at your workstation (if you are using RCONSOLE).

UPS (Uninterruptible Power Supply)

Protect your file server against electric power-line failures with an Uninterruptible Power Supply. File servers are more susceptible to data corruption during a power outage than ordinary computers because network operating systems use a write cache system to speed up their performance. Novell NetWare, for example, temporarily stores incoming data—data that should be written to the file server's hard disk—in file server memory. Unfortunately, this is memory that will forget everything if the power is turned off. Every 3 seconds, NetWare writes all this data stored in memory to the hard disk. So it takes NetWare about 5 seconds after a power failure to shut down normally, without danger of losing or corrupting data. Your UPS **must** provide those 5 seconds.

Figure 206 *Larger Uninterruptable Power Supplies will support larger/longer current draws when commercial power fails. Photo courtesy of Viteq Corporation.*

Look for a UPS that protects against power line surges, sags, and impulses, as well as complete power failure. National Power Laboratory, a division of Best Power Technology (which manufactures and sells power supplies), has released preliminary data for the first year of its five-year power quality study. Power-line monitors at the wall outlet show that only 5-9 percent of power line disturbances are power failures (zero volts at the outlet), according to this study. Most disturbances are sags (brownouts of 104 volts or less). Surges (short periods of 127 volts or more) and impulses (instantaneous blips of high or low voltage—spikes) are less common than sags. The brownout threshold used in the study (104 volts) is used by the Computer Business Equipment Manufacturers Association as a suggested operational design range for computers. Meanwhile, *PC Week* Labs tested eight name-brand PCs in brownouts and found them all working fine at 90 volts input. Confusing? You bet. Nevertheless, none of the authors would bet our jobs on a file server running at 90 volts.

Don't blame the electric company for all your power problems. Power company brownouts are common during peak air-conditioning hours in the summer, but in-house power-hogs (motors, elevators, fluorescent lights, and heavy tools) can also cause momentary brownouts as they start up. Conversely, turning these power-hogs off can produce a momentary voltage surge at your outlet.

Where to Install a UPS in your LAN

Put your file server on a UPS, of course. If you also install a UPS monitor card in the file server, most network operating systems will automatically warn your users to log out, then down the server properly. We strongly recommend using a monitor card. Some UPSs talk to the file server through the serial port or a special connection on a Novell disk coprocessor board. In any case, use a feedback mechanism that automatically shuts down the file server.

Do you need to protect any other parts of the network? Yes. You want to protect bridges, routers, and repeaters if you want the LAN to keep running during a power problem. Usually the real danger is data loss or data corruption at the file server, not loss of LAN functionality (we assume you're not supporting the space shuttle). If you really need to keep the LAN running in a power failure you'll need a UPS for each vital workstation as well.

Don't bother with a UPS for the printer. When the lights come back on your user can reissue the print command and continue where she left off. Do put an expensive laser printer on a surge protector, however.

Figure 207 *We install this standalone UPS monitor card in the file server, then connect its cable to a DB-9 connector on the UPS, so the NetWare UPS module in the file server will know when commercial power has failed and we're running on the UPS batteries.*

Phone lines and long printer cables can also conduct spikes to your file server. Consider using a telephone-line or data-line surge suppressor if your network experiences data corruption problems. Definitely use one if the area is susceptible to lightning storms.

How a UPS Works

Three major UPS designs are competing for the network manager's UPS dollar, and the UPS manufacturers are waging a white-paper battle to prove which is the best design. The big three are:

1. Standby UPS, which provides commercial line voltage to the computer until a power disturbance or interruption causes the UPS to switch to battery power. Filtering for spikes on the commercial power line varies by manufacturer.
2. On-line UPS (also called Full Time UPS), which sends commercial line power into a battery charger. Once started, the computer is powered by the battery at all times. When the computer is first turned on, though, it requires a big shot of electricity (some experts say as much as 40 times the normal operating current). Some on-line UPSs use an AC bypass to provide this first surge (they use line voltage from your commercial power source). Others do not, so you must buy a larger UPS to accommodate the turn-on current draw.
3. Standby UPS with a Ferro Transformer, which drives the computer off a ferroresonant transformer whether operating on commercial power or on battery backup. Like standby UPS designs, this UPS uses commercial power (from your outlet) under most conditions, and battery power only when there is a power disturbance. But neither battery power nor commercial power drive the computer directly, they both drive a ferroresonant transformer which in turn drives the computer. The transformer levels out voltage surges and sags, but it is not intended to address spike problems. Therefore, these UPSs require surge protection circuitry too.

Power glitches have become one of the major finger-pointing favorites for network troubleshooters. If you don't have the troubleshooter's favorite UPS technology, they'll insist that your problems are power related and refuse to check further until you have installed the preferred UPS design and retested your network.

Despite the white-paper wars, everyone agrees that power failures will obliterate any data stored in your file server's write cache. Eventually someone will do a definitive study proving that "on-line," "standby," or "standby with ferro transformer" UPSs are superior to the others. Until then, pick a brand with a good reputation and install it. You can easily lose more dollars worth of time and data in an unprotected crash than you'll lose by picking the second-best UPS design.

Use your experience with your local power company to decide which level of UPS is necessary. If the lights dim and flicker regularly, and the power goes totally out whenever a big storm hits, you clearly need an on-line UPS running full time off a battery backup.

If you see the lights dim, but the power never, never goes full dead, you may be all right with a surge suppressor and a voltage leveler (the ferroresonant transformer without any associated standby UPS). Remember, even if your utility provides clean, constant power the fluorescent lights and motors in your building will distort that power at your outlet.

How to Test Your UPS

Uninterruptible Power Supplies rely on battery backup. The batteries wear out, much as your automobile battery does. A recent letter to *BYTE* from a UPS design engineer suggested a normal battery life of three to five years for a UPS. Because on-line power supplies use their batteries continuously, they may need to be replaced much sooner.

Batteries wear out quickly when continuously charged and depleted, especially if repeatedly depleted to the same level. We borrowed a true on-line UPS from Viteq for our test LAN. Viteq and Panasonic (the big name in UPS batteries) maintain that the special ripple-circuit battery charger in this UPS will keep the batteries healthy for five years plus.

No matter which UPS design you use, it makes sense to test the battery backup capability every six months. Pull the plug and watch the file server, preferably while running a batch copy program that exercises the file server's hard disk. You need to know how many minutes your UPS will support this load.

Remember, the UPS monitor card knows when commercial power has been cut to the UPS, but most monitors don't actually measure the power remaining in your UPS. Instead, they count the minutes until it's time to broadcast the message "The file server will shut down in one minute" and down the server. If you, the LAN manager, have told this UPS monitor program to wait 20 minutes before downing the file server, it will wait 20 minutes whether the UPS has enough juice to run the server for 20 minutes or not. Therefore, you should test the batteries every six months to be sure that your run time estimates are still accurate. We don't have to tell you to do this test with everyone else logged off the network, do we?

For maximum battery life, run the UPS in a cool, dry place. Because batteries tend to go dead when lightly discharged, then fully charged, then lightly discharged, fully drain your UPS battery pack every six months, perhaps at the same time you test the UPS run time capability. A full discharge and full recharge every once in a while is good for a battery pack. This is true for laptop computer batteries too. Run them to full dead every week or two to make them last longer. Viteq, by the way, says that batteries on a ripple circuit charger don't need to be discharged every six months.

How to Remove and Install a UPS

First, test the wall outlet you're planning to use with a plug-in circuit tester, like the ones available for $10-$20 from Jensen Tools, Specialized Products Company, and many other electronic supply houses. The circuit tester will spot open grounds, reverse polarity, etc.—the typical problems caused by miswired outlets. If your outlet passes this preliminary test, plug your network file server into a UPS and plug the UPS into the wall.

We have been called to troubleshoot networks protected by all kinds of fancy surge protectors and a UPS, but everything plugs into the wall at an ungrounded (2-prong) outlet. Or they have a 3-prong to 2-prong adapter at the outlet and the little green wire is hanging loose in the air. Hook up that little green ground wire to the center screw on the outlet cover. Test it with your 3-prong outlet tester, it should be fine now.

Install the UPS monitoring and control card as you would install any other computer expansion card. The directions shipped with the UPS card give recommended switch settings. Be sure to plug in the UPS-to-monitor-card cable tightly; a poor connection can make troubleshooting difficult. The NetWare UPS STATUS utility gives you the UPS condition, or to be exact, it tells you what your file server software believes about the UPS condition. Use UPS STATUS to confirm that the server thinks you are on commercial power when the UPS is plugged into the wall and on battery power when the UPS is unplugged. If the server is confused and thinks you are on battery power when, in fact, the UPS is plugged into a working outlet, you've got the monitor board switch settings wrong.

You'll need to give the UPS software a recharge time estimate for this UPS. Eight times the number of minutes the UPS will power the network is a reasonable rule of thumb.

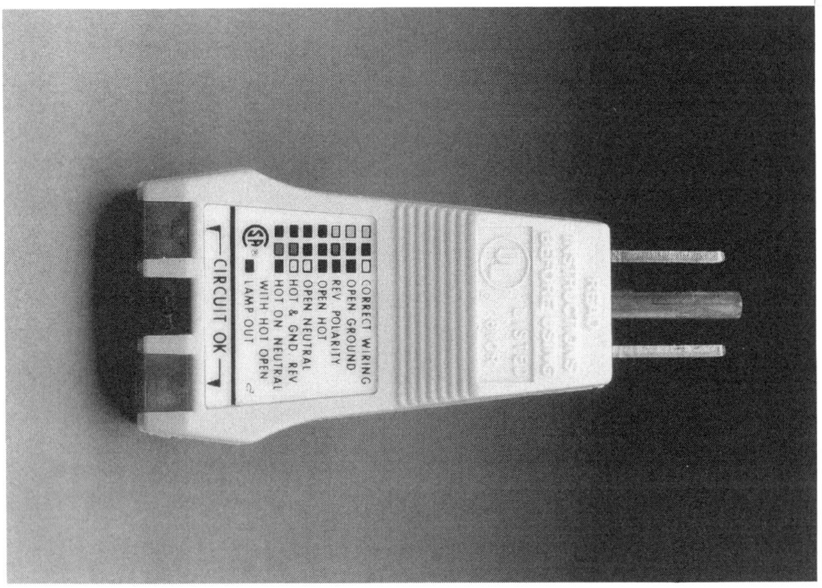

Figure 208 *Three-prong outlet tester. Photo courtesy of Specialized Products Company.*

Here are rough figures to help you decide how much UPS capacity you need. They are provided by American Power Conversion, and are in Volt-Amps (a rough measure of power usage).

Compaq 386	230 VA
AT clone	200 VA
Multisync monitor	110-200 VA (depends on monitor size)
B/W monitor	50 VA (many file servers use monochrome)
Laser printer	1000 VA (you see why it doesn't pay to UPS a Laser printer?)

Print Server

A Print Server is actually a software function on your LAN, not a physical piece of hardware. When people speak casually about "the print server," though, they're often referring to the hardware that this software is loaded on. We'll consider both hardware and print server software in this Data Sheet.

Print server software transports print jobs from a print queue on the file server (temporary storage) to the appropriate network printer. It's a combination traffic cop and freight forwarder.

How a Print Server Works

Here's a quick-and-dirty sketch of network printing:

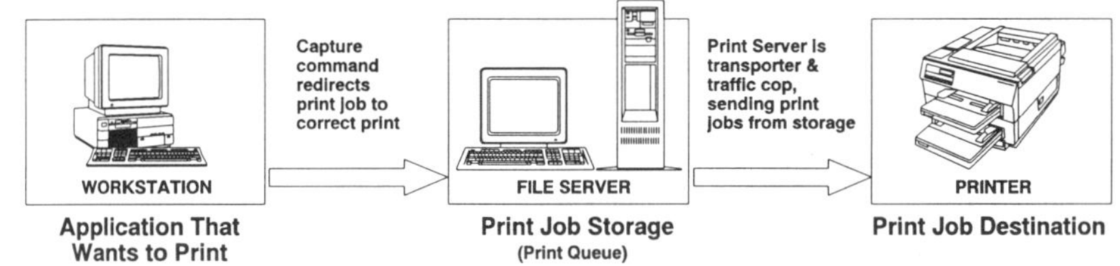

Figure 209 *Network printing.*

You'll notice that users store network print jobs in queues rather than sending them directly to a particular printer. Each queue is a subdirectory of the SYSTEM directory on the file server. The supervisor sets up bottom-line print queue defaults with the SPOOL and CAPTURE commands. Any user may override these system-wide defaults in her personal login script, or she may issue a new CAPTURE command from the DOS command line at any time.

Your print server software forwards files from print queues on this or other file servers (the queues don't have to be on the same file server as the print server!). Your print server watches both print queue and the printers it serves, sending a job to the printer if it's free and the job has no "hold" on it.

NetWare 2.x and 3.x allow you to run the print server software on three forms of hardware: on the file server, on a dedicated workstation, or on a Netware 286 "bridge." In addition, some third party manufacturers sell printer adapter hardware which contains the print server software and also connects printers to the network cable.

Where to Find Print Server Software on your LAN

1. On the file server—Use the INSTALL NLM to look at the AUTOEXEC.NCF file and see if there is a line to load PSERVER.NLM (NetWare 3.x). It will look something like this:

   LOAD PSERVER printserver

   If you have a multi-server LAN, with both NetWare 3.x server(s) and NetWare 2.x server(s), you may have installed the PSERVER software on one of the 286 servers or on a 286 NetWare bridge, rather than on one of the 386 servers. If you did, however, you used PSERVER.VAP rather than PSERVER.NLM (2.x servers and bridges use VAPs, 3.x servers use NLMs). At the 2.x file server console (or at the bridge), use the VAP command to list the Value Added Processes installed on this file server. Simply type VAP to see the list.
2. On a dedicated workstation print server (a PC that does only print server duty), the workstation monitor will show the 8-box Novell Print Server screen.
3. In a special-purpose print server (e.g., Intel's NetPort, Castelle's LANPress, or Hewlett Packard's Network-Printer adapter cards), use PCONSOLE to look for a print server name that you cannot trace to print server software running on a file server, dedicated workstation, or bridge. These adapters attach to the LAN cable out in the work area where you need printers. The boxes have serial and parallel ports to drive multiple printers. The adapter cards slide right into an HP LaserJet, and connect it directly to the LAN cable. Some of these special-purpose print adapters use standard NetWare print server software, but others use a proprietary substitute for Novell's print server which does the same job, often faster.

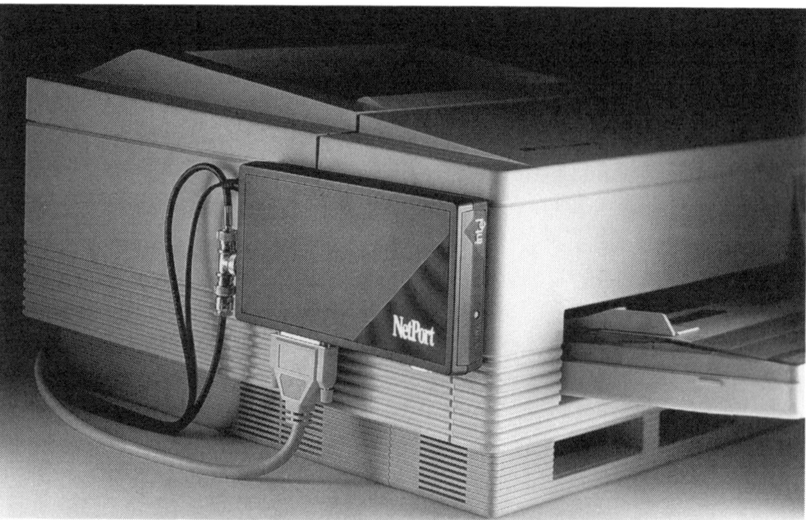

Figure 211 *This NetPort print server connects a laser printer to the thin Ethernet network cable. Like most special-purpose network print adapters, it is unobtrusive and easy to install. Photo courtesy of Intel Personal Computer Enhancement Operation.*

How to Install the Print Server

Let's first review the steps to set up network printing so you see where installing the print server fits into the process:

1. **Plan a printing layout** (plan which printers will be local and which will be network printers). There are five ways to set up a network printer, and you must choose which technique you will use for each printer. See Chapter 9 for our recommendations. When you first start out, set up a clear print-queue-to-printer path. Start with a one-to-one printer/print-queue correspondence until you know that everything is going right. Yes, you can direct two queues to one printer and one queue to two (or more) printers, but don't mess with that fancy stuff until you are sure the basics are performing flawlessly.
2. **Run PCONSOLE.** Before we can create a print server we must describe it and its associated print queues with PCONSOLE (we

draft the blueprints). In these blueprints we specify which print queue feeds which printer, we name and describe the print server, and we authorize specific users as Print Server Operators, or Print Queue Operators and queue users. Once these relationships are set up, supervisors and authorized Print Server Operators can manipulate these queue-to-printer vectors (pointers) with PCONSOLE. Ordinary users are locked out of this level, so they must be sure to send their documents to the correct print queue, the queue which feeds the network printer they want to use.

a. Create print queue(s).

b. Create print server(s).

c. Define printers.

d. On multiple-file-server networks, set up traffic flow to the right file servers, print queues, and print-servers.

e. Assign queues to printers.

3. **Create spooler mappings to provide a default print queue (if none is specified in the CAPTURE or NPRINT commands).**
4. **Load PSERVER.NLM, start PSERVER.VAP, run PSERVER.EXE, or start your special-purpose print server as per its installation instructions to activate the print server** (see below which one to use when). As it loads, your print server software reads the print queue/server/printer blueprints you set up in PCONSOLE. To actually bring a print server to life, run the print server software. In NetWare, the print server software is separate from the rest of the operating system, so it does not necessarily need to run on the file server.
5. **If you are using remote printer(s), run RPRINTER at the printer's home workstation.** Put RPRINTER in the workstation's AUTOEXEC.BAT file rather than the user's loginscript so the remote printer will be available to the network, whether the user is logged in or not.

Your application should now print normally whenever you issue a CAPTURE command. You may customize your printing with PRINTCON (a way to set up a standard printing configuration that includes all your preferred print options) and PRINTDEF (the database of printer definitions you need for PRINTCON), but the basic network printing is active.

Loading the Print Server Software

Note: Make certain you are using the correct software for your implementation.

1. **A print server on the network file server:** Use the PSERVER.NLM software if you have a NetWare 3.x file server. Use the PSERVER.VAP if you have multiple file servers on your network, and one or more are running NetWare 3.x, but you're running this print server software on one of your 2.1x file servers. If you use PSERVER.VAP you must also load the NetWare 3.x printing utilities onto your NetWare 2.1x file server.
2. **A dedicated workstation print server:** Run PSERVER from the workstation's DOS command line. Like PSERVER.NLM, this print server sends print jobs from a queue on a file server to printers connected here at the print server, or to remote printers connected to local workstations. Put this line in your SHELL.CFG file for this dedicated workstation print server:

   SPX CONNECTIONS = 60

   A 256K XT-class PC works fine as a dedicated print server. Novell says their engineers have found no evidence of faster printing with a faster (e.g., AT class) computer.

3. **Third-party printer ports, (like the Intel NetPort and Castelle LANPress):** Follow the directions packed with your special-purpose print server. These servers contain ROM-resident print server software. For our test LAN we installed and operated an Intel NetPort. It was as smooth as silk; easy to set up as a print server, easy to set it up a second time as a remote printer. Total time for the two installations, setting up print queues, etc., about half an hour. We needed to know little or nothing about NetWare to do the job.

It was very well-documented: clear directions, and clear recommendations when we had to make choices. In short, a breeze. We had no chance to use the troubleshooting info since nothing went wrong.

Using Remote Printers with a Print Server

Any print server can send data to a local printer attached to a workstation (Novell calls this a "remote printer"), but you must first run RPRINTER.EXE on the workstation. RPRINTER, a TSR (Terminate-and-Stay-Resident program), permits the print server to use a printer attached directly to your workstation. It takes only 4K of memory. You will need to put

SPX CONNECTIONS = 60

in the workstation's SHELL.CFG file, then run RPRINTER.EXE from the DOS command line at the remote printer's workstation. Check the Novell **Print Server** manual for syntax, or just type RPRINTER if you prefer the menu version.

If you want to use the local printer for network printing when the workstation's user is not there, it is a potential security loophole if the workstation is logged in but no user is watching the station. On the other hand, a user has access to the files in the LOGIN subdirectory, without logging in. Therefore, the totally hip supervisor puts RPRINTER.EXE and related files in the LOGIN subdirectory on the file server, so you can run IPX, NETx and RPRINTER.EXE in the workstation's AUTOEXEC.BAT file without logging any particular user in to the network. You will need access to the following files, so copy them all to the LOGIN subdirectory:

IBM$RUN.OVL

RPRINTER.EXE

RPRINT$$.EXE

SYS$HELP.DAT

RPRINTER.HLP

SYS$MSG.DAT

SYS$ERR.DAT

Testing a Print Server

The PCONSOLE utility shows "Printer status"—a good idea, but it lies. Don't believe PCONSOLE on this. Walk down to the printer and look for yourself. The same with the PSC command line version of the PCONSOLE commands—liar, liar, pants on fire. They could say the printer is "Waiting for job" when in fact it's out of paper or unplugged or the boss took it home for the weekend.

If you are having trouble printing, quickly inspect the printer visually for power, paper, and a tight connection at the printer cable, then use the printer's self-test to be sure the printer itself is not choked. Next, try setting up a test print queue served by this print server and pointing toward the known-good printer. If the queue fails to print, you can try servicing the same queue from another print server. If the other server makes the print jobs in the queue print correctly, you must have some kind of problem with your first print server. Perhaps it has corrupted setup data, or perhaps the print server software itself has become corrupted (unlikely, but anything is possible).

Don't forget to thoroughly check the hardware before you consider software suspects—a bad printer cable or printer port disables a network printer just as effectively as it disables a local printer on a standalone computer. Use QAPlus/fe with a printer port wrap plug to test the port. On a file server this means down the server and boot it from a DOS diskette, then test it. Test the cable the old-fashioned way, by swapping in a known-good one.

If you want any changes to take effect you must unload the print server, whether NLM, VAP, or PSERVER.EXE, then reload it. For example, if you use PCONSOLE to set up a new print server and queue, then try to assign the queue to the print server, the print server won't "Attach" to the queue. Unload the NLM, then reload it so it reads the new info.

Tape Backup Units

Most file server hard disks are so big that tape backup is the only rational choice. You probably need to back up your server every day, though the frequency depends on the volume of information your organization stores on the LAN each day and the value of that information. The system administrator may also be expected to back up the hard disks on individual workstations.

How a Tape Backup Works

Tape backup units come in two forms:

1. The backup software runs on the file server (an NLM or VAP) and the tape drive is attached directly to the file server or
2. The backup software runs on the workstation.

The first type (software on the file server) is much more expensive, but it's a hell of a lot quicker. Because the tape drive is connected to the server's bus with an adapter board (often a SCSI controller, often the same SCSI controller that runs your big file server hard disk) this design avoids loading the LAN cable with gigabytes of backup data. The best choice in this category is ARCServe.

We think the best choices in the second category are CPBackup and Palindrome's Network Archivist. We discuss backup utilities in Chapter 5. CPBACKUP is available with PCTools version 6.0 and above, but get version 7.1 or above because it's much more flexible.

Features to look for when you buy your tape backup drive and accompanying software:

- The required time to backup your drive.
- The ability to back up multiple volumes (both on the file server and on workstations).
- A tape big enough to back up the entire hard drive. You can set it to back up automatically at 2 a.m. when everybody is off the LAN. Otherwise you have to wait around until 3 a.m. to swap tapes.

How to Install and Test Tape Backup Units

Follow the manufacturer's directions carefully. You'll have to take normal precautions when installing the tape drive adapter cards—they may require an interrupt, use an I/O address, and/or use a DMA channel.

Clean the tape drive heads periodically with alcohol and a cotton swab just as you would on your home cassette tape machine.

Network Cards and Cables

Network Interface Card

A Network Interface Card links a computer (whether functioning as file server, workstation, bridge, or printer server) to the network cable. The card has an in/out data door from card to computer, called the I/O port. Once you install the card, by plugging it into the computer bus, the I/O port is wired into the computer. The exact I/O port address is determined by setting DIP-switches or jumpers on the card—see Installation on page 112 for more details.

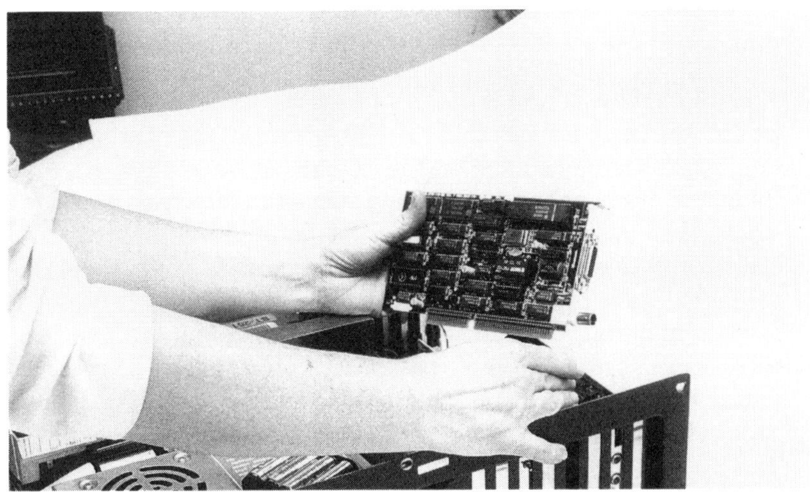

Figure 212 *This NE2000 Ethernet card has a round BNC connector for thin Ethernet cable, and the standard 15-pin AUI slide-lock connector for a thick Ethernet MAU drop cable or a transceiver.*

On the end of the card, sticking out the back of the computer, you'll find a second in/out door, the network cable connector socket. Some network cards have more than one physical cable connector — for example, one of the Thomas-Conrad Ethernet adapter cards in Figure 215 has three connector sockets. It can be used with any of the three popular types of Ethernet cable, but only one cable connector at a time can be activated and attached to the network. Most network cards only have a single cable connector, so you must order the right card for your particular network cable — an Ethernet card with a BNC coax cable connector won't hook up to twisted-pair wire, for example, nor will a Token Ring card do you much good in an ARCNET network.

Network Interface Cards are also called NICs, LAN cards, network boards, and NIUs (Network Interface Units)—all generic names for network adapter cards. When referring to cards designed for the three most popular network standards, we call them Ethernet cards, Token Ring cards, and ARCNET cards.

Where to Find the Network Cards in Your LAN

Experts—feel free to jump ahead to *How Network Cards Work* on page 106, *How to Test a Network Interface Card* on page 109, or *How to Install a Network Card* on page 112. The next few paragraphs are for first-time network explorers.

Look for a network card in each computer attached to the LAN: in workstations, file servers (up to four network cards per server), and in print servers, plus two or more network cards in each bridge.

A network cable connects to the back of the card. Look for coax cable (round and thick as a pencil, it looks like cable TV cable) or twisted-pair (looks like telephone line), or possibly a fiber optic cable (it's usually thinner than a pencil and looks like a stereo duplex speaker wire with a small half-twist or screw-on connector at the card). Shielded twisted-pair cable for Token Ring is about 3/8" in diameter with a 9-pin D-B9 connector at the card. Thick Ethernet, also called 10Base5, uses a drop cable from the big Ethernet cable in the wall or ceiling to the back of the workstation. This drop cable has an AUI (also called DIX) connector, which looks like a DB-15 game port connector, but the AUI uses a slidelock to hold the connector firmly onto the network card. See Figures 213-216.

You will have to sort through the cables on the back of the computer until you find the right one. Just work through them, one by one, ruling out the power cord (it plugs into a 110 volt wall outlet), the video monitor cable (it runs up to the back of the video monitor), your modem's phone cable

Figure 213 *A thin Ethernet cable is often black with a silver T connector.*

Figure 214 *Round BNC connector and 15-pin AUI connector on an Ethernet card.*

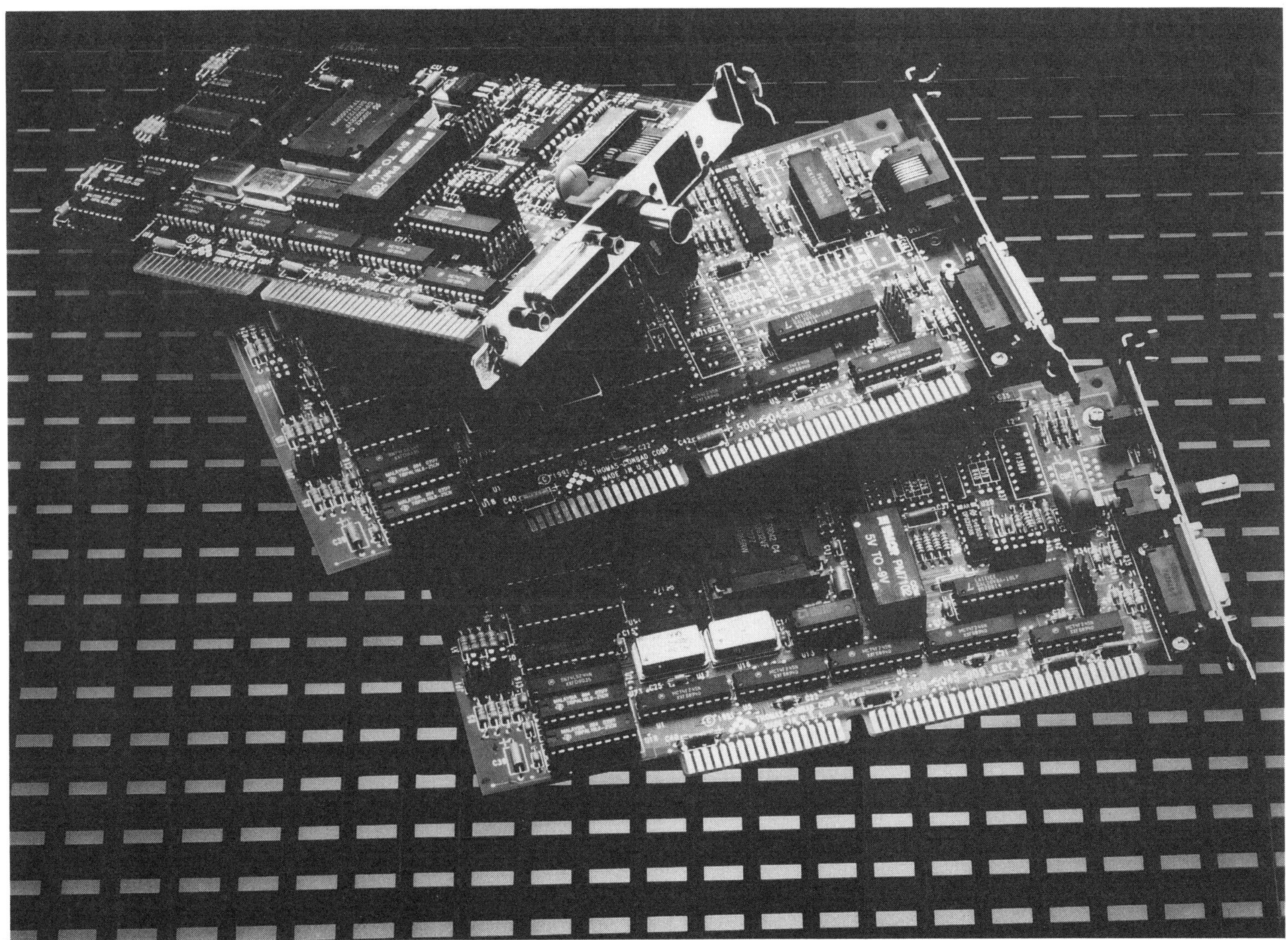

Figure 215 *The top card in this stack of Ethernet adapters from Thomas-Conrad has AUI, BNC, and RJ-45 connectors. Photo courtesy of Thomas-Conrad.*

(twisted-pair has 4, 6, or 8 wires, so it's about 1-1/2 times as thick as regular telephone cable, though it looks about the same), and your printer cable (that goes to the printer).

> **Warning:** Many Token Ring cards have a DB-9 connector that looks identical to a monochrome monitor connector on a video card—don't plug the Token Ring network cable into the video card, or the monitor into the network card. Token Ring cable often has "IBM" and a part number printed on the cable jacket. Once you have these cables sorted out, label them.

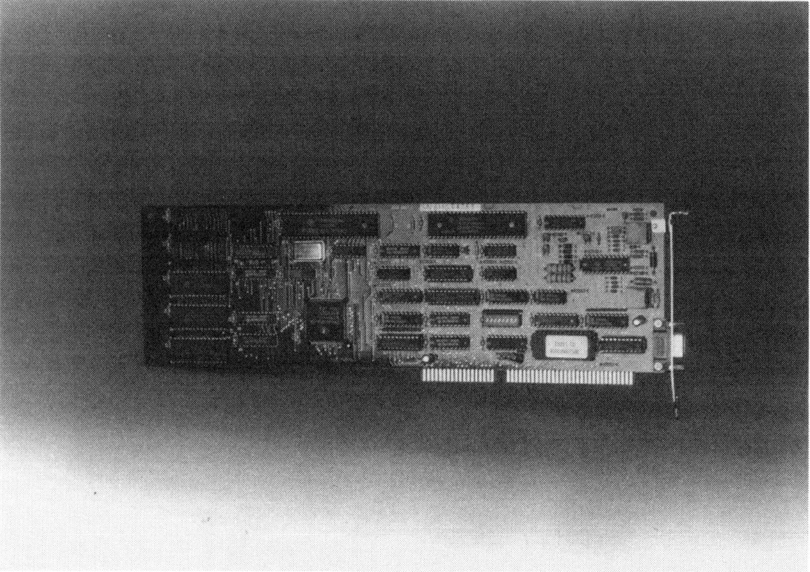

Figure 216 *Token Ring card with a DB-9 cable connection on the end. Photo courtesy of Computer System Products Incorporated.*

If you're having trouble sorting out the cables and cards, check out the photos. We show you BNC connections for COAX cable (Figure 214), RJ-45 sockets for twisted-pair wire (Figure 214), and DB-9 ports for a Token Ring (Figure 216). There's also a fiber optic cable section with a closeup of an ST fiber optic connector in Figure 239.

There are also a few wireless network designs that use either infrared or radio waves to send data from card to card. These network cards use a short antenna which runs directly off the back of the card.

How Network Cards Work

Workstations and file servers use interchangeable network cards. There is no distinction between file server and workstation, print server, or communications server at the card-and-cable level. Each network card sees all the other network cards as co-equal nodes. Luckily each card broadcasts a unique node number, so they can tell each other apart.

A network card receives information from its host computer (the computer it's installed in), processes it into data packets suitable for the network, then broadcasts the packets onto the network. If it has any information for its host computer, whether internally generated feedback or external data from the network, the network card sends an interrupt to the host computer's CPU. Upon receiving an interrupt, the CPU sets aside its present work to check the network card. This is called servicing the interrupt. So the I/O port, the door between computer and network card, only has a handle on the CPU side. The CPU can freely open the door to speak to the network card. The network card can only send an interrupt and wait for the CPU to open the door to see what the card needs.

The host computer (the one this card is installed in) runs a special software driver that tells the computer how to interact with this particular network card. That driver information is combined with the specific hardware settings on this particular network board (for instance, I/O port address and interrupt) when you generate the NetWare shell for this station. The Data Sheet section for the Network Operating System, pages 84-92, explores the software side of your network. Look there for more details about the workstation NetWare shell and the NetWare file server operating system.

Let's look at the cable for a moment—the physical connection between all these cards. We have to distinguish between the Topology (the shape of the network cable run), the Cable Medium (the physical cable, what it's made of), and the Access Scheme (who gets to talk on the cable, and when).

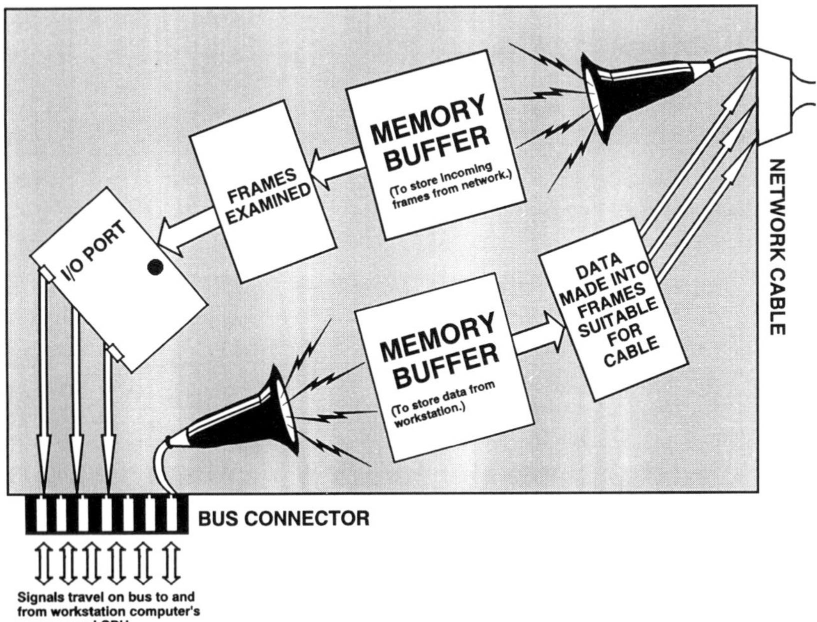

Figure 217 *How network cards communicate with the PC and the network cable.*

Topology

The three biggies are linear bus, star bus (series of stars), and ring (also called star ring).

Two of the bus topologies share a "party-line" quality—whenever any card on the bus sends a signal, every card on the bus hears that signal. The linear bus uses a single trunk cable (the common bus) with individual nodes connected like ribs on a backbone. Star bus topology uses signal splitters (hubs) to send the signal out in different directions on a bus cable shaped like interconnected stars. Both active and passive hubs are allowed, with the active hubs able to transmit a stronger signal to feed a longer cable and/or additional signal splitters. Figures 224 and 225 show linear bus Ethernet networks.

Ring (or star ring) topology has no party-line bus. Instead, each workstation's output port is connected to the next station in the circle until the output cable of the last station is connected to the input port of the first station. To make cabling easier, star ring networks use a wiring concentrator (a hub) located in the center of the star. This hub connects each work station to its appropriate neighbors, so the installer need only run cables from the hub to each workstation rather than from workstation to workstation in a big, messy cable ring. These Token Ring hubs are also called MAUs (Media Access Units) and IBM 8228s. Figure 238 shows two Token Ring networks, which use the ring topology.

Cable Medium

Networks run on coax cable, twisted-pair wire, fiber optic cable, and on infrared and radio transmitters. Each network card is designed to work with one or more of these media. A typical Ethernet card (such as the NE2000 card shown in so many of our lab photos, or the Thomas-Conrad Ethernet adapter shown in Figure 215) will work with two or even three different cables. See the sections on coax, fiber optic, twisted-pair, or wireless NICs if you want more details about specific cables.

All of these cabling media work fine, but not all of them are normally used in every topology. Token Ring networks typically use 8-wire twisted-pair cable, and all Token Ring networks use the star ring topology. ARCNET comes in coax, fiber optic, and twisted-pair designs, but no one has yet manufactured packet radio ARCNET cards. The Ethernet access scheme has been the most flexible in terms of media, running on thick or thin coax, on fiber optic or twisted-pair, as well as on packet radio and infrared transmitters. For years you had to pick one of these media and use only that medium for a segment of your Ethernet network. New Ethernet hubs are starting to break down that limitation. They seamlessly connect coax, fiber optic and/or twisted-pair, so you can cable together six workstations and a file server with thin coax, then connect the next eight workstations on this same Ethernet network with twisted-pair. Though these hubs allow you to run twisted-pair cable in a star topology, the signal is still running on a common bus cable where each workstation's transmissions are audible to all the other workstations on the bus.

Bridges and routers provide even more media flexibility. They are designed to translate one protocol to another (eg., ARCNET to Ethernet and vice versa) and one medium to another (eg., fiber optic to twisted-pair). See the table of Interconnection Devices on page 150 for precise distinctions between bridges, routers, and gateways.

Access Scheme

Okay, we have our network card connected to a cable. Other entities on the network communicate with this particular card by broadcasting a packet of data addressed to this card (to its node address). Though all parties on the network hear the broadcast message, only the card that is addressed receives the message into its input memory buffer. It's like the PA system at the airport: "blah, blah, ... blah-blah ... Ronnie Smith, Ronnie Smith. Please meet your party at gate 15. ... blah-blah ... " Ronnie Smith puts only her message into her memory buffer.

So how do these cards know who gets to talk when? We can't have all 20 cards on the network blabbing simultaneously. Time to discuss network access schemes, also called access protocols. Ethernet, ARCNET, and Token Ring each uses its own access protocol, so it makes sense to discuss them separately. Go to the section on your particular access scheme.

The CSMA/CD Protocol Used by Ethernet Cards

Ethernet networks use the CSMA/CD access protocol (Carrier Sense Multiple Access with Collision Detect). Each Ethernet card listens to the cable, waiting for a quiet moment to broadcast its messages. That's the Carrier Sense part. CSMA/CD is used with a Linear Bus Topology, a cabling scheme which puts all the Ethernet nodes on the same bus (the same party-line), so if one card broadcasts, every other card on the bus hears it. The party-line bus is the Multiple Access part. And Collision Detect works like this: In a quiet moment your Ethernet card sends a data signal out along the cable. If all is normal, this signal travels the length of the cable without interference, finally hitting the terminating resistor on the end of the cable where 90 percent of the signal goes right "through" the resistor and out of the cable. If the signal is garbled because of collisions with another card's broadcast, the card waits a random few moments, then sends the data signal again. If there has been a collision, any other broadcasting cards will realize it because they will also hear gibberish on the cable. The other cards also wait a random amount of time, then send their messages again.

The Token-Passing Protocol Used by ARCNET Cards

ARCNET employs a token-passing access scheme. It transfers the right to broadcast from one node to the next higher-addressed station. When you power up an ARCNET network the stations reconfigure themselves, each one discovering and noting the next-higher node address on the network (there can be gaps, for example, no stations between number 45 and number 79). When a token-holding node finishes transmitting it passes the token the way an emcee passes the microphone. "And now, I turn the mic over to you, station 79." Station 45 counts the microseconds until it receives the token again. It will force a network reconfiguration if the token doesn't return quickly enough (often caused by turning off a station). When you turn on your workstation for the day your ARCNET card transmits a reconfiguration burst on the network cable to force a network reconfiguration.

ARCNET uses the star bus cable topology. Whenever one card sends a signal out on the bus all the cards hear that signal, no matter how many hubs (signal splitters or signal repeaters) the signal may have to travel through. Therefore, a renegade card that broadcasts gibberish all the time, whether it has the token or not, will bring down an ARCNET network. A typical example would be an ARCNET card with broken receiver circuitry—it would keep broadcasting the reconfiguration signal because it never gets an answer. Setting two ARCNET cards to the same node address also thwarts the token bus access scheme. Be careful of this; you, the installer, are responsible for setting each new or replacement card to a unique address.

Ethernet is an IEEE/ANSI/ISO standard, and Token Ring is an IEEE/ANSI standard. (The IEEE is the Institute of Electrical and Electronics Engineers, ANSI is the American National Standards Institute, and ISO is the International Standards Organization.) ARCNET (and ARCNETplus, when it's released) is a proprietary standard created by Datapoint Corporation. Datapoint is now trying to make ARCNET an ANSI standard.

The Token Ring Access Protocol Used by Token Ring Cards

Token Ring networks use ring topology with the Token Ring access protocol, another token-passing access scheme. Whereas ARCNET passes the token by numerical node address, Token Ring passes the right-to-transmit token downstream to the next workstation on the circular network cable. Signals flow only in one direction. A signal from your node to its upstream neighbor must flow through each node on the ring before it reaches your upstream neighbor, the node that sends signals directly to you.

The multi-station access unit (the hub in the center of a Token Ring network) shunts the signals past a node whenever that node is turned off. Some intelligent MAUs also cut malfunctioning cards out of the ring.

A Token Ring network runs at the speed of the slowest card in the ring, so don't expect to pep up one workstation by substituting a 16 MB/sec card for its old 4 MB/sec card in a 4 MB/sec ring.

How to Test a Network Interface Card

We will cover the most likely network card malfunctions in this section, and give you some ideas for quick card testing. But do you know for sure that the network card is the culprit? We developed Troubleshooting Flowcharts because a step-by-step technique for locating the problem is faster than random guesses (even if they are educated guesses). You'll find these charts in Part 3 of this book.

If you just can't stand to go to the Troubleshooting Flowcharts, here are the techniques we use when we're pretty sure we've isolated the problem to this network card.

First, quickly check the computer as a standalone desktop PC—if it isn't working right as a standalone, don't waste your time trying to test the network card. Diagnostics like QAPlus/fe and CheckIt will give you a good, quick analysis if you have any doubts.

Next, consider the boot diskette. Many workstations operated fine yesterday, but won't connect to the network today. 80 percent of the time, we find that the network card is fine, but the IPX, NETx, or boot files on the boot diskette have gotten trashed. Try your backup copy of this workstation's boot diskette. If for some reason you don't have a backup copy, it makes sense to create a new workstation boot disk, formatting it with the /S parameter. Copy NETx to the diskette. IPX must be custom-generated for the network card configuration in this particular machine. If you have a copy of IPX for this machine, copy it to your new boot disk. If not, regenerate IPX with SHGEN and add it to the boot disk. (Use WSGEN if you've got NetWare 2.2 or 3.11.)

Test the workstation with this plain-vanilla diskette (no CONFIG.SYS, no AUTOEXEC.BAT, no SHELL.CFG files). If it works, add your SHELL.CFG, CONFIG.SYS, and AUTOEXEC.BAT files from the old diskette and test the workstation again.

If one of these files makes the station choke, you'll have to go through each file, line by line, looking for the culprit. Start with only one of these suspect files on your new boot diskette (temporarily rename the other two so the computer won't use them). Working with the suspect file, use a plain ASCII text editor (e.g., EDLIN or the Norton Editor) to put the letters REM in front of each line of the file. Any line marked REM is, as you know, ignored as the file loads. Remove the REM from one line. Reboot the computer and test it. If that line is not the culprit, remove the REM from a second line, etc., until you find which one is causing a conflict with the IPX or NETx files.

If a good boot diskette doesn't revive the workstation, we'll have to check the physical card and cable.

See if the Card Can Talk to the Cable

It's a good idea to do simple tests first. COMCHECK, a Novell utility provided with NetWare, can test the network card and cable using only the IPX protocol. We review other utilities capable of revealing subtle malfunctions in operational network cards (the cards that walk and talk, but can't run a marathon) in Chapter 5, *Choosing and Using Network Utilities*. For now, we're concentrating on lifeless workstations. Use COMCHECK if you can't log in to the network from a particular station and you're wondering if the card and cable are minimally functional. It gives a quick "connected" versus "unable to connect" test for each workstation—without getting the NetWare shell or operating system variables involved. We have included a short course in COMCHECK in Appendix B. If your workstation card won't even run IPX, go to *Checking a Brand New Card*, below, or to *Checking a Previously Working Card*, on the next page. And if you're wondering about the cable, why not connect another workstation (a known-good one) to this cable? A portable computer with a parallel-port-to-Ethernet adapter or a parallel-port-to-ARCNET adapter would work very well.

Checking a Brand New Card

If this is a new network card, one that has never worked in another workstation, please check, double-check, and triple-check that you're installing it correctly, without creating an interrupt, memory, I/O address, or DMA conflict with the other hardware in this workstation or file server. We give you detailed configuration instructions in the Installation section, pages 112-116—read that section and follow the instructions carefully when you install the card. Type IPX/i and check the IPX configuration specs against the physical card jumpers—does your IPX match your card? Right network card driver? Right IRQ, DMA, and I/O address?

If the IPX configuration matches your card's physical configuration, IPX will display a message like this when it loads successfully:

> Novell IPX/SPX v3.01 Rev. B (9000605)
>
> (C) Copyright 1985, 1990 Novell Inc. All Rights Reserved.
>
> LAN Option: NetWare Ethernet NE2000 V1.03EC (891227)
>
> Hardware Configuration: IRQ = 5, I/O Base = 340h,
> no DMA or RAM

If the IPX configuration is wrong, you may get a message like this:

> ******* ETHERNET HARDWARE FAILS TO RESPOND *******

Or the workstation may just hang when you load IPX.

If the network card still malfunctions you'd be wise to pull it out and replace it with a second new card or a known-good network card from another workstation. If this new card works but your first one choked, you've got a bad card. If neither of the network cards work, you probably have a conflict at this particular computer, not bad cards. Try one of these cards in a working workstation with a working network card (replace the workstation's network card with your suspect). It should work. If not, it's a turkey.

Assuming you've found a known-good network card, it's time to get this card working in the suspect workstation. To minimize possible conflicts, try pulling all cards out of the workstation except the floppy controller and the video card. Install the known-good network card. It should work. If it doesn't, yank the video card and replace it with a simple monochrome card and monitor (fancy EGA and VGA cards conflict with network cards more often than their humble monochrome brothers). Now it should work. If it does, install one item that you pulled out and retest. When the network card stops working again, you've found the conflict. Use your diagnostic programs, your brain, and the telephone tech support lines for your hardware item and your network card. You're not the first person whose network card conflicted with her scanner or her incredibly hot hard disk controller. Tech support at the scanner or the controller manufacturer will walk you through a solution.

If IPX works, and you still can't get this new network card to work in this suspect computer it's time to double-check the cable. Move a well-functioning workstation over here and plug it into the cable. If this workstation works when connected to your cable, but your workstation with only a monochrome card, a floppy controller, and a good network card doesn't, then you must have some subtle and expensive lunacy in your workstation computer. This is very unlikely—maybe one in a million. Start from the top and make absolutely sure you're here. We think you probably skipped a step or answered one of these questions wrong.

If you have a dead network card in a NetWare 286 server, the server may not come up at all. It may just hang halfway through the boot process, or NetWare may come up and shut down. NetWare 386 is more forgiving; it usually gives a message like "No token ring out there" if the card is bad or misconfigured.

Checking a Previously Working Card

Has this network card been working fine in this computer? If so, did you just put a new piece of hardware in the computer? Maybe something that uses memory or interrupts—what doesn't? Better pull the new piece of hardware back out of the computer and check it again. If the computer works fine without the new goody, but chokes with it in, you clearly have a configuration conflict. Check the installation instructions on pages 112-116, paying particular attention to the popular sites of conflict: interrupts, base I/O address, memory address, and DMA channel.

No new hardware in the computer? Too bad. Be sure you've got a good workstation boot disk. We mentioned this above, but it bears repeating: We have found that 80 percent of malfunctioning workstations, when only a single workstation is malfunctioning, have trashed boot files or trashed NETx and IPX files.

A loose or bad cable is another popular culprit. Check your cable connection at the back of the computer. Many NICs have diagnostic lights on the back of the NIC that show activity (transmit, receive, collision) and connection status. If not, visually inspect the cable—it should not be crushed, twisted into knots, or mangled. We have directions for testing the LAN cable in the sections on twisted-pair, Token Ring, coax, fiber optic, and wireless networks. The COMCHECK utility from Novell is also helpful here.

If the card works, but not as well as it should — e.g., workstation has slow performance, workstation hangs, etc.—you may have a bad cable, not a bad card. In either case, though, use the Frye Utilities or run point-to-point tests with Thomas-Conrad Corporation's TXD to analyze the traffic between this suspect card and the other stations on the network. TXD is very complete, but it requires a very sophisticated user. Frye Utilities for Networks is much more accessible.

If you still doubt the card, or you don't own any diagnostics, swap in a known-good card and put this suspect card in a trouble-free workstation. If the problem moves to the new machine with the card, the card is bad.

Sometimes a card works, but it is being overwhelmed by the network traffic to this particular node. The system administrator at a major international organization, for example, ran into problems with a workstation that locked up intermittently under heavy load. The problem moved to another machine when the card was moved, so she knew the card itself caused the problem. The administrator thought of the Input/Output buffer (a storage area of RAM chips installed right on the network card so the card doesn't drop incoming packets when the network is sending packets faster than it can process them). New 10Base-T cards, for example, typically have a 16K to 64K buffer, with the larger buffer used in a file server or another heavily-used node (e.g., a graphics station). If the buffer is too small, the workstation may drop packets, or even freeze. The card in question was old, with only 8K of memory in the buffer.

When the network administrator added RAM chips (she added 8K more to the I/O buffer), the workstation stopped locking up. There was just too much traffic for the small buffer to handle. Older designs used these separate RAM chips on the network card. In most new cards, the buffer RAM is integrated into the VLSI chip (the big, square, flat-mounted chip), so you can't add additional RAM in the field.

This Network Card Kills the Whole Network

An Ethernet card that broadcasts continuously will, of course, crash an entire coax network. Twisted-pair Ethernet with concentrators (10Base-T) looks like Ethernet from heaven. If the concentrator is working right, it will disconnect any out of control card that is continuously jabbering. If the concentrator malfunctions, however, a bad 10Base-T card can bring down the network.

An ARCNET card with a busted receive circuit will continuously try to reconfigure the network because it never receives replies from other cards.

A card that shorts the cable, or one that produces signal voltage higher than normal, can also bring the whole network down.

In all cases, swap the suspect card with a known-good card from a trouble-free workstation. If the problem follows the card, the card is bad. If the trouble stays with the original workstation, the workstation computer itself or the cable running to this workstation is the culprit.

How to Install a Network Card

Each network card is designed to fit a particular computer's physical bus connection, so check out the computer before ordering a new network card. The host computer will be ISA bus (Industry Standard Architecture; the XT, AT, and 386-AT bus), EISA (Extended Industry Architecture), or MCA (Micro Channel Architecture; the PS/2 bus). ISA network cards come in 8-bit or 16-bit versions. If you're installing the card in an XT or XT clone, you will need an 8-bit card. 286/AT clones (286 machines) and 386/

Figure 218 *The 8-bit Ethernet card on the bottom has a single bus connector. The top card is for the 16-bit AT-style bus ISA bus found in 286/AT, 386/AT, and 486/AT computers.*

ATs have a 16-bit bus. Either 8 or 16-bit network cards will fit in these computers. 16-bit cards are faster than 8-bit cards, so it makes sense to put a 16-bit card in your ISA file server, even if you have to economize with 8-bit workstation cards. You would be well advised to put fast cards in your I/O intensive workstations too (CAD, graphics, and dBase users). MCA network cards are 16-bit. EISA cards are 32-bit cards, and often very fast indeed.

If you need advice about 1) Removing the workstation case and cover or 2) Removing and Installing Expansion cards, consider buying our first book, *Fix Your Own PC*. Chapters 1 and 11 cover these elementary repair skills. Most of you have replaced a PC card or two in your time, so we're not repeating the directions again in this book. But if you haven't, don't get distressed. Either buy the book and follow the directions or get an experienced friend to help you with your first couple of network board installations. The mechanics are not difficult—if you can use a screwdriver, you can install Network Interface Cards.

Setting the Switches

Every network card needs to be set up with jumpers or DIP-switches before you install it into the workstation or file server. We were all confused about the purpose of the DIP-switches when we first installed network cards, so let's go over eight parameters we can set with DIP-switches and/or jumpers. With any luck the default switch settings (the ones the card was shipped with) will be usable most of the time.

The first four parameters set up friendly relations between the network card and the computer it's installed in. In each case, the network card must not conflict with another piece of hardware (a card or other computer gadget) in this particular computer. So no two devices can share the same I/O address, interrupt, memory address, or DMA channel. Don't panic if these are new terms, when we look at them one by one they'll make sense.

I/O port address (also called I/O decode or base I/O address in some literature): The data path between the operating system and the LAN board is located here, at the I/O address. The workstation's operating system (DOS, OS/2 or UNIX) or Novell NetWare (the file server's operating system) and the network card use this I/O address to pass information back and forth.

The I/O port address on a network card must be unique in this computer (no other items already installed at that I/O address). Ever try to visit an old friend when you've got the wrong street address? The same thing happens to the computer's CPU if you set the network card to an incorrect or previously-assigned I/O address. If no one's home, you're out of luck. If someone answers, but it's the wrong person, you're out of luck again. So be sure to

- set the I/O address to a free address and
- accurately tell the computer what address you used (this telling-the-computer happens when you generate workstation boot diskettes).

Network card I/O addresses are typically in the range 2E0h to 380h, far above the I/O addresses used by DMA, the keyboard, interrupt controllers, or the hard disk. On the other hand, the second serial port (COM2) and the parallel port (LPT1) are located in this area (hex 2E0 to hex 380). COM2 (at 2F8h) is an 8-bit port, so it uses addresses 2F8-2FFh inclusive, leaving the very next address (hex value 300h) likely to be available. LPT1 (at 378h) is also an 8-bit port which uses addresses 378-37Fh inclusive, leaving the memory block starting at address 380h likely to be free.

Use QAPlus/fe or CheckIt to see the I/O addresses already in use in your host computer. We reviewed these diagnostic programs and other troubleshooting utilities in Chapter 5.

Interrupt (IRQ): Interrupts get the CPU's attention. When the network card has information for the CPU it sends an interrupt to the CPU. This signal asks the CPU to look at the network card (at the right I/O address, of course) and find out what's there. Most network cards for ISA bus computers (that's XT and AT clones, 386/ATs and 486/ATs) support three or four interrupts in the IRQ2, IRQ3 to IRQ7 range. MicroChannel Cards sometimes support high interrupts (IRQ9 or IRQ12, for example). The trick is to set the network card interrupt so it is unique (different from the interrupt used by any other card in the computer).

Use QAPlus/fe or CheckIt to look at the interrupts already in use in your host computer. We reviewed these diagnostic programs in Chapter 5. QAPlus/fe is particularly useful when shoehorning a second or third network card into a computer because it displays the interrupt(s) your network cards are already using.

IRQ4 is normally assigned to COM1, the first serial port. And IRQ3 is used by COM2, the second serial port. If you have a modem or serial port installed in your computer, better use a program like QAPlus/fe to inspect the interrupts assigned to these cards. If you use the same interrupt for two cards in the machine the computer will become confused. IRQ5 is assigned to the second parallel port, LPT2. Since few computers have two parallel ports, IRQ5 is a good candidate for network card interrupt. One warning: The hard disk controller in an XT clone uses IRQ5, so you'll have to pick another interrupt or yank the hard disk.

Even well-laid plans can go awry, though. When we first installed NetWare 3.10 in our test LAN we set our file server NIC to IRQ5. This seemed reasonable, since IRQ5 is for LPT2 (the second printer port) and we only had one printer port in the computer. That printer port was properly set up for LPT1, using IRQ7 (the right interrupt for LPT1). The file server and the network card worked fine, but the Print Server NLM wouldn't work—we couldn't run printers off the file server. Apparently the print server freaked out when it realized that IRQ5 was in use, and assumed that we had a second printer port on this file server. When it tried to poll the second printer port, the port wouldn't answer, so the print server choked. All worked fine when we changed the NIC to a different interrupt.

Here's another example of interrupt trouble. We had a multi-server network (in this case with two servers). Our users could log in to one of the servers just fine. They could see the other server on the network with the SLIST (server list) command, but they couldn't log in to it. Even the supervisor couldn't log in. Everybody got the error message "No response from Server NUMBER2." The NIC in the unlogable file server had the wrong interrupt, an interrupt the server associated with a serial port. The server could speak to the NIC, and the NIC could talk to the network cable, so the server could broadcast its name to the other server and to the workstations. When other workstations on the cable sent info to this NIC, though, the NIC could not get the CPU's attention. The CPU thought it was getting a serial port interrupt, not the network card calling for the CPU's attention. So the server never received any login messages from the wire.

One final interrupt warning: A lot of installers have had trouble using interrupt 2 in AT bus computers (a 286, 386, or 486 with an Industry Standard or EISA bus). Interrupt 2, the cascade interrupt, is assigned to the high interrupt controller in an AT or AT clone. When interrupt 2 triggers, the CPU knows that one of the high interrupts (#8 to #15) needs attention, so it switches control of the bus to the high-interrupt controller. If the network card, not the high interrupt controller, sent the interrupt, the computer chokes.

Base memory address (also called Mem Decode): The network card ROM must fit into the reserved memory area between 640K and 1024K (in Hex, that's addresses A000h to FFFFh). Most LAN cards use addresses like C000h, D000h and D800h, and use approximately 8K of memory. EGA/VGA cards and hard disk controllers use memory in the C000h to CFFFh area, so this memory probably won't be free in a power-user's computer.

Token Ring cards also set up RAM buffers in the reserved memory area (these buffers hold input from the network that the computer's CPU can't deal with immediately), so be prepared to check both the NIC ROM and the NIC RAM buffer memory blocks for conflicts with other memory users.

Use QAPlus/fe, ASQ, or CheckIt to identify the base memory addresses already in use in your host computer. The chart in Figure 8.1 will show you where things ought to be located, but only a memory diagnostic program can check the facts in your particular computer—cards sometimes use memory that they shouldn't be using.

DMA Channel: Very few LAN cards use DMA Channels (Direct Memory Access Channels), but some do (e.g., 3COM's Etherlink Plus 3C505). If you're installing a network card that uses DMA, use QAPlus/fe or CheckIt to identify the DMA channels already in use in your host computer.

Novell says DMA channels 1 and 3 are usually reserved for workstation network boards. Other DMA channels may be dedicated to memory refresh (channel 0 if it's an XT or XT clone), to XT hard disk drives (channel 3), or to floppy disk drives (channel 2). DMA channel 1 is reserved for SDLC (that's IBM talk for network cards and IBM SNA cards), so it looks like a good prospect. DMA channel 4 is the cascade.

If you set the next four configuration parameters properly, you'll foster peaceful relations between the Network Interface Card, the cable it's attached to, and other nodes on the network.

Cable type (thick versus thin Ethernet cable versus twisted-pair): Many Ethernet cards will work with either thick or thin Ethernet (often called Cheapernet) cable, and some will work with twisted-pair wiring as well. Thick Ethernet cable requires a heavy duty external transmitting/receiving unit (transceiver) called an MAU (a Medium Attachment Unit) and a twisted-pair drop cable from the MAU to the workstation. Thin Ethernet uses a lightweight coax transceiver built right into the network card. Twisted-pair Ethernet also uses a transceiver on the card.

Node address: On a network, no two nodes (cards) can have the same personal (node) address. Ethernet cards are hardwired at the factory with unique node addresses. So are Token Ring cards. In ARCNET, however, it is up to the installer to make sure no two nodes on your network have the same address, so write down the ARCNET node address you use in each machine. The node addresses are set with DIP-switches on the card. ARCNET cards come from the factory set to address 0 (which, by the way, is an illegal address). Never set a card to address 0. An ARCNET system administrator can save herself some hassle by setting the node addresses with forethought. Set all the workstations to 1xx (e.g., 101, 102, 103, etc.) and all the bridges to 00x, for example. Then make sure you note the node address settings, with workstation location and username, in your network journal. When you have an error pinpointed to a particular node address you'll be able to quickly find that node. By the way, you're setting a binary number when you set ARCNET node address switches, so keep alert as you translate from binary (switches) to decimal (your notes).

Reconfiguration Timeout (also called Propagation Delay or Extended Timeout): ARCNET cards allow you to set the reconfiguration timeout to accommodate extra-long cable runs. Because long cables require extra signal propagation time, the card must wait longer for a reply before it decides the network is malfunctioning and forces a reconfiguration. All cards in an ARCNET network must be set to the same Reconfiguration Timeout value—and in most cases the default (shortest) value will be fine.

Remote Boot PROM (also called a Remote Reset PROM): Use the PROM to boot this workstation off the network file server rather than booting it from a floppy disk or the workstation's internal hard disk. Not all network cards come with a remote boot PROM socket. If your card does, and you want the remote boot feature, you'll need to activate the socket and install a PROM (get it from your network board manufacturer). When you install a new version of NetWare, be sure your remote boot PROM is up to date—they usually change with each major NetWare upgrade.

Mixing Brands and Speeds of Network Cards

We do not believe in mixing card brands. We have seen some weird network problems in mix-and-match networks—and not necessarily with the workstations running the cheaper network card. Pick a network card you like, even if it's a cheap one, and stick to it.

If you're using really cheap, no-name network cards (and why would you? the hardware cost is the smallest cost in most networks) be certain you stick to one brand. At least your cards will all have the same idiosyncracies if they almost (but don't quite) meet some aspect of the Ethernet or ARCNET standards.

Even when dealing with major brands, like 3COM, you need to be aware of idiosyncracies. For example, the special 3COM cards capable of transmitting across longer-than-IEEE-standard coax cable lengths can only be used with similar 3COM cards. Adding even one standard Ethernet card to an extra-length network equipped with 3COM long-distance cards can bring the whole network down. The normal Ethernet card broadcasts with less power than needed to carry the length of the network, other cards interpret the low signal as a collision, and the network slows as these "collisions" overload the cable.

Token Ring cards come in two speeds, 4Mbps (megabits per second) and 16 Mbps. The ring will run at the speed of the slowest card, so it makes sense to match the cards that are already installed.

ARCNET cards also come in two speeds, ARCNET at 2.5 Mbps and ARCNETplus at 20 Mbps. Unlike Token Ring, ARCNET networks allow fast cards to talk fast to other fast cards—and talk slow to the slow cards. Put your 20 Mbps ARCNETplus cards in the file server and those workstations that really work the file server hard—the ones that heavily use databases (if the database is not a network client-server design), or workstations using Windows or other graphics applications stored on the network server. Datapoint says that ARCNETplus will be compatible with ARCNET, but you will need to install ARCNETplus active and passive hubs wherever the data path between two ARCNETplus cards crosses a hub.

Network-To-Parallel-Port Adapters for Laptops

External network adapters use the parallel port to send data to the network without using a network card. This is particularly useful for laptop computers since they seldom have space for a standard Network Interface Card.

Figure 222 Ethernet-to-parallel port adapter. Photo courtesy of Xircom.

By comparison, some portable computers provide an expansion slot for the card of your choice. We wrote much of this book, for example, on a Toshiba 5200 equipped with a standard NE2000 Ethernet card. During the day the Toshiba was a full-speed network workstation. At night we unplugged it from the ThinNet cable and took it home to use as a standalone. Remember, standard network cards provide much faster response than a parallel port adapter (typically 5 times the speed). In Figure 3.3 the authors are installing a network card in this Toshiba before hooking it up to the test LAN.

The Toshiba 5200 is an anomaly, most laptops have no room for a network card. If your laptop needs to be integrated into the network, consider using a parallel-port-to-network external adapter. They're more expensive than a network card, but a single parallel port adapter can serve a number of laptop users who only need network access on an intermittent basis. In addition, an external adapter connects to any computer with a printer port, whether AT bus, MCA (MicroChannel Architecture—the PS/2 bus) or EISA (Extended Industry Architecture) bus, and the adapter uses no additional interrupts or memory blocks, so it can't conflict with anything already installed in the computer.

Connecting an External Network Adapter to your LAN

These adapters are small and portable, like your laptop. We tried out the LAN in a CAN kit from EXOS, which weighs only 15 ounces for both the adapter and power supply. About the size and weight of a pack of cigarettes, the adapter slips easily into a pocket. Its power supply is not much bigger, though heavier.

ARCNET, 10Base-T (Ethernet on twisted-pair), 10Base2 (thin Ethernet), and Token Ring versions of these adapters plug right in once you set up a hook-in point on your network cable system. You may connect or disconnect any of these adapters while the network is up and running. Token Ring, 10Base-T, and ARCNET running on the newer Model 9490 passive hubs are tolerant of disconnections—just unplug the network wire and carry the laptop away. 10Base2 is easy too—detach the stub of the network T connector from the external adapter, but leave the T connector itself in the coax cable run. One warning: Old style ARCNET passive hubs must be terminated on each connector, so you may run into troubles if you leave an ARCNET cable hanging loose. Check with your adapter supplier for details.

How an External Network Adapter Works

These external adapters use the parallel port instead of a separate network card I/O port. They use the I/O address and interrupt of the parallel port to communicate with the portable computer. Therefore, you must create a custom IPX.COM file on the portable which recognizes that the parallel port is the gateway to the network. On the other end of the adapter, at the network cable end, the adapter speaks standard ARCNET, Ethernet, or Token Ring (depending, of course, on the kind of adapter you bought).

How to Test an External Network Adapter

Your adapter's manual will tell you how to interpret the diagnostic lights on your adapter. If you are having difficulty connecting to the network, remember to test the cable with a known-good workstation before you condemn the external network adapter.

Because these adapters use the computer's parallel port, better test the parallel port, too, if the adapter won't work. Use QAPlus/fe with the parallel port wrap plug test to test the circuits in the port. Remember, too, that ordinary printers often work fine without an active interrupt at the parallel port—but these adapters need to use the interrupt. So check out the interrupt with a good diagnostic program, too.

How to Remove and Install External Network Adapters

There is nothing to it. Plug it into your computer's parallel port, connect the LAN cable, and make up a workstation diskette with appropriate IPX and NETx files. A few external adapters are designed to connect to the serial port. In general, parallel port connection is faster.

Ethernet on Coax Cable

Coax cable carries electrical signals among workstations, file servers(s) and printer(s). So what is coax? Just a single signal-conducting wire which is carefully shielded, both from physical damage and from electrical interference. Network Interface Cards send electrical pulses out onto the wire.

The IEEE (the Institute of Electrical and Electronics Engineers, the national LAN standard-setting body) specifies a solid copper central wire for thick Ethernet coax, and a stranded, tinned copper conductor wire for thin coax Ethernet networks. This wire is surrounded by a layer of electrical insulator (a dielectric, often polyethylene), then covered with a braided metal shield to buffer the data signal against electrical interference. Without this shielding the electromagnetic fields from electric power lines, fluorescent lights, and the electrical appliances found in a typical office would create random electrical fluctuations on the data conductor—in other words, they would add random bits to your data. The outermost layer is a sturdy jacket that is waterproof and tough enough to protect the cable from injury.

By the time all the shielding is added, thin coax is about the diameter of a pencil. Typically covered with a black, clear, or grey plastic jacket, thin coax cable is labeled with numbers like RG-58 (thin Ethernet type) or RG-62 (ARCNET coax). Cable TV cable is RG-59. Thick coax for Ethernet is roughly 1/2 inch in diameter and wears a brightly-colored outer jacket (often orange or yellow). It has annular rings every 2.5 meters to show where the installer may tap the cable for a station.

The access scheme controls who is broadcasting when on the wire, and provides standards for constructing data packets to send on the wire.

When you see thick coax cable you know you're dealing with Ethernet. When you see thin coax, the network could be using either the Ethernet or the ARCNET cable access scheme. We cover ARCNET networks running on coax cable in the Data Sheet section, *ARCNET on Coax and/or Twisted-Pair*, pages 133-140.

If you're not sure whether your network is ARCNET or Ethernet, we'll show you how to differentiate between the two kinds of coax in the next section—but first you need to find the network cable at the back of your workstation.

Finding Your LAN Coax

Look at the back of your workstation. There will be a heavy, black 115 volt power cord which plugs into the wall electrical socket. You'll also have a video cable running from the back of the video monitor to a video card connector on the back of the computer. The keyboard cable often runs around to the back of the computer, too. You may also have a mouse or a printer cable. Okay, none of those is the coax.

But is there another pencil-sized, plastic-coated cable attached in back there? One that runs into one end of a shiny T connector and out the other side? See Figure 223. Okay, you've probably got thin Ethernet, also called Cheapernet cable and 10Base2, and the round half-twist connectors at the T fitting are called BNC connectors. The cable type should be printed right on the cable—10Base2 Ethernet cable is Type RG-58. A few ARCNET bus installations also use these T connectors, but ARCNET uses RG-62 or RG-59/U coax cable. Some of these ARCNET cards use two coax connectors on the card (input and output) rather than an external T.

Most ARCNETs use the star topology, with coax connected directly to the back of the card. See Figure 233. Look for RG-62 or RG-59/U printed on the cable. Yes? You've got ARCNET. Go to the ARCNET on Coax and/or Twisted-Pair section, page 133.

Thick Ethernet, the IEEE's 10Base5 Ethernet standard, uses a drop cable from a transceiver on the big Ethernet cable in the wall (or ceiling) to the workstation. This cable uses an AUI connector, which looks like a DB-15 game port connector but the AUI has a slidelock to hold the connector onto the network card. These AUI connectors are also called DIX connectors by some manufacturers (e.g., Novell). Figure 212 shows the thick Ethernet connector on a network card.

Coax Cable for LANs:

Cable Type	Impedance	Diameter	Connector	
Ethernet thin cable—RG-58	50 ohms	3/16"	BNC connector	Photo Figure 223
ARCNET—RG-62	93 ohms	3/16"	BNC connector	
or RG-59/U	75 ohms	3/16"	Uses an RG-62 pigtail at the end with BNC	
Ethernet thick cable	50 ohms	3/8"	MAU at the thick cable with a twisted-pair drop cable to the network card	
Drop cable for thick Ethernet (it's not coax, it's shielded pair cable)		3/8"	DIX/AUI connector	Photo Figure 215

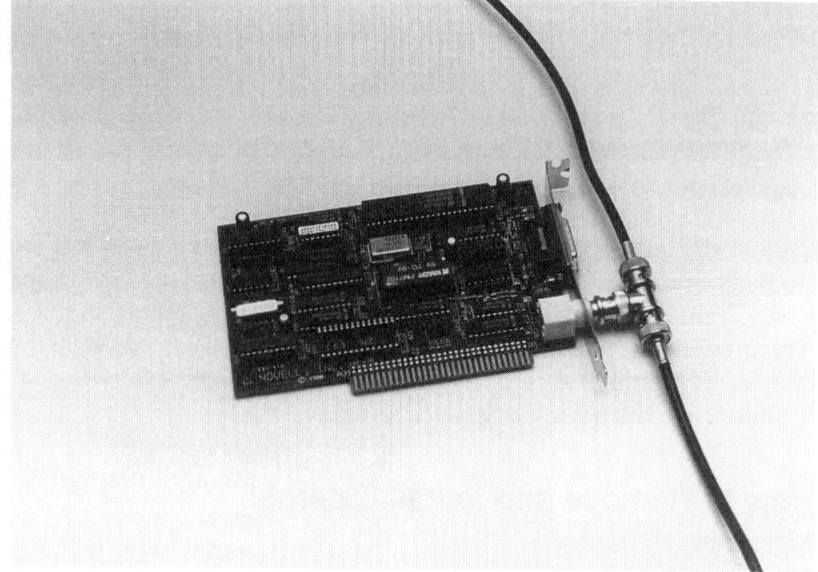

Figure 223 *Ethernet card connected to RG-58 ThinNet cable.*

How Coax Works

Your data signal travels on the wire in the center of your coax cable. Because of the shielding, coax cable broadcasts no EMF (Electromagnetic Frequency) waves. What about external interference? It's hard for EMF waves to get in through the electromagnetic shielding on coax, but not impossible. Avoid heavy electrical fields when you run this stuff. If, for example, you put coax in an elevator shaft, you can watch your network get woozy each time the elevator goes up or down. There is a tremendously powerful electric motor bolted to the bottom of the elevator, and the field it puts out is too strong for coax EMF shielding. Frankly, there aren't that many places to run cable vertically in a highrise building—you can hardly toss it out the sixth floor window and haul it in again three floors down to connect up with Accounting. Though there are phone line conduits between floors, they are often full of cable already. That is why many multi-floor networks are specified with the riser (the vertical run of cable between floors) made of fiber optic and installed in the elevator shaft. Fiber is fast and it's EMF-proof, but comparatively expensive. A typical fiber/coax installation has at least one server and network on each floor, cabled with coax. The fiber backbone ties these networks together.

Be careful to specify plenum-grade coax cable if you're intending to lay the cable in the ceiling (the typical place) and if the area between the drop ceiling and the floor above is a plenum (functions as an air-return duct for the building ventilation system). Plenum-grade cable is manufactured with fire-resistant and low-smoke materials in the insulation and cable jacket, to minimize poisonous chemical fumes in the building during a fire. Your local fire code gives details.

A terminator (terminating resistor) at each end of the cable keeps a data signal from reflecting back when it hits the end of the cable. In effect, the signal keeps traveling out the end of the cable and into the resistor rather than bouncing off the dead end of the cable the way waves bounce off the end of a swimming pool. Reflected signals would bounce up and down the cable, interfering with new signals on the bus. Use a 50 ohm terminator on 50 ohm thin Ethernet cable.

Document Your Network

Network specialists recommend that you carefully document the network when it's installed, and keep that documentation up to date to reflect any and all changes. You will need a cable diagram and a list of node addresses with each node's physical location and user. Do it now. Don't wait until your network monitoring software shows that a node is failing.

The workstation node address and the station number shown on Novell NetWare information screens are not related to physical workstation location. They will not help you troubleshoot, unless you've documented the network first. The node address is assigned to each Ethernet card when it's manufactured, and the station number is assigned to each workstation by NetWare when the workstation logs in to the network. The station number is only a server connection number, with nothing to do with the physical station itself. So neither of these helpful-sounding numbers will help you figure what stations are connected to which cable, or where a particular cable goes next.

Many network utilities create network topology maps and/or user-lists for you. These network management utilities should always be supplemented with an accurate cabling diagram—often drawn on a copy of your building's floorplan blueprints. Professional installers should provide first-class documentation (cable test results, cable diagram, etc.). Ask for them. Your installer should also label the cables, indicating the cable segment name and where it's going. Make sure the labels match the names on your cable diagram.

How to Install and Test Coax Cable

Coax is used on bus topology networks—on networks that work like telephone party lines. When a station broadcasts a signal on the bus, that signal propagates (travels) along the bus in both directions until it reaches the terminators at the far ends of the bus cable. It takes time for this signal to travel through the wire. If the wire is very long, you may need repeaters to rebroadcast the signal, sending it along to the farther reaches of the bus. Each repeater adds to the total propagation time (the IEEE specifies a 9.6 microsecond maximum for repeater delay).

Ethernet has very specific cable-length specifications for a reason. When designing Ethernet, the IEEE balanced the desire for large networks against an inconveniently long propagation time. They calculated precise cable lengths, and their associated propagation delays, then set the minimum frame size and the minimum time between frame transmissions that were suitable for the maximum cable segment lengths that they chose. If the IEEE allows a maximum of four repeaters between any two workstations on an Ethernet network, they mean it. When they say 600 feet of cable per thin Ethernet coax segment, they don't mean 611 feet.

Because thick and thin Ethernet cabling rules are so different, we wrote two separate sections. *Installing and Testing Thin Ethernet Cable* is the section that follows. If you are particularly interested in thick Ethernet cable, skip to page 123. Remember, though, that most large Ethernet networks are a mixture of thick and thin coax segments, mixed with 10Base-T segments running on twisted-pair wire. As long as you join each new cable medium to its brethren with a repeater, all will be well.

Installing and Testing Thin Ethernet Cable (Cheapernet or 10Base2):

We installed our test LAN on thin Ethernet. See Chapter 1 for war stories and photos of a typical ThinNet installation.

Ethernet uses a bus topology. That means that the cable is, in effect, all one piece of cable. If a network card transmits on any segment, that signal is audible on every segment of the coax cable—it's audible to all the other workstations and servers on this network. We describe Ethernet's CSMA/CD access scheme on page 108 in the Network Interface Card section of these Data Sheets.

Ethernet workstations are like bumps on a coaxial cable backbone, with file servers treated like any other node on the cable. The IEEE standards for thin Ethernet allow no "drop cable" from the bus T connector to a workstation, so connect the T connector directly to the back of your workstation's network card. Figure 224 shows a typical 10Base2 (thin Ethernet) Ethernet cable design. A summary of the IEEE 10Base2 cabling specs starts on page 121.

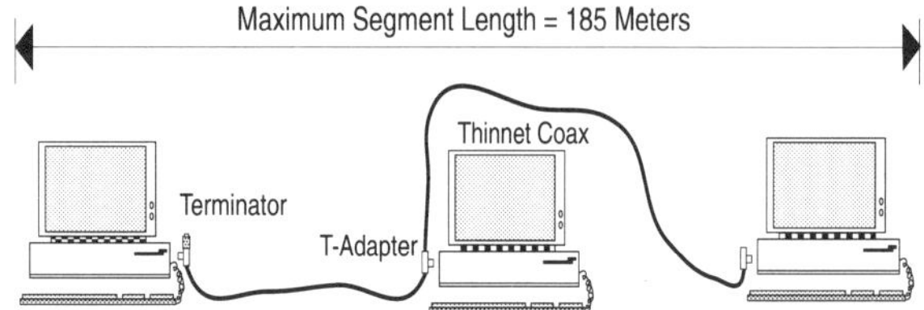

Figure 224 *Ethernet 10Base2 network. Diagram by Allyson Almieda of Computer System Products.*

Please note the terminating resistors on this diagram. Make sure that one of the terminators is grounded to a first-class earth ground. We often ground one terminator to the PC case and rely on the standard three-wire PC power cable at that workstation for the ground. This technique is only as good as the ground connection between terminator and case, the connection through the power supply to the ground wire in the power cord, and (most important) the quality of the ground at the outlet. Buy a ground and polarity checker to test your outlet (see Figure 208). Running the network without a ground may allow uncontrolled voltage surges to build up in the cable. These surges can cook your network cards.

The bigger the network (longer runs, more workstations), and the more heavily it is loaded, the closer you must adhere to IEEE specs when installing cable if you want to avoid disaster. Because troubleshooting is so difficult after the network is in place, and because marginal design errors which degrade signal transmissions often show up only as the network gets heavily loaded, do it right the first time. Nine out of ten "LANs From Hell" are cable plant disasters.

Most office and professional environments demand a professional cable installer. Computer people seldom have the skills to run cable through the walls without leaving tacky-looking wallboard cuts and patches.

Wall people and regular electricians don't understand the Ethernet specs. One LAN which was cabled by non-professionals (somebody's brother-in-law) had big coils of cable in the ceiling over each workstation "in case you need more cable later." The poor LAN was choking on these huge cable runs and intermittently failing.

Adding an extra workstation, replacing a bad T connector, or moving a workstation requires no special skills. The BNC connectors on the cable ends twist off a card or a T connector with a slight-push-and-half-twist motion. Buy pre-made lengths of coax—the BNC connectors are properly installed at the factory. If you must make custom cables, installers say the twist-on connectors are easier for amateurs than soldered or crimped BNC connectors.

Most cable installers will use a TDR (Time Domain Reflectometer) to test the cable integrity while the cable is still on the reel. After installation they will test it again, but it's useful to know you started with a good reel of cable. A TDR will also measure the installed length of each cable segment—essential when you're running cable segments that are close to the IEEE length limits.

Before installing any little piece of cable, make sure it meets IEEE 802.3 specs for 10Base2. Introducing a length of IBM terminal coax or ARCNET coax into the network will cause malfunctions (slowdowns and/or complete network crash). Be sure you're using the right grade cable, too. Underwriter's Laboratory tests and certifies cable suitable for general uses (e.g., in walls or conduit, from wall to computer) or for persnickety uses (e.g., suitable for use in the plenum space that modern office buildings use in lieu of air return ducts).

As you run your coax, avoid strong EMF fields, such as elevators, heat pumps, and AC units. Avoid physical interference—please, not under the rug where chairs roll over it, and no sharp bends (IEEE gives a minimum bend radius of 5 centimeters).

IEEE 10Base2 (Thin Ethernet) Cabling Specs

The IEEE envisioned using 10Base2 (thin Ethernet) to interconnect workstations in a small department or work area. The 10Base2 cable is likely to be moved frequently as work areas are rearranged and stations are moved. Unlike 10Base5 (thick Ethernet), no drop cables are allowed—if you move a workstation, you must move the main trunk cable too. You may connect two 10Base2 (thin Ethernet) segments with a 10Base5 (thick Ethernet) segment. You may not connect two thick coax segments with a thin coax segment.

A trunk segment will be made of a length of coax, then a T connector, then a length of coax, then a T for the next workstation, etc. Each length of coax between T connectors must be at least 0.5 meter long, so minimum workstation spacing is also 0.5 meter. Use BNC connectors at each connection point. Maximum trunk segment length is 185 meters (600 feet). Terminate both ends of a trunk with a 50 ohm resistor. One of these terminating resistors must be grounded.

Link segments are **not** trunk segments, they are point-to-point segments connecting two repeaters. No workstations may be attached to a link segment. The IEEE gives a propagation-delay specification as well as explicit length specifications (it depends on the medium) for these link segments. Coax links of 500 meters (10Base5) or 185 meters (10Base2) are acceptable. FOIRL links may be up to 500 or 1000 meters long (depending on the rest of the LAN topology) and are typically used to connect two buildings or two floors in a highrise building. We discuss the IEEE fiber optic inter repeater link (FOIRL) standard on page 132 of these Data Sheets.

The maximum path between any two stations is five segments, connected through four repeaters. Of those segments, three may be trunk segments (the coax cable which is tapped with T connectors for workstations) and two segments may be link segments (the point-to-point segments connecting a pair of repeaters).

A maximum of 30 workstations and repeaters are allowed per cable segment. Thirty workstations is realistic only if the users load the cable lightly, like E-Mail or word processing.

Set the LAN board in each workstation to use an internal transceiver. (Set this up with jumpers on those NICs that can function in both thick and thin Ethernet environments. See the Network Interface Card section in these Data Sheets for card jumper information.)

The minimum bend radius for 10Base2 cable is 5 centimeters.

Troubleshooting a Thin Ethernet Installation

The first question is always "What has changed?" If you have just moved a workstation, added cable, or installed a new card in a workstation, go right back where you were working and look for a problem. It's easy enough to carelessly connect a T connector or wiggle a cable loose. If you added a section of cable, is the cable still terminated properly at each end (with one of the terminators grounded)? Is it now longer than 600 feet? Nine times out of ten you created the problem yourself.

If you can't find any problem where you were just working, or the problem started without your help, use COMCHECK and your TDR (Time Delay Reflectometer) to look for a broken or shorted cable. See Appendix B for COMCHECK hints. A TDR is also handy because it measures the total cable length (in case you're over the Ethernet limit). Using COMCHECK (or your TDR) and your network diagram, identify the bad section of coax cable, then replace it. By the way, Thomas-Conrad's TXD diagnostic software will reveal stone-dead network cables, just like COMCHECK does, but it's far more discriminating. It's capable of locating and documenting subtle card or cable errors as well as egregious ones. In Chapter 5 we discuss a range of network diagnostic software.

If you don't have a TDR, you can use a pocket-sized coax cable tester, available at Jensen Tools. It's not as quick as the TDR (the TDR says how many feet down the cable the problem is located), and it won't find poor quality connections like a TDR will, but it works and it costs well under $100 (even a basic TDR is close to $900). Put the BNC test cap on one end of the cable—it's got a diode connecting the center conductor to the cable shield. Then attach the battery-powered pocket tester to the opposite end. The tester reveals shorts between the cable shield and center conductor, and it checks the cable continuity (no continuity means the cable conductor is broken).

Use an ohmmeter to test the terminators too. A 50 ohm terminator should have 50 ohms resistance between the center connector and the outer shell.

Ethernet T connectors go bad a lot (seems silly, since there's almost nothing to them, but it's true). Swap them out to test them—BORING! Cheap T connectors die faster. You might as well pay a little more to install decent quality T connectors and avoid the swap-out hassle.

Do not underestimate the human factor. People trip over the coax cable and rip it out of the connector, then feel foolish and try to repair the problem themselves. Tug gently on any suspicious connections. Repair any that are held together with Scotch tape.

The cable will not tell you that it is the problem. There are no "Shorted Ethernet cable" error messages in NetWare. Instead, you must deduce that the coax cable is malfunctioning. As a general rule, slowing response throughout the network leads a person to suspect the cabling system—especially if the trouble occurs on multiple file servers, on multiple workstations, with many different users, and with many different applications. Pretty bad cable causes slow network response. Really bad cable can bring the entire network down. A downed network is easier to fix; test it with COMCHECK, find the busted cable, and replace it. Moderately bad cable is much harder to pinpoint. Here are two case histories.

An electrician used a piece of coax to patch an additional workstation into a thin Ethernet network. He used IBM coax (normally used to connect a 3270 terminal on mainframe installations), not RG-62 Ethernet cable, because computer cable is computer cable. Workstations stopped working, some in this end of the building, some in the other end. Note, the "bad" workstations were not necessarily on the incorrect cable segment, or even near it. Meanwhile, the operating system files started to get corrupted on the server. If they were reinstalled, the server would work okay for a few hours, then get corrupted again.

What happened? Using the wrong cable caused so many hardware interrupts at the file server NIC that the server CPU freaked out and started to mishandle the hard disk controller. Since some OS files are written to the hard disk during use (e.g., the bindery files), there you are, operating system corruption. Please note that the organization was running an early 2.x version of NetWare. The new stuff is much tougher and it's more thoroughly insulated from hardware freakouts.

A network in a major government department failed only in the winter. It failed by midmorning and miraculously recovered some time around 4:30 p.m. each day. The problem was finally traced to a cable installed under a coat rack. By midmorning, the coat rack was heavy enough to crush the coax, eventually shorting it. When people removed their coats in the evening the rack became lighter and lighter.

It is wise to set up a service contract covering your LAN cable if it's a complex installation. (Actually, it is foolish not to.) The equipment you need to thoroughly test a big Ethernet network costs way too much for anybody who doesn't troubleshoot cabling for a living. A TDR (Time Domain Reflectometer) alone costs $900, even for the stripped down models. Sophisticated traffic analyzers cost thousands, and they are sometimes necessary to pinpoint a subtle problem.

If you like LAN troubleshooting gossip, check out *Managing an Ethernet Installation: Case Studies from the Front Lines*, a tale of troubleshooting in Northeastern University's Ethernet network, which was published in *Computer Communication Review*, October 1990. The authors located cable fault after cable fault, and documented each fault's effect on the network with a monitor.

Installing and Testing Thick Ethernet Cable (10Base5)

Thick Ethernet cable doesn't look like coaxial cable at the workstation because installers use an MAU (Media Access Unit) to tap into the big coax cable in the wall or ceiling, then run a short twisted-pair drop cable from the MAU to a 15-pin network connector on the back of the LAN card in your workstation or file server. Vampire tap MAUs clamp onto the cable sheath while a probe penetrates the cable insulation to contact the current-carrying center conductor. In-series MAUs are harder to install, since the network must be powered off while the installer cuts the Thick Ethernet cable and installs threaded N-type connectors to patch the MAU into the cable. Maximum length for the drop cable from an MAU to a workstation is 50 meters.

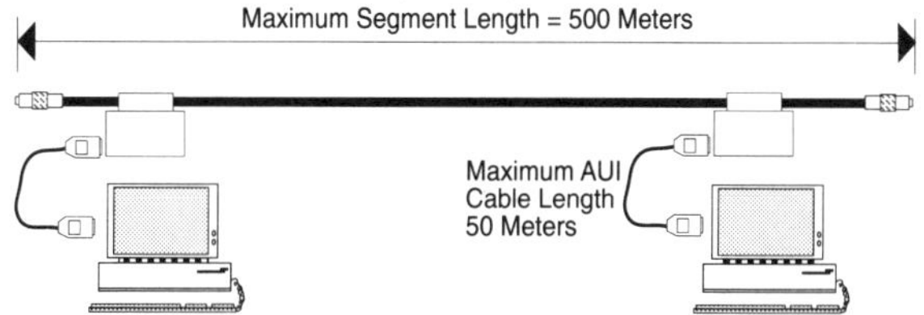

Figure 225 *Ethernet 10Base5 network. Diagram by Allyson Almieda of Computer System Products.*

The bigger the network (longer runs, more workstations), and the more heavily loaded, the closer you must adhere to IEEE specs when installing cable if you want to avoid disaster. We summarize the IEEE specs for 10Base5 (thick Ethernet) on the next page. Because troubleshooting is so difficult after the network is in place, and because marginal design errors which degrade signal transmissions often show up only as the network gets heavily loaded, do it right the first time.

Do not plan on doing your own 10Base5 cable installation. Professional installers are expensive, but troubleshooting a lousy cable plant is worse. We recommend you go with one of the higher bids, and be sure to check the installer's references. They should have many happy customers—with networks in the same size and complexity range as the network you're planning.

Make sure your installer uses coax that meets the IEEE 802.3 10Base5 specifications. Underwriter's Laboratory tests and certifies cable suitable for general uses (e.g., in walls or conduit), and plenum grade cable for the plenum space above the ceiling. Most installers will use a TDR (Time Domain Reflectometer) to test the cable integrity on the reel before they start installing it. Not a bad idea.

Avoid routing coax through strong EMF fields—near elevators, heat pumps, and AC units. Avoid physical damage or stress on to the cable: no sharp bends, hang the cable from cable hangers rather than asking it to support it's own weight (most coax is not strong enough), don't scrape it on sharp edges while installing it, and keep it off the basement floor so rats don't nibble through the waterproof covering and short everything out.

IEEE 10Base5 (Thick Ethernet) Cabling Specs

The IEEE envisioned using 10Base5 (thick Ethernet) to connect workstations throughout a large department or a single building. They planned on using 10Base5 as a trunk cable, leaving it in place permanently, and adapting to workstation movement with drop cables off the main 10Base5 trunk, or with 10Base2 (thin Ethernet) segments in local workgroups.

You may connect two thin Ethernet segments with a thick coax segment. You may not connect two thick coax segments with a thin coax segment.

The maximum trunk coax segment length is 500 meters (1640 feet). Terminate both ends of a trunk with a 50 ohm resistor. One of these resistors must be grounded.

A maximum of 100 workstation-plus-repeater-or-bridge connections are allowed per trunk segment.

If possible, each coax trunk segment should be a single, unbroken length of coax cable. Specify cable from the same production lot when you order multiple reels of cable for your original installation. If it is necessary to make up a segment from a couple coax sections joined with coaxial barrel connectors, the IEEE recommends using cable from the original manufacturer and the original cable production lot. If that is not possible (for example, you need to extend a trunk segment and have no cable left from the original lot), the cable will exhibit minimal signal reflection problems at the cable-join point if each piece used to make the total 500 meter trunk cable is 23.4, 70.2, or 117 meters long. Don't mix cable manufacturers. Arbitrary combinations of cable and cable length are a last resort. This can only be acceptable if you can measure the signal reflection at each cable joint and determine that the reflection is no more than 7 percent of the original signal issued by a workstation MAU. In our experience, it's best to use a repeater between two segments unless your additional cable comes from the same manufacturer and production lot—it's too easy to get subtle signal reflection problems that will slow down your network under heavy traffic.

The minimum distance between workstation or repeater transceivers is 2.5 meters (8 feet). Thick Ethernet cable has annular rings on the cable (every 2.5 meters) to show where you can tap in a transceiver MAU.

Link segments are not trunk segments, they are point-to-point segments connecting two repeaters. No workstations may be connected to a link segment. The IEEE give a propagation-delay specifications for these link segments, which translate into 10Base5 links of 500 meters maximum and 10Base2 links of 185 meters maximum. FOIRL links (Fiber Optic Inter Repeater Links) may be up to 500 or 1000 meters long (depending on the particular LAN topology), and are typically used to connect two buildings or two floors in a highrise building. We cover the IEEE fiber optic inter repeater link (FOIRL) standard on page 132 of these Data Sheets.

The maximum path between any two stations is five coax segments, connected through four repeaters. Of those segments, three may be trunk segments (the coax cable tapped with MAUs for workstations) and two segments may be link segments (the point-to-point segments connecting two repeaters).

Minimum bend radius for 10Base5 cable is 10 inches (254 millimeters).

Set the workstation's LAN board to use an external transceiver (the MAU). Most network cards allow you to set this up with jumpers on the NIC.

The maximum distance from PC to MAU transceiver (the drop cable length) is 50 meters (164 feet). Use an AUI (also called DIX) connector at drop-cable-to-NIC and drop-cable-to-MAU connections.

Troubleshooting a Thick Ethernet Installation

It makes sense to set up a service contract covering your LAN cable. The equipment you need to thoroughly test a big Ethernet network costs way too much for anybody who doesn't troubleshoot cabling for a living. A TDR (Time Domain Reflectometer) alone costs $900, even for the stripped down models. Sophisticated traffic analyzers can cost thousands.

If you insist on troubleshooting your own cable, you will find that most of the troubleshooting hints discussed in the thin Ethernet troubleshooting section are applicable.

Ethernet on Unshielded Twisted-Pair (UTP)—10Base-T Ethernet

Most 10Base-T networks are wired in a star (octopus) pattern, with repeater hubs (also called concentrators or wiring centers) in the center of the star and workstations at the end of the tentacles. Twisted-pair wiring carries electrical signals between these concentrators (wiring hubs) and the workstations, file servers, and other nodes on the network. Because the wire is a bus (a party line), all stations hear any signals on the bus. Therefore, 10Base-T has a bus topology, even though the wiring diagram looks star-shaped.

The IEEE (Institute of Electrical and Electronics Engineers) 10Base-T Ethernet twisted-pair standard specifies two pairs of wires to each node, one pair to transmit and one to receive. The wires in each pair are twisted together in a helix to minimize electrical interference, but they are not shielded with metal foil or metal braid like the shielded twisted-pair cable used in most Token Ring installations.

10Base-T networks use an Ethernet-style cable access scheme. (The access scheme controls who is broadcasting on the wire when, and provides standards for constructing data packets to send on the wire.) Therefore, it's simple to connect 10Base-T networks to other Ethernet networks on different media (coax, fiber optic, or wireless infrared or radio wave) with a repeater.

Note: If you're looking for information about Token Ring networks on twisted-pair cable, go to the Token Ring Cabling section of these Data Sheets. ARCNET is also covered in a separate section. We're only dealing with 10Base-T (Ethernet on twisted-pair) here.

By the way, Synoptics Corporation's Lattisnet products were among the first and most popular Ethernet-on-twisted-pair products, so don't be surprised when some technicians casually call all 10Base-T products "Lattisnet." Lattisnet is **not** 10Base-T, though they are similar. The data signals are slightly different. On the other hand, 3COM and others make dual-purpose Lattisnet/10Base-T cards that can be configured for either protocol with jumpers.

Finding Twisted-Pair Wiring in your LAN

Look at the back of your workstation. You'll see a heavy, black 115 volt power cord which plugs into the wall electrical socket. You'll also have a video cable running from the back of the video monitor to a video card connector on the back of the computer. The keyboard cable often runs around to the back of the computer as well, and you may have a mouse or a printer cable. None of those is the twisted-pair network cable.

Look for another cable attached back there, one that resembles the ordinary flat telephone wire running from the wall jack to your telephone answering machine, extension phone, or modem. Twisted-pair looks like ordinary phone wire (even to the RJ-45 telephone-style modular connector)—but twisted-pair is 1-1/2 times the diameter of phone wire, designed bigger specifically to help you differentiate your modem phone cord from your LAN cable. By the way, a few 10Base-T cards (e.g., Hewlett-Packard) use the small RJ-11 connector, the same as the one used on ordinary phone equipment. Sorry, sometimes they don't make it easy for us.

Under the 10Base-T standard, each node (each workstation or file server computer or bridge/router/gateway to another section of network) is connected to an intelligent wiring hub. The hubs, also called repeaters and concentrators, are usually clustered in a central wiring closet, with twisted-pair wire running a maximum of 100 meters (330 feet) from repeater to workstation. Ordinary telephone-style UTP (Unshielded Twisted-Pair) wiring runs from the wiring closet, through the ceiling and walls or under the carpet to the workstation. Most often the building's wiring terminates at a data outlet plate on the wall. The network administrator hooks up a workstation with a short UTP cable (RJ-45 connectors on both ends) from the wall plate to the back of this workstation's 10Base-T network card.

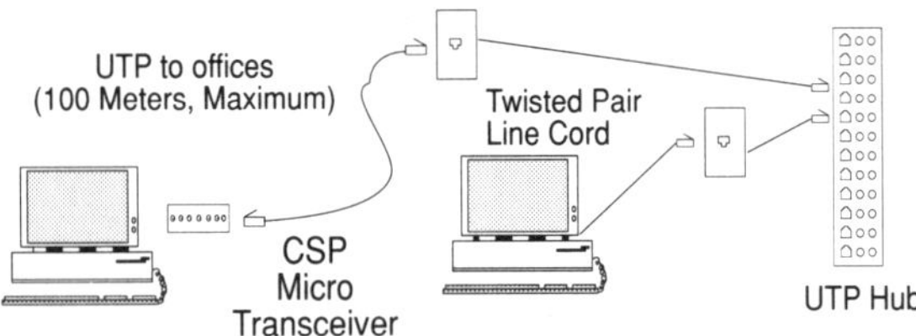

Figure 226 *Simple 10Base-T running on twisted-pair to a hub. Diagram by Allyson Almieda of Computer System Products.*

A large 10Base-T network with multiple, widely separated repeater hubs often uses a coax or fiber optic "backbone" cable to connect all these hubs. Most wiring concentrators permit easy connection to other Ethernet cabling schemes. Some have BNC plugs for thin coax and/or fiber optic cable connectors. Almost all concentrators have AUI connectors, which accommodate a standard transceiver cable. You can connect a fiber optic transceiver (a transmitter/receiver tap into fiber optic cable), a thick coax transceiver (to tap into a thick coaxial cable trunk), or a thin coax transceiver to the AUI connector on the concentrator hub. It makes sense to isolate individual high-traffic hubs from the backbone with a bridge. A bridge limits traffic between the hub and the backbone because it forwards only those data packets whose destination address lies across the bridge.

Figure 227 *A twisted-pair 10Base-T transceiver (AUI port on one end, RJ-45 on the other), used to adapt an ordinary Ethernet card with AUI port to 10Base-T wiring. Note the SQE on-off switch. Photo courtesy of Computer System Products Incorporated.*

Figure 228 *Volksnet's twisted-pair 10Base-T hub with telephone-style, 25-pin, twisted-pair cable connector. Photo courtesy of Computer System Products Incorporated.*

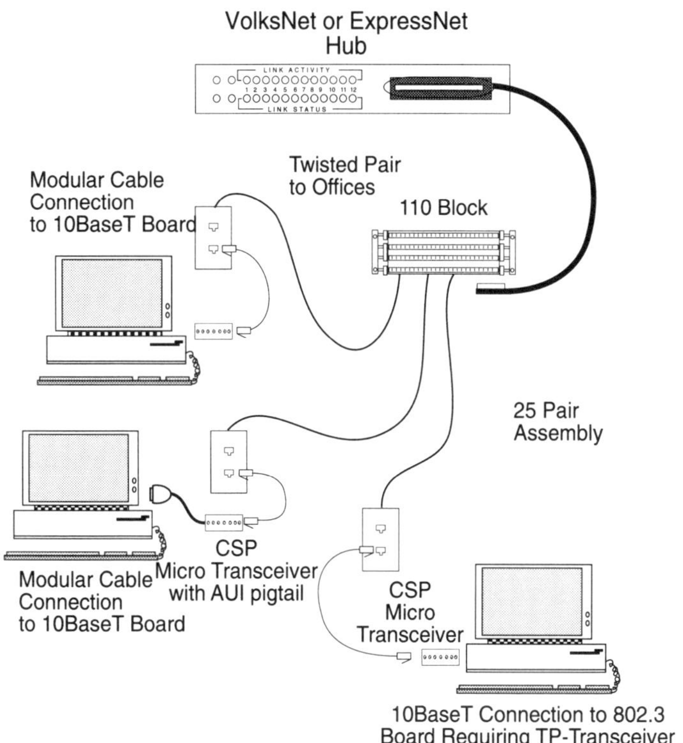

Figure 229 *Ethernet 10Base-T running on telephone-style twisted-pair with a Volksnet Hub. Diagram by Allyson Almieda of Computer System Products.*

How Twisted-Pair Cable Works

A twisted-pair network card transmits on one twisted-pair and receives on a second twisted-pair of wires. This two-pair cable connects to an intelligent multi-port repeater unit (the wiring hub which is typically installed in a central wiring closet). Because the repeater unit is capable of automatically disconnecting a malfunctioning workstation's transmit side from the rest of the network, excessive collisions on that workstation's connection cable will not spread and bring the entire network down. The repeater reconnects the station when the collisions stop.

10Base-T is an extension of the Ethernet standard. It uses the CSMA/CD (Carrier Sense Multiple Access with Collision Detect) access protocol like other versions of Ethernet. Read page 108 in the Network Interface Card section of these Data Sheets for more information about CSMA/CD.

How to Install and Test Twisted-Pair Wiring

10Base-T (Ethernet on twisted-pair) is in vogue. Very high speed Ethernet networks run on fiber optic cable, and the vast majority of Ethernet networks in place today are coax, but 10Base-T is gaining ground because it's easy to wire, easy to troubleshoot, and tolerant of minor cable faults. Market researchers project over half of new Ethernet networks will be installed on twisted-pair wire by the mid-90s.

When buying hubs for a large 10base-T network, check whether they have agents for SNMP to query (Simple Network Management Protocol, the coming standard in network management). SNMP allows remote monitoring and control of network hardware from any vendor who adheres to the SNMP protocol—with a single SNMP network management program.

Use a UPS in the wiring closet with your 10Base-T hubs if you have a UPS on both file server and the workstations and you must keep the complete circuit operating during a power failure. If only your file server is protected, don't bother to UPS the hubs because the workstations are going to fail anyway.

Should I Use New Cable, or my Existing UTP Cable?

Forget everything the salesman told you about running 10Base-T on your existing office phone lines. Theoretically, you could employ the unused twisted-pairs in your PBX telephone cable. The newest 4-pair twisted-pair wires for PBX (Private Branch Exchange) telephone cable are of data quality, and less susceptible to electromagnetic interference than ordinary residential quad (the round 4-wire phone wire used in homes). Silver Satin (a flat, silver-colored commercial and residential phone wire) is not even twisted-pair and should never, never be used.

In real life, though, most offices are not wired with 4-pair PBX. Even if you have two good, unused pairs of PBX twisted-pair, they are usually not connected to the right pins at the wall jack. Figure 232 shows the three competing RJ-45 wall jack standards. You'll notice that only two of the three are compatible with 10Base-T networks. And most experts agree that data and voice transmissions should never move in the same cable sheath unless you're using shielded twisted-pair cable.

So what connects the workstations to the concentrator? The IEEE says they designed 10Base-T for telephone wire. "The performance specifications are generally met by 100 m of 0.5 mm telephone twisted-pair." In section 14.4.1 of the 10Base-T standards the IEEE discusses connecting a workstation (a DTE) to a repeater MAU (the transmit/receive connection layer in the repeater).

> "The medium for 10Base-T is twisted-pair wiring. Since a significant number of 10Base-T networks are expected to be installed utilizing in-place unshielded telephone wiring and typical telephony installation practices, the end-to-end path including different types of wiring, cable connectors, and cross connects must be considered. Typically a DTE connects to a wall outlet using a twisted-pair patch cord. Wall outlets connect through building wiring and a cross connect to the repeater MAU in a wiring closet."

The IEEE also recommends that you use twisted-pair wiring installed according to the EIA/TIA Commercial Building Telecommunications Wiring Standards (approved July 1991).

These EIA/TIA standards will ensure that new buildings and new renovations are compatible with 10Base-T networks. The standards define both the backbone cabling systems that interconnect the telecommunications closets, and the horizontal wiring from the telecommunications closet to the wall plate where you plug in your phones and computer workstations. This horizontal wiring must include two separate cables:

1. a four-pair UTP (unshielded twisted-pair) cable for phones, and
2. a separate data cable of four-pair UTP, two-pair shielded twisted-pair, or 50 ohm coax cable.

Since horizontal wiring is limited to 90 meters maximum, it meets 10Base-T segment length requirements if the 10Base-T repeater hub is located in the wiring closet. And EIA/TIA specifies cable which meets 10Base-T standards. This specification also specifically prohibits flat, non-twisted cabling in the wiring closet (a common source of signal degradation).

Figure 230 shows the twisted-pair classification scheme proposed by Anixter Brothers, a major cable distributor. Cable manufacturers, distributors, and installers have started using this twisted-pair level system to make twisted-pair cable comparisons easier—especially for customers who wanted to compare bids for cabling jobs. It's easier to know if the bids specify the same level of cable quality. You can see in the figure that 10Base-T requires Level 3 or Level 4 cable.

Unfortunately, many older buildings were not wired to the EIA/TIA standards. If they have only a single 4-pair UTP cable carrying telephone signals to the workstation wall plate, you're not likely to get acceptable performance if you try to employ the unused twisted-pairs on this cable to carry LAN data signals. Even if you have separate voice and data cables, the data UTP may not be up to 10Base-T standards for impedance or crosstalk.

A cable specialist can check your present wiring. Remember, though, that cable companies are in business to sell and install cable. Nevertheless, only cable installers have the test equipment (it's not cheap) and the expertise to thoroughly check out existing UTP. So if you have an older

Twisted Pair Level Program℠

Level		Impedance	Attenuation dB/1000 ft	NEXT[1]	Mutual Capacitance	Applicable Standard	Typical Usage
1 Voice		N/A	N/A	N/A	N/A	UL 444 ICEA S-80-576	Voice RS232
2 ISDN & Low Speed Data		84-113 ohm @ 1MHz	4.0 @ 256 kHz 5.66 @ 512 kHz 6.73 @ 772 kHz 8.0 @ 1 MHz	N/A	N/A	UL 444 ICEA S-80-576 IBM Type 3 Media	IBM 3270 IBM 3X-AS/400 4 Mbps Token Ring
3 LAN & Medium Speed Data		100 ohm ± 15% 1-16 MHz	7.8 @ 1MHz 17 @ 4 MHz 30 @ 10 MHz 40 @ 16 MHz	41 dB @ 1 MHz 32 dB @ 4 MHz 26 dB @ 10 MHz 23 dB @ 16 MHz	20 pF/ft Max.	UL 444 ICEA S-80-576 ANSI/EIA/TIA-568 Category 3	10BASE-T OPEN DECconnect SynOptics Starlan 10
4 Extended Distance LAN		100 ohm ± 15% 1-20 MHz	6.5 @ 1 MHz 13 @ 4 MHz 22 @ 10 MHz 27 @ 16 MHz 31 @ 20 MHz	56 dB @ 1 MHz 47 dB @ 4 MHz 41 dB @ 10 MHz 38 dB @ 16 MHz 36 dB @ 20 MHz	17 pF/ft Max.	UL 444 ICEA S-80-576 TIA TR41.8.1 Category 4 NEMA "Low Loss"	Extended Distance 10BASE-T 16 Mbps Token Ring
5 High Speed LAN	4 pr.	100 ohm ± 15% 1-100 MHz	6.3 @ 1 MHz 13 @ 4 MHz 20 @ 10 MHz 25 @ 16 MHz 28 @ 20 MHz 32 @ 25 MHz 36 @ 31.25 MHz 52 @ 62.5 MHz 67 @ 100 MHz	62 dB @ 1 MHz 53 dB @ 4 MHz 47 dB @ 10 MHz 44 dB @ 16 MHz 42 dB @ 20 MHz 41 dB @ 25 MHz 40 dB @ 31.25 MHz 35 dB @ 62.5 MHz 32 dB @ 100 MHz	17 pF/ft Max.	UL 444 ICEA S-80-576 TIA TR41.8.1 Category 5 NEMA "Low Loss" Extended Frequency	Extended Distance 10BASE-T 16 Mbps Token Ring CDDI[2]
	2 pr.	150 ohm ± 10%	3.2 @ 1 MHz 6.7 @ 4 MHz 10.6 @ 10 MHz 13.7 @ 16 MHz 39 @ 62.5 MHz	58 dB @ 1 MHz 58 dB @ 4 MHz - 40 dB @ 16 MHz	9 pF/ft Max.	IBM Data Grade Media FDDI (STP)[3]	IBM 4/16 Mbps Token Ring CDDI

1. Worst Pair Near End Cross-Talk
2. 100 ohm CDDI Applications Require Continued Study
3. FDDI applications for STP is defined in "An Interoperable Solution for FDDI Signaling Over Shielded Twisted Pair," Version 1.0, May 21, 1991, released jointly by DEC, AMD, Motorola, SynOptics, and Chipcom Corp.

NOTE: Program specifications subject to change as standards or other industry developments warrant.

Figure 230 *Courtesy of Anixter Brothers.*

building, plan on running fresh twisted-pair wiring for your LAN, or paying almost cable-installation costs to a cable company to test your wiring and correct any problems.

Troubleshooting Twisted-Pair Wiring

According to *PC Magazine*, October 16, 1990,

> "During our testing, we completely changed our wiring hubs without taking down the network. We worked quickly to let NetWare retry connections, but we swapped between hubs from different companies without a blink or reset. The combination of 10Base-T wiring and NetWare tries hard and succeeds in keeping the network working."

PC Magazine's tests show that 10Base-T is very tough, nevertheless we do not recommend messing with electronic equipment while the power is on. Yes, it might be helpful to change a card or a repeater hub without bringing the whole network down, but what are your users doing? Saving critical data to their database? Down the network before changing hubs unless the hardware is specifically designed for safe "hot swapping."

10Base-T has some troubleshooting advantages over other Ethernet implementations because 10Base-T concentrators are intelligent. They will cut a bad node (broken wire, shorted wire) out of the network, then use LEDs to show you which node is the problem. Always check these LEDs first thing if you have one or two workstations out, but the rest of the stations on the concentrator seem to be working fine. Be sure the hub has power!

If you find no complaining LEDs at the concentrator, consider the malfunctioning workstation. Is it behaving correctly? Make sure it boots, then loads the IPX protocol and NETx. Can you log in? If so, it may make sense to use some of the testing and troubleshooting utilities we discuss in Chapter 5. If the workstation won't boot, or it won't load IPX and/or NETx.COM, better get the workstation working right before you start thinking about possible cable problems. Some troubleshooters keep a portable computer and a parallel-port-to-10Base-T adapter around to test suspect cables. If the portable works on this cable you know the trouble is in your workstation, not your wire.

Don't forget to check for diagnostic lights on the 10Base-T Network Interface Card in the workstation. Many of these network cards have diagnostic LEDs on board to show transmit, receive, collision/jabber, and link status.

If you have a number of downed workstations, better break out your network cabling diagram. Perhaps you have a bad hub, or a bad wire to this hub from the rest of the network. Perhaps you have a bad bridge or router. Using your network diagram and the COMCHECK utility, find out which cable runs are working and which are down.

Once you know which cable run is down, methodically check each section of the run, from network card through patch cable to the data connector on the wall, through the horizontal wiring to the wiring closet, through a cross-connect cable at the wiring closet to the 10Base-T concentrator. Inside the wiring closet, look for loose connections and poor wiring contacts. Never use Silver Satin cable (which does not meet the 10Base-T specs) for cross connect cables, even for short ones.

Twisted-pair test tools can help. Jensen Tools sells a cute little modular twisted-pair cable tester for $120. Attach the remote unit to the far end of the twisted-pair cable, then check for opens, shorts, and miswired cables with an LED readout on this end of the cable. Unfortunately, the test tells you only that you have a problem, not where. So you'll have to test each segment until you find the guilty patch cord or cable connection.

If you have a higher repair tool budget, and especially if you have to troubleshoot both coax and twisted-pair cable runs, consider the Quick Scanner from Microtest (also available from Jensen Tools) which lists for $995. The Quick Scanner's TDR (Time Domain Reflectometer) sends a signal down the cable, whether coax or twisted-pair, then calculates the cable length from the time it takes for the signal to echo back. Since excessive cable length will choke an otherwise good LAN, and since the

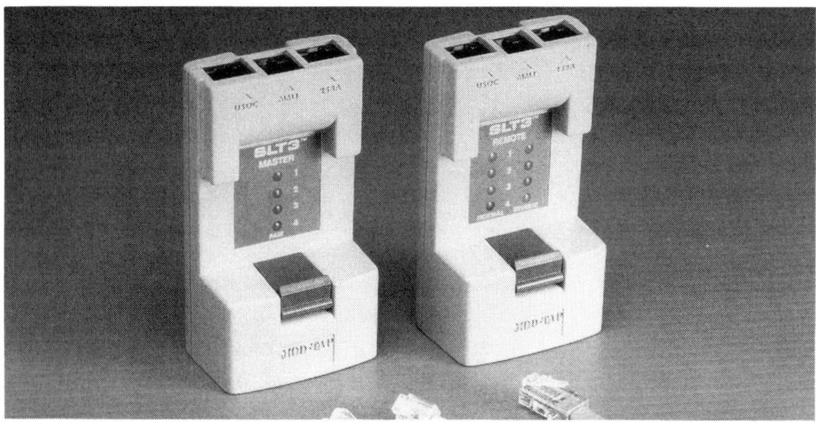

Figure 231 Modular cable tester for USOC, TIA, and AT&T 258A twisted-pair wiring. Photo courtesy of Jensen Tools.

cable is usually in the wall and ceiling so you can't use a tape measure to check each cable run, a TDR can be very helpful. If the TDR detects a malformed echo, the Quick Scanner recognizes the short, open, or bad connection that caused the poor signal, and can tell you how many feet down the cable this problem is occurring.

Not all twisted-pair wiring is connected the same, even when the different schemes use an identical RJ-45 connector. If your building is wired with the USOC standard, but your patch cables are AT&T 258A standard, the network is going to choke.

Figure 232 shows three ways to connect the same 4-pair twisted-pair wire to an RJ-45 connector. EIA/TIA has approved two incompatible pin/pair wiring assignments. Pin 1 on the preferred design, for example, connects to the white-green wire and pin 2 connects to the green wire—together, they are called pair 3. The alternate design is the AT&T 258A standard which uses pin 1 for the white-orange wire and pin 2 for the orange wire, the wires called pair 2 by cable manufacturers. At least both these schemes keep twisted-pairs together carrying paired signals. Consider the third standard, the USOC standard at the bottom of Figure 232. The USOC standard connects pin 1 and pin 8 to a twisted-pair set (the brown

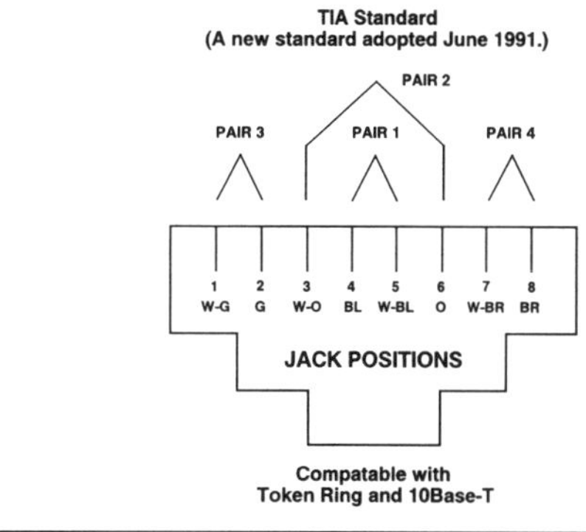

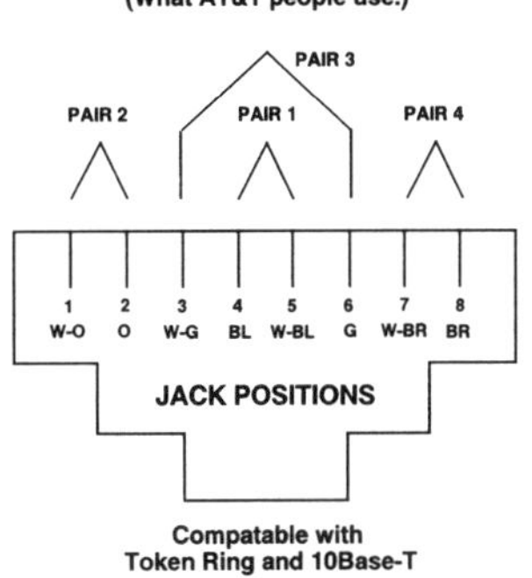

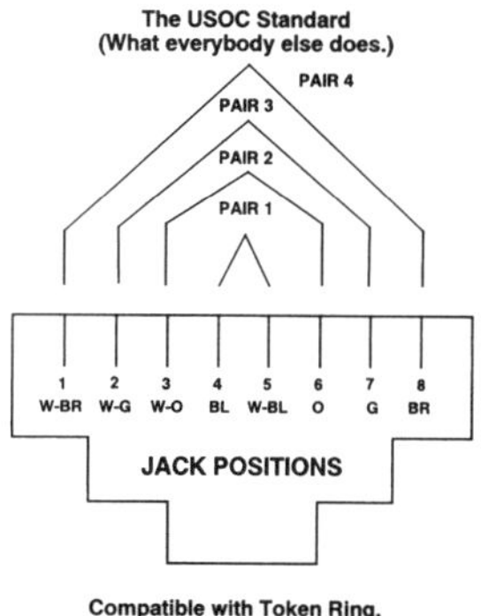

Figure 232 Three ways to wire RJ-45 connectors.

set, pair 4 according to the cable manufacturers). If you have USOC cable connected to equipment wired for either of the EIA/TIA standards, the signals in pins 1 and 2, which should be sent in a twisted-pair set so the wire twists will minimize electrical interference, will instead be sent in one wire from pair 4 and one wire from pair 3. This is called pair-splitting, and is a major cause of intermittent network problems (e.g., workstation temporarily goes off line) in poorly wired twisted-pair networks.

It is not unusual to end up with a combination of old and new twisted-pair cables, especially if you are combining multiple, small twisted-pair networks into a large department-wide network. A state agency in Richmond had this situation, and the network was always going down. They finally decided to rewire the entire building with new, all-the-same-electrical-characteristics twisted-pair, and they've had minimal network problems since.

One final caution. Be careful when using RJ-45 plugs—there are two kinds. The old "silver satin" flat phone line used RJ-45s with spike connectors that work fine with stranded wire (telephone twisted-pair). 10Base-T specs solid wire, not stranded. You'll need to use the new RJ-45 connectors for solid wire or you'll get severe cable angst. Thanks to Phil Raidt for this tip.

Fiber Optic Inter Repeater Link (FOIRL)

IRLs (Inter Repeater Links) are point-to-point, repeater-to-repeater connections with no workstations tapped into the link segment. Using IRLs, you can install a longer network than the legal number of coax-segments-tapped-for-workstations would allow. FOIRL uses fiber optic cable for the inter repeater link. A FOIRL repeater picks up signals from one Ethernet coax or twisted-pair network segment and transmits the signals through a fiber optic link cable. At the far end of the link cable, a second repeater picks up the optical signal and rebroadcasts it on another coaxial or twisted-pair Ethernet segment. Ethernet IRL (Inter Repeater Link) segments may be coax or fiber. See the section on repeaters in these Data Sheets for more information about coax IRL segments. We're dealing solely with fiber optic IRLs here.

Where to Use FOIRL Repeaters in Your LAN

Use FOIRL repeaters wherever your network requires cable runs that exceed the maximum segment-length limitations. FOIRL segments are particularly appropriate when connecting two coax segments, one on each floor, or when connecting two buildings because fiber optic cable doesn't pick up noise from electromagnetic fields in elevator shafts or conduits and it doesn't conduct electrical current between buildings.

How FOIRL Works

A FOIRL link preserves the Ethernet bus. Any signal on the coax cable gets sent down the fiber optic cable to the other FOIRL repeater. Any signal on the fiber optic cable is broadcast on the coax cable.

FOIRL uses a two-fiber optical cable: one fiber for transmit, one for receive. Data bits are transmitted on the cable when a laser turns off and on, sending light flashes. The IEEE specifies a repeater on each end of the FOIRL cable, with each repeater connected in turn to a coax cable segment or a 10Base-T hub.

IEEE standards allow a maximum of four repeaters along the signal path between any two stations on a network. This signal path may include up to three segments of coax cable tapped for workstations and up to two IRL segments (Inter Repeater Link segments, the point-to-point links with no workstations tapped into the link segment). If your network includes any 10Base-T segments, and most do, the IEEE sets the maximum FOIRL segment length to 500 meters (if you are using a five segment network). If your network has only four segments and three repeater sets, you may run 1000 meter FOIRL link segments.

Installing and Testing FOIRL

Get an experienced fiber optic cable company to run the cable. The cable itself just screws onto a connector on the repeater (if you're using the SMA connection). ST-type connectors attach with a slight push and a half-twist, much like the BNC connectors used with thin coax cable.

Check the diagnostic lights on your FOIRL repeaters. If a light shows troubles with the FOIRL link, call the vendor.

ARCNET on Coax and/or Twisted-Pair Cable

ARCNET topology is a series of stars, with a hub at the center of each star and coax or twisted-pair cable running to each station from the hub. The hubs are connected with coax or fiber optic cable links.

Unlike most networks, ARCNET lets an installer mix different kinds of cable in the network to carry the electrical signals between workstations, file server, and network printers or other peripherals. According to Datapoint's *ARCNET Cabling Guide*, "Every link between RIM (Resource Interface Module—an ARCNET card) and hub or between a pair of hubs can be a different type of cable, as long as the limitations of each type of cable are observed."

Though you can use coax or twisted-pair cable on any particular segment, maximum length limits are always much shorter for twisted-pair, whether shielded or unshielded, than for coax. If we compare the two cable designs we'll understand why.

Coax cable is a single signal-conducting wire which is carefully shielded from physical damage and from electrical interference. The central copper wire is surrounded by a layer of electrical insulator (a dielectric, often Teflon), then covered with a braided metal shield to buffer the data signal against electrical interference. Without this shielding the electromagnetic fields from electric power lines, fluorescent lights, and the electrical appliances found in a typical office would create random electrical fluctuations on the data conductor—in other words, they would add random additional bits to your data. The outermost layer on coax cable is a sturdy jacket, waterproof and tough enough to protect the cable from injury.

Alternatively, you may use a single pair of wires in a twisted-pair cable to carry the ARCNET data signal. Because each pair of wires in the cable is twisted together in a helix, the wires tend to emit (and receive) less electromagnetic interference than ordinary untwisted wires receive.

An ordinary wire, or pair of wires, is an antenna, so a LAN on ordinary wire would be unacceptable to the FCC because of the electrical noise it would emit when high frequency data is transmitted over the wire. Unshielded twisted-pair is better; ARCNET specs allow UTP (Unshielded Twisted-Pair) cables up to 330 feet (100 meters) in length. Shielded twisted-pair is better yet; maximum cable length is 660 feet (200 meters). But compare this to coax. Datapoint recommends two types of coax cable, RG-62 and RG-59/U, which are suitable for 2000-foot or 1500-foot segment lengths, respectively. For really long runs you should use a fiber optic link between two fiber optic hubs, then go back to copper wire as you fan out from the fiber hub at the remote site. ARCNET allows fiber optic runs of 15,000 feet. No, that's not a typo, we're talking close to 3 miles between the fiber hubs.

Finding the ARCNET Cable in Your LAN

Let's start with the cable running to an individual station. Look at the back of your workstation. You'll see a heavy, black 115 volt power cord which plugs into the wall electrical socket. You'll also have a video cable running from the back of the video monitor to a video card connector on the back of the computer. The keyboard cable often runs around to the back of the computer too, and you may have a mouse or a printer cable. Okay, none of those is the network cable.

Look for another cable attached back there, one that resembles the ordinary flat telephone wire running from the wall jack to your telephone answering machine, extension phone, or modem. Twisted-pair looks like

Figure 233 *Thomas-Conrad's ARCNET cards have BNC connectors for coax star or coax bus cabling, as well as twisted-pair RJ-45 ports. Photo courtesy of Thomas-Conrad.*

ordinary phone wire (even to the RJ-45 or RJ-11 telephone-style modular connector)—but twisted-pair is 1-1/2 times the diameter of phone wire, designed bigger specifically to help you differentiate between your modem phone cable and your LAN cable.

Some ARCNET cards have two twisted-pair ports for RJ-11 or RJ-45 twisted-pair connector plugs. Most ARCNET cards have a bank of eight switches on the rear of the card so you can reset the card's node address without taking the cover off the workstation computer. This should help you distinguish twisted-pair ARCNET cards with RJ-45 or RJ-11 connectors from modem cards with RJ-45 or RJ-11 connectors. Most modems don't have the bank of switches on the back of the card next to the RJ-11 or RJ-45 connectors.

If you don't have twisted-pair, maybe you have coax at the card. By the time all the shielding is added, coax is about the diameter of a pencil. Typically manufactured with a black, clear, or gray plastic jacket, ARCNET coax has RG-62 or RG-59/U printed on the jacket. The cable might be attached to the back of the network card directly with a round, half-twist connector called a BNC (see Figure 233). There is also a bus version of ARCNET that uses a T connector at the card, much like thin Ethernet (see Figure 223). You should be able to tell ARCNET from Ethernet by the cable ID numbers printed right on the cable jacket (see the coax cable chart below). Unfortunately, some of the really messed up LANs, the ones that desperately need a troubleshooter, have been miswired with Ethernet cable in an ARCNET LAN or vice versa. So read the cable numbers, but double-check the cards against the cables if you think something is suspicious. If you've got a thin Ethernet LAN, go to page 117 for Ethernet on coax.

Coax Cables:

Cable Type	Impedance	Connector	Application
RG-62	93 ohms	BNC connector	Recommended for ARCNET —the standard
RG-59/U	75 ohms	BNC connector	Recommended for ARCNET when you will also use the cable to conduct MINX video originals
RG-11/U	75 ohms	RG-59/U pigtail	Acceptable for ARCNET with MINX video
RG-58	50 ohms	BNC connector	Only cable suitable for thin Ethernet

ARCNET allows both active and passive hubs. Look for ARCNET active hubs in the central wiring closets on each floor. These active hubs send a signal down the cable to other hubs, or directly to workstations and file servers equipped with ARCNET cards. Passive hubs were designed to split the signal from an active hub between two or three stations. For example, you could run a single cable from the active hub in the wiring closet to two workstations in a shared office, then split the signal with a passive hub.

Datapoint recommends that you install passive hubs out in the work area, close to the end user. When using passive hubs you risk two typical ARCNET cabling sins: running a cable from one passive hub to another, and leaving one of the ports on an old-style passive hub unterminated. Either sin will choke your network. And either is easy to commit if you put passive hubs in the wiring closet or the ceiling where you might forget them. When locating parts and documenting your existing cable plant, look carefully for hidden passive hubs. If you're installing a new network, follow Datapoint's recommendations in their *ARCNET Cabling Guide*.

Figure 234 *Coax and twisted-pair versions of ARCNET active hubs. Photo courtesy of Computer System Products Incorporated.*

How to Install and Test ARCNET Cable

We can't give you complete specifications and directions for installing an ARCNET network here. Datapoint Corporation, the inventor and authoritative guardian of the ARCNET standard, has published two useful guides: the *ARCNET Cabling Guide*, and the *ARCNET Designers Handbook*. Both are available from Datapoint Corporation at (800) 733-1500. We recommend you purchase a copy of each if you need more details than we can give you here.

ARCNET was originally designed for coax cable. Datapoint still specifies coax between any two hubs—and only the recommended types of coax (RG-62 or RG-59/U) and the recommended manufacturers, at that.

The original ARCNET topology is a series of stars. Individual stations equipped with ARCNET cards (Datapoint calls them RIMs in their literature) are connected to hubs. Active hubs regenerate and retransmit the signals they receive, so active hubs can drive long cable lengths, either hub-to-hub or hub-to-RIM. Passive hubs are simple signal-splitters. They take a strong signal and split it into two or three identical signals, but each of the three is much weaker than the original. A small ARCNET network of four RIMs or less can use a single passive hub and short cables to connect the four stations. Anything bigger requires active hubs.

Passive hubs are confusing and troublesome. The old-style passive hub (Datapoint's Model Code 9485) must be terminated on any unused port, and it allows a maximum of 200 feet of cable between any two stations connected to the hub with RG-62 cable. This hub is obsolete. You should not install this kind of hub in any new networks. The new passive hub (Model 9490) has a longer distance range, 300 feet with RG-62 cable, and it does not need to be terminated on all unused ports like Model 9485 does.

Datapoint also makes two kinds of active hubs: ordinary active hubs, and intelligent hubs that can be monitored remotely. In addition, many other manufacturers produce ARCNET cards and hubs with widely varying topologies and features—for example, ARCNET cards that can be daisy-chained together instead of using a passive hub. We haven't tried to make

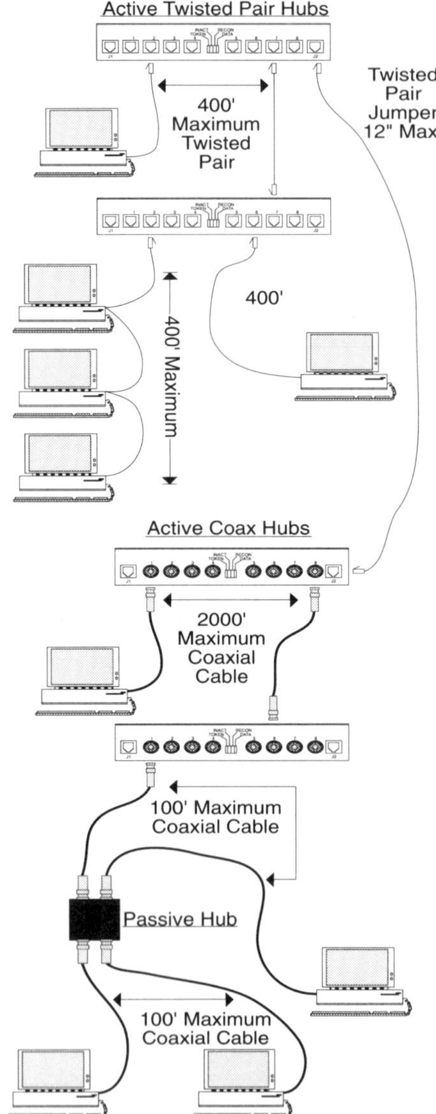

Figure 235 *ARCNET networks. Diagram by Allyson Almieda of Computer System Products.*

a comprehensive survey, preferring to concentrate on the original ARCNET standard instead. Figure 235 shows the classic ARCNET on coax cable with passive hubs, and ARCNET on twisted-pair with a daisy-chain of three workstations.

By the time you read this, ARCNETplus will be shipping with 20 megabit per second cards instead of the 2.5 megabit per second ARCNET cards conforming to the original standard. ARCNETplus promises to be downward compatible, but it's hard to believe that marginal cabling plans that can barely carry 2.5 megabit per second ARCNET will work well with ARCNETplus. Datapoint has also announced that you will need ARCNETplus hubs (both active and passive) if they are in the signal path between any two ARCNETplus cards.

ARCNET is an incredibly robust standard because it's incredibly paranoid. For example, each data transmission involves a four-step send/acknowledge sequence between transmitting card and receiving card. When the transmitter-to-be receives the token, it sends an enquiry to the receiving card called an FBE (free buffer enquiry) to make sure the receiver has space to receive the data packet. When the receiver says yes (sends back a positive ACK frame), the transmitter sends the data packet and awaits another positive acknowledgement from the receiver.

ARCNET is so reliable because it demands confirmation for each step. It can tolerate sleazy cabling, busted cables, and powered-off workstations that would choke any other network. In addition, it's not hard to make an ARCNET card. Most ARCNET hardware works very well. Nevertheless, people will offer to sell you ultra-cheap ARCNET cards and passive hubs that just plain don't work. Use some sense and buy from a reputable manufacturer.

ARCNET Cabling Specs

Datapoint allows many different types of cables in an ARCNET network.

Shielded Twisted-Pair—Datapoint says ARCNET will run on IBM Type 1 shielded twisted-pair cable. If you use Type 1 cable you'll need a balun (impedance matcher) to match the 150 ohm twisted-pair to the lower-impedance coax cable. IBM Type 1 cable is equivalent to Level 5 cable under the twisted-pair level grading system (see Figure 230 on page 129).

Maximum cable length, any link

Type 1—660 feet

Unshielded Twisted-Pair—According to Datapoint, ARCNET segments on IBM Type 3 twisted-pair will work fine if you use a balun (an impedance matcher) to match the twisted-pair cable to the coax. IBM Type 3 cable is equivalent to Level 3 cable under the new twisted-pair level grading system (see Figure 230 on page 129).

Maximum cable length, any link

IBM Type 3—330 feet

Datapoint 3-pair or 6-pair Cable—Use these cables only if they are already installed in your building.

Fiber Optic—If you have long fiber optic links you will find that the rest of the network must be down-sized to meet the ARCNET specs for maximum signal propagation time (the time it takes for a signal to get from any workstation to the farthest workstation on the network).

Maximum cable length, any link

Single-conductor fiber optic—15,000 feet

Coax—Datapoint recommends using RG-62. If you need to use the cable for Datapoint's MINX video as well as ARCNET, use RG-59/U (recommended, but only top quality) or RG-11/U.

Maximum cable length, any link

RG-62—2000 feet

RG-59/U—1500 feet for ARCNET, 1000 feet for ARCNET and MINX

RG-11/U—1750 feet for ARCNET and/or ARCNET and MINX

If you are planning to use anything but the original RG-62 coax, or if you're planning a large network, it makes sense to get the Datapoint design and cabling brochures. You will need to consider what adapters you require to match the impedance of different kinds of wire. You'll want to calculate the length of the network in terms of signal attenuation (the way a signal loses strength as it travels through a long cable and through passive hubs). And you'll need to calculate the network length in terms of propagation time. If you're installing a small ARCNET LAN, the recommendations we give below should do.

RG-62 Coax Cable— The maximum number of hubs between any two stations is 10 hubs, if using maximum cable lengths. If you use shorter cable lengths you can use more hubs, but Datapoint gives no clear guidance on this except to say that accumulated timing distortions in the signal (which increase as the signal traverses each hub) eventually limit the number of hubs. Our recommendation: Minimize the number of hubs—why make your life difficult?

Maximum distance station to active hub—2000 feet

Maximum distance between any two active nodes connected by a Model 9490 passive hub—330 feet; that means active-hub-to-passive-hub-to-station or station-to-passive-hub-to-station should be, at most, 330 feet

Maximum distance active hub to active hub—2000 feet

Maximum distance active hub to Model 9490 passive hub—300 feet; unused node connectors on Model 9490 active hubs need not be terminated

Unused node connectors on old-style Model 9485 passive hubs must be terminated with a 93 ohm resistor.

You may not cable a passive hub to a passive hub.

You cannot connect two active hubs with a passive hub.

The maximum node-to-node distance (the farthest apart nodes in the network)—22,000 feet

Yes, You Can Run Your Own Cable

ARCNET goes far, works well, and is very, very forgiving. Therefore, ARCNET is the network of choice for rough service (warehouses, classrooms, factories). Aesthetics is not a big factor in most of these environments, so you may choose to do your own ARCNET cabling. You'll still have to religiously abide by the ARCNET specifications, and by good practice for network cable. Avoid strong EMF fields, like elevators, heat pumps, fluorescent lights, and AC units, especially with twisted-pair cable. Avoid physical damage or stress to the cable. Coax hates sharp bends. Hang coax cable from cable hangers rather than asking it to support its own weight (most coax is not strong enough), don't scrape it on sharp edges while installing it, and keep it off the basement floor so rats don't nibble through the waterproof covering and short everything out.

Underwriter's Laboratory tests and certifies cable suitable for general uses (e.g., in walls or conduit, from wall to computer) or for plenum installation. Be careful to spec plenum-grade coax cable if you're intending to lay the cable in the ceiling (the typical place) and if the area between the drop ceiling and the floor above is a plenum (functions as an air-return duct for the building ventilation system). Plenum-grade cable is manufactured with fire-resistant and low-smoke materials in the insulation and cable jacket to minimize poisonous chemical fumes in the building during a fire. Your local fire code gives details.

Most cable installers use a TDR (Time Domain Reflectometer) to test the cable integrity while the cable is still on the reel. After installation they will test it again, but it's useful to know you started with a good reel of cable. A TDR will also measure the installed length of each cable segment—essential when you're running cable segments that are close to the IEEE length limits.

Adding an extra workstation, replacing a bad T connector, or moving a workstation requires no special skills. The BNC connectors on the cable ends twist off a card or a T connector with a slight-push-and-half-twist motion. Buy pre-made lengths of coax—the BNC connectors are properly installed at the factory. If you must make custom cables, installers say the twist-on connectors are easier for amateurs than soldered or crimped BNC connectors.

On the other hand, most office and professional environments demand a professional cable installer. Computer people seldom have the skills to run cable through the walls without leaving tacky-looking wallboard cuts and patches. Wall people and regular electricians don't understand network cabling specifications and they're used to dealing with electrical wires, which are much more robust than coax cable. They tend to snag network cable, kink it, or leave coils of cable in the ceiling over each workstation "in case you need more cable later."

Document Your Network

Network experts recommend that you carefully document the network when it's installed, and keep that documentation up to date to reflect any and all changes. You will need a cable diagram and a list of node addresses with the physical location of each node address, and that node's user. Do it now. Don't wait until your network monitoring software shows that a node is failing. Perhaps you think you'll figure it out when the time comes. After all, you know both the station number and the node address of the failing workstation. Don't kid yourself, save grief and document now.

The station number shown on Novell NetWare information screens is unrelated to physical workstation location. This number is assigned to each workstation by NetWare when the workstation logs in to the network—it's really a server connection number, and has nothing to do with the physical station itself. You might use some meaningful node address numbering system when you install your ARCNET cards (you get to set ARCNET node numbers yourself)—but we bet you didn't. So neither of these helpful-sounding numbers will tell you what stations are connected to which cable, or where a particular cable goes next.

Troubleshooting ARCNET Cabling

ARCNET is designed to run even if one or two cables are broken. If only one or two stations are down, but the rest work fine, you can be pretty sure the problem is in these workstations, or in the network cable that connects them to the rest of the world. If that's your situation, go to the dead workstation. If it seems to work fine, but it won't hook up to the network, we'll do a quick local card-and-cable survey.

The first question is always "What has changed?" If you have just moved a workstation, added cable, or installed a new card, go right back where you were working and look for a problem. It's easy enough to carelessly connect a cable. If you removed a workstation, was it cabled to a passive hub that needs to be terminated? If so, did you terminate the hub with a 93 ohm resistor (we're assuming you're using the standard RG-62 coax cable). If you added a section of cable, is it longer now than the ARCNET standards allow? Nine times out of ten you created the problem yourself.

Remember, too, that people trip over cables and rip them out of the wall connector, then feel foolish and try to repair the problem themselves. Tug gently on any suspicious connections. Repair any that are held together with Scotch tape.

If you see nothing obvious, it's wise to swap in a known-good workstation to find out if the problem is workstation/card/user or a cabling fault. If the new workstation chokes too, we'll assume there is a cable problem and start testing.

Use COMCHECK to look for a broken, shorted, or miswired cable. We have detailed directions for COMCHECK in Appendix B. Use your network diagram, COMCHECK, and cable test tools to identify the bad section of cable, then replace it. By the way, Thomas-Conrad's TXD diagnostic software will reveal stone-dead network cables, just like COMCHECK does. But it's far more discriminating; it's capable of locating and documenting subtle card or cable errors as well as egregious ones. In Chapter 5 we discuss a wide range of network diagnostic software.

If you're using twisted-pair cable, the modular cable twisted-pair cable tester that Jensen Tools sells for $120 can be handy (see Figure 231). Attach the remote unit to the far end of the twisted-pair cable, then check for opens, shorts, and miswired cables with an LED readout on this end of the cable. Unfortunately, the test tells you only that you have a problem, not where. So you'll have to test each segment until you find the guilty patch cord or cable connection. Methodically check each section of the run from network card through the patch cable to the data connector on the wall, through the horizontal wiring to the wiring closet, through a cross-connect cable at the wiring closet to the ARCNET hub. In the wiring closet, look for loose connections and poor wiring contacts.

If you have a higher repair tool budget, and especially if you have to troubleshoot both coax and twisted-pair cable runs, consider the Quick Scanner from Microtest (also available from Jensen Tools) which lists for $995. The Quick Scanner's TDR (Time Domain Reflectometer) sends a signal down the cable, whether coax or twisted-pair, then calculates the cable length from the time it takes for the signal to echo back. Since excessive cable length will choke an otherwise good LAN, and since the cable is usually in the wall and ceiling so you can't use a tape measure to check each cable run, a TDR can be very helpful. If the TDR detects a malformed echo, the Quick Scanner recognizes the short, open, or bad connection that caused the poor signal, and can tell you how many feet down the cable this problem is occurring.

A TDR will measure your ARCNET cable just fine if the cable is disconnected at the far end. You're likely to get some weird readings, though, if you shoot the TDR toward a passive hub, because the passive hub splits the TDR signal and sends it down all the cable branches attached to the passive hub. And how is a TDR supposed to make sense of the echoes from three different-length cables, all returning at about a tenth of the signal strength you'd normally expect? So disconnect any cable you want to measure on both ends before you shoot it with the TDR.

If you don't have a TDR, you can use a pocket-sized coax cable tester, also available from Jensen Tools. It's not as quick as the TDR (the TDR says how many feet down the cable the problem is located), and it won't find a poor quality connection like a TDR will, but it works, and costs well under $100 (even a basic TDR is close to $1000). Put the BNC test cap on one end of the cable—it's got a diode connecting the center conductor to the cable shield. Then attach the battery-powered pocket tester to the opposite end. The tester reveals shorts between the cable shield and center conductor, and it checks the cable continuity (no continuity means the cable conductor is broken).

If you have no repair budget at all, you can always use the old swap-in-a-good-one technique. Run a temporary cable from the bad workstation to the active hub. If the workstation is fine now, install the new cable someplace unobtrusive and forget it, or call in cabling experts if you need a clean, professional job.

Use an ohmmeter to test the terminators too. A 93 ohm terminator should have 93 ohms resistance between the center connector and the outer shell.

T connectors go bad a lot (seems silly, since there's almost nothing to them, but it's true). Swap them out to test them.

Troubleshooting ARCNET Hubs

Old-style Model 9485 ARCNET passive hubs must be terminated on all unused ports. If not, sometimes the network will work okay and sometimes it gets hung up with ARCNET trying and retrying to configure itself. Some network designers think that passive hubs fail more often than active hubs. Therefore, when designing an ARCNET network they won't even tell the customer that passive hubs exist. They design everything with active hubs.

Is the power okay to the active hubs? If no power, no network. Do you have a blown fuse in one or more of your active hubs? If so, part of the network would be up, and the part running on the dead active hub(s) would be down. Most active hubs have LED indicator lights to help you troubleshoot a bad cable or a bad workstation at the other end of the cable.

Token Ring Twisted-Pair Cable

Token Ring cabling connects the workstations and the file server(s) on a Token Ring network to the concentrator. The concentrator is also called a MultiStation Access Unit (MSAU or MAU), or an 8228 unit. When your Token Ring network requires more than one 8-node MAU (in other words, if you've got more than eight workstations and/or servers), connect multiple MAUs together to make a single large network ring.

Though the Token Ring network is a logical ring (the signal passes from station to station in a ring), the actual wiring looks like a star. Cable installers run twisted-pair cable from the workstation to a wall plate and from the wall plate to the wiring closet where the centrally-located MAU lives.

Finding Token Ring Cabling in Your LAN

Look for Token Ring cable running from the MAU to each workstation, file server, bridge, gateway, etc.—in short, to each node on the network. Figure 238 shows two Token Ring network cable diagrams.

Each concentrator has a Ring Out (RO) port and a Ring In (RI) port. To complete the loop, the Ring Out is connected with a patch cable to Ring In. If you have more than one MAU, connect RO on the first MAU to RI on the second MAU, RO on the second to RI on the third, etc., until you finally connect RO on the last MAU to Ring In on the first MAU we started with.

Token Ring was originally designed to run at 4 Mbps (Mbps is megabits per second, a data speed rating in millions of bits per second), on 150 ohm shielded twisted-pair cable. Now, designers often run 4 Mbps Token Ring networks entirely on unshielded twisted-pair wiring (typically a 4-pair cable), and they're starting to implement 16 Mbps Token Rings on UTP. But most Token Ring networks run on shielded twisted-pair, or a combination of shielded and unshielded twisted-pair cables. Mixed media implementations often use UTP (Unshielded Twisted-Pair) from the workstation to the wiring closet, but for long runs from one wiring

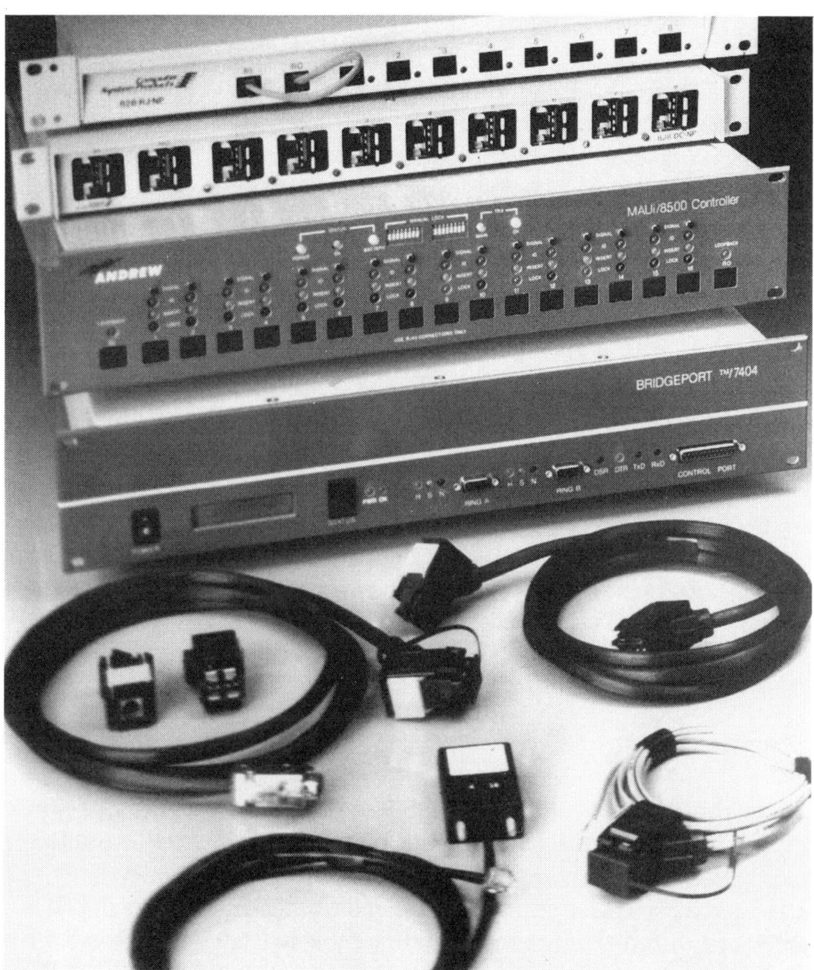

Figure 236 A Token Ring parts medley (MAUs, cables, baluns). Photo courtesy of Computer System Products Incorporated.

closet to another, or for MAU-Ring-Out to the next MAU's Ring In, they fall back on shielded twisted-pair. The IEEE is trying to reach agreement on extensions to the Token Ring standard, specifically the proper use of unshielded cable, but none have been published as we write this. In general, we suggest you wait for standards, or pick a design that you know works well for a Token Ring network of equivalent size—your company probably can't afford either the time or the money to boldly go where none have gone before.

The following table shows the variety of Token Ring cables manufactured, each with a specific purpose. These cable types are not interchangeable, no matter how similar they may look externally, but you don't need to worry about the various cable types—your network designer will worry about them.

IBM Cable Type	Number of data-grade pairs	Number of voice-grade pairs	Conductor	Sheilding (data pairs)	Twisted-Pair Level Program Equivalent
Type 1 Cable	2	N/A	22 AWG solid wire	Shielded	Level 5 twisted-pair of 22 AWG is electrically equivalent to Type 1
Type 2 Cable	2	4	22 AWG solid wire	Shielded	
Type 6 Cable	2	N/A	26 AWG stranded wire	Shielded	
Type 9 Cable	2	N/A	26 AWG solid wire	Shielded	
Type 3 Cable	2	N/A	22 or 24 AWG solid wire	Unshielded	Level 3 twisted-pair meets or exceeds the Type 3 specifications

Token Ring cards usually have a DB-9 connector on the back. See Figure 216 for a photo of a typical Token Ring network card. This DB-9 connector looks exactly like a monochrome or CGA color video connector (9 pins arranged in two rows, 5 in one row, 4 in the other). If you're using classic shielded twisted-pair cabling, your first cable will have a DB-9 connector at the workstation card end and the classic hermaphroditic Token Ring connector at the other end (see Figure 237). If you are using Type 3 cables (that's unshielded twisted-pair cable), you may use an RJ-11 or an RJ-45 plug connector (like a modular telephone connector plug) at the network card. Or you could also use a DB-9 connector there, but you'll switch to RJ-11 or RJ-45 modular plugs at the work area wall plate and at the Token Ring MAU hub in the wiring closet.

Figure 237 *Clunky hermaphroditic Token Ring cable end connector, and the balun needed to adapt this connector to unshielded twisted-pair cable using RJ-45 connectors. Photo courtesy of Jensen Tools.*

How Token Ring Cabling Works

One twisted-pair carries the signal coming into the workstation card (the receive pair), a second pair carries the signal out (transmit). Unlike ARCNET or Ethernet twisted-pair, Token Ring twisted-pair wiring carries a continuous current. The MAU monitors this current, bypassing this Token Ring card (cutting it out of the ring) when the current fails—for example, when you turn off your workstation.

Reversing transmit/receive polarity may damage the MAU or Token Ring card, so Token Ring connectors are designed to prevent misinstallation. You could mess things up, though, if you carelessly mixed up the wires while replacing a cable connector.

How to Test Token Ring Cabling

You should purchase a cable maintenance contract from a reputable cabling company—perhaps the one that originally installed your Token Ring cable. Most Token Ring test equipment is too expensive and the necessary skills are too esoteric to do it yourself, unless you're dealing with a very small LAN.

How to Remove and Install Token Ring Cabling

You can easily replace a bad cable or a malfunctioning MAU, but don't try to design and set up a Token Ring network from scratch. Token Ring is very picky—some say arcane—and the standards must be followed precisely. Besides, if you're going with Token Ring your organization has the money to pay an experienced Token Ring network designer and an authorized Token Ring cable installer. Be sure to check references — only Token Ring installations are relevant here.

The original IBM cabling plan called for two kinds of Token Ring cables, adapter cable and patch cable, both made of four-wire, shielded twisted-pair cable. In this scheme, adapter cables were 8 feet long, with a MAU connector on one end and a DB-9 connector on the network card end. The MAU end connector in this original wiring scheme was the big, square, clunky hermaphroditic connector shown in Figure 237, which would snap into an identical MAU connector on another cable or on the MAU itself.

Because not all workstations are within 8 feet of an MAU, you could extend the adapter cable with a patch cable, which came in 8 foot, 30 foot, 75 foot, and 150 foot lengths. The patch cable plugged into an adapter cable on one end and the MAU on the other.

New Token Ring cabling designs use mixed shielded and unshielded twisted-pair. Until there is an IEEE standard for these mixed media cabling systems, it will be hard to know what works for sure under maximum load and adverse circumstances. Here, though, are some generally accepted guidelines for Token Ring on IBM cable:

No more than 33 MAUs on the main ring.

Number of nodes per network (depends on main ring cable type)

Type 1 or 2 cable—260 nodes
Type 3 or 6 cable—72 nodes

Maximum MAU-to-workstation lobe cable length

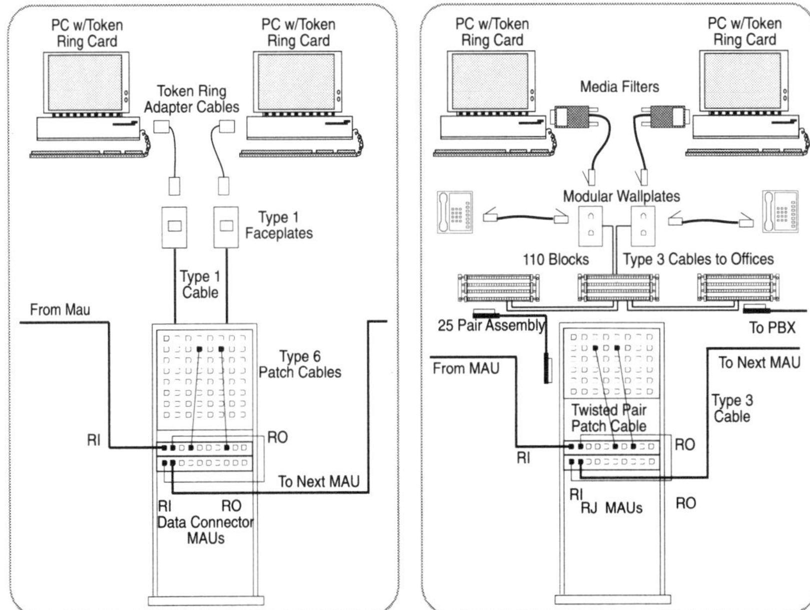

Figure 238 *Token Ring networks. On left: Shielded pair. On right: Unshielded pair. Diagram by Allyson Almieda of Computer System Products.*

Type 1 or 2 cable—330 feet
Type 3 or 6 cable—150 feet

Minimum cable length between any two devices

All cable types—8 feet

Maximum length of main ring cable (each MAU counts as 16 feet of ring cable, but we're not counting the lobe cables here)

Type 1 or 2 cable—660 feet
Type 3 cable—400 feet
Type 6 cable—150 feet

Maximum total length of main ring cable — dual ring Token Ring

Type 1 or 2 cable—1200 feet
Type 3 cable— 700 feet
Type 6 cable—400 feet

Don't mix shielded and unshielded twisted-pair cables on the same MAU

Think twice about moving a workstation down the hall and adding a 30-foot patch cable. Token Ring just can't handle that kind of spontaneity.

Let's suppose you have to replace a cable or an MAU. Get the new cable from your Token Ring supplier, ordering one of the same length and cable type. To disconnect the cable at the MAU, squeeze the square connector and pull out. The adapter cables at the card ends are similar to ordinary telephone connectors or to DB-9 connectors (remember to unscrew the little screws holding the connector to the card). If you're replacing an MAU, look for the setup tool that comes with the MAU. Plug it into each MAU port in turn, waiting a couple of seconds for the click. This will initialize each MAU port before you install the cables.

Fiber Optic Cable

Many new LANs use a fiber optic backbone between floors, between buildings, or between widely-separated concentrators, usually an Ethernet Fiber Optic Inter Repeater Link (FOIRL), an ARCNET Fiber Optic Link, or FDDI (Fiber Distributed Data Interface).

The FOIRL links connect two widely separated metal-wired (usually coax) segments of an Ethernet LAN with a point-to-point link from one repeater to another repeater. FOIRL does not serve individual workstations, it is strictly repeater-to-repeater. We have a separate Data Sheet on FOIRL starting on page 132.

Like FOIRL, ARCNET's fiber optic link is point-to-point, from one ARCNET fiber hub to another ARCNET fiber hub as much as 15,000 feet away. Each fiber hub sprouts standard metal-wired ARCNET segments connected to ordinary ARCNET BNC ports on the hub. Long fiber optic links affect the maximum station-to-station cable lengths allowed in the rest of the ARCNET network. Consult Datapoint's *Cabling Guide* for details.

FDDI is an extremely high-speed fiber optic network which is particularly suitable as a backbone to connect Ethernet or Token Ring networks. The FDDI standard has been adopted by the International Standards Organization (the authors of the OSI Seven-Layer Network Model which we discuss in Chapter 7). FDDI stations are wired in a ring with two fiber optic cables, but the stations normally send on only one fiber. If the fiber optic cable is injured, the second ring will start transmitting (but in the opposite direction around the circle), so a single cable break does not disable the system.

Though fiber optic backbones and links between repeater hubs are fairly common, fiber optic to the desktop (to each workstation) is rare outside the defense industry and other secure environments. Nevertheless, Ethernet, ARCNET, and Token Ring network cards for fiber optic cable are available, and the IEEE is drafting a fiber optic Ethernet standard (fiber optic to the desktop). A number of hardware manufacturers guarantee compatibility with the new IEEE standard soon after it is issued.

Finding Fiber Optic Cable in Your LAN

Fiber optics has traditionally been limited to high-speed and high-security installations because it has been so expensive. The price of cable and fiber optic equipment is dropping, though, so many high-end office buildings are being constructed with fiber optic cable in the walls, even if the tenants are not ready to light the cable yet.

Fiber optic cables are particularly appropriate when connecting two LAN segments in separate buildings (because of lightning, you don't want wire). And many LANs must traverse areas of high EMI (electromagnetic interference)—for instance, a factory floor where the EMI noise would destroy the data signal on a wire, or the elevator shaft in a highrise.

In addition, fiber optic is the cable of choice for high-security installations because it's so hard to eavesdrop on fiber. You probably know that a sophisticated sniffer can pick up subtle variations in the electromagnetic field emitted by a metal wire carrying data signals. From those variations we can reconstruct the electrical signal that must have been travelling over the wire. Therefore, no wire-based LAN can ever be completely secure. Fiber optics does not react to external electromagnetic interference, and it emits no electromagnetic field.

How Fiber Optic Cable Works

Fiber optic is almost always a point-to-point link, mostly because the technology to split a fiber optic signal is still very expensive, but the cable itself is fairly cheap. A typical fiber optic link uses a duplex cable, one fiber for transmit and a second for receive. In the case of FDDI, one fiber carries data clockwise and a second carries data counterclockwise. ARCNET fiber links use a single fiber between the two fiber optic hubs. A laser in the transmit end (driven by blips of electricity) sends blips of light down the cable to a PIN photodiode which converts the light back into electrical blips.

Installing and Testing Fiber Optic Cable

Use an experienced fiber optic installation company to run the cable. Once the cable is installed, it's easy to hook the cable to your repeater, transceiver, or concentrator (if you've specified appropriate connectors on the cable). SMA connectors screw on; ST-type connectors slip on with a half-twist.

AMP Incorporated has developed a fiber optic ST-type connector that is much easier to install than traditional fiber optic terminators. They swear a sixth grader could do it. Nevertheless, most LAN administrators turn all fiber optic repairs over to the experts.

The indicator lights on your fiber optic equipment give you good preliminary information, since most hardware has transmit, receive, and power LEDs. Some even have a link-continuity LED, which is helpful. But fiber optic test equipment is expensive, so administrators usually rely on their cable installation company to maintain and test their fiber optic links as necessary.

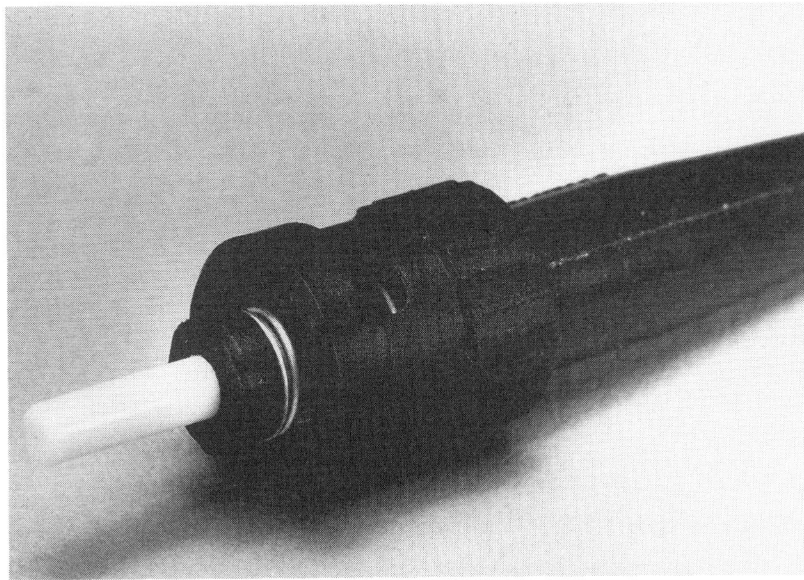

Figure 239 *Close-up of ST-type fiber optic end connector. Photo courtesy of Amphenol Corporation.*

Wireless Network Card

Wireless network cards communicate via packet radio, infrared beams, or microwaves rather than a network cable. These cards are ideal for temporary network setups or when conditions make conventional cable installation more hassle than it's worth. For example, some buildings have no space left to run cables, or you may wish to rearrange workgroups so frequently that the cost of rewiring (and the time lost) is too high to justify physical cabling.

Wireless card manufacturers maintain that these cards pay for themselves the first time you have to move a workstation. Consider packet radio. NCR estimates $700 per node (workstation or file server) for initial cable installation, and $700 more the first time you have to recable to move the workstation. Then add the cost of a conventional Ethernet card ($200-$400 is typical). If their figures are accurate for your cabling installation, and if you expect to need the flexibility to rearrange workstations often, the $1400 list price for WaveLAN cards doesn't look too bad. One warning, though: At present, WaveLAN's packet radio runs at a fifth of the speed (2Mbps) of conventional Ethernet (10Mbps). Motorola's Altair network, by comparison, runs at conventional Ethernet speeds.

Persoft makes a wireless bridge using one wire-capable Ethernet card and one wireless Ethernet card per bridge. With a pair of these bridges you may join two wired networks located on separate floors or in separate buildings. The packet radio card they are presently using has a range of 800 feet in unobstructed air using an omnidirectional antenna (the range is slightly less through concrete floors and other massive obstacles). If you use outdoor directional antennas, the range is five miles, ample for most across-campus building-to-building links.

How a Wireless Network Card Works

Infrared beams travel like visible light: in straight lines and exceedingly poorly through walls or other obstacles. They are often used in warehouses or open offices. One example is InfraLAN, the Token Ring infrared LAN manufactured by BICC Communications. Arranged in a logical ring, the InfraLAN base units receive data from an upstream unit and transmit it downstream to the next hub in the ring. Each base unit supports up to six workstations, which are hard-wired to the unit. This system requires an infrared base unit at each work group junction, and a standard Token Ring card in each workstation. BICC says their InfraLAN meets IEEE 802.5 specs for Token Ring, and will run either at 4 Mbps or at 16 Mbps. InfraLAN range is 5 to 80 feet between a pair of base unit transceivers.

Motorola's Altair network uses low-power 18 Gigahertz radio to transmit data signals from control modules attached to your Ethernet cable. Altair provides wireless branches on a wired Ethernet network with multi-station user modules as far as 40 to 130 feet from the control module (and the Ethernet cable). The shorter distance, they say, allows the radio signal to penetrate three interior walls. These low-power 18 Gigahertz waves do not pass through load-bearing walls, exterior walls, or floors, though they are not restricted to line-of-sight like infrared wireless LANs.

By comparison, spread spectrum radio transmitters do not have to be within line-of-sight, and the radio waves penetrate load-bearing walls and floors. To set up NCR's WaveLAN, for example, which conforms to the IEEE 802.3 standard used by Ethernet, install packet radio cards in each workstation and mount the antenna on the wall. The workstations need no base unit or hub on a wired portion of the network, and the signal carries a couple hundred feet through building walls and floors.

The spread-spectrum cards broadcast data in a low-power, wide-frequency band. Because the FCC has approved three frequency ranges for packet radio, users need no special license. To increase security, the data is encrypted. To allow multiple packet radio networks to operate in the same signal area, each packet is addressed by network number, then by station number. NCR's WaveLAN, for example, allows eight separate networks to operate in overlapping broadcast ranges.

Wireless network cards using radio transmission typically support Ethernet networks. This is not surprising; the University of Hawaii developed the precursor to Ethernet (the ALOHA network access system) for island-to-island communication via packet radio.

How to Test a Wireless Network Card

Use the diagnostic utilities supplied with your wireless LAN cards.

How to Remove and Install a Wireless Network Card

Install these cards in your workstations like ordinary network cards, check the Network Interface Card section of these Data Sheets for details.

Infrared card transmitters and receivers must be precisely aligned. The same is true for directional spread-spectrum radio cards. Even the omnidirectional antennas on radio cards broadcast an egg-shaped field rather than a perfect sphere. The antenna on NCR WaveLAN cards, for example, has a slightly longer range perpendicular to the flat sides of the antenna than on any other axis. Therefore, it makes sense to mount the antenna horizontally if you are communicating with other WaveLAN cards on the floor above or below. If you are using a pair of WaveLAN cards in a pair of bridges between two buildings, mount the antenna box vertically.

Interconnection Devices

Locating Interconnection Devices in The ISO (International Standards Organization) 7-Layer Network Scheme

ISO Layer Name and Number	Device	Device Characteristics and Features
7 Application Layer	Gateways	Suitable for WAN (Wide Area Network) to WAN connections (eg., SNA to X.25), LAN to WAN connections (eg. Novell's IPX to X.25), or LAN to mainframe (eg., Ethernet to IBM SNA) Translate one protocol into another (eg., IBM's SNA network protocol to Novell's IPX, or to TCP/IP in a UNIX network)
	Remote Bridges	Translate one protocol into another (eg., Ethernet to X.25 packet switching network protocol)
6 Presentation Layer		
5 Session Layer		
4 Transport Layer		
3 Network Layer	Routers	Examine only those packets addressed to this router Forward packets, routing them according to the ultimate destination address Operates with specific network-layer protocols (eg., Novell's BRGEN/ROUTEGEN router software which will route Novell IPX packets only)
2 DataLink Layer		
LLC sublayer		
MAC sublayer	MAC-LayerBridges	Can change physical medium (eg., connect coax to fiber optic) Some bridges can translate access protocols (eg., connect Ethernet to Token Ring) Other bridges limit themselves to a single protocol (connecting Ethernet to Ethernet, for example) Can deal with any network-layer protocol (DECnet, IPX, TCP/IP, etc.) because it reads the destination address on the access-protocol packet (the Ethernet, ARCNET, or Token Ring packet), not the network-layer information enclosed inside the access-protocol packet Forwards only those packets with a destination address across the bridge
1 Physical Layer	Repeaters	Can change physical medium (eg., connect coax cable to fiber optic cable) Must be Ethernet to Ethernet, or Token Ring to Token Ring (cannot translate between two different access-protocols)

Repeaters

A repeater is a device used to extend an Ethernet LAN beyond the length limits of a single cable segment. Repeaters receive signals on a network segment (could be any kind of segment— coax, fiber optic, twisted-pair) and rebroadcast them on another segment after restoring the signal to good-as-new condition. Two segments may be connected directly by a repeater, or by pairs of repeater units joined by Inter Repeater Links (IRLs). IRLs are point-to-point, repeater-to-repeater cables with no workstations tapped into the link segment.

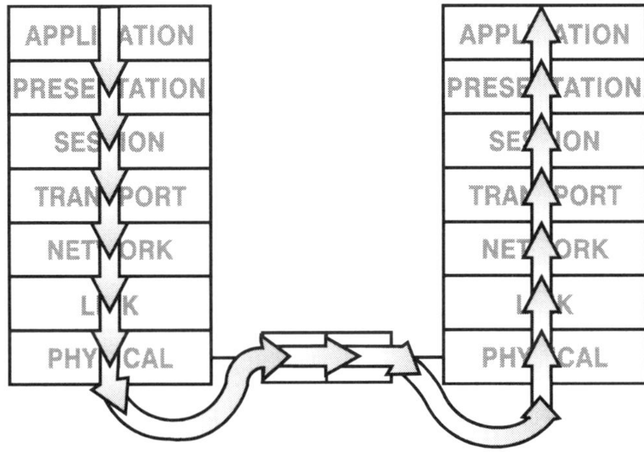

Figure 241 *A repeater functions on the Physical Layer.*

ARCNET does not use repeaters, because ARCNET active hubs perform the same function (receive the signal and rebroadcast it good-as-new). Token Ring does not need repeaters either (if cable limits are respected) because each Token Ring node acts like a repeater (receiving the signal and rebroadcasting it good-as-new). You've probably heard about Token Ring networks with one workstation on the far end of a very long cable run that loses connection to the network intermittently. The problem is cured by turning on an intermediate workstation that rebroadcasts the signal with enough pep to the far station.

Where to Find Repeaters in Your LAN

10Base-T networks rely on multi-port repeaters (hubs). These repeaters are usually clustered in a central wiring closet, with twisted-pair wire running a maximum of 100 meters (330 feet) from the repeater to each workstation. Most 10Base-T repeaters permit easy connection to other Ethernet segments running on different cable media. Some repeaters have BNC plugs for thin coax and/or fiber optic cable connectors. Almost all of these concentrators have an AUI connector, which accommodates the standard transceiver cable, so you may connect a fiber optic transceiver (a transmitter/receiver tap into fiber optic cable), a thick coax transceiver (to tap into a thick coaxial cable trunk), or a thin coax transceiver at this AUI port.

On standard Ethernet networks running coax cable, look for repeaters wherever your network requires long cable runs that exceed the maximum segment-length limitations. FOIRL (Fiber Optic Inter Repeater Link) segments made of fiber optic cable are particularly appropriate when connecting two coax segments, one on each floor, or when connecting two buildings, because the fiber optic cable doesn't pick up noise from electromagnetic fields in elevator shafts and it doesn't conduct electrical currents between buildings.

Network designers often split long coax cable runs on a single floor into two segments joined by a repeater. Because coax cable is normally installed in the ceiling, look for the repeater in the ceiling too.

How a Repeater Works

When a signal travels along a cable it loses strength (they call it cable loss or attenuation), gets degraded (distorted), and picks up noise. A once-perfect signal gets deformed, becoming less symmetrical. The timing gets sloppy, with the signal voltage-changes arriving a fraction of a second before or after they should (that's called jitter).

A repeater hears the signals with all these errors, massages the signal it hears, and transmits a clean signal. A repeater should produce an output signal equal in quality to the original signal that left the broadcasting station.

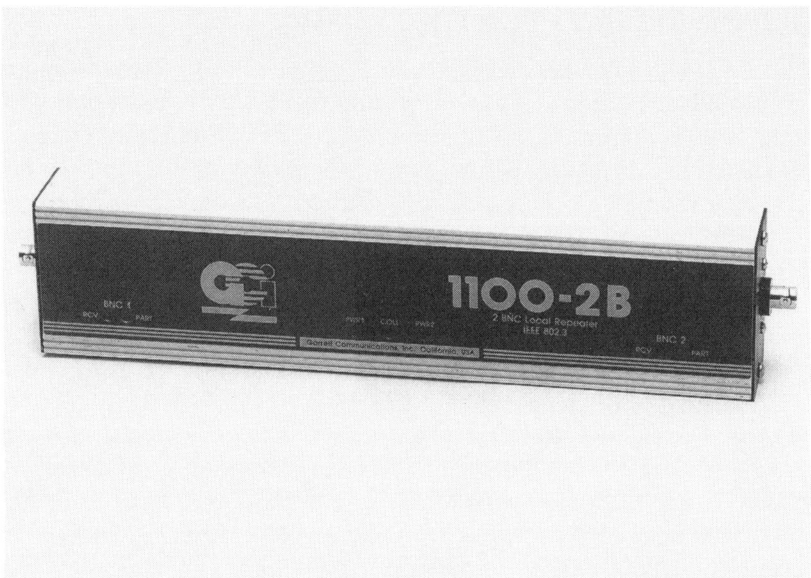

Figure 242 *Repeater with BNC connectors on both ends, for thin Ethernet network. Photo courtesy of Computer System Products Incorporated.*

The IEEE (Institute for Electrical and Electronics Engineers) standards allow a maximum of four repeaters along the signal path between any two stations on the network. This signal path may include up to three segments of coax cable tapped for workstations and up to two IRL segments (Inter Repeater Link segments, the point-to-point links with no workstations tapped into the link segment). If you are willing to put two coax cable IRL segments back-to-back, you may eliminate the central repeater and run one double-long IRL segment—but if you do, that double-length segment counts as two segments when you consider the maximum allowable path length between any two stations. Therefore, the longest path between two workstations may be either 1) three coax segments, four repeaters, and two link segments or 2) three coax segments, three repeaters, and a double-length link segment. While frantically cutting and pasting your dream network diagram, please remember that only one active signal path is allowed between any two points on an Ethernet network (so no circles).

10Base-T repeaters, and Ethernet repeaters designed for large multi-segment LANs, implement the IEEE auto-partition algorithm. They automatically disconnect a malfunctioning segment of the network when collisions on the suspect segment are out of control. A cable break, an unterminated cable, or a faulty connector could easily cause massive collisions that would interfere with the rest of the network if the repeater forwarded this gibberish. When the segment has calmed down (no collisions for a while), the repeater will reconnect it back into the network. Check the diagnostic lights on these repeaters, first thing, if you think you may have a cable or repeater problem.

How to Test a Repeater

If this repeater runs on AC power, be sure it's plugged in and the fuse is good. Check for loose cable connections, and examine the diagnostic lights. If you find nothing wrong, pull the repeater out and replace it with a known-good one.

How to Remove and Install a Repeater

Make sure the network is powered down on both sides of the repeater. It's stupid to fool around with electronic equipment when it's live. We've seen "network experts" melt LAN cards because they were too macho to down the network before disconnecting a cable.

Find the repeater in the ceiling (especially likely with thick coax networks) or in a wiring closet. Unplug it and plug the new one in.

According to IEEE 802.3 specs, repeaters should not be connected to transceivers (cable attachment devices) that generate an SQE test signal. So be certain the SQE (Signal Quality Error test) is disabled on the transceivers that connect your repeater to the coax or fiber optic cable. 10Base-T repeaters are usually connected directly to twisted-pair wire without any transceiver, but you will normally need a transceiver between a repeater and coax or fiber optic cable.

IEEE MAC-Layer Bridges

What's a bridge? Ask three network specialists and you'll get one of three answers.

1. The IEEE (Institute of Electrical and Electronics Engineers) answer: A Media Access Control Bridge as defined in specification 802.1D. An IEEE bridge may connect any combination of Ethernet, Token Ring, and token bus LANS (not ARCNET, they mean the IEEE token bus, which is usually used in factories for process control). The bridge is compatible at the Media Access Control level with each of the networks it will join. So an Ethernet-to-Token Ring bridge looks like an Ethernet node on the Ethernet side, and it looks like a Token Ring node on the Token Ring side. The bridge receives and transmits Ethernet frames (the basic data-package on the cable is called a frame) on the Ethernet side. If the frame should be forwarded to the Token Ring side, the bridge repackages the data into a Token Ring frame and transmits it on the Token Ring network.

These IEEE bridges "allow the interconnection of stations attached to separate LANs as if they were attached to a single LAN," so the bridge is transparent to the workstations. The IEEE suggests three reasons to use a MAC bridge:

1) to connect LANs using different Media Access Control protocols (e.g., Token Ring to Ethernet),
2) to effectively increase the physical size of a LAN (for example, to connect one Ethernet LAN to another Ethernet LAN, with the two together exceeding the length or number-of-stations allowed on a single Ethernet LAN),
3) to partition a single legal-size LAN for administrative or maintenance reasons.

2. The Novell answer: NetWare software running on a file server or a dedicated workstation. This Novell NetWare software is really router software, even though older versions of NetWare called these things

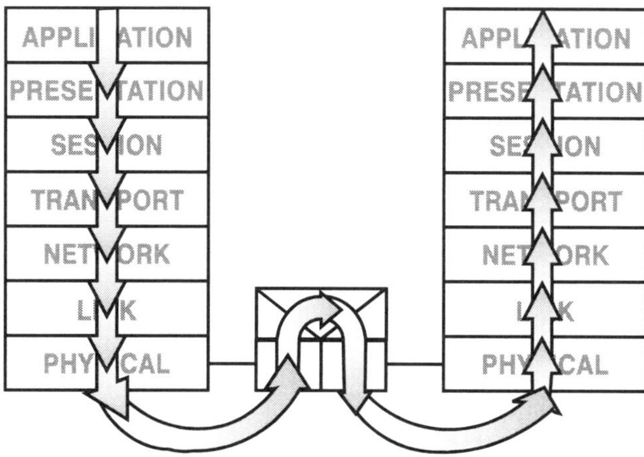

Figure 243 An IEEE MAC bridge functions on the MAC sublayer of the Link Layer.

"bridges." Novell gives some network terms different meanings than the ones used by the rest of the world. We'll be discussing IEEE MAC-Layer bridges in this Data Sheet. If you're dealing with a Novell "bridge," jump to the Data Sheet entitled *A Novell NetWare Router or Bridge* on page 155.

3. Remote Bridges: Network users and manufacturers also commonly use the term "bridge" for LAN-to-WAN (Wide Area Network) hardware. These products link Ethernet, Token Ring, or ARCNET via V.35, RS-232, or RS-422 connectors to T-1 (leased digital telephone line service), to Switched 56 (leased 56 kilobaud digital telephone line service), to X.25 (the packet-switching protocol used by public data networks like Telenet and Tymenet), or even to microwave and satellite connections. If you're dealing with a remote bridge rather than an IEEE MAC-Layer bridge, go to the Data Sheet on gateways. We prefer to call these machines gateways rather than bridges because they do so much more than the simple MAC-Layer bridge described by the IEEE, but some other writers and equipment manufacturers call them bridges. Unfortunately, the terminology hasn't settled down yet.

Where to Find an IEEE MAC Bridge in Your LAN

Many multimedia Ethernet networks use concentrators to connect the twisted-pair segments to the coax and fiber optic cable segments. These concentrators are usually modular, with space for bridge, router, and repeater modules as well as the basic twisted-pair, coax, or fiber optic modules. Some manufacturers design concentrators for both Ethernet and Token Ring modules, and provide Ethernet-to-Token Ring bridge modules as well.

Standalone bridge units are also available, some of which are attractive enough for office use, though we recommend you lock these bridges into a wiring closet with the rest of the delicate networking hardware.

How a MAC-Layer Bridge Works— the Spanning Tree Ethernet Version

A MAC bridge receives a frame, considers the destination address encoded in the frame, and forwards the frame if it should be retransmitted on the other port attached to the other LAN. The bridge is a translator, able to hear Ethernet and speak Token Ring or vice versa. Most bridges have two ports (one to each LAN) though multi-port bridges connecting more than two LANs also exist. In fact, most bridges don't need to translate protocols—many organizations need to partition a network for administrative reasons or wish to connect Ethernet to Ethernet or Token Ring to Token Ring. Therefore, the majority of bridges actually manufactured speak the same protocol on both ports.

A bridge should not forward all the frames it hears. It's not useful to forward frames (retransmit them on the other LAN) if they are not destined for a workstation on the other LAN—these frames would just clutter up the wire. Therefore, each bridge builds a filtering database listing all of the workstations located on the far side of the bridge. Before forwarding a packet, the bridge compares the packet's destination address to this database.

Bridges learn the location of workstations and of other bridges by observing the source address of packets on the wire. If packets from Station A arrive at Port 1, it's safe to assume that Station A is somewhere down the wire on the Port 1 side of this bridge.

Some bridges allow the network manager to explicitly configure the filtering database, specifying which workstations may transmit and receive from which bridge port(s). This allows a manager to connect a local workgroup network to the large company-wide network with a bridge, but limit the workgroup's access to sensitive data stored on the company-wide network.

There must not be two pathways between any two workstations. Network designers should carefully avoid creating loops when they bridge to another network (which may bridge to a third and a fourth network). On the other hand, a failed bridge or a severed cable leading to the bridge leaves the two network segments completely isolated. The IEEE's 802.1(d) Spanning Tree algorithm allows redundant bridge connections between network segments. The redundant bridge(s) act as a backup in case a primary connection fails. When the bridges are powered up they automatically configure themselves to produce one and only one path between any two stations (for some bridges, this means disabling ports that would create a second pathway from one LAN segment to another). If a cable is severed or one of the bridges fails, the other bridges will notice that something is amiss and attempt to reconfigure themselves to provide a single connection between any pair of workstations.

How a MAC-Layer Bridge Works— the Source Routing Token Ring Version

Each Token Ring workstation keeps a copy of the routing table. Token Ring frames contain the routing information right in the frame, so the bridge need only read the frame's routing data, not develop independent routing tables of its own. This is called source routing because the source of the frame, not the bridge, makes all routing decisions.

How to Test a Bridge

Talk to your vendor. The bridge should come with troubleshooting instructions and a warranty.

How to Remove and Install a Bridge

At the cable level, bridges are pretty simple to install. Just plug in the cable and let it rip. A spanning tree bridge is self-configuring. (It automatically learns which stations are on which side of the bridge and which ports should be disabled to prevent duplicate pathways between pairs of workstations.).

A Novell NetWare Router or Bridge

Novell router/bridge is software in NetWare 2.x and 3.x which will:

1. connect Ethernet, ARCNET, and Token Ring network topologies together as long as they are both (or all three) using NetWare,
2. allow you to create a super-size internetwork out of two independent smaller networks (in ARCNET, for example, you are limited to 255 stations—you could use a NetWare router/bridge to allow 300 ARCNET stations to communicate—by setting the 300 stations up on two networks), or
3. partition a network for administrative or maintenance reasons (divide a heavily-trafficked Ethernet segment into two segments, for example, with a separate network card in the file server serving each segment).

All this is done at the Network Layer, working with NetWare's IPX packets and NetWare-assigned network addresses. Novell's router/bridge looks inside the Ethernet, ARCNET, or Token Ring frame, reads the IPX data packet to find the ultimate destination address, then decides whether to forward the packet or not and decides which route the packet should take to its final destination (see Figure 9.3, which shows the NetWare protocol layers).

By comparison, the IEEE has defined a MAC-Layer bridge which works with the Ethernet or Token Ring frame destination address (the outer layer of data address wrappings), not the contents of the frame. If you're looking for information on IEEE's MAC-Layer bridges, see the Data Sheet entitled *IEEE MAC-Layer Bridges* on page 152.

The rest of the world calls these Novell "bridges" routers. Novell has traditionally used idiosyncratic network terminology, and a Novell "bridge" is a good example of Novell-speak. In 1990, Novell decided to conform to conventional definitions of the terms "bridge" and "router," so the old Novell usage is being phased out—for example, the successor to Novell's BRGEN (Bridge Generation) program is named ROUTEGEN. We're with Novell. For the rest of this section we will use the term "router," whether talking about the old NetWare "bridge" or the new stuff.

Where to Find a Novell NetWare Router in Your LAN

In a Novell network, the router is software, not hardware. Router software may, as it happens, be running on this or that particular workstation, but it is the software that makes the router, not any special attribute in the computer that runs that software.

Netware routers located inside the file server are internal routers. The MONITOR utility on your file server console shows the LANs you are connected to—go down to the Available Options box and highlight LAN Information. If you have an internal router you'll see two or more LAN drivers listed, one LAN driver for each Network Interface Card installed in this file server.

Multiple Network Interface Cards and the router software can also be installed in an ordinary workstation computer. This is an external router.

How a NetWare Router Works

Each file server can support up to four Network Interface Cards. If you install more than one card in the file server you've created an internal router (internal for inside the file server). For example, a file server with an Ethernet card and an ARCNET card installed could serve as a router between the two networks. Router software installed on this file server passes data from one network to the other only if the data is addressed to a destination on the far side of the router.

If you don't want to burden the file server with router duties (screening each incoming packet for rebroadcast on the other network), set up a dedicated workstation router (an external router). Install an Ethernet and an ARCNET card in the workstation, then run router software on the workstation. NetWare routers come in both dedicated and non-dedicated modes (a non-dedicated router also runs normal workstation software and functions as a regular workstation as well as a router). Non-dedicated routers sound good, but don't use them. What happens when the workstation application hangs and the operator has to reboot the workstation? The router also comes down, and all the half-transmitted messages between networks are left hanging. A simple XT works fine as a dedicated router, and it's cheap compared to the hassles it deflects.

A router (either internal or external) can connect up to four Ethernet and/or ARCNET networks. But a NetWare router can connect only two Token Ring networks, not four.

Here's an old Ethernet trick to cut the traffic on an overburdened network: Cut the network in half with an internal router at the file server, attaching each of the new networks to a separate Ethernet card in the file server. You've now cut the traffic on each segment in half. Yes, some of the traffic from the other segment will have to be transferred across the router and rebroadcast on this segment, but if you plan carefully you can probably divide the big network into two pieces that send data internally most of the time. For example, put the secretaries and the laser printer on the same segment, with the printer conveniently close to the secretaries that use it. Put the order-takers, and the dot matrix printer they use for invoices, on the other segment. Taking printer traffic off the main network bus can dramatically speed up both segments.

How to Test a NetWare Router

Use COMCHECK or TDX from Thomas-Conrad—we have directions for COMCHECK in Appendix B. If no traffic crosses the router, check the power and network cables at the router. Cables tight? Router software still running? If not, test the computer as a standalone with QAPlus/fe or another reliable diagnostic utility. The router computer must operate flawlessly as a standalone or you're going to have breakdown after breakdown.

Carefully test the cables running from the router to each LAN. They must, of course, be healthy or the router will fail to pass traffic.

The router software could be corrupted, of course. If nothing else works, it might make sense to reload the router software again from the original diskettes and regenerate the router software.

For new router installations: Does each LAN card have a unique address (on the LAN it's attached to)? Did you use the right NetWare LAN driver, interrupt, and I/O address for each network card? Does each network have a unique network address? The router card on a particular LAN cable should use the same network address as the file server(s) on that cable.

If the router is functioning erratically, but there is still communication across it, you're going to have a heck of a time isolating the problem. The network will slow down, of course, but there are many other reasons why the network could slow. It makes sense to check all the other card-and-cable and router-software possibilities before you decide to replace the router.

How to Remove and Install a NetWare Router

Follow the directions in your red NetWare manuals.

Routers

Network routers are star-like packet-sorting machines with multiple networks connected to the router. When a packet comes in, the router reads the destination address enclosed in the packet and sends it out on the correct cable.

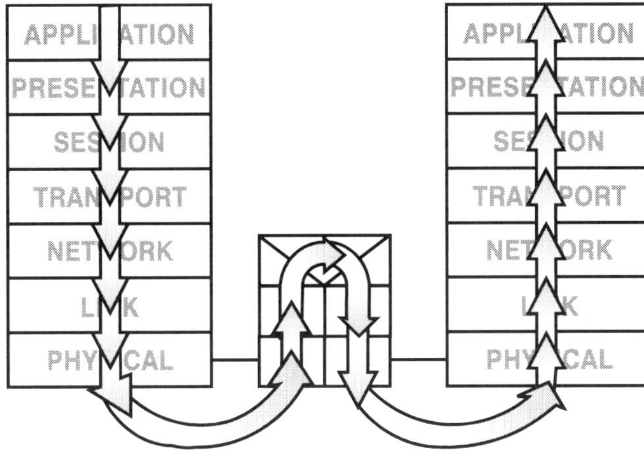

Figure 244 *A router functions on the Network Layer.*

Where to Find A Router in Your LAN

Some routers are PCs running special router software and connected to each network segment with an ordinary Network Interface Card. Other routers are sleek standalone boxes or modules to install in your multimedia wiring hub.

Hardware router boxes are heavy iron. Few small networks need them. If you're trying to segment a heavily-trafficked network into two smaller ones, you're probably better off with a bridge, or with Novell's router/bridge software if it's a NetWare network.

Again, pick a bridge if you merely want to connect one IEEE 802.3 LAN (that means Ethernet or Token Ring) to another 802.3 LAN, or you want to connect a 10Base-T Ethernet network running on twisted-pair cable to a 10Base2 Ethernet network running on coax.

How A Router Works

Routers are designed to work with one (or occasionally more than one) high level network protocol, so all the network segments attached to a router should share the same protocol. NetWare networks use the IPX protocol. UNIX uses the TCP/IP protocol, as do SUN and DEC. NetWare 3.11 and the new UNIX-based Novell NetWare for huge networks are pretty smart, they can use either TCP/IP or IPX. The router knows how to decode the destination address used by the protocol it understands. It compares this address (or often only the first few digits of the address) against the information in its routing tables. The table tells where the packet goes next (what router it goes to next), but it doesn't tell the router the final destination of the packet.

Novell furnishes router software with their NetWare operating system. Set up a PC equipped with a network card for each network segment the router will connect, then use the ROUTEGEN utility to create customized router software for this machine. Though early versions of NetWare called these things "bridges," they are really routers. See *A Novell NetWare Router or Bridge* on page 155 for details.

Most routers are standalone boxes, however, or they are modules for a manufacturer's patented wiring hub. Some routers pass TCP/IP, some pass IPX. Some connect to one cabled network and a digital telephone line (like T-1 or FT-1, Fractional T-1). Other routers have multiple ports, so they simultaneously sort and route the inputs from 3, 6, or 7 networks.

Consider a sophisticated IPX router connected to three Ethernet networks running NetWare and a T-I digital telephone line. This router receives any Ethernet frame addressed to it, on any of the three networks. It opens the Ethernet frame and looks for an IPX packet inside. If it finds the IPX packet, it reads the IPX packet's destination address, looks up this destination in its routing tables, and sends the IPX packet on its way (either down one of the Ethernet cables or across the country on the T-1 line to another router in California). If our router opens an Ethernet frame and finds a Banyan Vines packet inside it throws the packet away. The router doesn't know how Banyan Vines is addressed, so it looks to the router like a malformed IPX packet (garbage!). When data arrives on the T-1 line, the router reads the IPX destination address, looks up the destination in its routing tables, repackages the data in an Ethernet packet, and sends it out on the correct cable.

How to Test A Router

Always check cables and connections before you look for exotic hardware or software failures. Consider all the low-tech possibilities. Does the router have power? Does each of the segments that the router connects function properly on its own (when disconnected from the router)? If the router is software running in a dedicated PC, does the PC function properly as a standalone computer?

When you are convinced that the router itself is suspect, try the diagnostic software the manufacturer should have included with the router. If that doesn't work, call the manufacturer's help line.

How to Remove and Install a Router

Each manufacturer makes a slightly different product; follow their installation instructions. Expensive, self-configuring routers with dynamic routing tables are plug-and-go. But routers with static routing tables can't teach themselves which networks are located where on the grid of intersecting networks. You must enter the routing information in the router's routing table yourself.

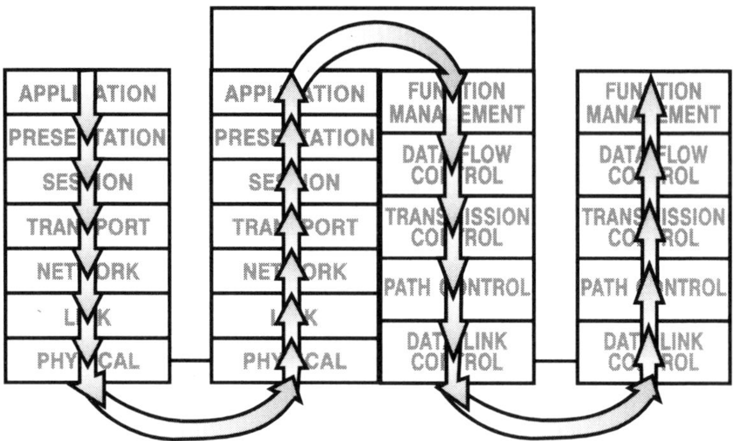

Figure 245 *A gateway from a network to a mainframe using the SNA protocol.*

Gateways

Gateways connect LANs to WANs (Wide Area Networks) and they connects WANs to other WANs.

What Wide Area Networks might you connect to your LAN? You might need to link your LAN to an X.25 packet switching network capable of transferring LAN data across the city or across the country to your organization's remote LAN. You might want to connect an Ethernet or Token Ring network to your IBM mainframe (the mainframe probably uses IBM's SNA protocol). You might use a fast T-1 cross-country data line to link the New York Ethernet LAN to your company's LAN in Boise.

Where to Find Gateways in Your LAN

Gateways are expensive. They're self-contained, so there's no need for the network administrator or the users to check them on a daily basis. Install them in the server-room with the rest of the exotic LAN hardware.

How a Gateway Works

The gateway looks like a regular node to your LAN (for instance, it transmits and receives Ethernet on the Ethernet LAN side). On the WAN side, the gateway uses the WAN protocol (speaking, for example, SNA on the IBM mainframe side of the gateway). If you're using a WAN to connect two LANs you'll obviously require two gateways, one at each end of the WAN.

Here's a quick list of WANs/media:

Phone lines:

T-1 (leased data-grade digital phone line)

Fractional T-1 (a piece of a T-1 line's data-carrying capacity)

Switched 56 (56 kilobaud data-grade dial-up digital phone call)

E-1 (leased data-grade digital phone line, European version of T-1)

Mainframe and Minicomputer connections:

SNA (IBM's WAN, which connects directly to an IBM mainframe. The next Data Sheet section covers 3270 terminal emulation and 3270 gateways, the most common LAN-to-IBM-mainframe connections).

X.25 (the data protocol used by most non-IBM mainframe makers to connect their mainframes to anything in the outside world, including your LAN).

DECnet (Digital Equipment uses the DECnet standard to connect DEC minis, PCs, and Macintoshes. You may use a LAN-to-DECnet gateway to connect your LAN to DEC's LAN).

Public Data Networks:

Tymenet, Telenet, Sprint, and other public packet-switching networks use the X.25 protocol to move your data from one X.25 connection on their network to another X.25 connection, for a fee.

Internet, the national educational/university network, uses the TCP/IP protocol.

How to Test Gateways

These things are black boxes—the vendor sells them to you, you plug them in. If anything goes wrong, call the vendor.

Installing Gateways

If you're planning to install T-1 or Switched 56 gateways, the gateway box itself will have to be approved by the vendor of the T-1 line. This is not usually a problem, but check it before you buy. A lousy T-1 box (one that doesn't conform to the T-1 standards) could crash an entire telephone switch, which controls 30,000 T-1 lines, so it's reasonable to require prior approval.

3270 Cards and 3270 Gateways

Mainframes expect to communicate with dumb terminals, not with PCs. 3270 Cards allow PCs to emulate these dumb terminals. These cards are popular because users don't want two machines (a PC and a dumb terminal) on their desks. 3270 gateways provide multiple 3270-style connections to the mainframe. These connections are typically pooled, so a few connections may be shared by multiple LAN workstations on demand.

Where to Find 3270 Cards and 3270 Gateways in Your LAN

Single-user 3270 cards fit in a workstation and provide only one connection to the IBM mainframe over a coax cable. This cable looks like thin Ethernet ("Cheapernet") complete with BNC connector, but the cable has different impedance, so don't try substituting Ethernet cable for true IBM coax. Very few installations use coax from the workstation card all the way back to the mainframe. Most of the time the wire in the wall is 8-wire 100 ohm twisted-pair cable. 3270 coax cable is 93 ohm. This is a problem because the signal hits the twisted-pair, sees a different impedance, and part of it bounces back—much like light reflects off a window (the

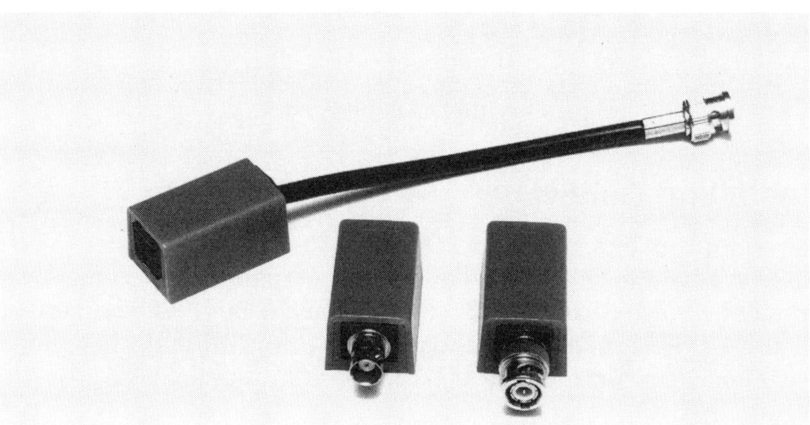

Figure 246 *Baluns to adapt 3270 coax to twisted-pair cable. Photo courtesy of Computer System Products Incorporated.*

impedance of glass and air are very different). An impedance matcher (a balun) allows the signal to make the transmission smoothly, much like non-reflecting coatings on glass minimize reflections. Figure 246 shows typical 3270 baluns.

3270 gateways require a PC (usually dedicated), 3270 cards, and 3270 gateway software, so they are often locked up with the file server to prevent tampering. These gateways may be either directly connected to mainframe concentrators with coax, with an impedance matcher and twisted-pair cable, or they may be remotely connected through T-1 lines or modems.

How a 3270 Card or 3270 Gateway Works

3270 cards and gateways impersonate one or more dumb terminals with a combination of card hardware and software running on the PC. They do not connect your LAN to the mainframe. Instead, they connect one or more workstations on the LAN to the mainframe.

How to Test a 3270 Card

Some manufacturers provide test programs for their 3270 cards, but in general, once you've installed the card and the software it either works and works fine, or it doesn't work at all. If it doesn't work at all, check for proper installation (interrupts!) and recheck your software installation. If you have doubts about the mainframe cable, test it by connecting another computer with a working 3270 card to the suspect cable.

How to Remove and Install 3270 Cards

You'll need a telecommunications expert to sort out the protocols your card needs to communicate with your particular mainframe (they've changed over the years). Work with an expert or a 3270 equipment manufacturer who comes highly recommended, most LAN managers are too busy to also become experts in 3270 emulation.

If you're installing a 3270 card in a PC, be sure you're using a unique interrupt. QAPlus/fe will help here because it lists the interrupts already in use at the workstation, including the network interface card and its interrupts.

Communications Servers

Communications servers allow networked PCs to dial out and/or allow off-site LAN-users to dial in. Modem servers provide dial-out access to a pool of modems shared by network users. Access servers allow one or more remote users to dial in to the network. Some writers call a gateway to a mainframe a communications server, but we treat it separately. See *Gateways*, on page 158, if you're talking about PC to mainframe communication.

These communications servers allow users to upload or download documents from the LAN. They are not intended to allow a remote user to work on the LAN like a regular workstation—the data transfer speeds across a phone line are too slow to do this without driving your users crazy.

Where to Find the Communications Server in Your LAN

Most LANs have no specialized communications servers. Most LANs do not need networked modems, nor do they need to support remote dial-in access. If you have a modem in your workstation, but no other user on the network can use your modem, then you have a local modem. Troubleshoot local modem problems with our standalone PC troubleshooting book, *Fix Your Own PC*. Remember that your workstation's network card uses an interrupt—so be sure to check for interrupt conflicts between modem and network card.

Most communications servers are dedicated computers that only do communications, they cannot simultaneously function as workstations. This makes sense, since communications take so much processing power.

It also makes sense to lock these communications servers in the file server room with the rest of the exotic LAN hardware. No one except the system administrator should be meddling with it.

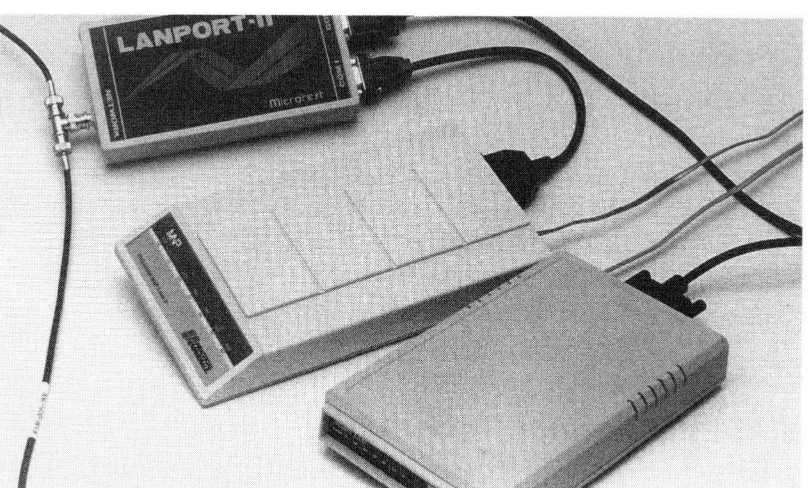

Figure 247 *The LANPORT-II, a special modem server, is on a thin Ethernet network with a pair of shared modems.*

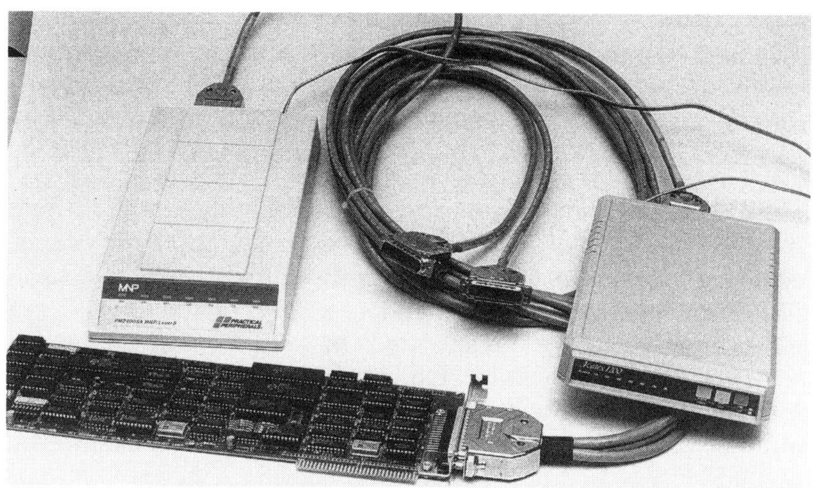

Figure 248 *Novell's WNIM+ card is installed in a dedicated 386 PC. A single WNIM+ card can drive four paired modems.*

How a Communications Server Works

There are two categories of communications servers:

Type 1. The application program is running on a computer on the network, and the communications server paints the screens from that applications program on your remote terminal. Type 1 servers and software:

- require a lot of processing power in the machine(s) on the LAN that run the program
- use relatively little data transfer up and down the phone line
- require a high-speed 386 server loaded with memory to service many callers, or a slave computer on the LAN to service each caller. Some programs take the big-server tack (e.g., Novell's WINM+ board which can service four callers, and four boards

can be installed in a communications server for a total of 16 callers per communications server); other programs use one-machine-per-user (e.g., PCAnywhere, which will run on almost anything, but will only service a single user).

Type 2. The program is running on the remote computer and the distant computer sends pseudo-frames back to the communications server on the LAN, which translates these pseudo-frames into real frames and sends them out on the LAN cable. There are a number of versions of these programs, and each program uses its own tricks to compress data transfer. Nevertheless, it is an inherently inefficient way to do business over the phone.

- this is a relatively rare design
- it requires a lot of data transmission up and down the phone line
- it tends to be implemented in small, inexpensive, easy-to-install boxes.

How to Install and Test a Communications Server

This depends on the server. Follow the manufacturer's instructions carefully. Take the normal precautions when installing an internal card—which may require an interrupt, use an I/O address, and/or use a DMA channel.

These communications servers are really sophisticated pieces of equipment and have a lot of subtle angles. For example, most Type 1 servers equipped with a monochrome video screen will only be able to transmit monochrome video images out the phone wire—ergo, they can only run monochrome software. Certain kinds of software will just not run remotely. For example, Lotus Express (a very popular front end for MCI Mail) generally will not run remotely on one of these communications servers because it's a TSR and these communications servers don't like TSRs.

PART III
The Troubleshooting Flowcharts

Introduction to the Troubleshooting Flowcharts

Troubleshooting requires a clear mind and the ability to think about a problem without prejudice. Many different hardware or software malfunctions can cause the same error symptoms on a LAN. If you approach troubleshooting with preconceptions, with a fixed idea of what the problem is, you may never be able to fix the actual LAN because you are blinded by the theoretical LAN in your head. In these charts, and the preceding Data Sheets, we provide the information that you need to make good decisions—it is up to you, however, to make the right decisions.

The Biggest Time-Saving Secret We Know

Differentiate between individual-PC hardware malfunctions and network malfunctions.

If a particular problem is located on one machine, completely separate that machine from the network and make sure it works. QAPlus/fe is a very good starting point for analyzing problems. If you find any problems with the standalone machine, fix them. You might have to remove the network card if it is conflicting with other hardware in the PC. Yank the network card if you have any doubts. If you need any help, *Fix Your Own PC*, our standalone PC troubleshooting book, covers the specific steps.

We recommend you buy QAPlus/fe or some other standalone PC diagnostic software. Even the best diagnostic software is not 100 percent correct. Occasionally, it will warn you about problems that you do not have, and it will sometimes miss the troubles you do have. However, such programs do a good job of quickly catching the obvious problems. As you use your favorite diagnostic software with your own equipment you will gradually understand its quirks and it will become even more valuable.

Our Troubleshooting Flowcharts

We have broken network troubleshooting into simple steps and have outlined those steps in the flowcharts that follow. We think they cover almost every situation that you will run into. If they don't, let us know.

Problem Solved means we think you have found your problem. It is worth going through the flowcharts one more time, after you get problem solved, to make sure the problems are all fixed. Often a machine will have several different problems at once.

Wrong Turn means that we don't think you should be at this place. Go through the flowcharts again, with a helper if possible, and see if you get a different answer. If you end up at wrong turn again let us know. Logical inconsistency is a hobby of ours.

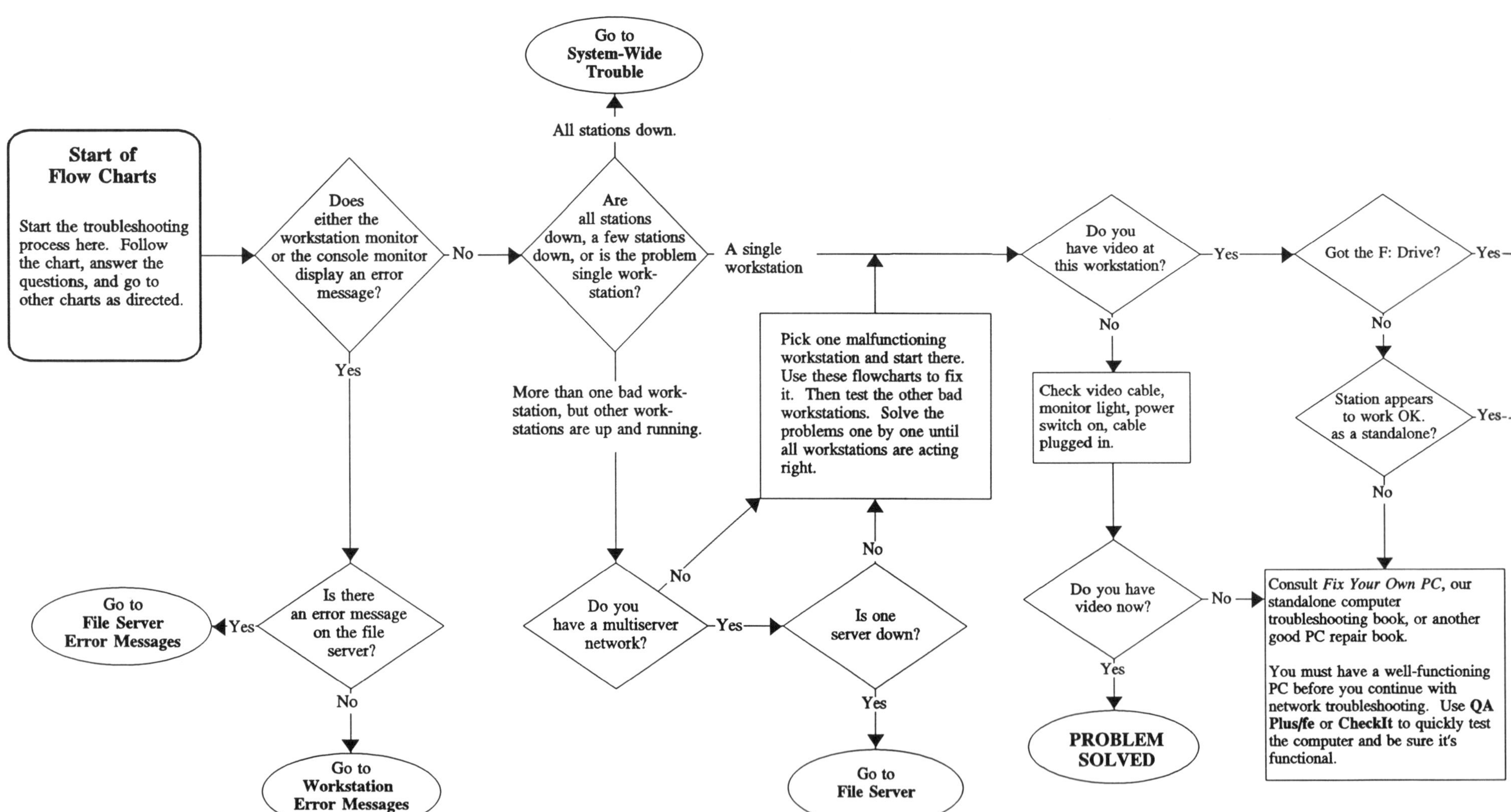
Start of Flow Charts
Start the troubleshooting process here. Follow the chart, answer the questions, and go to other charts as directed.
Does either the workstation monitor or the console monitor display an error message?
No
Yes
Is there an error message on the file server?
Yes
Go to File Server Error Messages
No
Go to Workstation Error Messages
Are all stations down, a few stations down, or is the problem single workstation?
All stations down.
Go to System-Wide Trouble
More than one bad workstation, but other workstations are up and running.
Do you have a multiserver network?
No
Yes
Is one server down?
No
Yes
Go to File Server
Pick one malfunctioning workstation and start there. Use these flowcharts to fix it. Then test the other bad workstations. Solve the problems one by one until all workstations are acting right.
A single workstation
Do you have video at this workstation?
Yes
No
Check video cable, monitor light, power switch on, cable plugged in.
Do you have video now?
Yes
PROBLEM SOLVED
No
Got the F: Drive?
Yes
No
Station appears to work OK. as a standalone?
Yes
No
Consult Fix Your Own PC, our standalone computer troubleshooting book, or another good PC repair book.
You must have a well-functioning PC before you continue with network troubleshooting. Use QA Plus/fe or CheckIt to quickly test the computer and be sure it's functional.

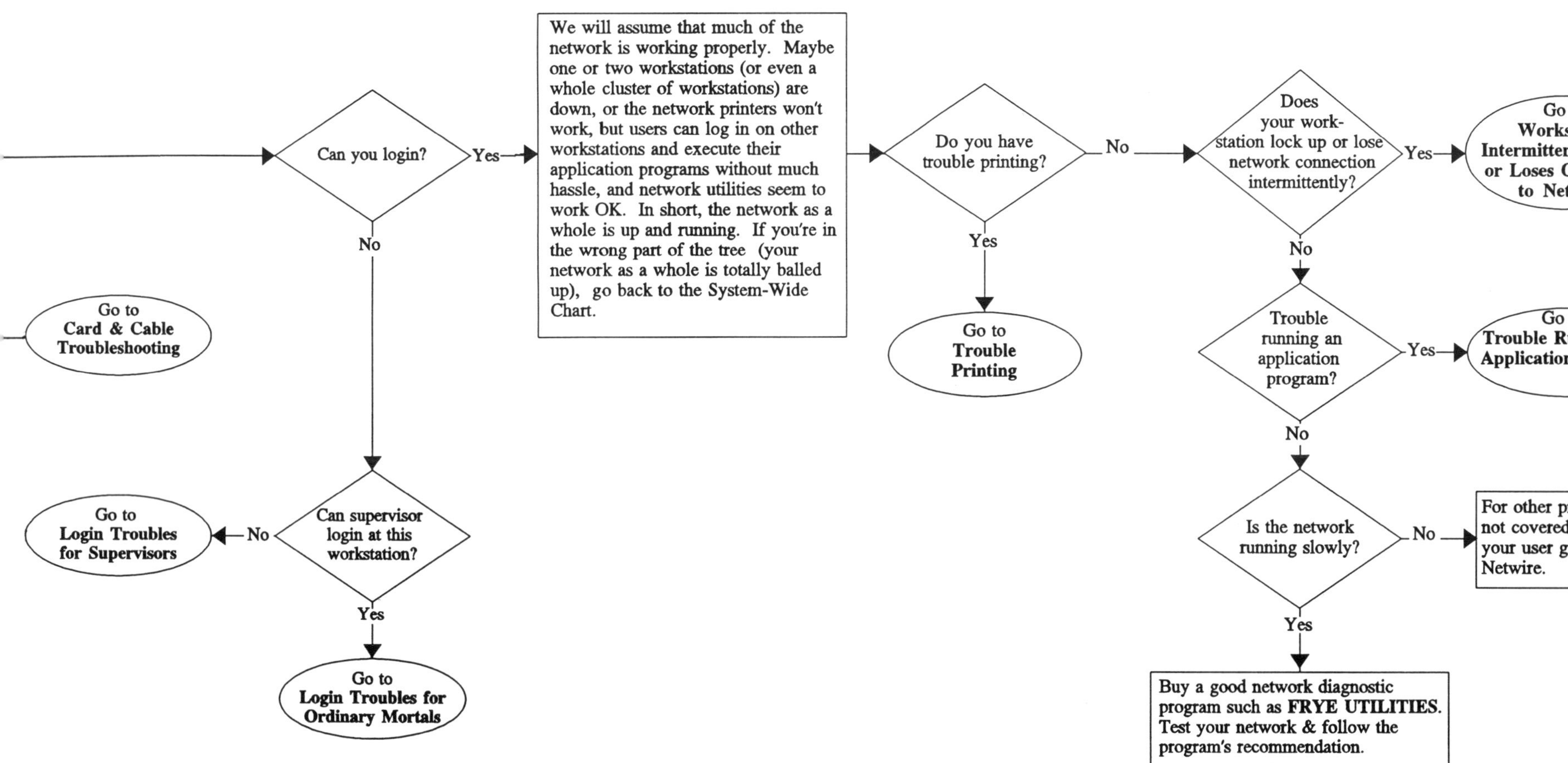

Can you login?
Yes
No
We will assume that much of the network is working properly. Maybe one or two workstations (or even a whole cluster of workstations) are down, or the network printers won't work, but users can log in on other workstations and execute their application programs without much hassle, and network utilities seem to work OK. In short, the network as a whole is up and running. If you're in the wrong part of the tree (your network as a whole is totally balled up), go back to the System-Wide Chart.
Do you have trouble printing?
No
Yes
Go to **Trouble Printing**
Does your work-station lock up or lose network connection intermittently?
Yes
Go to **Workstation Intermittently Locks or Loses Connection to Network**
No
Trouble running an application program?
Yes
Go to **Trouble Running an Application Program**
No
Is the network running slowly?
No
For other problems not covered here, try your user group or Netwire.
Yes
Buy a good network diagnostic program such as **FRYE UTILITIES**. Test your network & follow the program's recommendation.
Go to **Card & Cable Troubleshooting**
Can supervisor login at this workstation?
No
Go to **Login Troubles for Supervisors**
Yes
Go to **Login Troubles for Ordinary Mortals**

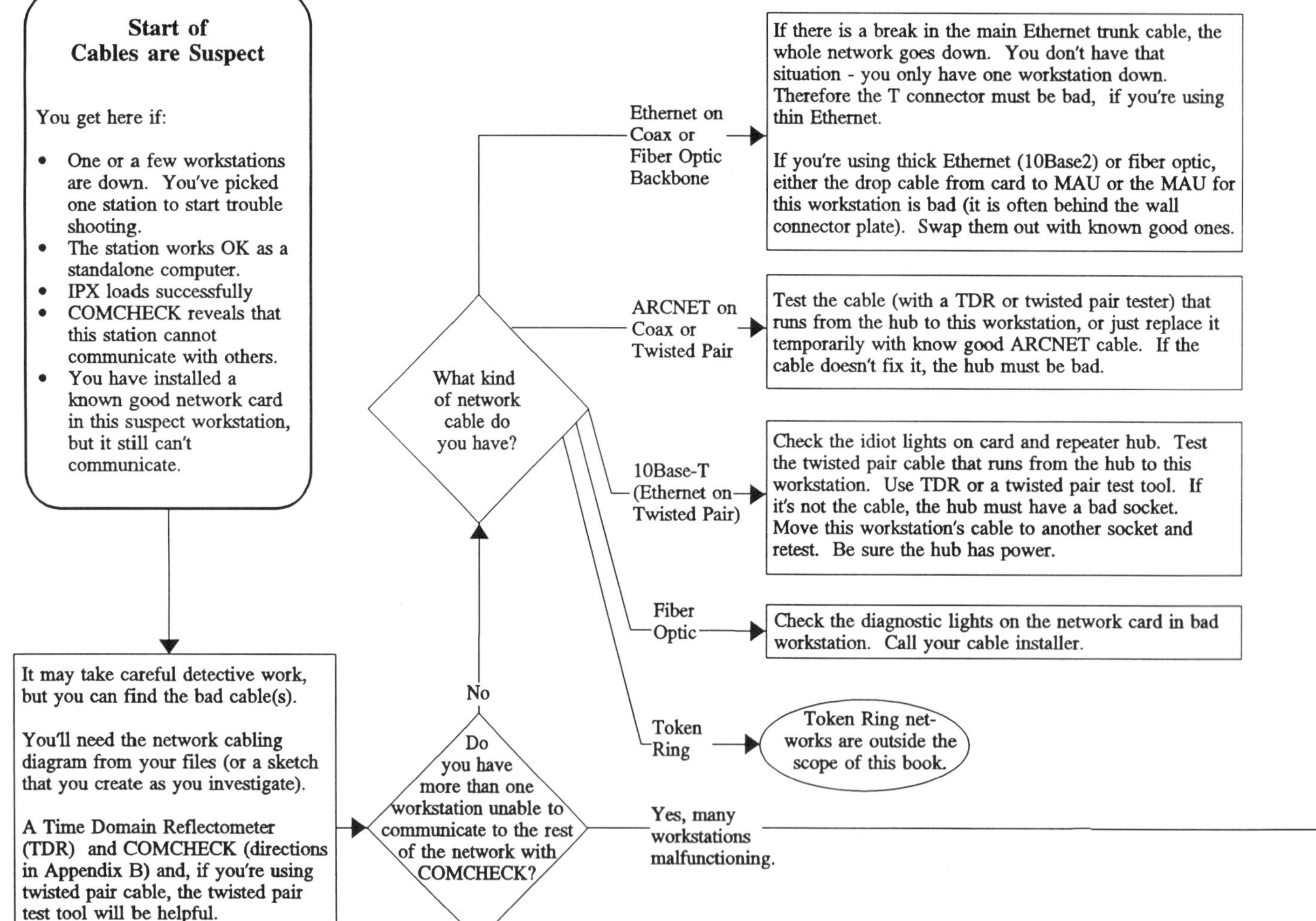
Start of
Cables are Suspect
You get here if:
• One or a few workstations are down. You've picked one station to start trouble shooting.
• The station works OK as a standalone computer.
• IPX loads successfully
• COMCHECK reveals that this station cannot communicate with others.
• You have installed a known good network card in this suspect workstation, but it still can't communicate.
It may take careful detective work, but you can find the bad cable(s).
You'll need the network cabling diagram from your files (or a sketch that you create as you investigate).
A Time Domain Reflectometer (TDR) and COMCHECK (directions in Appendix B) and, if you're using twisted pair cable, the twisted pair test tool will be helpful.
Do you have more than one workstation unable to communicate to the rest of the network with COMCHECK?
No
Yes, many workstations malfunctioning.
What kind of network cable do you have?
Ethernet on Coax or Fiber Optic Backbone
If there is a break in the main Ethernet trunk cable, the whole network goes down. You don't have that situation - you only have one workstation down. Therefore the T connector must be bad, if you're using thin Ethernet.
If you're using thick Ethernet (10Base2) or fiber optic, either the drop cable from card to MAU or the MAU for this workstation is bad (it is often behind the wall connector plate). Swap them out with known good ones.
ARCNET on Coax or Twisted Pair
Test the cable (with a TDR or twisted pair tester) that runs from the hub to this workstation, or just replace it temporarily with know good ARCNET cable. If the cable doesn't fix it, the hub must be bad.
10Base-T (Ethernet on Twisted Pair)
Check the idiot lights on card and repeater hub. Test the twisted pair cable that runs from the hub to this workstation. Use TDR or a twisted pair test tool. If it's not the cable, the hub must have a bad socket. Move this workstation's cable to another socket and retest. Be sure the hub has power.
Fiber Optic
Check the diagnostic lights on the network card in bad workstation. Call your cable installer.
Token Ring
Token Ring networks are outside the scope of this book.

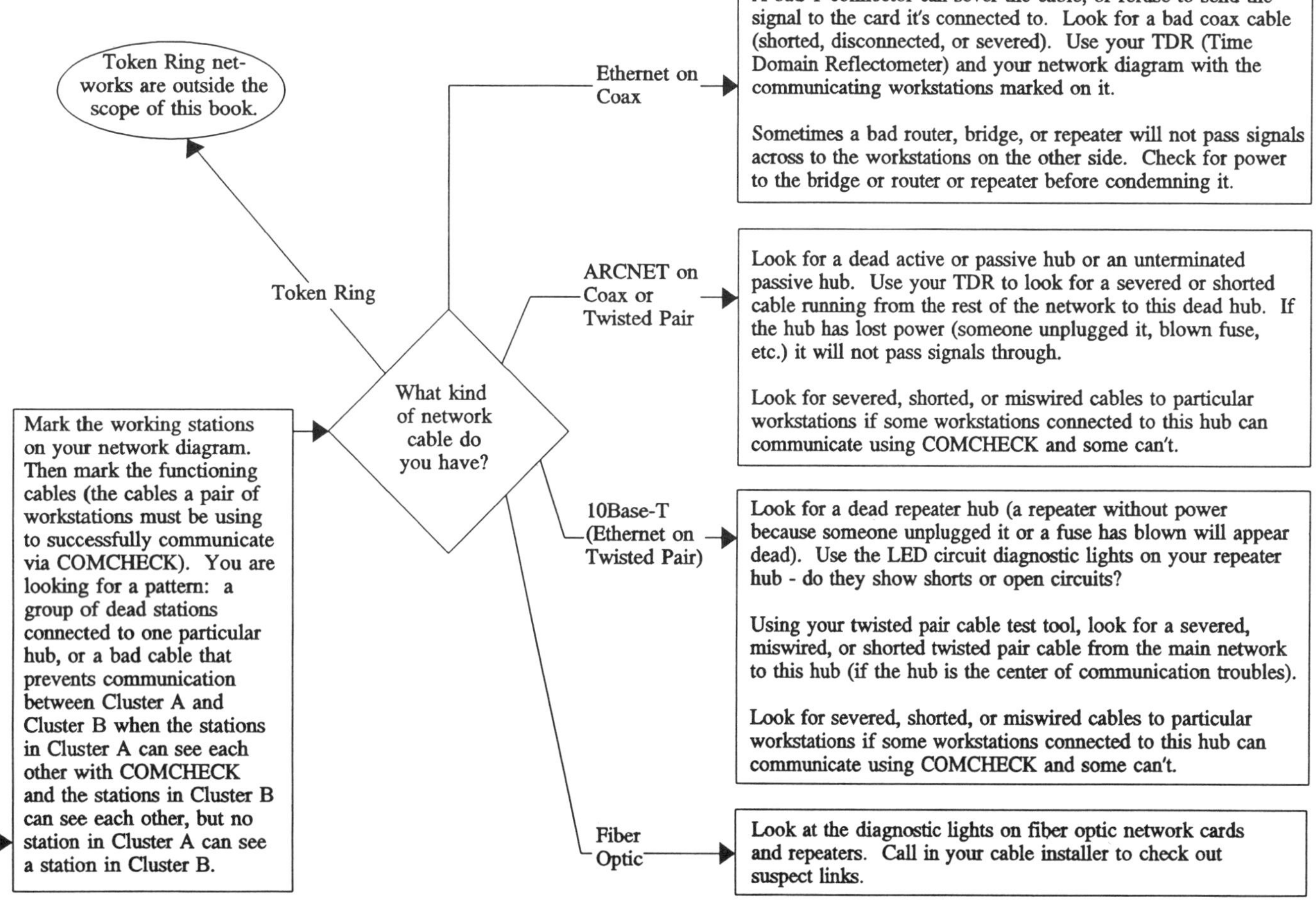
Token Ring networks are outside the scope of this book.
Token Ring
Mark the working stations on your network diagram. Then mark the functioning cables (the cables a pair of workstations must be using to successfully communicate via COMCHECK). You are looking for a pattern: a group of dead stations connected to one particular hub, or a bad cable that prevents communication between Cluster A and Cluster B when the stations in Cluster A can see each other with COMCHECK and the stations in Cluster B can see each other, but no station in Cluster A can see a station in Cluster B.
What kind of network cable do you have?
Ethernet on Coax
A bad T-connector can sever the cable, or refuse to send the signal to the card it's connected to. Look for a bad coax cable (shorted, disconnected, or severed). Use your TDR (Time Domain Reflectometer) and your network diagram with the communicating workstations marked on it.
Sometimes a bad router, bridge, or repeater will not pass signals across to the workstations on the other side. Check for power to the bridge or router or repeater before condemning it.
ARCNET on Coax or Twisted Pair
Look for a dead active or passive hub or an unterminated passive hub. Use your TDR to look for a severed or shorted cable running from the rest of the network to this dead hub. If the hub has lost power (someone unplugged it, blown fuse, etc.) it will not pass signals through.
Look for severed, shorted, or miswired cables to particular workstations if some workstations connected to this hub can communicate using COMCHECK and some can't.
10Base-T (Ethernet on Twisted Pair)
Look for a dead repeater hub (a repeater without power because someone unplugged it or a fuse has blown will appear dead). Use the LED circuit diagnostic lights on your repeater hub - do they show shorts or open circuits?
Using your twisted pair cable test tool, look for a severed, miswired, or shorted twisted pair cable from the main network to this hub (if the hub is the center of communication troubles).
Look for severed, shorted, or miswired cables to particular workstations if some workstations connected to this hub can communicate using COMCHECK and some can't.
Fiber Optic
Look at the diagnostic lights on fiber optic network cards and repeaters. Call in your cable installer to check out suspect links.

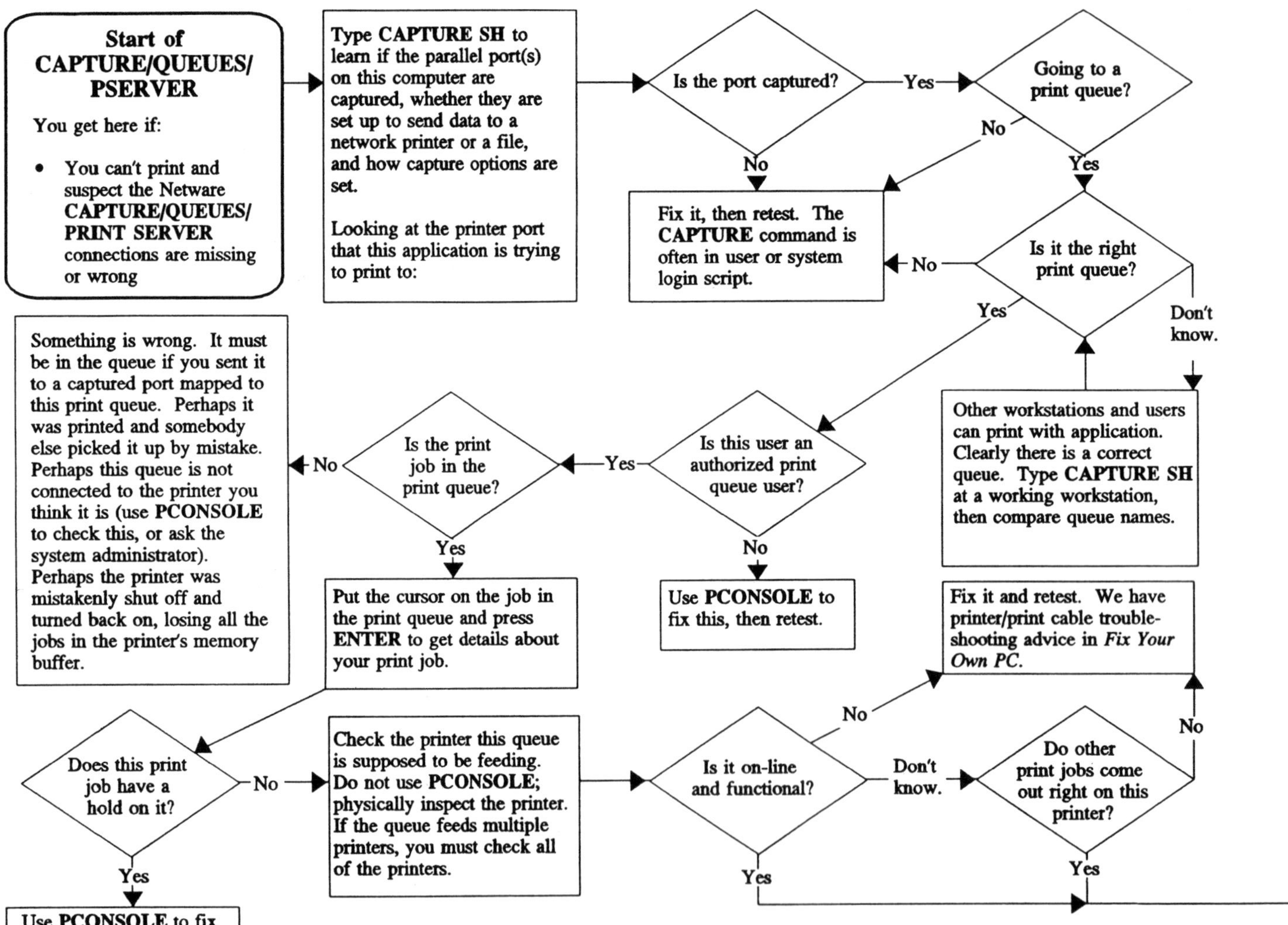
Start of CAPTURE/QUEUES/ PSERVER
You get here if:
• You can't print and suspect the Netware CAPTURE/QUEUES/ PRINT SERVER connections are missing or wrong
Type CAPTURE SH to learn if the parallel port(s) on this computer are captured, whether they are set up to send data to a network printer or a file, and how capture options are set.
Looking at the printer port that this application is trying to print to:
Is the port captured?
Yes
No
Going to a print queue?
No
Yes
Fix it, then retest. The CAPTURE command is often in user or system login script.
No
Is it the right print queue?
Yes
Don't know.
Other workstations and users can print with application. Clearly there is a correct queue. Type CAPTURE SH at a working workstation, then compare queue names.
Is this user an authorized print queue user?
Yes
No
Use PCONSOLE to fix this, then retest.
Is the print job in the print queue?
No
Yes
Something is wrong. It must be in the queue if you sent it to a captured port mapped to this print queue. Perhaps it was printed and somebody else picked it up by mistake. Perhaps this queue is not connected to the printer you think it is (use PCONSOLE to check this, or ask the system administrator). Perhaps the printer was mistakenly shut off and turned back on, losing all the jobs in the printer's memory buffer.
Put the cursor on the job in the print queue and press ENTER to get details about your print job.
Does this print job have a hold on it?
No
Yes
Use PCONSOLE to fix this, then retest.
Check the printer this queue is supposed to be feeding. Do not use PCONSOLE; physically inspect the printer. If the queue feeds multiple printers, you must check all of the printers.
Is it on-line and functional?
No
Don't know.
Yes
Fix it and retest. We have printer/print cable trouble-shooting advice in Fix Your Own PC.
Do other print jobs come out right on this printer?
No
Yes

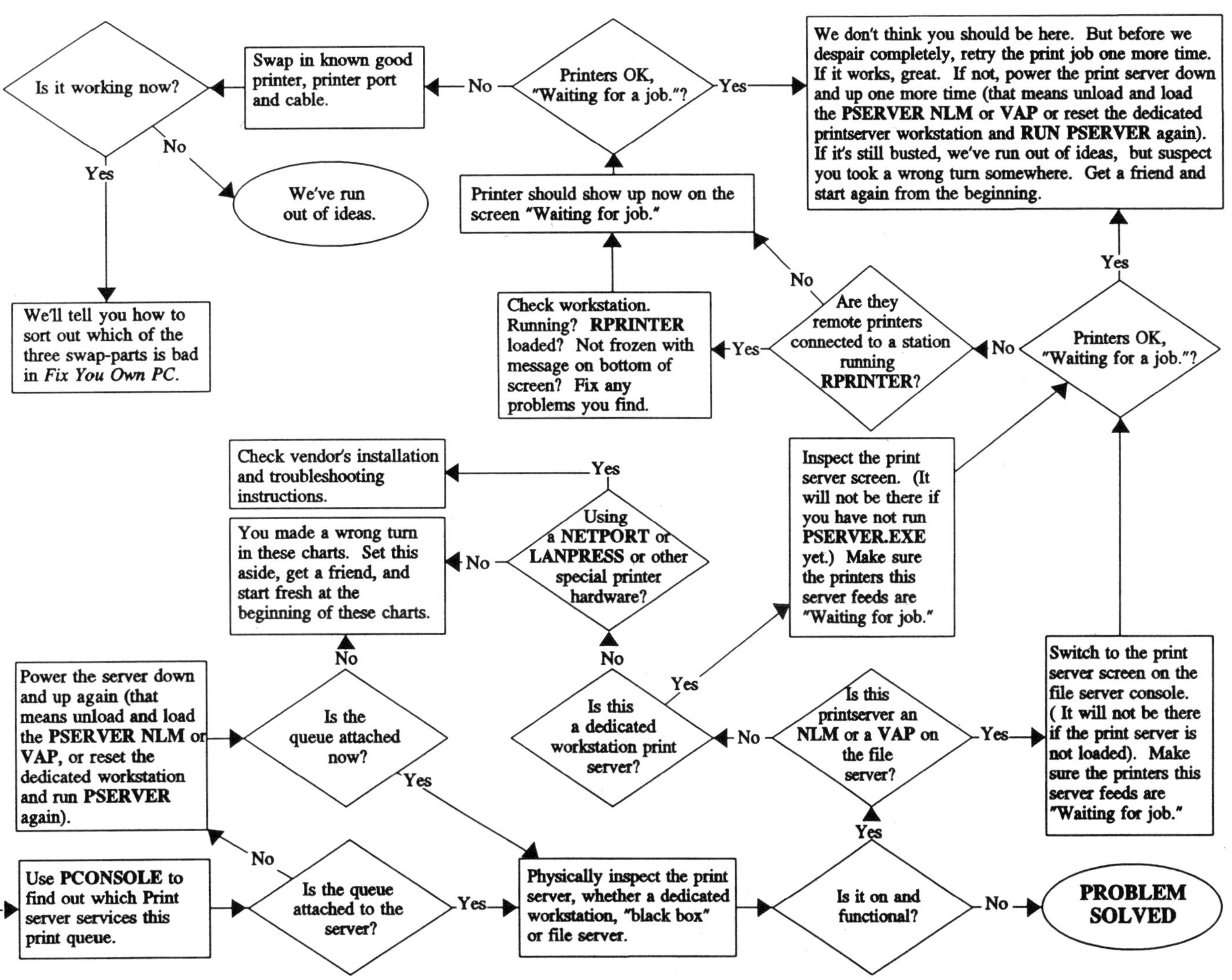

Is it working now?
Swap in known good printer, printer port and cable.
No
Printers OK, "Waiting for a job."?
Yes
We don't think you should be here. But before we despair completely, retry the print job one more time. If it works, great. If not, power the print server down and up one more time (that means unload and load the PSERVER NLM or VAP or reset the dedicated printserver workstation and RUN PSERVER again). If it's still busted, we've run out of ideas, but suspect you took a wrong turn somewhere. Get a friend and start again from the beginning.
No
Yes
We've run out of ideas.
Printer should show up now on the screen "Waiting for job."
We'll tell you how to sort out which of the three swap-parts is bad in Fix You Own PC.
Check workstation. Running? RPRINTER loaded? Not frozen with message on bottom of screen? Fix any problems you find.
Yes
Are they remote printers connected to a station running RPRINTER?
No
No
Printers OK, "Waiting for a job."?
Yes
Check vendor's installation and troubleshooting instructions.
Yes
Using a NETPORT or LANPRESS or other special printer hardware?
No
You made a wrong turn in these charts. Set this aside, get a friend, and start fresh at the beginning of these charts.
Inspect the print server screen. (It will not be there if you have not run PSERVER.EXE yet.) Make sure the printers this server feeds are "Waiting for job."
No
No
Power the server down and up again (that means unload and load the PSERVER NLM or VAP, or reset the dedicated workstation and run PSERVER again).
Is the queue attached now?
Yes
Is this a dedicated workstation print server?
Yes
No
Is this printserver an NLM or a VAP on the file server?
Yes
Switch to the print server screen on the file server console. (It will not be there if the print server is not loaded). Make sure the printers this server feeds are "Waiting for job."
No
Yes
Use PCONSOLE to find out which Print server services this print queue.
Is the queue attached to the server?
Yes
Physically inspect the print server, whether a dedicated workstation, "black box" or file server.
Is it on and functional?
No
PROBLEM SOLVED

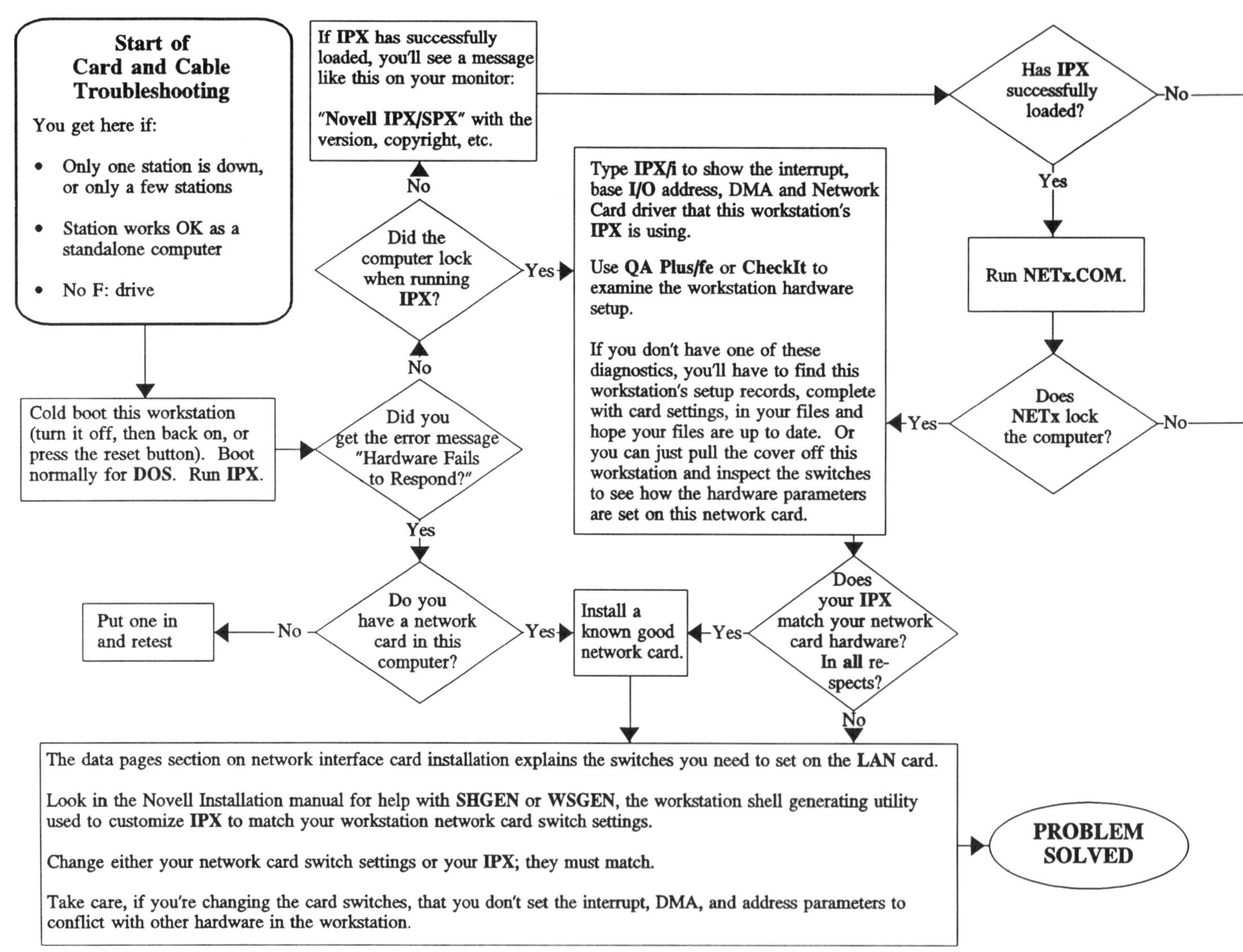
Start of
Card and Cable
Troubleshooting
You get here if:
• Only one station is down, or only a few stations
• Station works OK as a standalone computer
• No F: drive
Cold boot this workstation (turn it off, then back on, or press the reset button). Boot normally for DOS. Run IPX.
Did you get the error message "Hardware Fails to Respond?"
No
Did the computer lock when running IPX?
No
If IPX has successfully loaded, you'll see a message like this on your monitor:
"Novell IPX/SPX" with the version, copyright, etc.
Has IPX successfully loaded?
No
Yes
Run NETx.COM.
Does NETx lock the computer?
No
Yes
Yes
Type IPX/i to show the interrupt, base I/O address, DMA and Network Card driver that this workstation's IPX is using.
Use QA Plus/fe or CheckIt to examine the workstation hardware setup.
If you don't have one of these diagnostics, you'll have to find this workstation's setup records, complete with card settings, in your files and hope your files are up to date. Or you can just pull the cover off this workstation and inspect the switches to see how the hardware parameters are set on this network card.
Yes
Do you have a network card in this computer?
No
Put one in and retest
Yes
Install a known good network card.
Yes
Does your IPX match your network card hardware? In all respects?
No
The data pages section on network interface card installation explains the switches you need to set on the LAN card.
Look in the Novell Installation manual for help with SHGEN or WSGEN, the workstation shell generating utility used to customize IPX to match your workstation network card switch settings.
Change either your network card switch settings or your IPX; they must match.
Take care, if you're changing the card switches, that you don't set the interrupt, DMA, and address parameters to conflict with other hardware in the workstation.
PROBLEM SOLVED

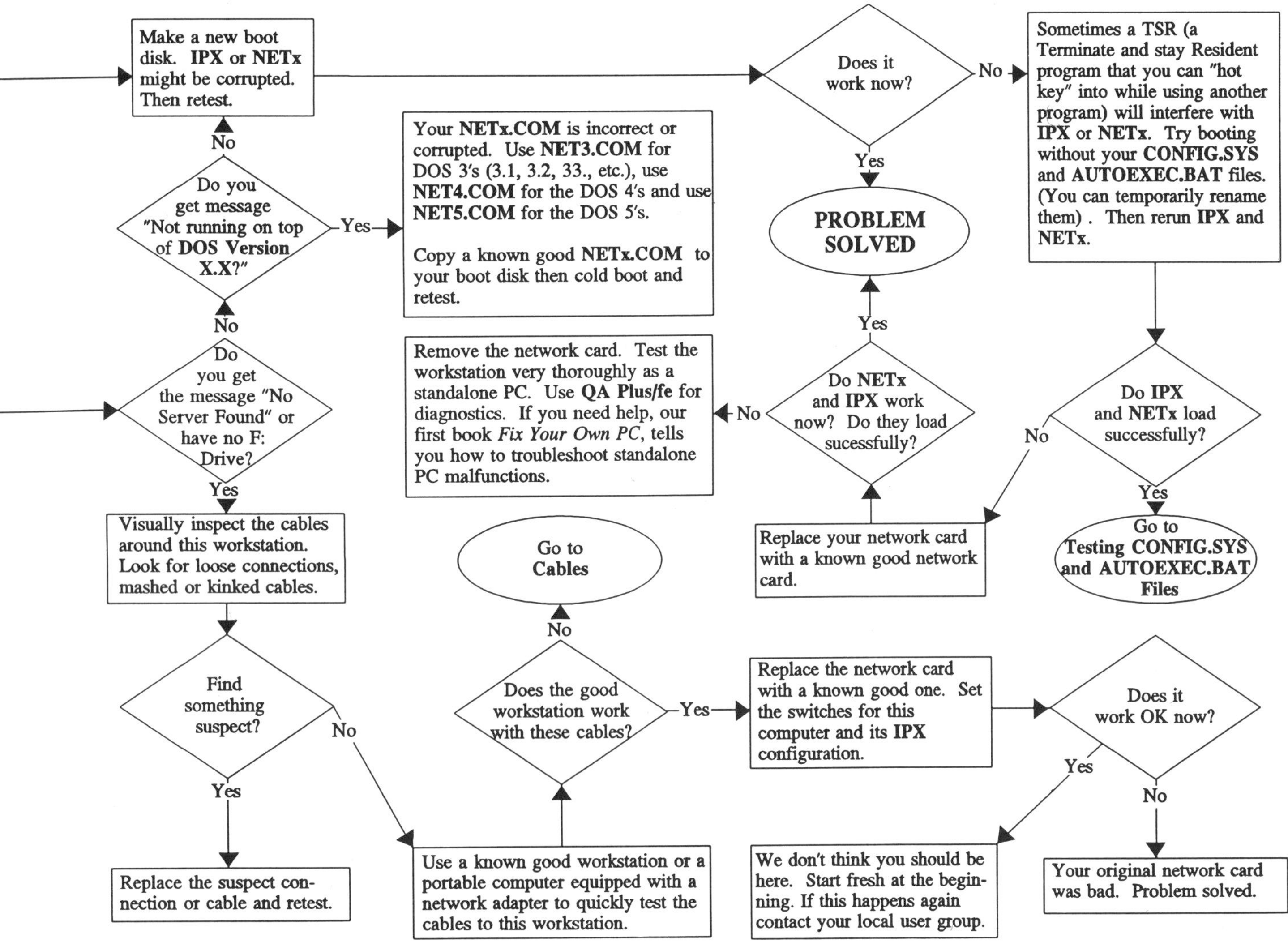

Make a new boot disk. IPX or NETx might be corrupted. Then retest.
Does it work now?
No
Sometimes a TSR (a Terminate and stay Resident program that you can "hot key" into while using another program) will interfere with IPX or NETx. Try booting without your CONFIG.SYS and AUTOEXEC.BAT files. (You can temporarily rename them) . Then rerun IPX and NETx.
No
Do you get message "Not running on top of DOS Version X.X?"
Yes
Your NETx.COM is incorrect or corrupted. Use NET3.COM for DOS 3's (3.1, 3.2, 33., etc.), use NET4.COM for the DOS 4's and use NET5.COM for the DOS 5's.
Copy a known good NETx.COM to your boot disk then cold boot and retest.
Yes
PROBLEM SOLVED
Yes
No
Do you get the message "No Server Found" or have no F: Drive?
Remove the network card. Test the workstation very thoroughly as a standalone PC. Use QA Plus/fe for diagnostics. If you need help, our first book Fix Your Own PC, tells you how to troubleshoot standalone PC malfunctions.
No
Do NETx and IPX work now? Do they load sucessfully?
Do IPX and NETx load successfully?
No
Yes
Yes
Visually inspect the cables around this workstation. Look for loose connections, mashed or kinked cables.
Go to Cables
Replace your network card with a known good network card.
Go to Testing CONFIG.SYS and AUTOEXEC.BAT Files
No
Find something suspect?
No
Does the good workstation work with these cables?
Yes
Replace the network card with a known good one. Set the switches for this computer and its IPX configuration.
Does it work OK now?
Yes
Yes
No
Replace the suspect connection or cable and retest.
Use a known good workstation or a portable computer equipped with a network adapter to quickly test the cables to this workstation.
We don't think you should be here. Start fresh at the beginning. If this happens again contact your local user group.
Your original network card was bad. Problem solved.

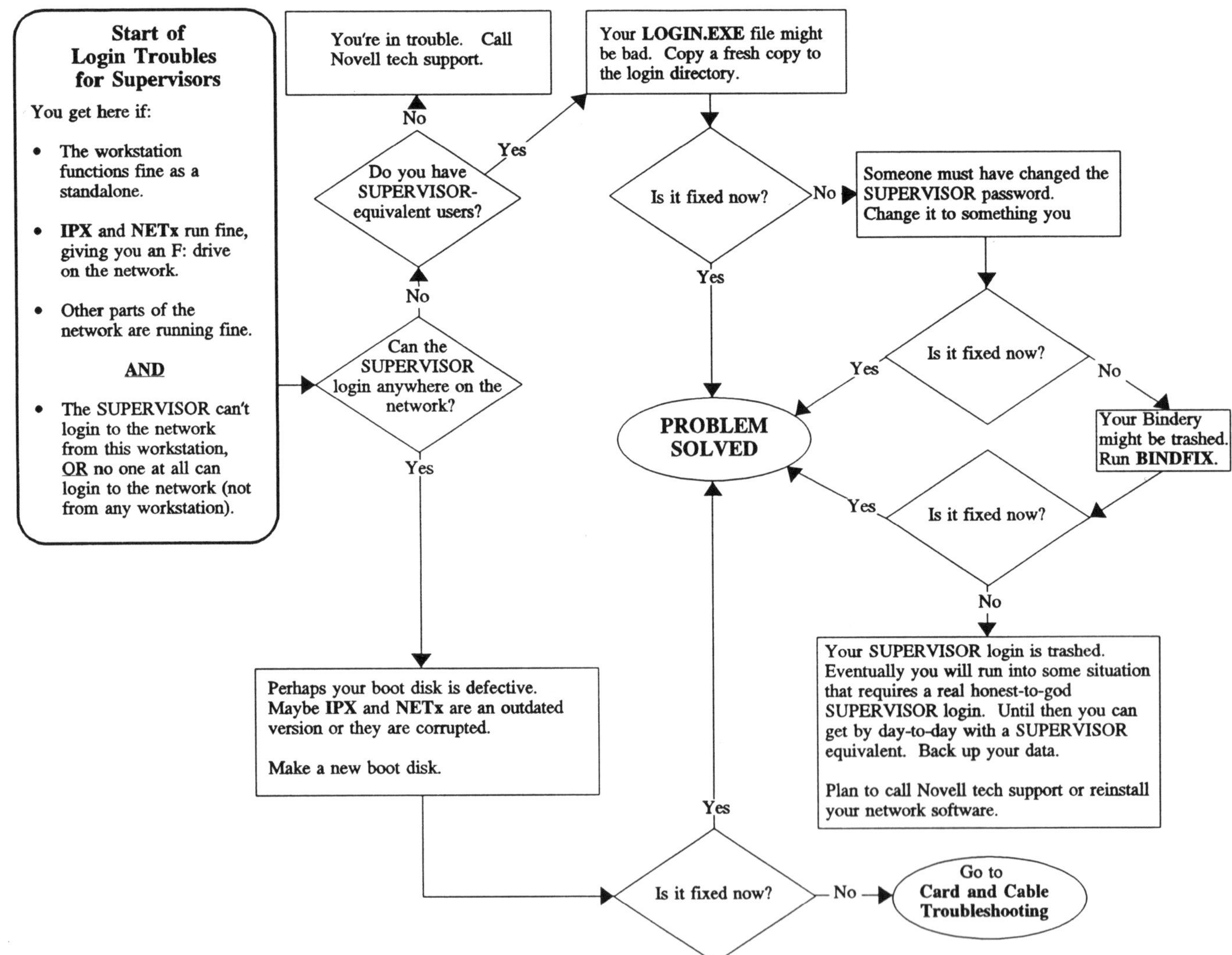
Start of
Login Troubles
for Supervisors
You get here if:
• The workstation functions fine as a standalone.
• IPX and NETx run fine, giving you an F: drive on the network.
• Other parts of the network are running fine.
AND
• The SUPERVISOR can't login to the network from this workstation, OR no one at all can login to the network (not from any workstation).
Can the SUPERVISOR login anywhere on the network?
No
Do you have SUPERVISOR-equivalent users?
No
You're in trouble. Call Novell tech support.
Yes
Your LOGIN.EXE file might be bad. Copy a fresh copy to the login directory.
Is it fixed now?
No
Someone must have changed the SUPERVISOR password. Change it to something you
Yes
Is it fixed now?
Yes
No
Your Bindery might be trashed. Run BINDFIX.
Is it fixed now?
Yes
No
Your SUPERVISOR login is trashed. Eventually you will run into some situation that requires a real honest-to-god SUPERVISOR login. Until then you can get by day-to-day with a SUPERVISOR equivalent. Back up your data.
Plan to call Novell tech support or reinstall your network software.
PROBLEM SOLVED
Yes
Perhaps your boot disk is defective. Maybe IPX and NETx are an outdated version or they are corrupted.
Make a new boot disk.
Is it fixed now?
Yes
No
Go to Card and Cable Troubleshooting

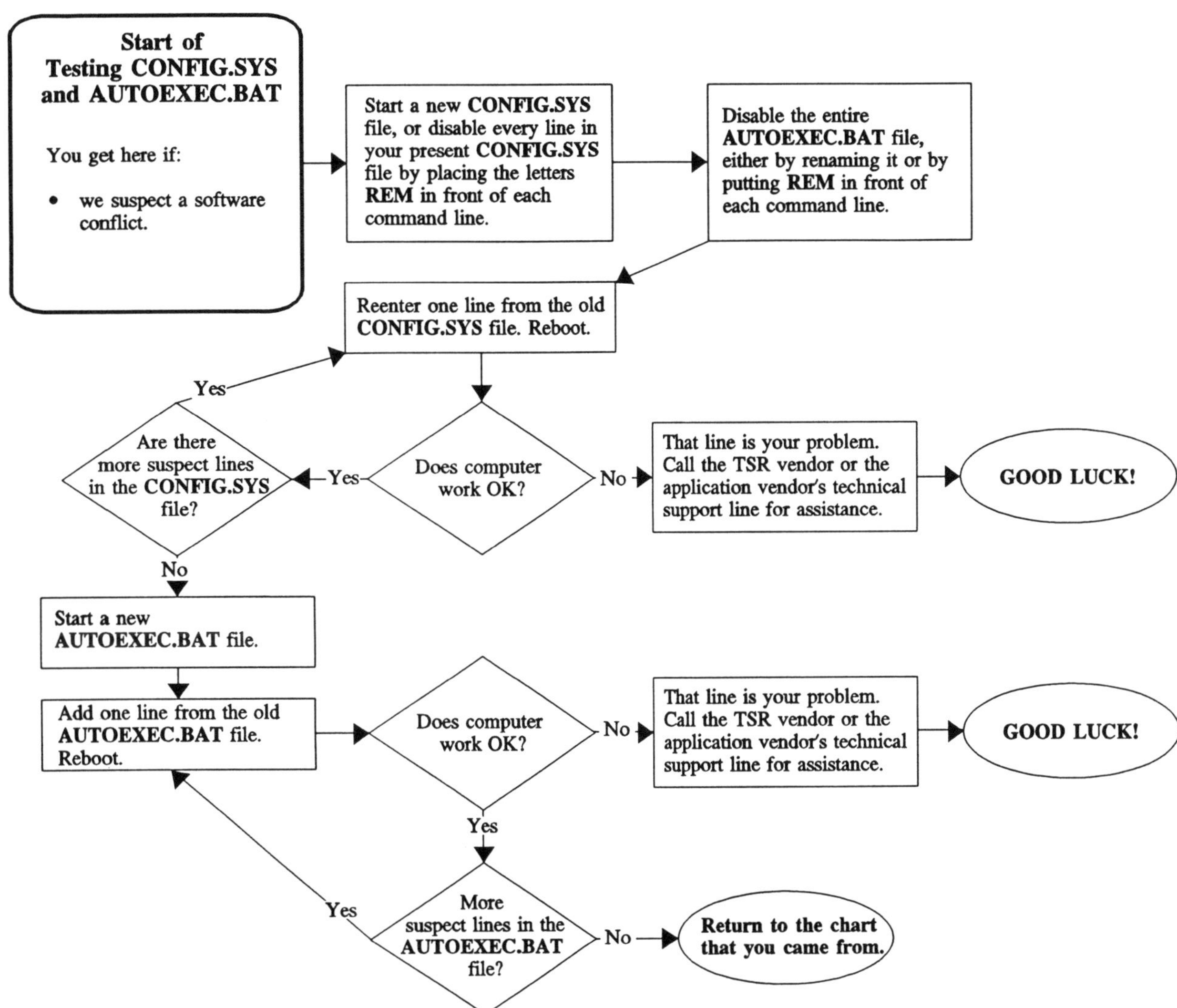

Start of Testing CONFIG.SYS and AUTOEXEC.BAT
You get here if:
• we suspect a software conflict.
Start a new CONFIG.SYS file, or disable every line in your present CONFIG.SYS file by placing the letters REM in front of each command line.
Disable the entire AUTOEXEC.BAT file, either by renaming it or by putting REM in front of each command line.
Reenter one line from the old CONFIG.SYS file. Reboot.
Yes
Are there more suspect lines in the CONFIG.SYS file?
Yes
Does computer work OK?
No
That line is your problem. Call the TSR vendor or the application vendor's technical support line for assistance.
GOOD LUCK!
No
Start a new AUTOEXEC.BAT file.
Add one line from the old AUTOEXEC.BAT file. Reboot.
Does computer work OK?
No
That line is your problem. Call the TSR vendor or the application vendor's technical support line for assistance.
GOOD LUCK!
Yes
Yes
More suspect lines in the AUTOEXEC.BAT file?
No
Return to the chart that you came from.

Start of File Server Error Messages

You get here if:

- Your **Netware 3.X** file server monitor displays an error message.

OR

- Both the file server and a workstation display error messages.

We need to figure out whether the error message is being generated by
the file server's BIOS ROM
DOS
Novell NetWare
or a Third Party NetWare Loadable Module (NLM)

When you first turn on the file server, it counts memory and goes though a power-on-self-test (POST) where it checks the keyboard, disk drives, etc. to make sure the hardware is functioning correctly. If you get an error during this POST, try to find it in the hardware manual that came with the computer you're using as a file server. If you can't find the manual, or the error's not listed there, try ***Fix Your Own PC***, our standalone PC repair book, looking especially in Appendices A and B.

With the POST successfully completed, the file server boots DOS. Your DOS boot disk, whether floppy disk or hard disk, has an **AUTOEXEC** batch file that automatically starts loading **SERVER.EXE**, the **NetWare 386** operating system kernel. If you get a DOS error during this boot process, consult your DOS manual.

You can tell that **SERVER.EXE** has started loading when NetWare puts the message "loading server" on the monitor. If you've made it this far, then get an error message, the message is probably from NetWare itself, or from 3rd party software (nonNovell software) that your NetWare **AUTOEXEC.NCF** file is automatically loading on the file server along with the NetWare operating system.

With this background, let's try to sort out who is giving you this error message on the file server.

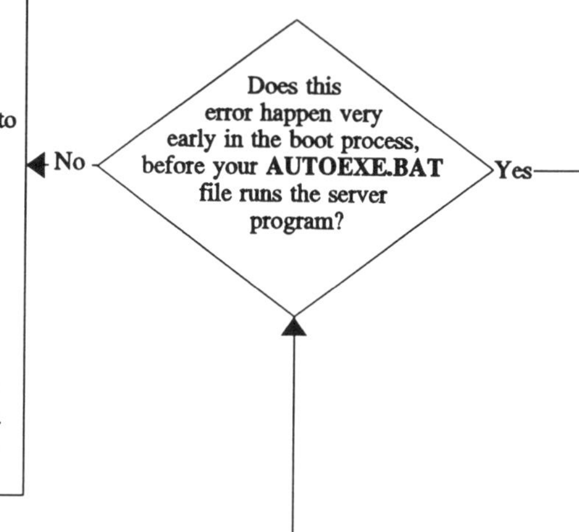
Does this error happen very early in the boot process, before your AUTOEXE.BAT file runs the server program?
No
Yes

This is either a Novell NetWare error or an error displayed by a 3rd party NLM (NetWare Loadable Module).

If any of your network workstations are functioning properly, use Novell's online help facility to look up the error message. (See Appendix A if you don't know how to operate the online help software). If no workstation is functional, or you prefer working with hard copy, use the Novell System Messages manual (use the index).

If you can't find the message online or in the manual, it might be an undocumented error message or a 3rd party software error message. Check the manuals for your 3rd party NLMs.

If all these leads fail, try Novell's tech support. They may have seen the message before and have it in their database. Call them. Expect to pay, but they're very, very good and should figure it out for you.

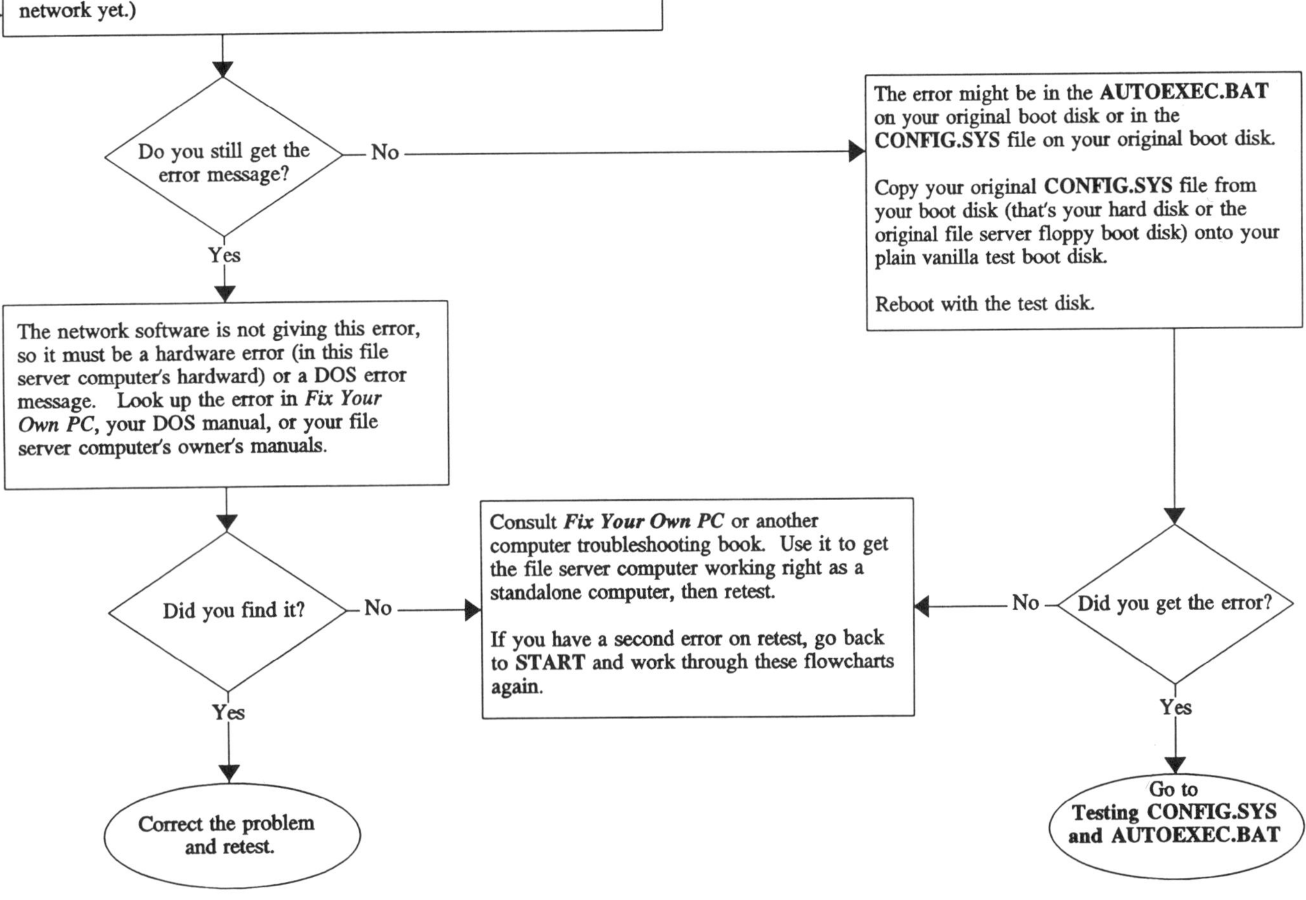
You're probably getting a BIOS ROM (hardware equipment) error or a DOS error. Try booting the file server with a plain vanilla DOS boot disk (no **AUTOEXEC.BAT** and no **CONFIG.SYS** files). Use the same DOS version you normally use with the file server. (Remember, your network won't fire up with a plain vanilla boot disk, but we're just checking that the hardware can boot DOS, we're not checking the network yet.)
Do you still get the error message?
No
Yes
The error might be in the **AUTOEXEC.BAT** on your original boot disk or in the **CONFIG.SYS** file on your original boot disk.
Copy your original **CONFIG.SYS** file from your boot disk (that's your hard disk or the original file server floppy boot disk) onto your plain vanilla test boot disk.
Reboot with the test disk.
The network software is not giving this error, so it must be a hardware error (in this file server computer's hardward) or a DOS error message. Look up the error in *Fix Your Own PC*, your DOS manual, or your file server computer's owner's manuals.
Did you find it?
No
Yes
Consult ***Fix Your Own PC*** or another computer troubleshooting book. Use it to get the file server computer working right as a standalone computer, then retest.
If you have a second error on retest, go back to **START** and work through these flowcharts again.
Did you get the error?
No
Yes
Correct the problem and retest.
Go to **Testing CONFIG.SYS and AUTOEXEC.BAT**

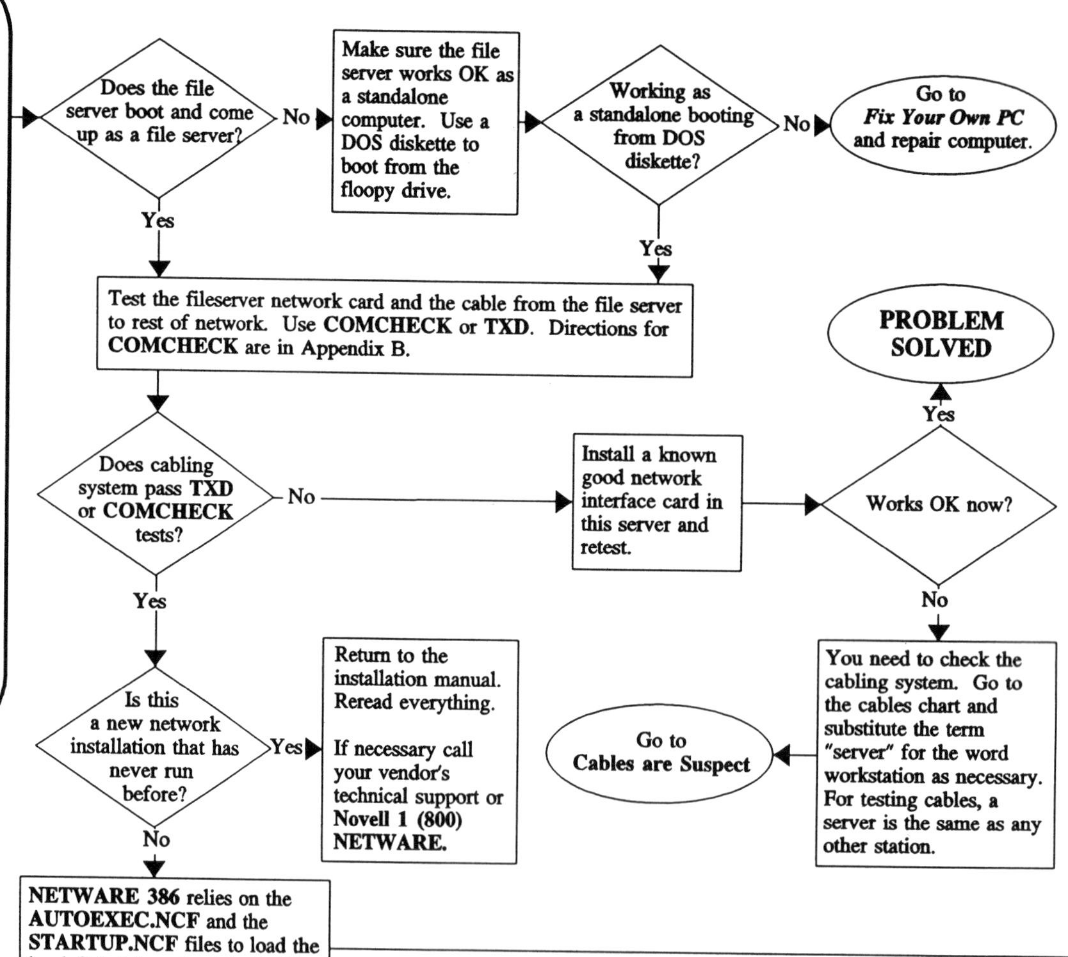
Start of
File Server
You get here if:
• There is a system-wide network problem.
• No workstations get an F: drive (one-server network).
or
Some workstations can't log onto one server in the multi-server network because one server is down.
• The file server is down and won't come back up when we power off and power on again.
or
The file server doesn't communicate with the rest of the network.
Does the file server boot and come up as a file server?
No
Yes
Make sure the file server works OK as a standalone computer. Use a DOS diskette to boot from the floppy drive.
Working as a standalone booting from DOS diskette?
No
Yes
Go to
Fix Your Own PC
and repair computer.
Test the fileserver network card and the cable from the file server to rest of network. Use COMCHECK or TXD. Directions for COMCHECK are in Appendix B.
PROBLEM SOLVED
Yes
Does cabling system pass TXD or COMCHECK tests?
No
Install a known good network interface card in this server and retest.
Works OK now?
Yes
No
Is this a new network installation that has never run before?
Yes
Return to the installation manual. Reread everything.
If necessary call your vendor's technical support or Novell 1 (800) NETWARE.
Go to
Cables are Suspect
You need to check the cabling system. Go to the cables chart and substitute the term "server" for the word workstation as necessary. For testing cables, a server is the same as any other station.
No
NETWARE 386 relies on the AUTOEXEC.NCF and the STARTUP.NCF files to load the hard disk driver, load the LAN card driver, and BIND IPX to the LAN card driver.

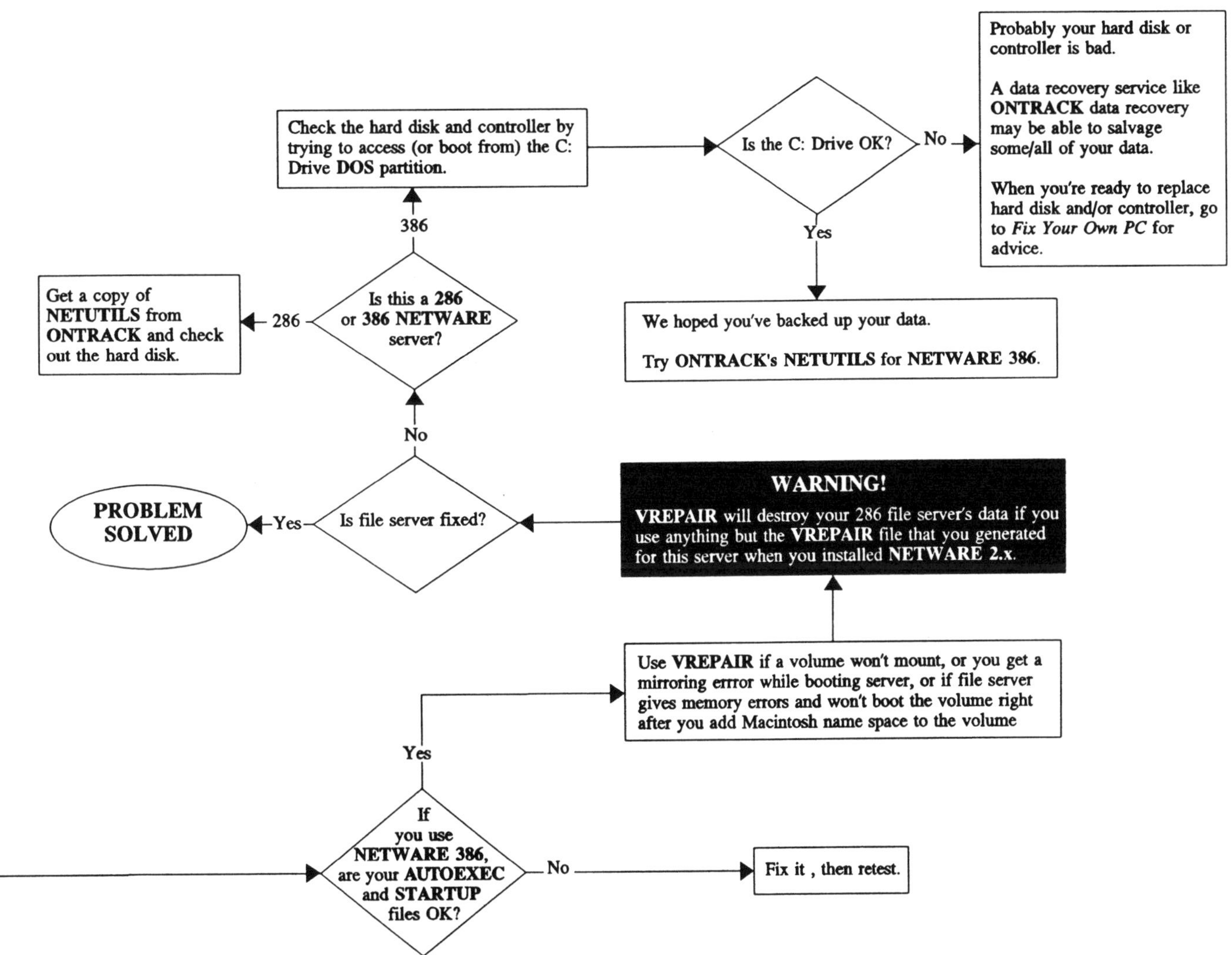
Check the hard disk and controller by trying to access (or boot from) the C: Drive DOS partition.
Is the C: Drive OK?
No
Probably your hard disk or controller is bad.
A data recovery service like ONTRACK data recovery may be able to salvage some/all of your data.
When you're ready to replace hard disk and/or controller, go to Fix Your Own PC for advice.
Yes
We hoped you've backed up your data.
Try ONTRACK's NETUTILS for NETWARE 386.
386
Is this a 286 or 386 NETWARE server?
286
Get a copy of NETUTILS from ONTRACK and check out the hard disk.
No
PROBLEM SOLVED
Yes
Is file server fixed?
WARNING!
VREPAIR will destroy your 286 file server's data if you use anything but the VREPAIR file that you generated for this server when you installed NETWARE 2.x.
Use VREPAIR if a volume won't mount, or you get a mirroring errror while booting server, or if file server gives memory errors and won't boot the volume right after you add Macintosh name space to the volume
Yes
If you use NETWARE 386, are your AUTOEXEC and STARTUP files OK?
No
Fix it , then retest.

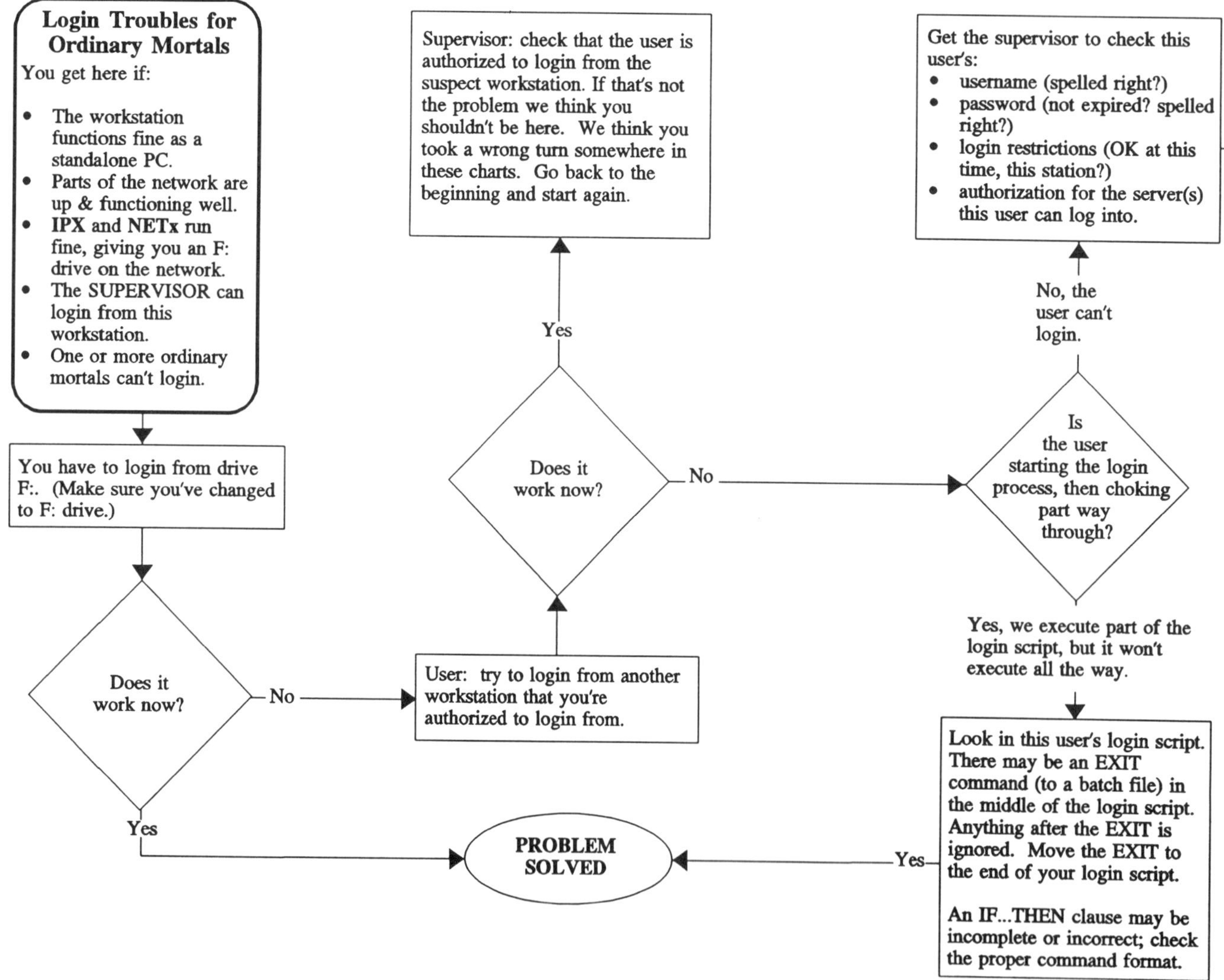
Login Troubles for Ordinary Mortals
You get here if:
• The workstation functions fine as a standalone PC.
• Parts of the network are up & functioning well.
• IPX and NETx run fine, giving you an F: drive on the network.
• The SUPERVISOR can login from this workstation.
• One or more ordinary mortals can't login.
You have to login from drive F:. (Make sure you've changed to F: drive.)
Does it work now?
No
Yes
User: try to login from another workstation that you're authorized to login from.
Does it work now?
Yes
Supervisor: check that the user is authorized to login from the suspect workstation. If that's not the problem we think you shouldn't be here. We think you took a wrong turn somewhere in these charts. Go back to the beginning and start again.
No
Is the user starting the login process, then choking part way through?
No, the user can't login.
Get the supervisor to check this user's:
• username (spelled right?)
• password (not expired? spelled right?)
• login restrictions (OK at this time, this station?)
• authorization for the server(s) this user can log into.
Yes, we execute part of the login script, but it won't execute all the way.
Look in this user's login script. There may be an EXIT command (to a batch file) in the middle of the login script. Anything after the EXIT is ignored. Move the EXIT to the end of your login script.
An IF...THEN clause may be incomplete or incorrect; check the proper command format.
Yes
PROBLEM SOLVED

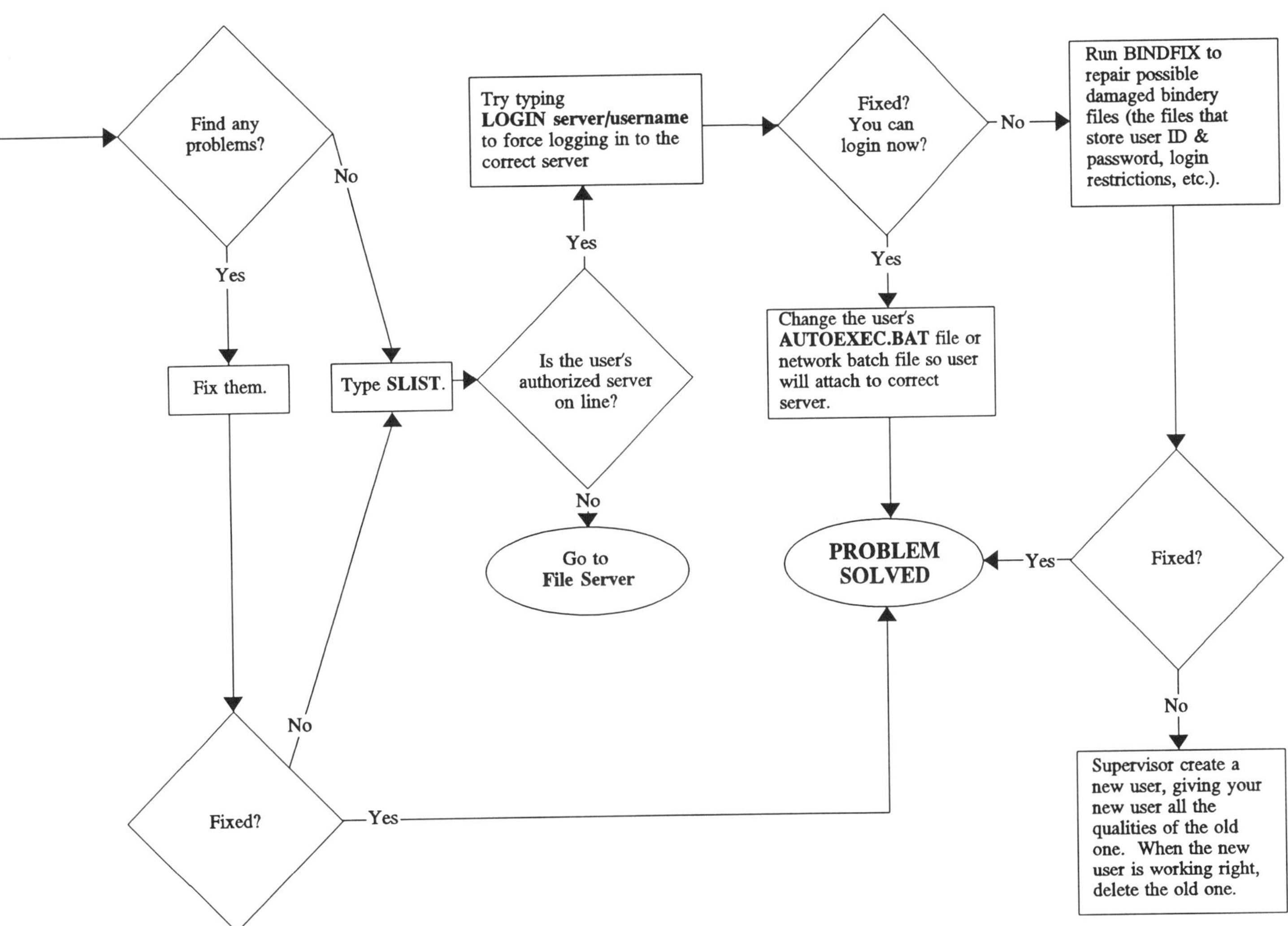
Find any problems?
Yes
No
Fix them.
Type SLIST.
Fixed?
No
Yes
Is the user's authorized server on line?
Yes
No
Try typing LOGIN server/username to force logging in to the correct server
Go to File Server
Fixed? You can login now?
No
Yes
Change the user's AUTOEXEC.BAT file or network batch file so user will attach to correct server.
PROBLEM SOLVED
Run BINDFIX to repair possible damaged bindery files (the files that store user ID & password, login restrictions, etc.).
Fixed?
Yes
No
Supervisor create a new user, giving your new user all the qualities of the old one. When the new user is working right, delete the old one.

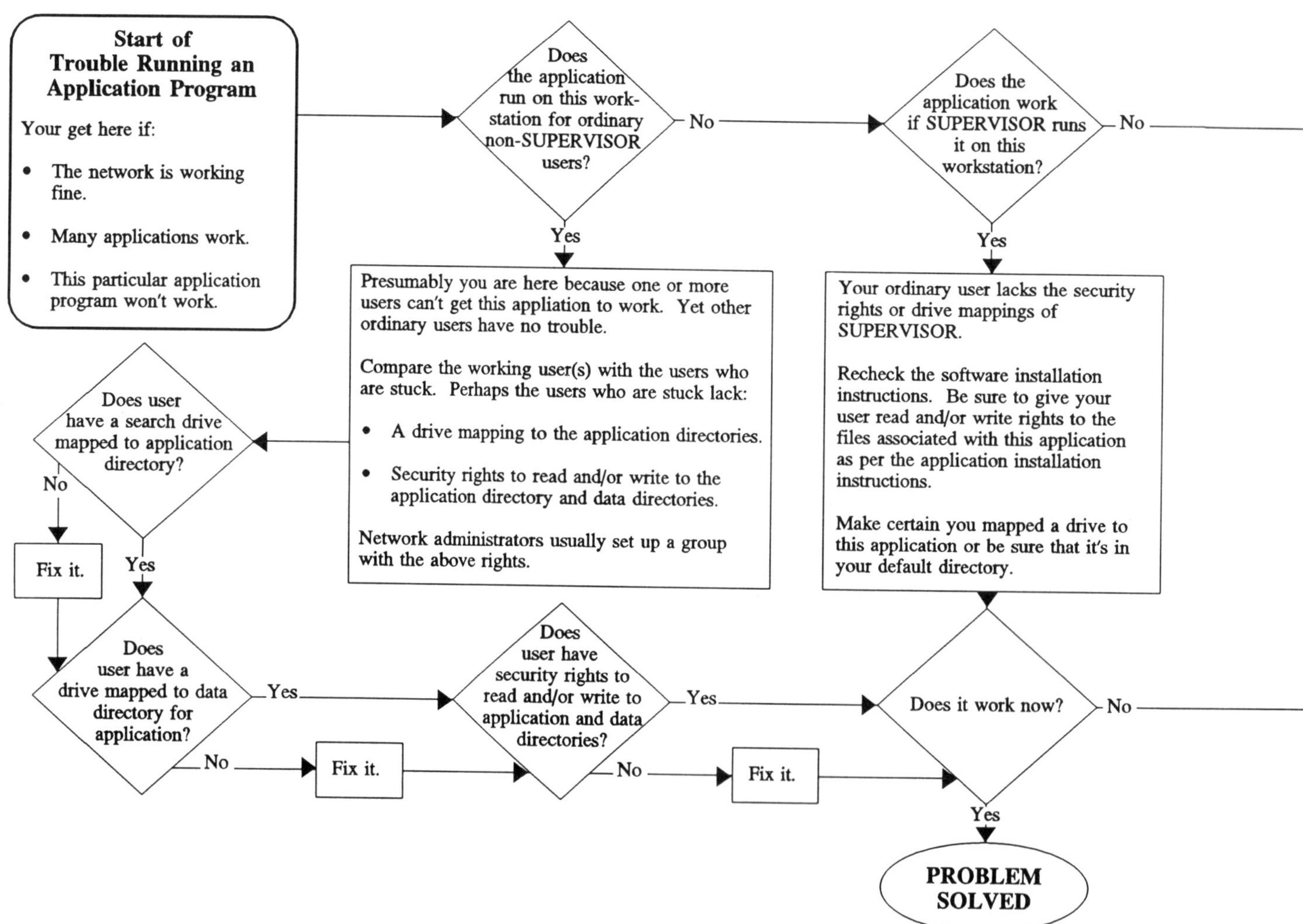
Start of
Trouble Running an
Application Program
Your get here if:
• The network is working fine.
• Many applications work.
• This particular application program won't work.
Does the application run on this work-station for ordinary non-SUPERVISOR users?
No
Does the application work if SUPERVISOR runs it on this workstation?
No
Yes
Presumably you are here because one or more users can't get this appliation to work. Yet other ordinary users have no trouble.
Compare the working user(s) with the users who are stuck. Perhaps the users who are stuck lack:
• A drive mapping to the application directories.
• Security rights to read and/or write to the application directory and data directories.
Network administrators usually set up a group with the above rights.
Yes
Your ordinary user lacks the security rights or drive mappings of SUPERVISOR.
Recheck the software installation instructions. Be sure to give your user read and/or write rights to the files associated with this application as per the application installation instructions.
Make certain you mapped a drive to this application or be sure that it's in your default directory.
Does user have a search drive mapped to application directory?
No
Fix it.
Yes
Does user have a drive mapped to data directory for application?
Yes
No
Fix it.
Does user have security rights to read and/or write to application and data directories?
Yes
No
Fix it.
Does it work now?
No
Yes
PROBLEM SOLVED

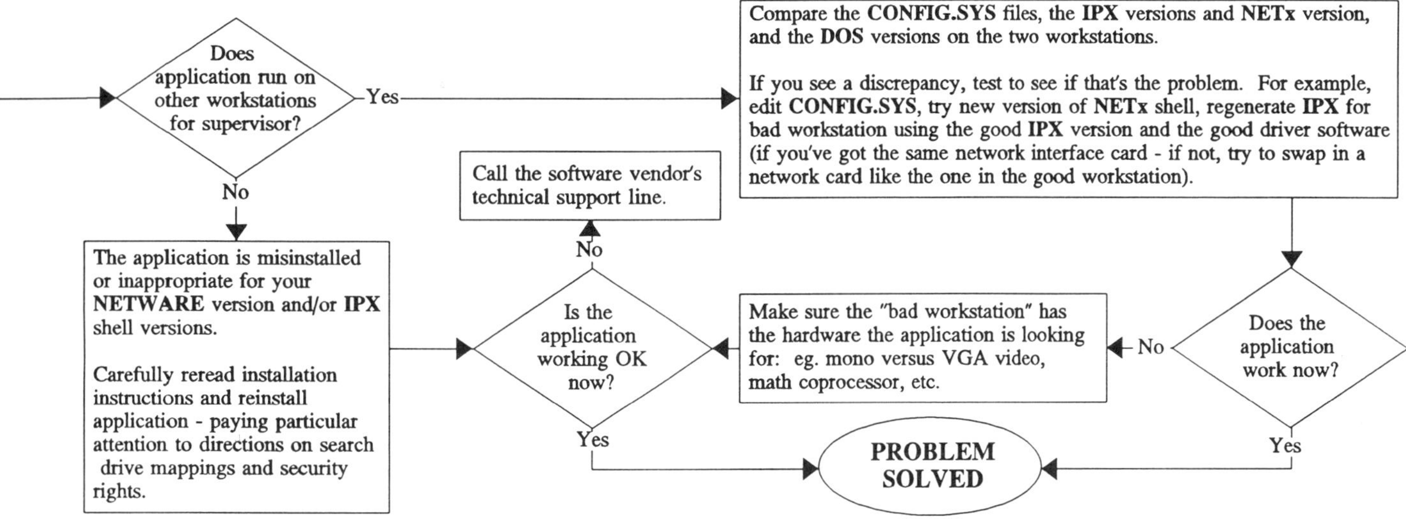
Does application run on other workstations for supervisor?
Yes
No
Compare the **CONFIG.SYS** files, the **IPX** versions and **NETx** version, and the **DOS** versions on the two workstations.
If you see a discrepancy, test to see if that's the problem. For example, edit **CONFIG.SYS**, try new version of **NETx** shell, regenerate **IPX** for bad workstation using the good **IPX** version and the good driver software (if you've got the same network interface card - if not, try to swap in a network card like the one in the good workstation).
Call the software vendor's technical support line.
The application is misinstalled or inappropriate for your **NETWARE** version and/or **IPX** shell versions.
Carefully reread installation instructions and reinstall application - paying particular attention to directions on search drive mappings and security rights.
No
Is the application working OK now?
Yes
Make sure the "bad workstation" has the hardware the application is looking for: eg. mono versus VGA video, math coprocessor, etc.
No
Does the application work now?
Yes
PROBLEM SOLVED

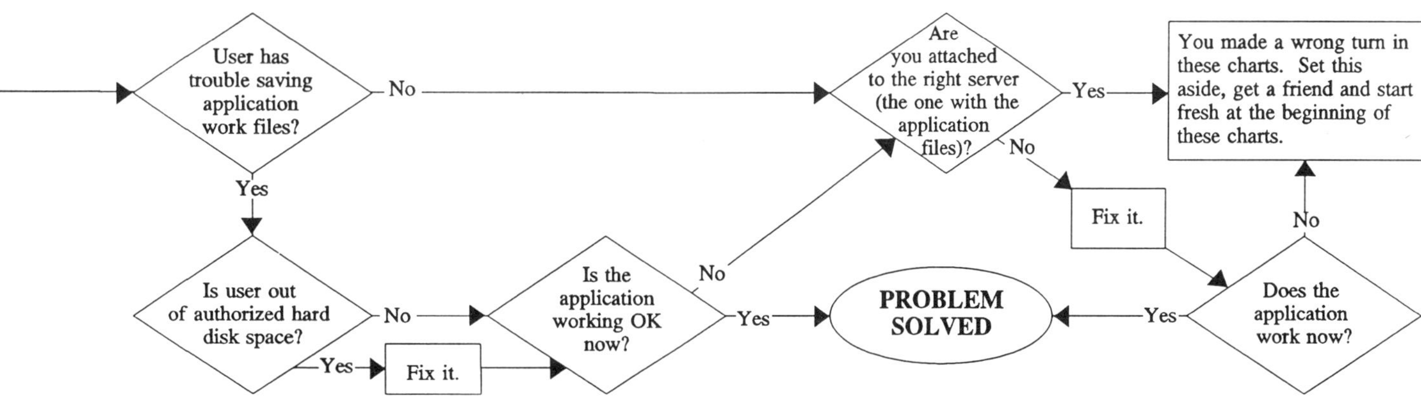
User has trouble saving application work files?
No
Yes
Are you attached to the right server (the one with the application files)?
Yes
No
You made a wrong turn in these charts. Set this aside, get a friend and start fresh at the beginning of these charts.
Fix it.
No
Is user out of authorized hard disk space?
No
Yes
Fix it.
Is the application working OK now?
No
Yes
PROBLEM SOLVED
Yes
Does the application work now?

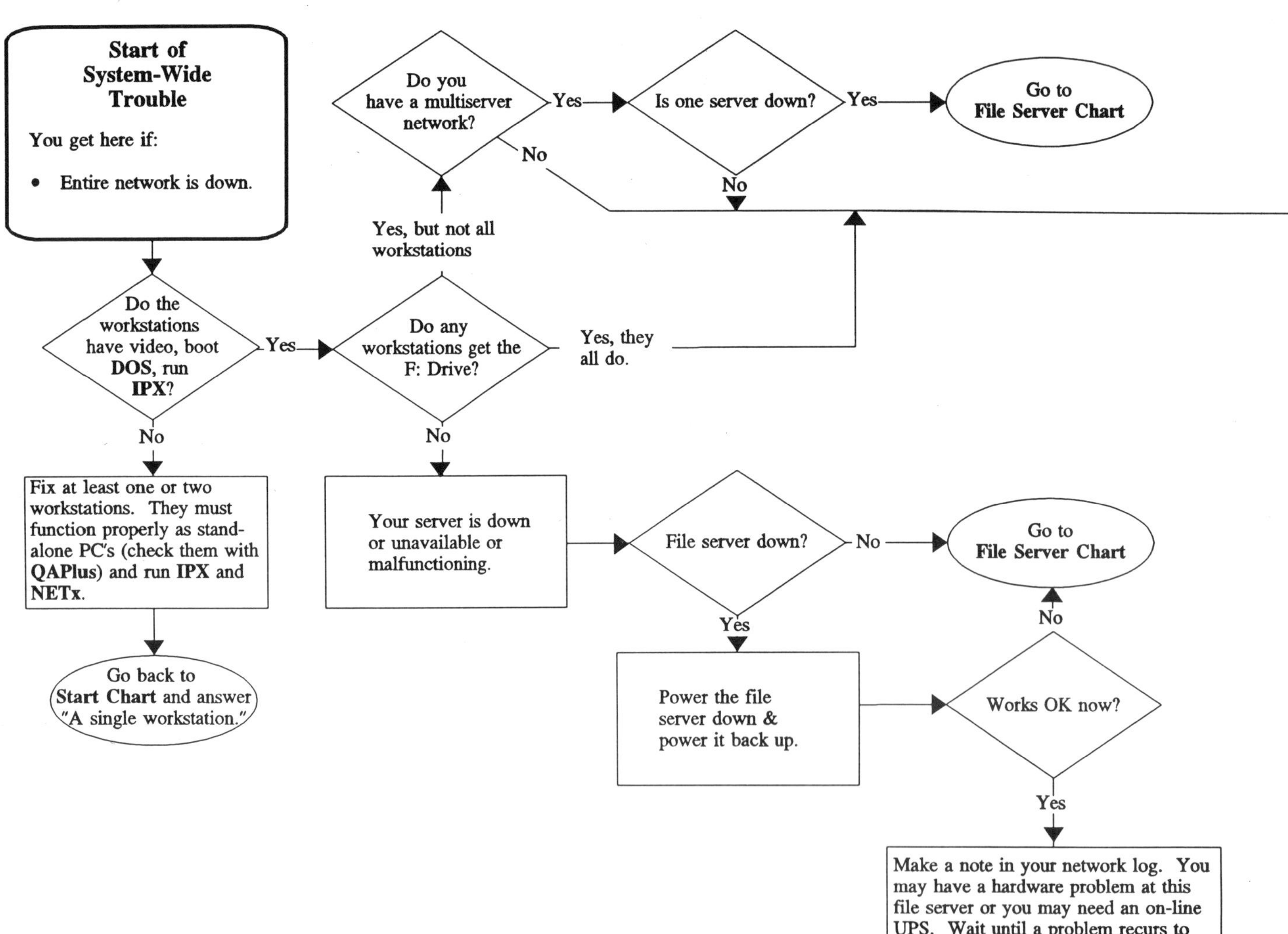
Start of System-Wide Trouble
You get here if:
• Entire network is down.
Do the workstations have video, boot DOS, run IPX?
Yes
No
Fix at least one or two workstations. They must function properly as stand-alone PC's (check them with QAPlus) and run IPX and NETx.
Go back to Start Chart and answer "A single workstation."
Do any workstations get the F: Drive?
Yes, but not all workstations
Yes, they all do.
No
Your server is down or unavailable or malfunctioning.
Do you have a multiserver network?
Yes
No
Is one server down?
Yes
No
Go to File Server Chart
File server down?
No
Yes
Go to File Server Chart
Power the file server down & power it back up.
Works OK now?
No
Yes
Make a note in your network log. You may have a hardware problem at this file server or you may need an on-line UPS. Wait until a problem recurs to check further.

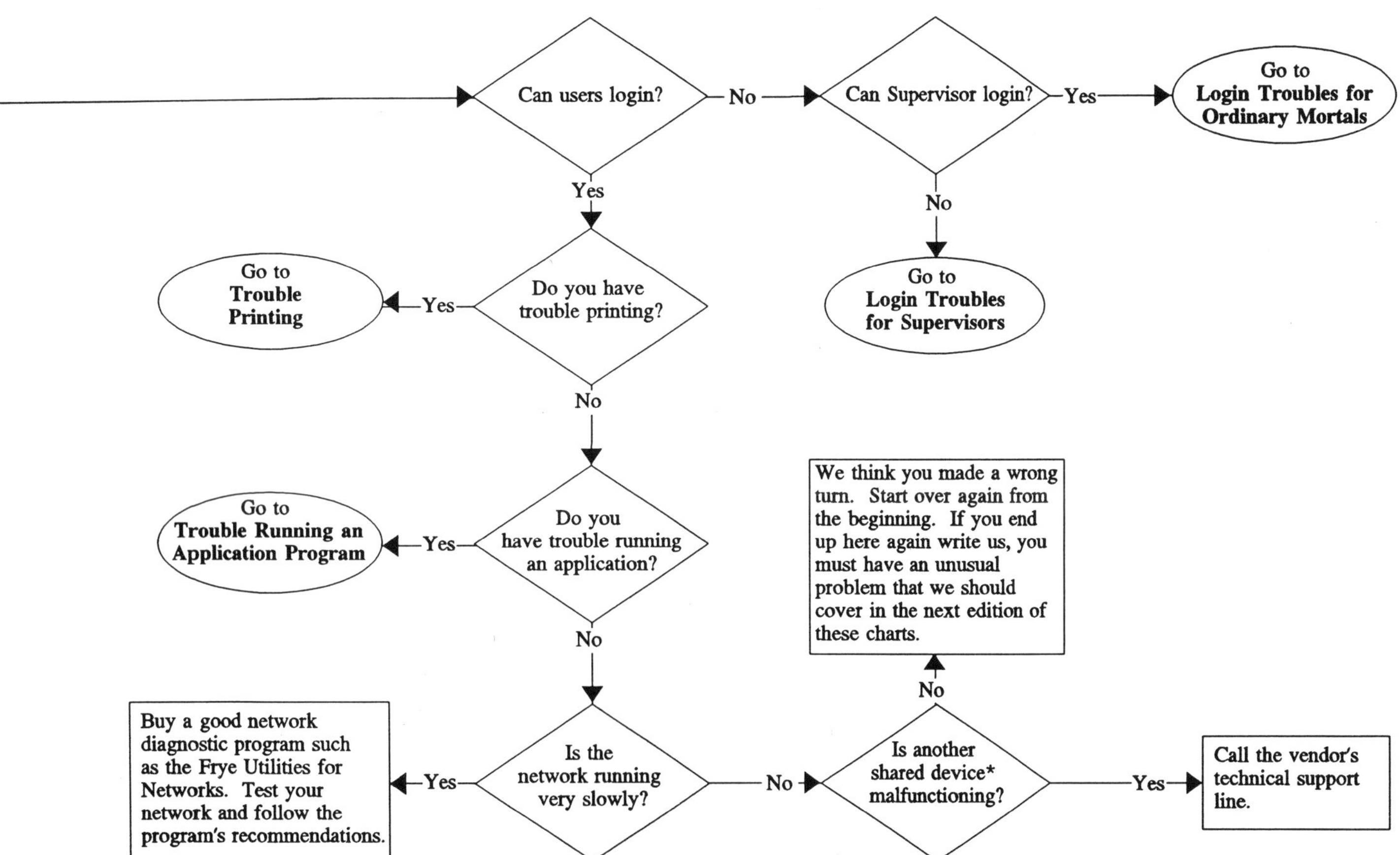

Can users login?
No
Can Supervisor login?
Yes
Go to **Login Troubles for Ordinary Mortals**
No
Go to **Login Troubles for Supervisors**
Yes
Do you have trouble printing?
Yes
Go to **Trouble Printing**
No
Do you have trouble running an application?
Yes
Go to **Trouble Running an Application Program**
No
Is the network running very slowly?
Yes
Buy a good network diagnostic program such as the Frye Utilities for Networks. Test your network and follow the program's recommendations.
No
Is another shared device* malfunctioning?
Yes
Call the vendor's technical support line.
No
We think you made a wrong turn. Start over again from the beginning. If you end up here again write us, you must have an unusual problem that we should cover in the next edition of these charts.

*e.g. modem server, CD ROM drive

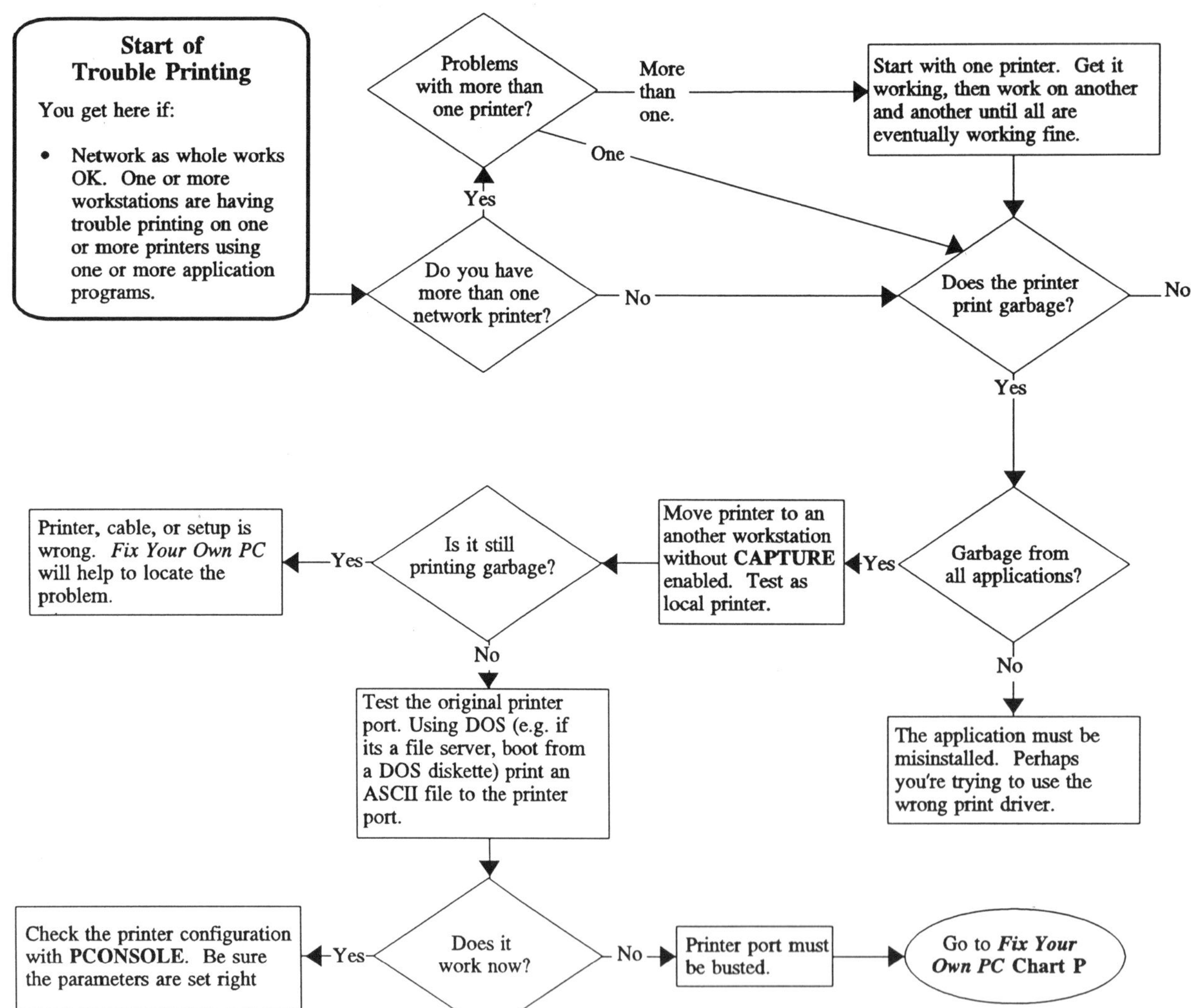
Start of
Trouble Printing
You get here if:
• Network as whole works OK. One or more workstations are having trouble printing on one or more printers using one or more application programs.
Problems with more than one printer?
More than one.
One
Start with one printer. Get it working, then work on another and another until all are eventually working fine.
Yes
Do you have more than one network printer?
No
Does the printer print garbage?
No
Yes
Printer, cable, or setup is wrong. *Fix Your Own PC* will help to locate the problem.
Yes
Is it still printing garbage?
Move printer to an another workstation without **CAPTURE** enabled. Test as local printer.
Yes
Garbage from all applications?
No
Test the original printer port. Using DOS (e.g. if its a file server, boot from a DOS diskette) print an ASCII file to the printer port.
No
The application must be misinstalled. Perhaps you're trying to use the wrong print driver.
Check the printer configuration with **PCONSOLE**. Be sure the parameters are set right
Yes
Does it work now?
No
Printer port must be busted.
Go to *Fix Your Own PC* Chart P

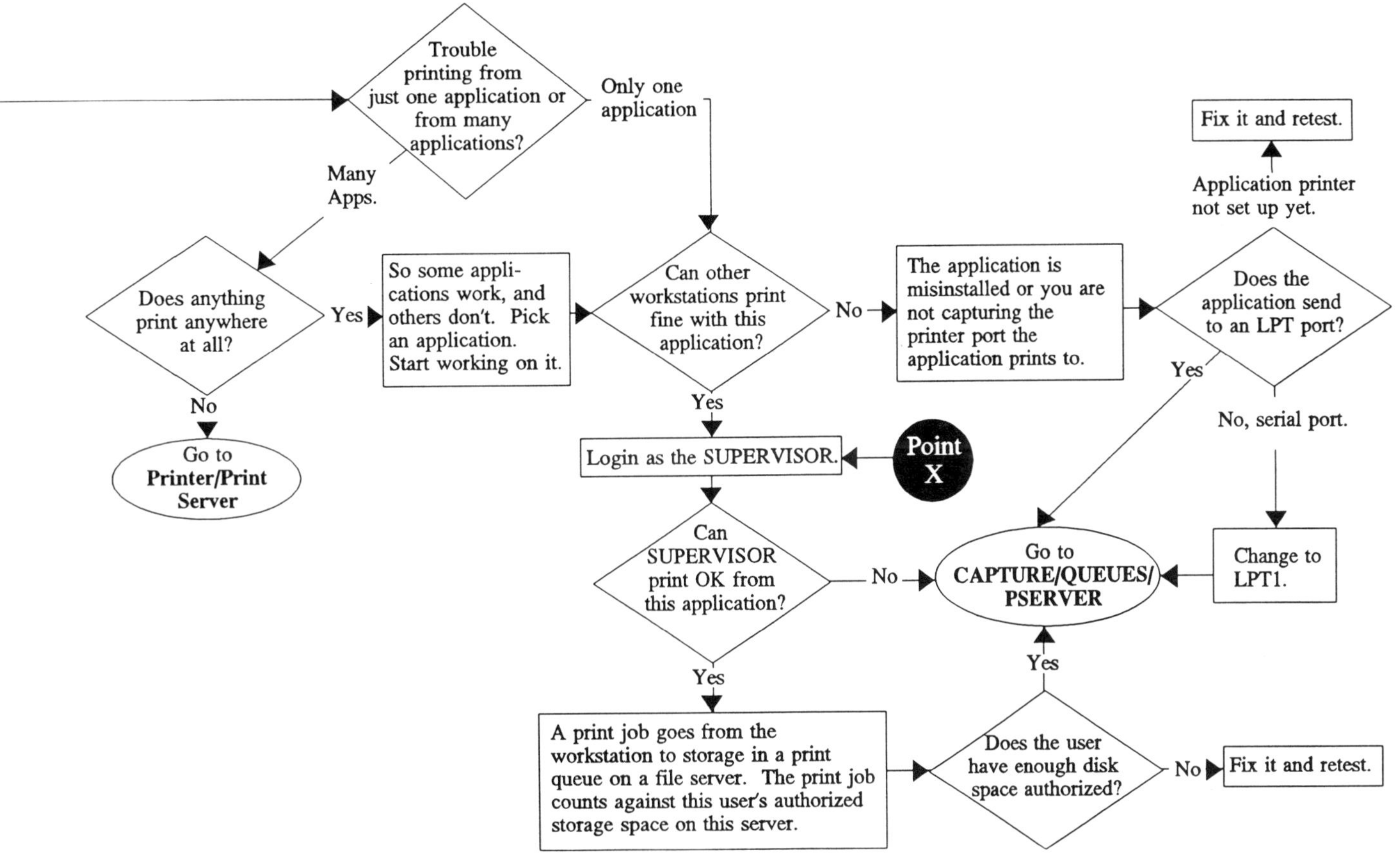
Trouble printing from just one application or from many applications?
Only one application
Many Apps.
Does anything print anywhere at all?
Yes
No
Go to **Printer/Print Server**
So some applications work, and others don't. Pick an application. Start working on it.
Can other workstations print fine with this application?
No
The application is misinstalled or you are not capturing the printer port the application prints to.
Does the application send to an LPT port?
Application printer not set up yet.
Fix it and retest.
Yes
No, serial port.
Change to LPT1.
Yes
Login as the SUPERVISOR.
Point X
Can SUPERVISOR print OK from this application?
No
Go to **CAPTURE/QUEUES/ PSERVER**
Yes
A print job goes from the workstation to storage in a print queue on a file server. The print job counts against this user's authorized storage space on this server.
Does the user have enough disk space authorized?
Yes
No
Fix it and retest.

Start of Workstation Error Messages

You get here if:

- Workstation(s) display an error message.

We need to figure out which hardware or software level is issuing the error message. Suspects are:
the workstation's ROM BIOS (a hardware error)
DOS
IPX (the NetWare datagram delivery service)
NETx.COM (the NetWare shell)
Application software (this includes your wordprocessor, database, spreadsheet, etc. as well as Windows, or a DOS shell like PCShell).

First we'll consider what each of our suspects do.

When you turn the workstation on, it counts memory and goes though a power-on-self-test (POST) where it checks the keyboard, disk drives, etc. to make sure the hardware is functioning correctly. The ROM BIOS (a chip on the mainboard) controls both the POST and any messages displayed during the POST. If you get an error during this POST, try to find the error message in the hardware manual that came with the computer you're using as a file server. If you can't find the manual, or the error's not listed there, try **Fix Your Own PC**, our standalone PC repair book, looking especially in Appendices A and B.

With the POST successfully completed, the workstation boots DOS, usually from the A: drive or from the local hard disk (the C: drive). You know we've reached the boot stage when the drive light for drive A or drive C stays on for a few seconds while the computer reads the DOS boot files off the disk. As DOS boots, your computer will display a DOS version copyright message (e.g. Toshiba Personal Computer MSDOS Version 4.0, etc., or Microsoft(R) MSDOS(R) Version 3.30, etc.). While booting, DOS reads the **CONFIG.SYS** file on your boot disk and sets its parameters accordingly. Next DOS executes the commands in your **AUTOEXEC.BAT** file.

Many workstation boot disks have the **IPX** and the **NETx** commands in their **AUTOEXEC.BAT** file, so the user is automatically attached to the network when booting the workstation. Some of these **AUTOEXEC** batch files lead the user directly to the network login and then to a network menu system. Other **AUTOEXEC** batch files leave the user on her local drive (typically on drive C:) and allow her to log into the network manually, if she chooses to do so.

Here are the login steps, whether carried out in an **AUTOEXEC.BAT** file or manually at the DOS command line. Run **IPX**. Run **NETx** (**NET3** for DOS Version 3.x, **NET4** for DOS 4.x, **NET5** for DOS 5.x). Switch to the F: drive. Type **LOGIN**. At the prompts, enter your name and password.

Once on the local drive (drives A:, B:, or C:) or a network drive (drives F: through Z: are typical network drive letters), the user starts an application. An error while running application software can be caused by malfunctions in any of the layers we've named (the workstation hardware, DOS, **IPX** and the network interface card, **NETx**, or the application software itself). In addition, an expired password, insufficient security rights, incorrect drive mapping, or a host of other user-controllable and supervisor-controllable parameters can cause errors, and it may not be obvious that improper NetWare settings are the culprit. Of course, a malfunctioning file server or defective network cables and hubs will give workstation errors too.

With this background, let's try to sort out who is giving you this error message on your workstation.

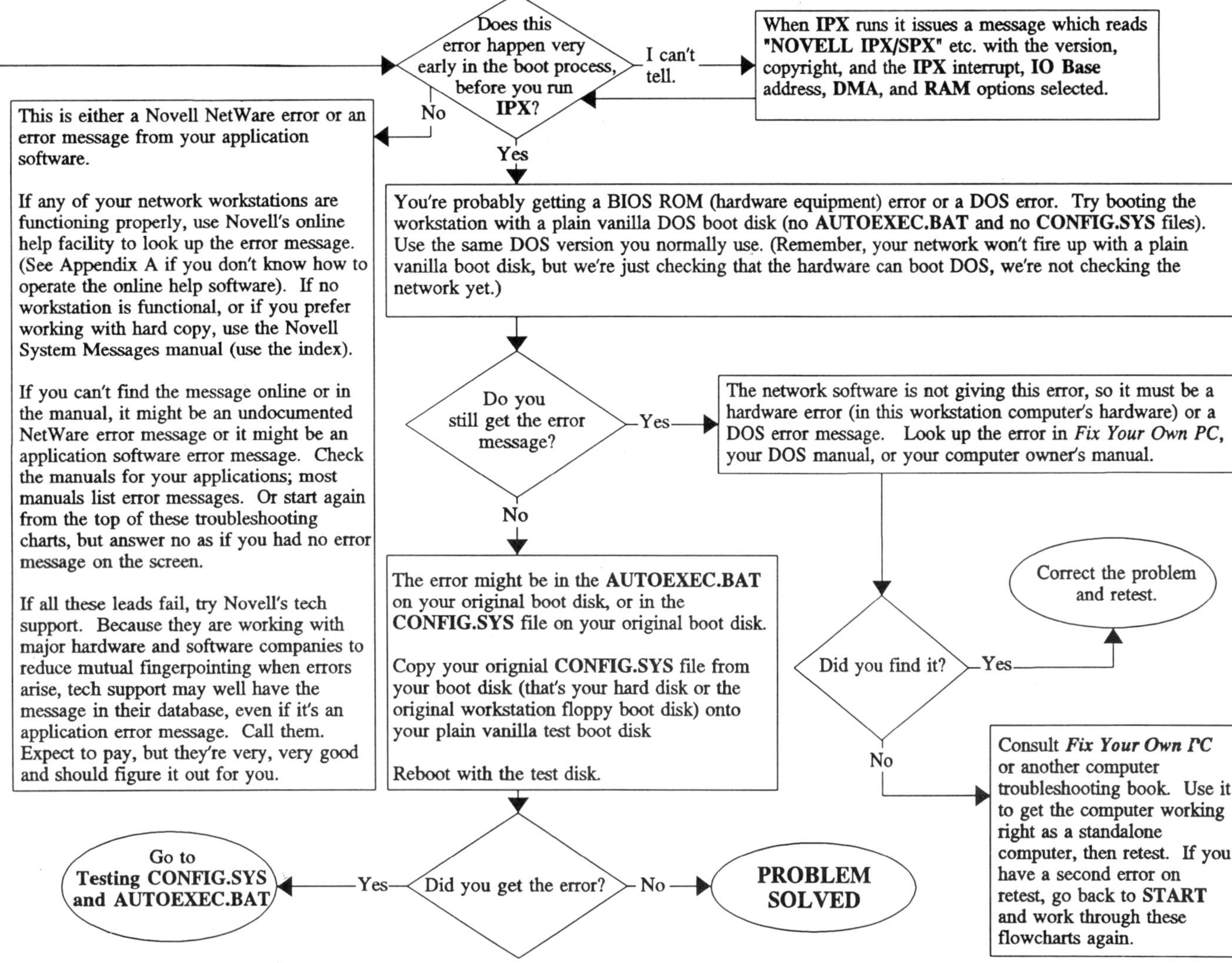
Does this error happen very early in the boot process, before you run IPX?
I can't tell.
When IPX runs it issues a message which reads "NOVELL IPX/SPX" etc. with the version, copyright, and the IPX interrupt, IO Base address, DMA, and RAM options selected.
No
This is either a Novell NetWare error or an error message from your application software.
If any of your network workstations are functioning properly, use Novell's online help facility to look up the error message. (See Appendix A if you don't know how to operate the online help software). If no workstation is functional, or if you prefer working with hard copy, use the Novell System Messages manual (use the index).
If you can't find the message online or in the manual, it might be an undocumented NetWare error message or it might be an application software error message. Check the manuals for your applications; most manuals list error messages. Or start again from the top of these troubleshooting charts, but answer no as if you had no error message on the screen.
If all these leads fail, try Novell's tech support. Because they are working with major hardware and software companies to reduce mutual fingerpointing when errors arise, tech support may well have the message in their database, even if it's an application error message. Call them. Expect to pay, but they're very, very good and should figure it out for you.
Yes
You're probably getting a BIOS ROM (hardware equipment) error or a DOS error. Try booting the workstation with a plain vanilla DOS boot disk (no AUTOEXEC.BAT and no CONFIG.SYS files). Use the same DOS version you normally use. (Remember, your network won't fire up with a plain vanilla boot disk, but we're just checking that the hardware can boot DOS, we're not checking the network yet.)
Do you still get the error message?
Yes
The network software is not giving this error, so it must be a hardware error (in this workstation computer's hardware) or a DOS error message. Look up the error in Fix Your Own PC, your DOS manual, or your computer owner's manual.
No
The error might be in the AUTOEXEC.BAT on your original boot disk, or in the CONFIG.SYS file on your original boot disk.
Copy your orignial CONFIG.SYS file from your boot disk (that's your hard disk or the original workstation floppy boot disk) onto your plain vanilla test boot disk
Reboot with the test disk.
Did you find it?
Yes
Correct the problem and retest.
No
Consult Fix Your Own PC or another computer troubleshooting book. Use it to get the computer working right as a standalone computer, then retest. If you have a second error on retest, go back to START and work through these flowcharts again.
Did you get the error?
Yes
Go to Testing CONFIG.SYS and AUTOEXEC.BAT
No
PROBLEM SOLVED

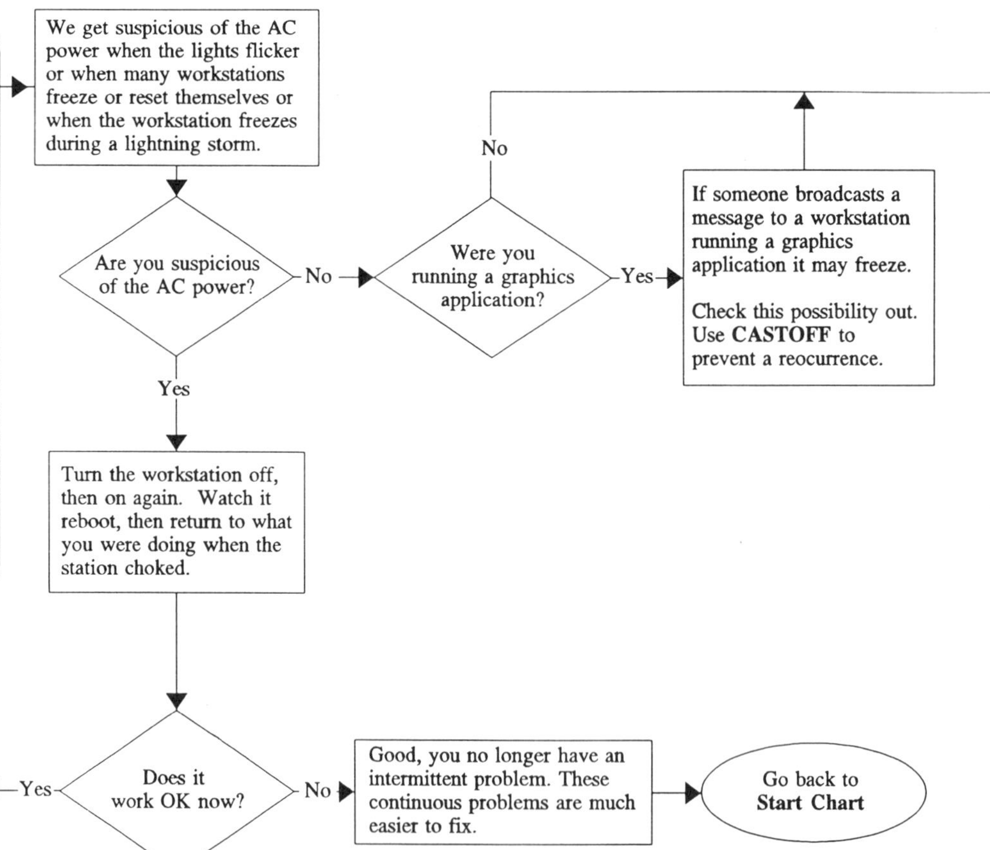
Start of
Workstation Intermittently
Locks up or Loses
Connection to Network
You get here if the network works fine much of the time:
BUT
• Your workstation intermittently locks up (screen and keyboard freeze).
or
• Your workstation intermittently loses connection with the network.
or
• You get many network read or write errors at this workstation.
We get suspicious of the AC power when the lights flicker or when many workstations freeze or reset themselves or when the workstation freezes during a lightning storm.
Are you suspicious of the AC power?
No
Yes
Were you running a graphics application?
No
Yes
If someone broadcasts a message to a workstation running a graphics application it may freeze.
Check this possibility out. Use CASTOFF to prevent a reocurrence.
Turn the workstation off, then on again. Watch it reboot, then return to what you were doing when the station choked.
Does it work OK now?
Yes
No
Don't make too much of it. Note this episode in your network log. If it recurs, we'll have to deal with it, but for now we'll guess it was a power flucution. If the workstation is crucial you may want to try an on-line power supply here.
Good, you no longer have an intermittent problem. These continuous problems are much easier to fix.
Go back to Start Chart

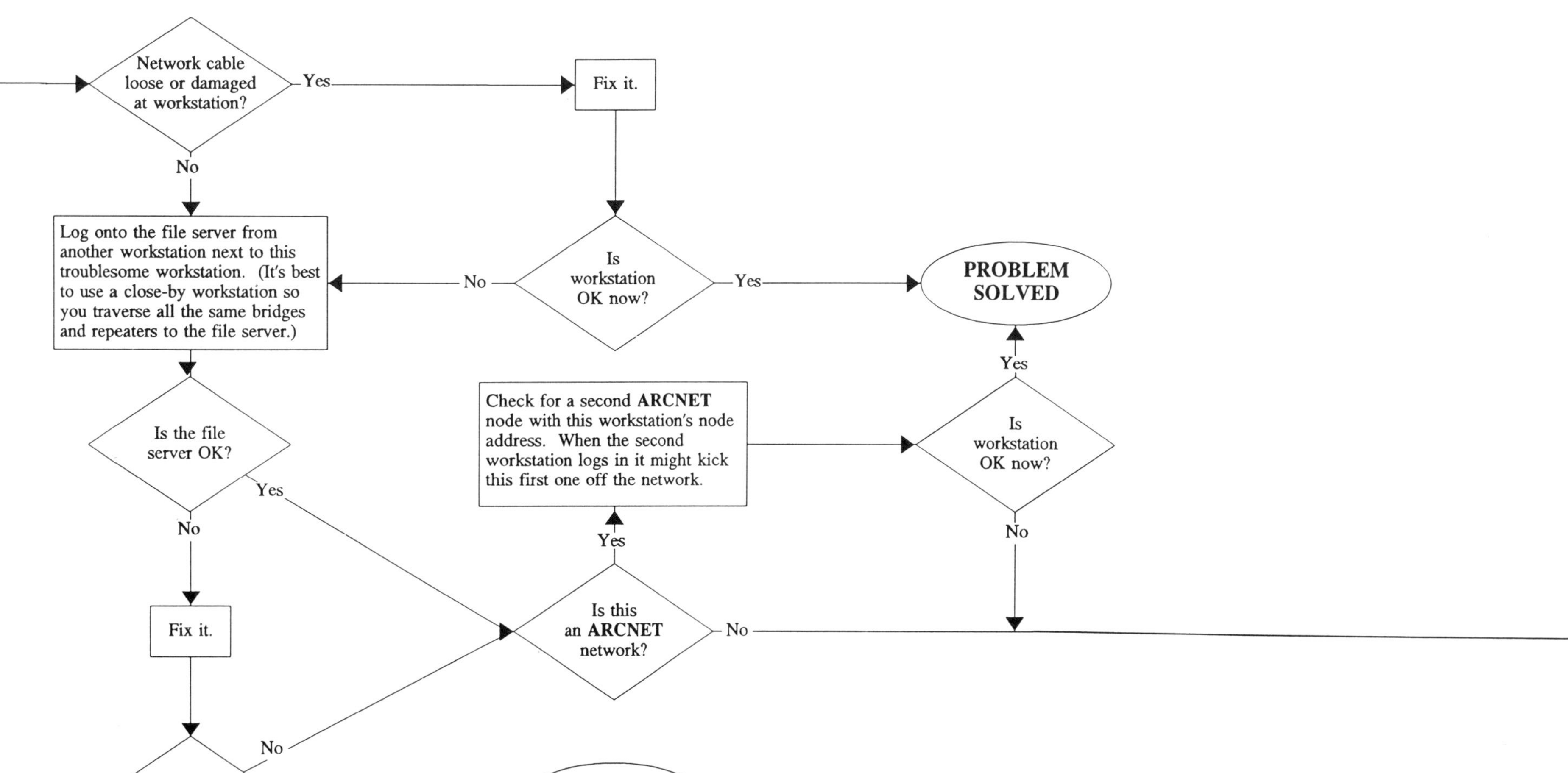

Network cable loose or damaged at workstation?
Yes
Fix it.
No
Log onto the file server from another workstation next to this troublesome workstation. (It's best to use a close-by workstation so you traverse all the same bridges and repeaters to the file server.)
No
Is workstation OK now?
Yes
PROBLEM SOLVED
Yes
Is the file server OK?
Yes
No
Check for a second **ARCNET** node with this workstation's node address. When the second workstation logs in it might kick this first one off the network.
Is workstation OK now?
No
Yes
Fix it.
Is this an **ARCNET** network?
No
No
Is workstation OK now?
Yes
PROBLEM SOLVED

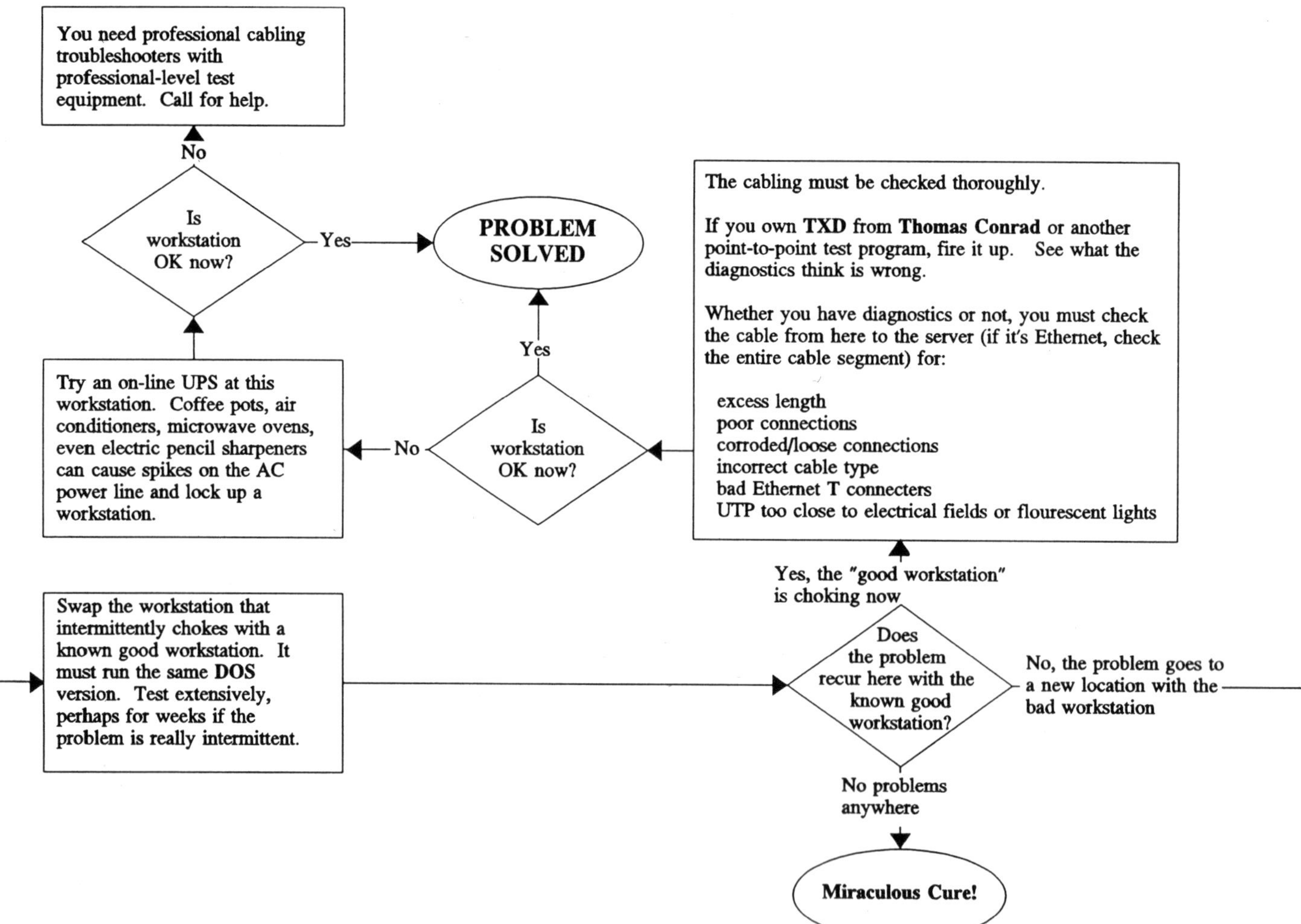
You need professional cabling troubleshooters with professional-level test equipment. Call for help.
No
Is workstation OK now?
Yes
PROBLEM SOLVED
Yes
Try an on-line UPS at this workstation. Coffee pots, air conditioners, microwave ovens, even electric pencil sharpeners can cause spikes on the AC power line and lock up a workstation.
No
Is workstation OK now?
The cabling must be checked thoroughly.
If you own TXD from Thomas Conrad or another point-to-point test program, fire it up. See what the diagnostics think is wrong.
Whether you have diagnostics or not, you must check the cable from here to the server (if it's Ethernet, check the entire cable segment) for:
excess length
poor connections
corroded/loose connections
incorrect cable type
bad Ethernet T connecters
UTP too close to electrical fields or flourescent lights
Yes, the "good workstation" is choking now
Swap the workstation that intermittently chokes with a known good workstation. It must run the same DOS version. Test extensively, perhaps for weeks if the problem is really intermittent.
Does the problem recur here with the known good workstation?
No, the problem goes to a new location with the bad workstation
No problems anywhere
Miraculous Cure!

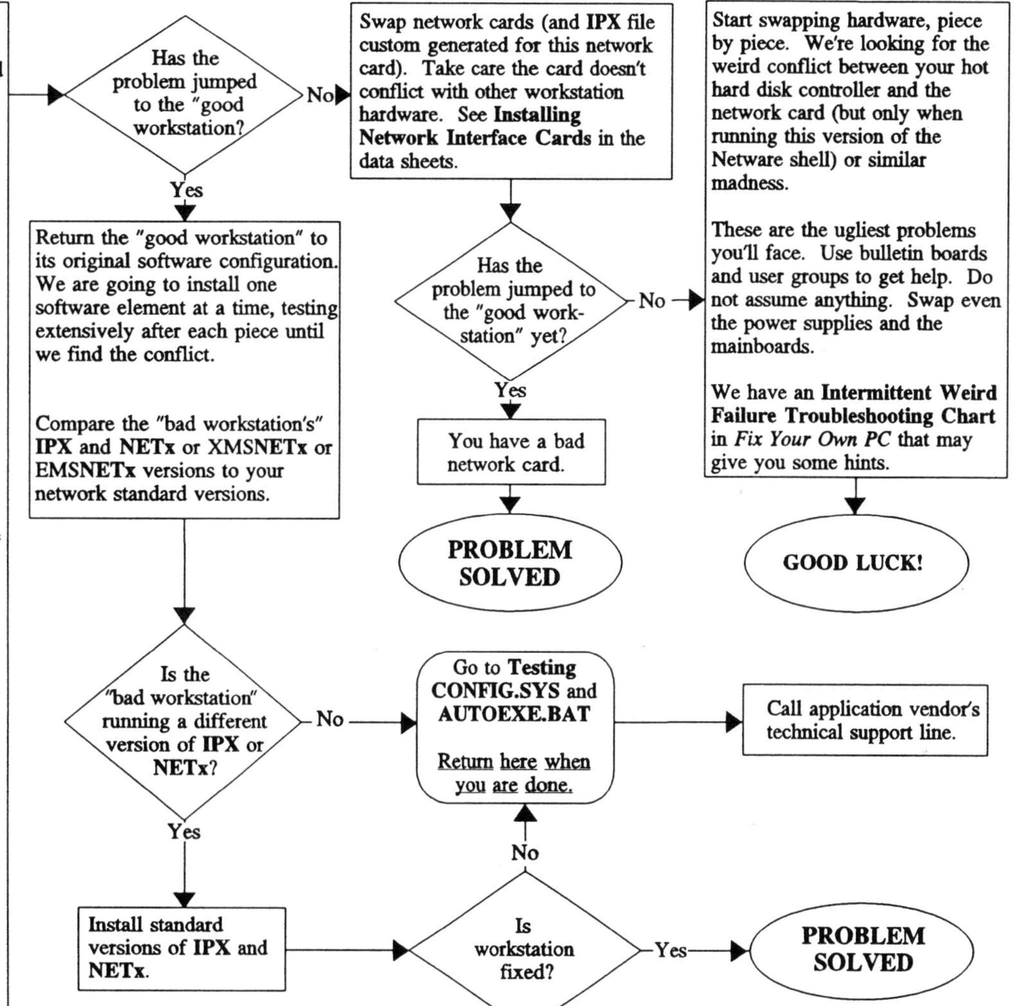
You will have to methodically transfer aspects of the bad workstation into the known-good workstation.
We'll start with the software. If that's not the problem, we'll try swapping hardware.
Throughout this process (which might take weeks if the problem is really intermittent)
1) Keep written notes
2) Test extensively after each change.
3) Change only one thing at a time
When the problem jumps to the "good workstation" we know the last thing we changed was the culprit.
Let's move all the software from the "bad workstation" to the "good workstation." If the problem moves to the good workstation we'll deal with the software piece-by-piece; if not, we'll consider hardware.
Move:
the application
AUTOEXEC.BAT
CONFIG.SYS
Test with the original user doing the original job on this test workstation.
Has the problem jumped to the "good workstation?
No
Yes
Return the "good workstation" to its original software configuration. We are going to install one software element at a time, testing extensively after each piece until we find the conflict.
Compare the "bad workstation's" IPX and NETx or XMSNETx or EMSNETx versions to your network standard versions.
Swap network cards (and IPX file custom generated for this network card). Take care the card doesn't conflict with other workstation hardware. See Installing Network Interface Cards in the data sheets.
Has the problem jumped to the "good work-station" yet?
No
Yes
You have a bad network card.
PROBLEM SOLVED
Start swapping hardware, piece by piece. We're looking for the weird conflict between your hot hard disk controller and the network card (but only when running this version of the Netware shell) or similar madness.
These are the ugliest problems you'll face. Use bulletin boards and user groups to get help. Do not assume anything. Swap even the power supplies and the mainboards.
We have an Intermittent Weird Failure Troubleshooting Chart in Fix Your Own PC that may give you some hints.
GOOD LUCK!
Is the "bad workstation" running a different version of IPX or NETx?
No
Yes
Go to Testing CONFIG.SYS and AUTOEXE.BAT
Return here when you are done.
Call application vendor's technical support line.
Install standard versions of IPX and NETx.
Is workstation fixed?
No
Yes
PROBLEM SOLVED

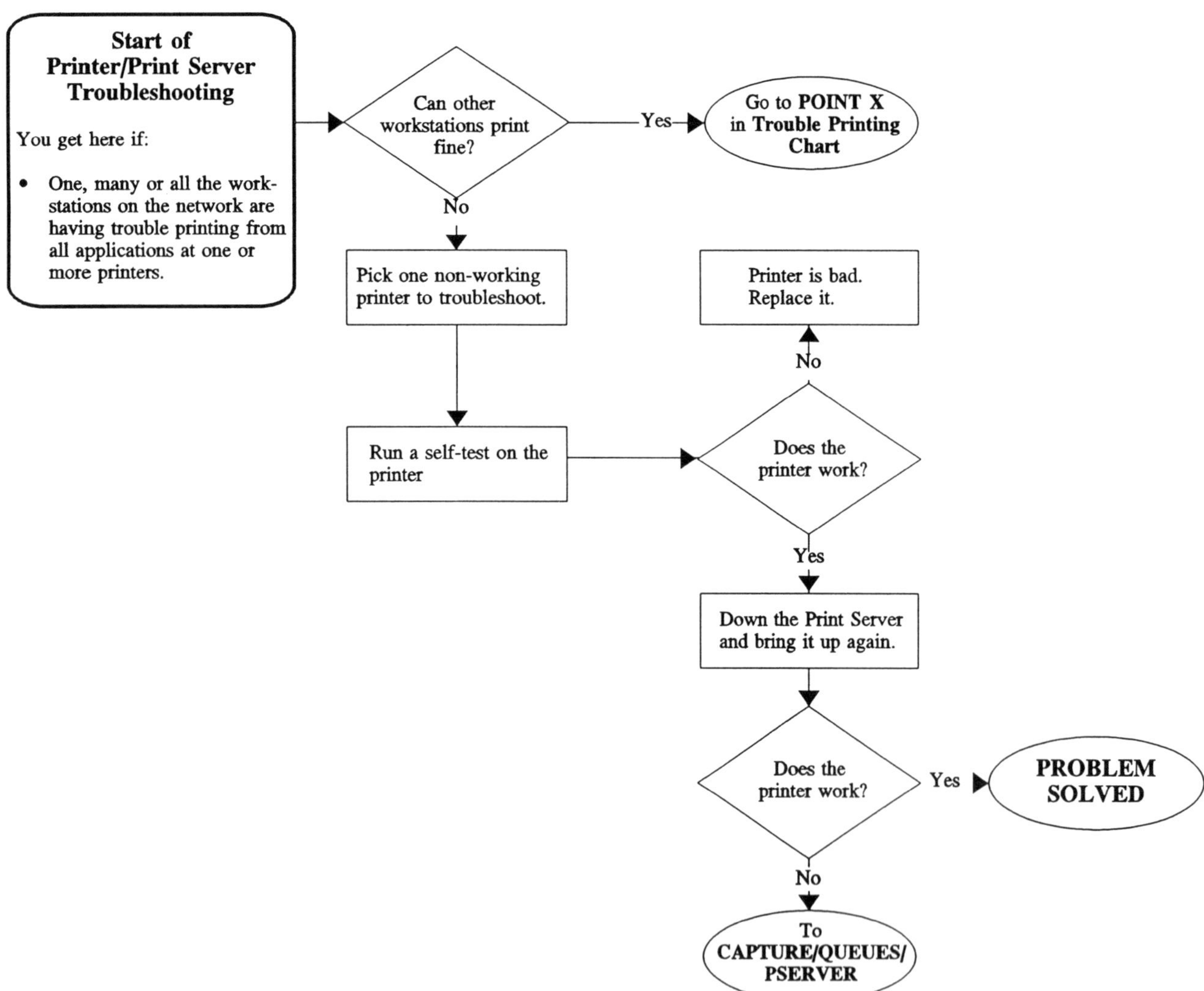
Start of
Printer/Print Server
Troubleshooting
You get here if:
• One, many or all the workstations on the network are having trouble printing from all applications at one or more printers.
Can other workstations print fine?
Yes
Go to POINT X in Trouble Printing Chart
No
Pick one non-working printer to troubleshoot.
Run a self-test on the printer
Does the printer work?
No
Printer is bad. Replace it.
Yes
Down the Print Server and bring it up again.
Does the printer work?
Yes
PROBLEM SOLVED
No
To CAPTURE/QUEUES/ PSERVER

APPENDIX A:

Novell NetWare Online HELP

At the > prompt, type HELP and press ENTER. You'll be at the NetWare Help Main Menu. Some people need no additional tutoring. Because the main menu is fairly intuitive, they can start looking up topics immediately by jumping from triangle to triangle. Put the cursor on the triangle, using either a mouse or the TAB and SHIFT-TAB keys, then press ENTER to jump to that topic.

Other people need more explicit instructions. Start with How to Use NetWare Help on the main menu, then explore Creating Infobases Using Folio VIEWS. This last is a useful tour of the software's capabilities that includes the text of the U.S. Constitution on which you can practice your search techniques. Supplement that introduction with the PreVIEW online user manual (PreVIEW is the software used to display the online help databases). Press F1 twice from a NetWare Online Help screen to call up the PreVIEW manual. The preVIEW folks call each herd of information an Infobase. NetWare Help is one infobase, the PreVIEW manual is another, and the U.S. Constitution infobase is a third. Because you can access multiple infobases simultaneously, things can get pretty confusing. Nevertheless, spend some time learning your way around NetWare Help. You won't regret the investment; it's like having a network guru at your fingertips.

Using Novell's Online Index to All Manuals

This index covers six major Novell manuals in one monster index. To access it, type

HELP INDEX

Use the search feature (press the space bar) and enter the first couple letters of your topic, or use the triangles to jump into the index midway (pick a key word which alphabetizes close to your desired topic), then press ENTER. Now you can go down the alphabet, but you won't be able to go back towards the letter A until you press ENTER again. The index abbreviates the Novell 3.10 manuals as follows:

B = The User Basics manual in the back of the System Administration manual
C = Concepts
I = Installation
P = Print Server
S = System Administration
U = Utilities

Unfortunately, the Novell **System Messages** manual (error messages) and the **Supplements** manual (hardware installation) are not included in this online index. We tell you how to look up error messages online in the next paragraph, but you'll need to page through the **Supplements** manual section-by-section for hardware info.

How to Look Up an Error Message

At the > prompt, type

HELP SYSTEM MESSAGES

Press ENTER. When the System Messages, error messages screen comes up, follow the directions, pressing first ENTER, then the space bar, then typing the first word or two of your error message in quotation marks (it will appear in the bottom box, the one marked QUERY). Stop when you've narrowed the field down to a manageable number of matches (the number of matches is below the query box). Press ENTER, and the data retrieved in your search will be displayed. If you want to go back to try reframing the search request, press the space bar and edit your query. Press ENTER to search using the new query.

Don't narrow your query too much, though, or you may miss out on useful information. Here is a typical example. When trying to read a file off the network file server hard disk, the following error appears on the workstation:

Network Error: IO error network disk during READ FROM A FILE
Abort, Retry?

When we type "Network Error: IO error" we get three matches to the search string, but none of the info is useful. We try again with a simpler, less explicit string "Network Error" and get 27 matches. When we page through the matches, we eventually reach

Network Error <cause> during <operation>.
File = <drive>:<filename>
Abort, Retry, Fail? or Abort, Retry?

That's our error! The <cause> is, of course, "IO error network disk" and the <operation> is "READ FROM A FILE."

By the way, if you were using a **System Messages** manual you'd run into a similar problem, but it's a bit easier to catch on to the <cause> and <operation> variables when working with the paper manual.

APPENDIX B:

COMCHECK—A NetWare Communications-Testing Utility

When troubleshooting a possible card or cable malfunction, it's a good idea to do the simple tests first.

COMCHECK, a Novell utility provided with NetWare, can test the network card and cable at a workstation, as long as the workstation functions well enough to load the IPX protocol. Perhaps "test" is too strong a word, because COMCHECK gives you very few details about the connection between your workstation and others on the network. It does, however, give a quick "connected" versus "unable to connect" test for each workstation—without getting into the NetWare shell or operating system.

Use COMCHECK if you can't log in to the network from a particular station, and you're wondering if the card and cable are minimally functional. We review other utilities, ones capable of revealing subtle malfunctions in operational network cards (the walking wounded), in Chapter 5, *Choosing and Using Network Utilities*.

To See if the Card Can Talk to the Cable

From a workstation: Boot DOS and run IPX from your workstation boot diskette, then run COMCHECK. We have found it is handy to create a workstation troubleshooting diskette ahead of time. If your workstation uses 1.2 Meg floppies or 3-1/2" floppies, this troubleshooting diskette can be a copy of the *DOS/DOS ODI Workstation Services* disk called SHGEN-1. If your workstation has only a 360K A: drive, be sure to include at least these files from DOS/DOS ODI: IPX.COM, COMCHECK.EXE and COMCHECK.HLP, and all the files with the DAT or the OVL extension. When you're done, test it to make sure you understand how it's supposed to work—it's a lot easier to practice your skills the first time with working equipment.

By the way, COMCHECK expects to find a file xxxx$RUN.OVL with the "xxxx" part of the file name equal to the Short Machine Name specified in your SHELL.CFG file for this workstation. If you specify no Short Machine Name, or you have no SHELL.CFG file, the default is

$RUN.OVL, which you copied to your workstation troubleshooting disk from the DOS/DOS ODI disk. You can use the $RUN.OVL default if you temporarily rename your SHELL.CFG file.

From a file server: Because non-dedicated file servers running NetWare 2.2 and all the NetWare 3.x versions boot first from DOS, you can use the COMCHECK utility just as you would use it at a workstation. File servers running earlier versions of NetWare 2.x don't boot from DOS in their file-server mode, but they are, after all, just ordinary computers that can boot from a DOS floppy diskette in the A: drive.

So get a DOS diskette for the file server's floppy, run IPX (customized with SHGEN or WSGEN for this file server NIC, as if the file server were any other workstation), then run COMCHECK. We prefer to make up a file server troubleshooting diskette ahead of time. It should be bootable and contain the files from the *DOS/DOS ODI Workstation Services* diskette called SHGEN-1, along with a copy of IPX.COM that matches this file server's network card configuration. If your file server has only a 360K A: drive, be sure to include at least these files if you want to run COMCHECK at the server computer: IPX.COM, COMCHECK.EXE, COMCHECK.HLP, and all the files with the DAT or the OVL extension. When you're done, test the diskette by running COMCHECK at the file server to make sure you understand how it's supposed to work.

To See if Other Workstations Receive this Card's Broadcast

Run COMCHECK from a number of workstations, making sure that each one lists all the other stations also running COMCHECK. Each station broadcasts a signal every 15 seconds (the default, it's changable). If COMCHECK doesn't hear from another station that has been broadcasting, it waits 60 seconds (the default), then highlights that station's name, and presumes the silent station is dead. If you're running COMCHECK on a monochrome screen you probably won't see the highlighting, so keep your eye on the time of last broadcast.

COMCHECK can locate a single bad station, of course. It also shows interesting patterns if a bridge or a repeater is malfunctioning—all stations on a particular side of the repeater can communicate, but none can communicate with stations on the far side of the busted repeater.

Therefore, use COMCHECK in conjunction with your network cabling diagram if you are having trouble with multiple dead stations. A single bad hub or cable can kill a whole group of workstations. Use COMCHECK to identify a suspect cable, then test the suspect with a TDR (Time Domain Reflectometer) or, if appropriate, a twisted-pair test tool. If necessary, you can always install a known good temporary cable in place of the suspect. If the workstations come back to life, call in a cabling installation specialist to run the permanent wire.

For cable troubleshooting hints, look in the Data Sheets.

Running COMCHECK When Logged In to the Network

You can run COMCHECK

- on top of IPX only
- on top of IPX and NETx
- or when logged in to the network.

If you run both IPX and NETx, or log in to the network before running COMCHECK, you'll test those operating system layers too. If you can log in, though, you don't need a simple "connected/not-connected" test, and there are plenty of sophisticated network troubleshooting packages available that can tell you far more than COMCHECK can. See Chapter 5 for our thoughts on network utilities.

APPENDIX C:

List of Suppliers

A

Amphenol Corporation
(fiber optic products)
(708) 960-1010

Anixter Brothers
(cables, Twisted Pair Level Program)
(800) 323-8166

ASP Computer Products, Inc.
(printer sharing devices)
(800) 445-6190

B

Belden
(cables)
(800) 235-3361

Best Power Technology
(UPS Maker)
(800) 565-2221

Brightwork Development
(maker of Sitelock)
(201) 530-0440

C

Castelle
(LANPress print server, network fax)
(800) 359-7654

Central Point Software
(publisher of PCTools)
(503) 690-8090

Cheyenne Utilities
(NetWare Utilities, ARCserve)
(800) 243-9462

Computer System Products
(cards, cables, baluns, repeaters, etc.)
(800) 422-2537

D

Datapoint
(ARCNET, ARCNETplus)
(800) 733-1500

DiagSoft
(makers of QAPlus/fe)
(408) 438-8247

F

Frye Computer Systems, Inc.
(Frye Utilities for Networks)
(617) 247-2300

Federal Technology Company
(EXOS pocket Ethernet and Token Ring Devices)
(408) 434-2200

G

Global Engineering Documents
(Source of Standards Documents)
(800) 854-7179

H

HP
(Laser Printers)
(800) 752-0900

I

Intel Corp.
(NetPort print server, PC enhancement parts)
(800) 538-3373

J

Jensen Tools
(LAN, computer, and electronic tools)
(602) 968-6231
(800) 366-9662 (FAX)

L

The LAN Support Group, Inc.
(makers of Bindview)
(713) 621-9166

M

Microtest
(maker of LANPort and LAN test tools)
(602) 971-6464

Motorola
(Altair wireless Ethernet)
(800) 233-0877

N

NCR Corp.
(for WaveLAN wireless Ethernet cards)
(800) 225-5627

Novell
(800) NET-WARE (technical assistance)

O

Ontrack Data Recovery, Inc.
(they recover corrupted data and data from dead hard drives)
(800) 872-2599

Ontrack Computer Systems, Inc.
(maker of Disk Manager - N and Netutils hard disk utilities)
(800) 752-1333

Q

Qualitas, Inc.
(maker of 386MAX)
(301) 907-6700

R

Retix
(X.400 Software for E-MAIL)
(213) 399-2200

S

Specialized Products Company
(LAN, electronics, and telecommunications tools)
(800) 527-5018

T

Thomas-Conrad
(makers of TXD)
(512) 836-1935

Toshiba
(800) 457-7777

TouchStone Software
(makers of CheckIt)
(213) 598-7746

V

Viteq Corporation
(Uninterruptible Power Supplies)
(800) 678-4877

W

Western Digital Corp.
(video, LAN, and hard disk controller cards)
(714) 863-0102

X

Xircom
(parallel-port-to-network adapters)
(818) 878-7600

GLOSSARY

Also consult the Concepts **manual that came with your NetWare.**

Numbers

1Base5: Unshielded Twisted-Pair Ethernet; 1 Mbps speed; maximum length between workstation and concentrator of 500 meters. Not widely used.

10Base2: CheaperNet, Thinnet, or Thin Ethernet; 10 Mbps speed; maximum cable segment length of 200 meters.

10Base5: Thick Ethernet, the cable system specified by DEC and Xerox; 10 Mbps speed; maximum cable segment length 500 meters.

10Base-F: Fiber Ethernet; used between workstations and a concentrator; 10 Mbps speed; estimated distance of 2.2 kilometers.

10Base-T: Twisted-Pair Ethernet; 10 Mbps speed. Very popular.

A

Active Hub: In ARCNET, a hub that amplifies and cleans up the signal between nodes.

AIX: IBM's version of UNIX. We have the feeling this will become the standard operating system on all IBM machines, whatever their size.

AppleTalk: Apple's peer-to-peer network.

ANSI: American National Standards Institute. The U.S. is the only industrial country in which standards are set by industry, not the government. ANSI does not write standards; it ensures that standards written by recognized industry groups such as the IEEE societies are developed through a process that is fair to all those involved. It has long been recognized that standardization is good for all manufacturers in the long run.

Application Software: The program your computer uses to do work, such as word processing or a spreadsheet program.

API: Application Program Interface. A way for a program to access NetWare.

ARCNET: Datapoint Corp.'s long-standing network system. It is slow (2.5 Mbs), hardy, and relatively cheap. It is not part of the IEEE 802 standards, although it is a token bus system.

ARCNETplus: The new high speed version of ARCNET. It is expected to operate at 20 Mbs, the fastest of any LAN on copper.

Attach: When a client opens a path of communication between itself and a server, it is said to be attached to the server.

AUI cable: Attachment Unit Interface. The cable from the back of an NIC to a Media Access Controller (MAC), such as found with 10Base-T.

B

Backbone: See **trunk**.

BALUN: BALanced, UNbalanced. An impedance-matching device, which allows networks that are intended to run over coax to run over twisted-pair.

Banner: A page placed by the print spooler at the beginning of a print job so the different jobs can be separated.

BIOS: Basic Input Output System. An IBMism for firmware; that is, software written and "burned" into a ROM (Read Only Memory) chip. The BIOS ROM tells the computer how to boot, provides a Power On Self Test (POST) routine, and acts as the interface between the hardware and the software. Cards such as EGA cards and hard disk controllers also contain ROMs with accompanying instructions (firmware) to tell them what to do.

Bit: The smallest "thing" or number in a digital computer. A bit is either ON or OFF; we say it has the value 1 or 0, or TRUE or FALSE.

BNC Connector: A twist connector, used to connect coax cables.

Boot: The process the computer goes through to load the operating system. There are two kinds of boot—hard and soft. When you turn on the computer or hit the reset button, the system performs a hard (cold) boot. A hard boot forces a check of all hardware, the type of floppy drives, the presence and size of the hard disk, etc., before it loads the operating system. When you press CTRL-ALT-DEL, the computer performs a soft (warm) boot and only reloads the operating system.

Bridge: A device that connects two networks at the Link Layer, sometimes called a MAC-Layer Bridge in LANs. To confuse matters, Novell used to call their routing software a "bridge," but began to use the standard term with release of NetWare 3.11 and 2.2.

Bus: The path that control information takes from the processor to components such as the hard disk and video card. The structure of the bus determines what sort of devices may be added to a computer and how fast the computer can perform certain types of operations. See also **bus board** and **bus connector**.

Bus Board: Some manufacturers have chosen to put the bus and bus connectors on one board, and the rest of the mainboard chips on a separate processor board. Examples are Kaypro, Wells American, and new modular PCs.

Bus Connector: Expansion cards are connected to the bus through bus connectors on the mainboard. XT clones and compatibles use 8-bit bus connectors, with a single 64-contact socket for each expansion card. 286-based machines use a 16-bit bus. They use a longer, double bus connector on the mainboard for 16-bit cards. Most 286/AT clones also provide a couple of the XT-style, short, 8-bit connectors for older cards that won't physically fit into 16-bit slots. 386 machines have the same bus connectors as 286/AT clones, though they may also have a special proprietary bus connector for their own custom memory expansion card.

Byte: Eight bits, the smallest unit of data moved about in a computer.

C

CCITT: Consultative Committee International for Telegraph and Telephone (translation from the French); an international standards body. Technically, it does not produce standards, but recommendations. It was started to ensure interoperability between international telegraph and telephone exchanges. You've seen its recommendations in such things as V.32 modems and the WAN X.25 protocol.

Chip: The name for a integrated circuit. Chips are silicon wafers with circuits photo-etched in layers into the silicon surface.

CMOS: Complementary Metal Oxide Semiconductor (CMOS) chips require very little electricity, so they are used to store information with battery backup.

Client-Server Architecture: Method of organizing interconnected computers in which a client process or device makes a request of another application or device for services, such as a copy of a file or printing services.

Co-processor: A chip that performs a function in parallel with the processor. It has no responsibility for control of the machine. The usual example is the x87 (8087, 80287, etc.) math co-processor that handles floating-point calculations for the microprocessor.

COMCHECK: Novell utility provided with NetWare that tests the network card and cable. Use COMCHECK if you can't log in to the network from a particular station and you're wondering if the card and cable are minimally functional.

Communications Server: A device designed to provide communications services to network users. Most used as a pool of modems for dialing in and out of the network.

Connection Number: A number assigned to a process when it logs into a NetWare server. Each time you log in, your connection number may be different.

Conventional Memory: The 640 Kb of PC memory also known as DOS memory.

CSA: Canadian Standards Authority; much more than the Canadian equivalent of ANSI—it has the force of law. Most of its standards are developed by ANSI, with which it has a close relationship.

Crash: An abrupt, abnormal end to a process, whether caused by hardware or software failure. When people say "the hard disk crashed," they may mean anything from a physical head-to-platter collision to garbage data caused by a power fluctuation. In the first case, all data is lost, though professional data recovery services may be able to rebuild the disk and recover some or all of your data. In the second case, VREPAIR, BINDFIX, or other hard disk utilities reviewed in Chapter 5 will probably take care of things. When network people say "the system crashed," they mean the file server and/or the cabling system malfunctioned, terminating network activity.

Crosstalk: Interference on one set of wires from another. Overhearing another conversation during your phone call is an example of crosstalk.

CSMA/CD: Carrier Sense Multiple Access with Collision Detect. The protocol used on Ethernet to determine if a node can talk now or not. Basically, the node listens to the wire and if it hears nothing, proceeds to send. If a node notices a collision or some other garbage on the wire, it sends out a short burst of noise to alert the other stations. The sending station detects this and re-sends after a random interval.

CPU: Central Processing Unit. In micro-computers, the chip that executes instructions and manipulates information. Also called the processor or the microprocessor.

D

DS0: A slot in a T1, DS1, or E1 line. Depending on the signalling used, has a speed of 64 KB or 56 KB. Fractional T1 is made up of DS0 units.

DS1: Digital Signal 1, the same thing as a T1 line.

Datagram: A message composed of one packet; independent of all preceding and following packets.

Data Separation Circuit: The circuit in the path between the controller and the heads on the hard disk. It encodes the data so it may be consistently read back from the media surface. See also **encoding scheme**.

Device Driver: An extension of the BIOS, a device driver allows DOS to access specific hardware in a hardware-blind fashion. DOS doesn't need to know about the hardware details in a mouse, for example. Instead, the mouse device driver is located at interrupt 33, and DOS just interrupts at hex 33 to access this mouse- control subroutine. Installable device drivers can be loaded with a line like DEVICE = name_of_device_driver in the CONFIG.SYS file. ANSI.SYS and DRIVER.SYS are installable device drivers, as are the special drivers shipped with a mouse, scanner, or other sophisticated hardware item.

DCB: Disk Co-Processor Board. A special kind of hard disk controller that allows mirroring and can greatly speed up a server.

DIF: Data Interchange Format. A standard text file format, often used in E-mail.

Distributed Processing: WARNING! Novellspeak! Most people do not consider it "distributed processing" when you download an application and associated data files from the file server to a workstation, then run that application at the workstation, but that was Novell's original definition of "distributed processing." Modern usage defines "distributed processing" as tasks that are split between nodes on the network with each doing part of the processing. A database engine on the file server with a database front-end at the workstation is an example of distributed processing. This is not just nitpicking. Try running a sort on a huge non-distributed-processing database. All 1 million (or whatever) records will have to be downloaded from file server to workstation and sorted at the workstation. This kind of traffic can really bog down a network. An SQL front-end, by comparison, sends the sort request to the database engine. Only the records that meet the sort criteria are downloaded to the workstation.

DMA: Direct Memory Access. Data is transferred inside a computer through the DMA chip, not through the microprocessor, thus increasing the transfer speed. The hard disk controller uses DMA to read data from the hard disk and store it directly into RAM.

DMA channel: A direct pathway between the bus and the memory. It allows devices to dump data into the computer quickly.

DOWN: File server console command which closes out the server before turning it off. According to Novell "DOWN ensures data integrity by writing all cache buffers to disk, closing all files, and updating the appropriate Directory and File Allocation Tables."

DIP-Switch: Dual Inline Package switch. A little module containing several tiny switches. It is designed as a dual-inline-package (two rows of little legs) so it can be mounted on a circuit board exactly like a chip.

DOS: Disk Operating System. As PC-DOS or MS-DOS, was originally written by Microsoft at the request of IBM in 1979. Since that time, many features from Xenix have been added (like directories, for example). It is an extension of the BIOS ROM, and allows simple access to peripherals by a higher (hardware-blind) program, such as COMMAND.COM. See *Inside The IBM PC* by Peter Norton (Brady Books, 1982, and often thereafter) for all the gory details.

E

E1: The European version of T1, with a band-width of 2.048 Mbs and the ability to carry 30 simultaneous conversations. It is offered in the U.S. by several companies.

EMS: Expanded Memory System. Also known as LIM (Lotus/Intel/Microsoft, for the vendors that defined the standard) and as bank-switched memory. See **expanded memory** in this glossary for a complete definition.

Encoding Scheme: Used to process data before it is stored on floppy diskettes, hard disks, tape, or other media. The encoding scheme massages "raw" data and turns it into a stream of signals designed to make error detection easier. Encoding schemes are also used to compress data.

ESDI: Enhanced Small Device Interface. Interface for hard drives in which the data separation circuit is in the hard drive. (The cabling scheme is the same as the ST412/ST506 interface, where the data separation circuits are on the hard drive controller). ESDI allows the manufacturer of the hard drive to use any encoding scheme they wish, so the manufacturer can pack more data onto the physical drive surface.

EISA: Extended Industry Standard Architecture. Extensions to the standard 16-bit AT bus to allow 32-bit transfers. This bus is one of the alternatives to IBM's MCA bus (used in the PS/2 line).

Expanded Memory: Also known as LIM, EMS, or bank-switched memory. This is a memory management scheme designed to get around the 1 MB memory barrier in 8088 CPU chips. EMS exploits a window of available address space between 640 KB and the 1 MB barrier. Banks of memory are switched in and out of the 16 KB window as needed, providing effective access to as much as 32 MB of additional memory. Many application programs have been written to utilize LIM to store data or to store programs until they are needed. Used by NetWare's EMSNETx.COM.

Extended Memory: The memory in an 80286 or 80386 machine with an address above 1 MB. This memory cannot be used by DOS (4.X or below) for anything other than a RAMDISK or print spooler. However, it can be used under DOS by some programs that throw the 286 or 386 CPU chip into protected mode, where it can take advantage of this memory. Microsoft HIMEM.SYS and Lotus 3.0 are examples.

External Bridge: A bridge or router external to the file server(s) running router software built with a special NetWare utility.

F

Format (high-level): The process of preparing the media (disk or tape) for addressing by DOS. DOS checks the media for defects and creates certain tables. These tables allow DOS to find the stored data.

Format (low-level): Process of placing marks on the media so data stored on the media can be found again.

File Server: Computer running the network operating system. It communicates packets of data to other devices on the LAN workstations, other file servers, print servers, communications servers, bridges, routers, brouters, and gateways. It usually provides mass storage for the network.

File Handles: DOS uses file handles to communicate with files on the disks. The FILES= command in CONFIG.SYS allocates the maximum number of files that can be opened on a disk. The number of file handles is set in the CONFIG.SYS file on the workstation boot disk.

Frame: Unit of data or supervisory information at the Data Link Layer. Ethernet and Token Ring speak in frames. Frames are the envelopes for packets.

FT1: Fractional T1. See **T1**, **leased line**, **E1**, **DS0** and **DS1**.

Functionality: Network Guy jargon, usually used to mean "it actually works." Sample usage: "Our product provides TCP/IP functionality on a NetWare network."

G

Gateway: A device that allows one type of network to talk to a different type of network.

Generate: In software, the process of uniquely combining a number of distinct elements to produce the piece of software that you individually require.

I

IDE: A type of hard disk controller where all but the most basic I/O and address selection reside in the drive. Currently very popular.

IEEE: Institute of Electrical and Electronic Engineers. Various societies of the IEEE are responsible for developing industry standards that are subsequently approved by ANSI and ISO.

IEEE 802: Committee responsible for the development of LAN standards.

IEEE 802.3: Ethernet.

IEEE 802.4: Token Bus (not ARCNET).

IEEE 802.5: Token Ring.

IEEE 802.6: Metropolitan Area Network (MAN).

Internal Bridge: Bridge inside the file server.

IP Tunnel: Novell program that allows IPX packets to be transmitted over a TCP/IP network.

IPX: Internet Packet Exchange, Novell's peer-to-peer communications protocol. This is a proprietary protocol, but Novell has such a high percentage of the network installed base that IPX has become a de facto standard. IPX is a NetWare datagram delivery service that creates, maintains, and ends connections between network devices, addressing and sending data packets out, receiving incoming data and routing it to the operating system. IPX is a child of XNS or the ordinal Ethernet LAN.

IBM clone: A computer that is functionally the same as an IBM PC, XT, or AT. Clone and compatible mean the same thing since the Phoenix and ERSO BIOSs came on the market. Some earlier IBM-compatible machines, such as the Sanyo, were unable to run standard software without modification.

iAPX86: Intel Advanced Processor. The name Intel uses for the 80x86 family of microprocessors and support devices. Examples include LAPX 86 (8086), LAPX 286 (80286), LAPX 386 (80386), and LAPX 486 (80486).

I/O, Input/Output: Process by which the computer communicates with the external world. Input comes from keyboards, mice, scanners, modems, digital tablets. Output goes to printers, monitors, modems, etc. The term I/O is very context dependent. For example, data that is output from a program may become input for another program.

Interleave: Data is loaded onto the hard disk one sector at a time, but not necessarily in contiguous sectors. An interleave of two uses every other sector. An interleave of three uses one sector, then skips two, then loads one, skips two, etc. Slow CPUs require higher interleave numbers if they are to successfully read a hard disk. Spinrite hard disk diagnostics will find your computer's ideal interleave number and set up the hard disk for maximum access speed.

Interrupt: There are three levels of interrupts. 1) Hardware interrupts break in on the CPU's internal meditations and ask for attention from the CPU. 2) NMI (NonMaskable Interrupts) demand attention right now. The CPU must suspend operations for an NMI. Most hardware interrupts are maskable, though; they are mediated by an interrupt controller chip. The interrupt controller chip queues up the interrupts and asks the CPU to service each one in its order of priority. 3) Software interrupts are a jump to a subroutine. The subroutine locations and the interrupt numbers assigned to each subroutine are stored in the Interrupt Vector Table.

Interrupt Vector Table: A table of 256 interrupts, located in the first K of memory, which contains the subroutine address assigned to each interrupt.

ISA: Industry Standard Architecture. The good old XT/AT bus.

ISO: International Standards Organization, the body composed of the many national standards bodies. It is represented by the ANSI for the U.S., and CSA for Canada.

K

Kernel: Core of an operating system.

K: Kilo, as in 1000. In computers, K means 1024.

L

Laser Printer: Essentially a Xerox™ machine which makes copies based on electronic signals from the computer, not on reflected light patterns from a paper original.

Leased Line: A telephone wire leased from a phone company that services only two points. T1, FT1, and E1 are examples.

LIM: Lotus-Intel-Microsoft (for the vendors who developed the standard). A technique to expand the amount of memory the computer can use for data. This method only works with special LIM or EMS cards and programs designed to use this memory. See **expanded memory**.

Logic: Name for the internal parts of the computer that perform functions defined by the rules of logic, as in philosophy.

M

Mainframe: Computer able to handle thousands of users at the same time with databases that are in the trillion bytes range. Prices start in the millions of dollars.

Media: Name for the actual channel of communication. Floppy disks and hard disks are magnetic media; CD/ROM is optical media.

Mega: Computer engineering term for a multiple of 1,048,576; casually used to mean a million. Also abbreviated as M (as in MB, megabyte).

Memory: That part of the computer that remembers things. Unlike human memory, it can not remember any context or any emotion. It can only remember a past state. See also **expanded memory**, **extended memory**, **nostalgia**, **RAM**, **ROM** and **system memory**.

MFM: Modified Frequency Modulation. One of many possible encoding schemes. MFM uses clock bits interspersed with the data. The ST412/ST506 standard for MFM was the most common hard disk controller encoding scheme for years. See also **RLL**, **ESDI** and **SCSI**, all competing hard disk controller designs.

Micro-computer: So-called because it is smaller than a mini-computer, a computer on a chip (although some mini-computers now are not much more than a computer on a chip). It can support a handful of users, depending on the operating system. Prices start at $500 or so.

Micro-controller: A microprocessor that is used in the control of a specific operation. The microprocessor in your microwave, your keyboard or your car engine is a micro-controller. Intel also calls micro-controllers "imbedded controllers."

Microprocessor: The part of the computer that processes. In micros, the chip that actually executes instructions and manipulates information. Also called the CPU (Central Processing Unit) or the processor.

Mini-computer: A computer smaller than a mainframe in both power and cost. These computers tend to support under a hundred users and cost several hundred thousand dollars.

MCA: Micro Channel Architecture. The name of the bus in the IBM PS/2 Model 50s and up. This bus is supposed to allow multi-processors. On any bus only one processor at a time can have control, but the MCA design allows any one of the processors in the machine to be in control. By comparison, ISA allows only the CPU to have control of the computer; all other processors are slaves to the CPU. See **PS/2**.

Multi-user: An operating system that allows many users doing different tasks to run on the same computer. Not so long ago, this was what was meant by operating system, since computers cost so much that every instant of processor time had to be used to justify the expense. Example: UNIX/XENIX.

Multi-tasking: An operating system that is able to do multiple jobs simultaneously.

N

NETGEN: The program that generates NetWare from the many possible elements into the complete operating system you need.

NetWare 286: Novell NetWare for a 286 computer. This software tends to have 2.X version numbers.

NetWare 386: Novell NetWare for a 386 computer. This software has 3.X version numbers.

NetWare Shell: The shell program running on your workstation. It is NETX.COM, NETX.COM, XMSNETX.COM OR EMSNETX.COM.

Network Address = cable address. Two separate sections of cable = two networks. Single section of cable = single network.

Network Interface Card (NIC): Card installed in the computer that talks to the network.

Network Operating System (NOS): Software that takes over a computer and turns it into a file server.

Network Resources: Shareable network services and hardware components, such as network printers, hard disks installed in the file server, a modem pool, a gateway to a mainframe computer, shared data, and application programs, or a tape backup system.

NFS: Network File System. Invented by SUN Systems and somewhat of a standard in UNIX; can be added to NetWare 3.11 as an option.

NIC: Network Interface Card.

NLM: NetWare Loadable Module. Add-on program for Novell 3.X that adds feature(s) to the network.

Node: Location where something is physically connected to the network. Servers, workstations, and special devices are all nodes on a network.

Numeric Co-processor: A special chip (8087, 80287, and 80387) designed to do rapid floating point calculations, logarithms, and trigonometry.

O

OSI: Open System Interface. A model for how telecommunications software should operate to provide standardization and ease of interoperability. See Chapter 7, *The Seven-Layer OSI Network Model*.

Operating System: Allows the computer to load programs and which controls the screen, the drives and other devices. The more the computer must do, the more complex the operating system.

P

Packet: Contents of a message between one Network Layer entity and another.

Packet Burst: A NetWare trick to improve performance over a leased line or phone line link. It works by increasing the packet window size from 7 to 127.

Partition (hard disk partition): A hard disk can be divided into distinct sections. The new versions of NetWare require a DOS partition and then a NetWare partition. The DOS partition is created with FDISK.

Passive Hub: In ARCNET, a simple signal splitter.

PC: Personal Computer, a term coined by *Byte Magazine* some 15 years ago, and adopted by IBM.

Peer-to-Peer Network: Network in which any node can request services from any other node. PC LAN, LANTASTIC, and NetWare Lite are examples of peer-to-peer LANs.

Print Server: Device/process that controls printers. In NetWare there are four types: 1) A print server running on the file server. 2) A print server running on a workstation that only handles printers. 3) A print server that runs on a workstation that is also being used for other purposes. 4) A "black box" such as LANport or a board in a laser printer.

Protocol: The rules for communications. The rules governing how one computer talks to another are telecommunications protocols or protocols for short.

Paged Memory: See **LIM** and **expanded memory**.

Processor: The part of the computer that executes instructions and manipulates information. In micros, this is a single chip. It is also called the CPU (Central Processing Unit) or the microprocessor. XT-compatible microcomputers are equipped with 8088 or 8086 microprocessors. AT-compatible computers use the 80286 microprocessor. 386 computers are built around the 80386 microprocessor. See **iAPX86**.

POST: Power On Self Test. The BIOS ROM contains a series of hardware test instructions (POST) that runs each time the computer is turned on.

Protected Mode: The mode in which a 80286 or 80386 processor executes instructions that are extensions to the original set of 8086 instructions. 80286 and 80386 chips are capable of operating either in real mode, where they are limited to the 8086 instruction set, or in protected mode.

PS/2: Personal System 2. (The PC, PC Jr., PC XT and PC AT were Personal System 1.) This 1987 IBM family of microcomputers incorporates a patented bus called MCA. We classic-bus partisans feel IBM designed this line to thwart cloning. See **MCA**.

R

Resources: See **network resources**.

Remote Printer: Printer attached to a standard work station shared with the rest of the network. Not a good idea, unless the work station is rarely and lightly used, since the remote printer software uses up RAM that applications need to perform acceptably.

RAM: Random Access Memory. Any part of this memory can be used by the microprocessor. Each storage location in RAM has a unique address, and each address can be either written to, or read, by the processor. System memory, maximum 640 Kilobytes, is the area DOS uses to manipulate programs. Expanded or extended memory (see these two terms in the glossary) are also RAM. When people are using the term RAM casually, as in "How much RAM does your computer have?", they are usually talking about the system memory plus expanded and extended memory. See also **ROM** (Read Only Memory).

Real Mode: 80286 microprocessors can operate in two modes—real mode and protected mode. 80386 and 386/SX microprocessors also have a virtual mode, one where the 386 can masquerade as multiple 8088 machines. In real mode these microprocessors pretend to be a very fast 8086 or 8088. This is the mode these processors operate under when running DOS, i.e., for most of the programs you will run.

RLL: Run Length Limited. This is a method of encoding data on hard disk surfaces. It is similar to MFM, but does not require clock bits, so it can record more data in the same space. Instead of clock bits, it uses a rule about the number of consecutive zeroes that are written in any data stream. The method was developed by IBM some 15 years ago for mainframe use. It is as reliable as MFM for recording data; however, the recording surface must be very good. If the hard disk is not RLL-certified by the manufacturer of the drive, don't use an RLL controller on the drive. See also **MFM**, **ESDI** and **SCSI**.

ROM: Read Only Memory. Recorded once, at the factory, ROM is the ideal way to hold instructions that should never change, such as the instructions your computer requires to access the disk drive. See also **RAM** (Random Access Memory) and **BIOS** (Basic Input Output System).

Router: Device used to route packets. It allows connection of several smaller networks into one efficient one.

S

Server: A special-purpose computer on a network which provides the other workstations with file storage service, printing services, or communications services. See also **file server**, **print server**, and **communications server**.

Shell: Program that allows your computer to talk with a file server. It intercepts DOS interrupts and translates them into Network Core Protocols (NCP), or NetWare-speak equivalents.

SHGEN: The NetWare program that generates the IPX you need for the network card in your machine.

SNA: Systems Network Architecture, IBM standards for mainframe communications. Gateways to IBM mainframes follow SNA protocols.

SNMP: Simple Network Management Protocol. Intended as a way to manage INTERNET, and therefore something of a LAN management standard. For it to work, bridges, routers, servers, hubs, and concentrators must all be SNMP aware. NetWare 3.11 is SNMP aware.

SPX: Novell's Sequence Packet Exchange. Used in NetWare version 2.1 and above. A "Return receipt requested" service to guarantee packet delivery.

SCSI (Small Computer Systems Interface): An industry standard 8-bit intelligent interface to exchange data. The standard covers hard drives and tape drives. A SCSI controller can support up to eight devices. The interface allows drive manufacturers to use any encoding scheme they choose. SCSI is not supported in a standard way by the BIOS in ATs, posing interesting installation problems at times.

Seek Time: The length of time it takes for a hard disk head to find a track; expressed in milliseconds (ms). Average seek time is how long it will take to find a track, on average. Though fast seek times are often touted as an indication of a fast hard disk, seek time alone is rather useless as an expression of hard disk speed. Transfer rate is more meaningful.

Settle Time: How long it takes for the heads to settle down to the process of reading the hard disk once the specified track is found.

Setup: A program used to store hardware information in the CMOS chip of a 286 or a 386 clone.

Single-user: An operating system that allows only one user to use the computer at a time. See also **multi-user** and **UNIX**.

Single-user, Single Task: A version of single user that allows only one user at a time to do one task at a time. DOS is an example.

Single-user, Multi-task: A version of single user that allows only one user to do multiple tasks simultaneously. Examples: OS/2, Windows 386, DesqView 386, and VM 386.

Stack: A scratch pad for the microprocessor. When the microprocessor is interrupted in the middle of a task by a more urgent task, it save notes to itself about the contents of registers, etc. These notes are essential if the microprocessor is to resume the first task where it left off.

Star: Network topology in which nodes are wired to a central place (hub or concentrator).

State: Condition, as in ON-OFF, HIGH-LOW, or ZERO-ONE. In computers this means the particular way all the memory locations, registers and logic gates are set, e.g., "wait state." State is also used casually to indicate the particular condition and status of the computer.

Spooler: Term for placing a print job in a file until the printer can get to it. The program that does this is called the spooler or print spooler.

ST412/ST506: The names of the original hard drives in micros. The drives are no longer made, but the interface Seagate developed for them is still used. This interface is used on standard XT and AT drives and controllers. See also **MFM** and **RLL**.

Switch 56KB: Service offered by some phone companies as a way to make an all-digital phone call.

System Console: The display and keyboard from which the file server is controlled.

System Memory: The memory in the computer that DOS (or the chosen operating system) can use to store information and execute programs. On most DOS computers, a maximum of 640 Kb.

T

T1: 1.544 Mbps lines designed to carry 24 simultaneous phone conversations. It is commonly leased from a service provider.

TCP/IP: Transport Control Protocol/Internet Protocol; the basis for the largest communications network in the world, INTERNET. Because most of INTERNET's nodes run UNIX, TCP/IP is strongly associated with UNIX. It is generally also used as a generic name for a family of protocols.

ThickNet: 10Base5 (Ethernet on thick coax cable).

Throughput: The real speed that data is transmitted over a wire. Generally there is some overhead associated with sending data and ensuring that it arrived safely. This overhead can be as high as 25 percent of the bits on the wire.

ThinNet: 10Base2 (Ethernet on thin coax cable).

Token: An electronic message that is passed from station to station. The station with the token has the right to transmit on the network wire. This station must pass the token along to the next station after broadcasting for a maximum time. See also **Token Ring**, **ARCNET**, **ARCNETplus**, and **Token Bus**.

Token Bus: Network topology in which all the stations can be placed on the same line, excluding hubs, and a token is used to give permission to send on the network. Examples are Token Ring, Token Bus, ARCNET, and ARCNETplus.

Token Ring: Network topology in which the nodes are arranged in a ring. Invented by IBM; some say it is over-engineered.

Topology: The way the nodes in a network are connected. Networks have two different topologies: The one the signals see and the one used to wire it. Token Ring is a ring only to the signal—from the standpoint of the wiring, it looks like a star. 10Base-T looks like a bus to the signal, but like a star to the wiring.

Third-Party Software: Software from a vendor other than the primary vendor. Frye Utilities, for example, is a third-party software for NetWare.

Transceiver: Device that sends and receives signals over a medium.

Trunk: A section of network designed to handle a great deal of traffic, connecting many sub-networks. Also called a backbone.

Task: The job (usually an application program) that the computer does. A task is not the same as a user—a task is what the computer is doing. One person can simultaneously perform multiple tasks on a single computer. See **multi-tasking**.

Transfer Rate: Amount of data, measured in bytes per second, the computer can read from the hard disk.

Track-to-Track Access Time: How long it takes for the heads of a drive to move from one track to another. This number determines much of the speed with which data is read from the drive.

TSR (Terminate and Stay Resident): A program that pops back into use when a hotkey sequence is pressed. Sidekick is an example. TSRs sometimes present problems when they clash with each other, or with programs loaded subsequent to them, and cause symptoms that seem to be hardware-related.

Twisted-Pair: Wiring arranged in pairs twisted around one another to reduce interference.

U

UNIX: An operating system developed by AT&T in the early 1970s to run its computerized phone switching system on PDP-11s. This operating system is known for low overhead with easy connecting of different tasks. Unlike DOS, UNIX is a true multi-user, multi-tasking system.

V

VAP (Value Added Process): Program running on a 2.X NetWare server that allows additional features to be added. VAPs can also be run on bridges in both 2.X and 3.X NetWare versions.

Video RAM or Video Memory: Memory on the video card.

Virtual Mode: 80386 and 386/SX mode in which the machine pretends to be multiple 8086/8s. This is the mode these processors operate in under Windows 386.

W

WAN: Wide Area Network.

Window Size: When a packet or frame is sent out and an acknowledgement of its being received is required, a limit is placed by the sender on the number of packets or frames it will send before it refuses to send any more until an acknowledgement is received. Generally, the window size is 7. For long distances and/or transmission over a reliable medium, the window size is increased greatly, resulting in an increase in transmission throughput.

Workstation: The user's computer.

Word: The smallest unit of data the processor can do anything with. For the 8088, a word is one byte. For the 8086, 80186, 80286, and 386/SX, a word is 2 bytes. For the 80386, a word is 4 bytes.

WSGEN: Workstation Generation, a program in Novell NetWare 2.2 that generates IPX.COM, etc. It is the equivalent of NetWare 3.x SHGEN.

Write Precompensation: As the head on a hard disk starts to write on the smallest inner tracks, data errors can occur if the data is recorded exactly as it was on the large outer tracks. Write precompensation—subtle timing changes as the data is recorded—provides clean, clear data storage even on the innermost tracks.

X

Xenix: A version of UNIX developed for microcomputers. Slowly being replaced by UNIX as the micro-computers of today develop the power of mini-computers of 10 years ago.

XMS driver: Driver that allows access to extended memory, such as HIMEM.SYS. An XMS version 2.0 driver is required to run XMSNETx.COM.

XMSNETx.COM: Version of NET intended to be used with an XMS driver such as HIMEM.SYS. Use this version with Windows.

XNS: Xerox Network System. The first network based on Ethernet, developed by Xerox PARC, the same group that gave us graphical user interfaces and the mouse.

INDEX

Numbers

10Base2 *see* Ethernet, thin coax cable
10Base5 *see* Ethernet, thick coax cable
10Base-T *see* Ethernet, twisted-pair cable
15-pin AUI (DIX) *see* AUI
16-bit cards 112
258A AT&T *see* AT&T 258A
286/AT *see* ISA bus
3270 card (or 3270 gateway) 54, 159-60*fig*
386/AT *see* ISA bus
386Max 55, 60, 203
3COM 85, 114, 125
  idiosyncracies of 115
48-bit universal address format
486/AT *see* ISA bus
8-bit cards 112*fig*
802 specification *see* IEEE LAN specification
8228 *see* MAU; Token Ring, MAU
9-pin *see* DB-9

A

Altair 145, 202
Anixter Brothers *see* Twisted-pair, classifications
ANSI 109, 205
APPL, APPS *see* Directories, applications
Appletalk 59
Application Layer (Layer 7) 150*tbl*
  definitions of 49
  see OSI network layers
ARCNET 206
  access protocol (or scheme) 108-9
  advantages of 137
  ARCNETplus 206
  cabling overview 107-8
  choosing 23-24
  coax cable 118*tbl*, 133, 135*fig*, 136*fig*
    troubleshooting 139-40
  disconnecting from network 116-17
  fiber optic cable 133
    specifications of 137
  Fiber Optic Link 144
  how it works 108-9
  hubs 135*fig*, 136*fig*
    troubleshooting 140
  installing 136-39
  maker of 202

(A continued)
mixing cables 133
Network Interface Card 134*fig*, 135
bad 112
ARCNETplus 137
and node addresses 115, 135
and OSI network layers 51*fig*
speed of 115-16
topology, star bus 108, 133, 136*fig*
troubleshooting 139-40
twisted-pair cable 133, 135*fig*, 136*fig*
specifications of 137
troubleshooting 139-40
ARCServe 37, 100
ASQ utility 58
AT bus *see* ISA bus
AT&T 258A twisted-pair cable 131*fig*
AT&T Easylink 72
ATTACH 30, 80
AUI (DIX) connector with slidelock 103*fig*, 105*fig*, 126*fig*, 151
definition of 206
AUTOEXEC.BAT
and LOGIN error loop 30
and MAP 43
AUTOEXEC.NCF
in authors' test LAN 80*fig*
function 90
and IPX parameters 80
and SPOOL 68

B

Backup 27-28, 38
comparing types of 28, 37
and MAIL directory 28, 86
and NetWare bindery 37
see ARCServe; CPBackup; NBACKUP; Palindrome's Network Archivist; Tape backup; WORM drives
Balun 142*fig*, 160*fig*
definition of 206
BIND 80
Bindery 37, 75, 79
BINDFIX 77, 79
BNC connector 103*fig*, 105*fig*, 118*tbl*, 121, 134*fig*, 135, 151, 152*fig*
BRGEN 155
Bridge 51-53
definition of 51, 206
MAC-Layer 150*tbl*, 153*fig*
definition of 50, 153
choosing 51
source-routing 52, 154
spanning tree 154
NetWare "bridge" *see* Router
remote 53, 150*tbl*
see Repeater; Router
BROADCAST 28
BTRIEVE 75
Bulletin boards *see* NetWire
Bus topologies *see* ARCNET; Ethernet; Token Ring; Topology

C

Cable
link segments 121
outdoor-rated 236
plenum-grade 119
topologies 107
troubleshooting 79-80
see Coax cable; Ethernet; Fiber optic cable; PBX; Token Ring; Twisted-pair cable; Type 1, 2, 3, 6, 9 cable
CAD 112
CAPTURE 14-15, 64-65, 97, 99
definition of 68
and Time Out variable 68
Card
see 3270 card; Network Interface Card; Uninterruptible Power Supply, monitor card
Carrier Sense Multiple Access with Collision Detect *see* CSMA/CD
CASTOFF 28
CCITT 71, 207
Centronics 65,66
Cheapernet *see* Ethernet, thin coax cable
CheckIt 58, 77, 82, 109, 113, 114
maker of 203
CHKVOL 43
Classes 25, 31-32
Coax cable 104

(C *continued*)
and electromagnetic interference 119
how it works 119
IEEE specification for 117
installing, general principles 119-20
terminators for 119
types of 107-8
see ARCNET; Ethernet; Token Ring
COM ports 113
COMCHECK 79, 110, 111, 122, 130, 139, 156, 199-200, 207
COMMAND.COM "Bad" error message 29
Communications server 160-62, 207
see WNIM+
COMPSURF 87, 89
compared to Disk Manager-N 81
CompuServe 32
see NetWire
COMSPEC environment variable 29
Concentrators *see* Hubs
Configuration 35-36
important in installations 57
utilities for 58
see LAN; SYSCON
Connectors *see* AUI; BNC; Centronics; DB-9; RJ-11; RJ-45; RS-232; RS-422; ST; T connectors; Twisted-pair, telephone-style
CPBackup 37
preferred version 101
Crosstalk 207
CSMA/CD 108, 207

D

DAT *see* Tape backup units
Databases 116
network 58
see Bindery, Dbase, Paradox
Data Link (or Datalink) Layer *see* Link Layer
Date recovery
see BINDFIX; Ontrack service; SALVAGE
DB-9 connector 95, 106*fig*, 142
DB-15 connector *see* AUI
Dbase 58, 112
Dealers, Novell 25
DECnet 159
Diagnostic utilities 37-38
see CHECKIT; COMCHECK; Frye Utilities; LAN Directory; LANSight; Monitrix; NetWare Management; NetWare Early Warning System; PCTools; QAPlus/fe; TXD
DIP-switches 113, 208
Directories
and applications (programs) 29
DOS 29
and DOS versions 29
LOGIN 86
MAIL 28, 86
and print queues 65, 68
PUBLIC 29, 86
structure 28-29
SYSTEM 86, 87
in test LAN 29
see FILER; LISTDIR; NDIR; RENDIR
Disk Manager-N 81, 89, 203
compared to Disk Manager-N 81
see Ontrack
Diskless workstation *see* Workstation
DIX connector *see* AUI
DMA channel 114
DOS 208
and NetWare 2.x 76
versions *see* Directories
see AUTOEXEC.BAT; COMMAND.COM; COMSPEC
DOWN 77, 208
DR DOS 59

E

E-1 159, 208
EIA/TIA standards *see* Twisted-pair cable
EISA bus 112
Electromagnetic interference 119, 144
strong fields 121
E-Mail 71-72
see MHS, CCITT
EMSNETx 59, 86
see NETx
Error messages 41
Ethernet
access protocol 108
addresses 115
bridge, spanning tree 52

(*E continued*)
cabling overview 107-8
connections to:
ARCNET LANs 54
other Ethernet LANs 51, 52
IBM mainframes 54
parallel ports 116*fig*
Token Ring LANs 52
hub 26
link segments 52
mixed cabling 120
Network Interface Card 58, 103*fig*, 104*fig*, 112*fig*, 118*fig*
bad 112
installing 10*figs*
troubleshooting
reducing traffic on 156
and OSI network layers 50, 51*fig*
thick coax cable (10Base5) 26, 103*fig*, 104, 115, 118*tbl*, 123*fig*
definition of 205
drop cable 118*tbl*
how it works 119
IEEE specification for (IEEE 802.3) 117, 124-25
installing 123-24
troubleshooting 125
thin coax cable (10Base2) 12*figs*, 13*fig*, 26, 98*fig*, 103*fig*, 105*fig*, 115, 118*fig*, *tbl*), 120*fig*
definition of 205
disconnecting from node 116
how it works 119
IEEE specification for (IEEE 802.3) 117, 121-22
installing 120-21
troubleshooting 122-23
twisted-pair cable (10Base-T) 112, 115, 126*fig*
advantages of 130
definition of 205
disconnecting nodes (IEEE 802.3) 116
how it works 127*fig*
hubs 126, 151
IEEE specification for 125, 126, 128
installing 127
Silver Satin 130
simplest to set up
troubleshooting 130-32
using new or existing 127-28
see Lattisnet; Twisted-pair cable
topology, linear bus 108
transceiver 126*fig*
Expanded memory *see* Memory
ExpressNet *see* Hubs
Extended memory *see* Memory
External network adapter, *see* Network-to-parallel-port adapter

F

FBE 137
FCONSOLE 80
FDDI 144-45
Ferroresonant transformer *see* Uninterruptible Power Supply
Fiber optic cable 104, 144-45*fig*
see ARCNET; Ethernet; FDDI; FOIRL
File server, 4*fig*
286-based 75
386-based 75, 76
configuration of 35
definition of 3, 209
hard disk 77-78
making room on 30
how it works 76-77
installing 81
memory requirements, NetWare 3.x 75
non-dedicated 76, 79
Novell-certified 76
operating system 78-79, 87
with attached print server 65*fig*
runs too slowly 80, 81
security of 76, 81, 92
time to shut down 94
troubleshooting 77
UNIX NFS 88
see COMCHECK; Network Interface Card; MAP; Uninterruptible Power Supply; VREPAIR
FILER 43
FOIRL 26, 144-45, 151
how it works 132
installing, troubleshooting 133
see Ethernet
ForComment 32

(F *continued*)
Frame 209
Frye Utilities for Networks 38, 80
  see LAN Directory; NetWare Management; NetWare Early Warning System
FT-1 53, 159

G

Gateway 150*tbl*, 159
  definition of 51, 158*fig*, 209
Graphics programs 64, 112, 116
Grounding cap 13*fig*
GUEST, and temporary users 31

H

HELP, NetWare online 41, 197-98
Help *see* Classes; Novell
HIMEM.SYS 61, 84
How it works
  see software and hardware entries
Hubs 107
  active 205
  and disconnecting nodes 116-17
  passive 212
  VolksNet 126*fig*, 127*fig*
  see ARCNET; Ethernet; Token Ring

I

IBM 8228 *see* MAU; Token Ring, MAU
IEEE 109, 210
IEEE LAN specification (802.x) 52, 121-22, 124-25, 126
  and network size 120
  see Coax cable; Ethernet; Bridge, MAC-Layer; Token Ring
IEEE MAC-Layer bridge, *see* Bridge, MAC-Layer
InfraLan 145
INSTALL 30, 92
Installing
  cards and drivers 57-61
  see software and hardware entries
Internet 76, 159
Interrupts (IRQs) 113-14
  definition of 210
  and AT (ISA) bus 114
  and XT clone hard disk controllers 113
I/O address 113
IP 76, 88, 210
IPX (and IPX.COM) 58, 59, 76, 79, 86-87
  definition of 210
  parameters 80
  troubleshooting Network Interface Cards 109-111
IRL, definition of 132, 151
IRQs *see* Interrupts
ISA bus 112*fig*, 210
ISO 109

J

JetPress 67
JUMPERS 92
Jumpers *see* Network Interface Cards

L

LAN
  administration
    as a career path 17-18
    utilities for *see* Diagnostic utilities
  and configuration reports 36
  and consultants, 1 24-25
  definition of 3
  designing
    for accounting departments 21-22
    for a computer lab 24
    to link two LANs 23
    for simple printer sharing 22-23
    see LAN, good and bad
  do-it-yourself 25-26
  good and bad 19-20
  IEEE specification for 121-22, 124-25, 126
  multiple 52
  politics of 19-20
  reasons for 20
  and software 32-33
  troubleshooting, general 123
LAN Directory
  see also NetWare Management; NetWare Early Warning System

(L continued)
LAN in a CAN 116
LANPort 65, 202
LANPORT-II 161*fig*
LANPress 65, 98, 99-100, 201
LANSight 36
LAN WorkPlace 88
Laserjet Network Printer Interface Cards 67, 98
Lattisnet, compared to 10Base-T 125
Layers *see* OSI network layers
Linear bus cabling *see* Cable, topology
Link Layer (Layer 2) 52, 85, 150*tbl*, 153*fig*
  definition of 47
  see OSI network layers
LISTDIR 42
LLC (Logical Link Control) Sublayer 50, 150*tbl*
  see OSI network layers
LOAD 93
  in AUTOEXEC.BAT 30
  and RPRINTER 100
  see Directories
Local Area Network *see* LAN
Login script
  and COMSPEC 29
  and SYSCON 43
  memory use of 61
  What it does 83
Lost files *see* Data recovery; NDIR
LPT ports 113

M

MAC-Layer (or MAC sublayer) 50, 150*tbl*, 153*fig*
  see OSI network layers
MAIL *see* Directories
Manuals *see* User manuals
MAP 29-30, 42-43
  and ATTACH 30
  and AUTOEXEC.BAT 43
  and DOS CD command 43
MAU (or MSAU) 107, 115
  see Token Ring, MAU
MCA bus *see* Micro Channel Architecture bus
MCI Mail 72
Memory 211
  CMOS 207
  conventional (or DOS) 60
  expanded 59, 60-61, 209
  extended 59, 60-61, 209
  high DOS 60, 61
  in a PC 60*fig*
  RAM, ROM 213
  software memory managers 59,60
MHS (Message Handling Service) 71-72
Micro Channel Architecture (MCA) bus 112, 211
MIS departments 19
MONITOR 81, 92, 155
Monitrix 38

N

NBACKUP 28
  deficiencies of 37
NCP 88
NDIR 42
NE1000/2000 cards 79, 103*fig*
  installing 82*figs*
  see Ethernet, Network Interface Card
NET.CFG 59
NETGEN 87, 212
NetPort 65, 98*fig*, 99-100, 202
NetUtils 77, 203
  see Ontrack
NetWare 2.x (or NetWare 286) 76, 212
  and bad Network Interface Cards
  choosing 2, 22-24
  and DOS 76
  dedicated vs. non-dedicated modes 87
  installing on a new hard disk 81
  problems 78, 79
  version 2.15 87
  and VREPAIR 78
  and FCONSOLE 80
NetWare 3.x (or NetWare 386) 2, 4, 76, 212
  addresses 58
  and applications (programs) 30
  in authors' test LAN 75
  bridge 155-56
  choosing 22-24, 85

(N continued)
compared to NetWare 286
configuration options 8-9
and directory structure 28
and file servers 87
and hard disks 77, 81
HELP, online 41, 197-98
how it works 86-87
installing 89-92
jumper settings *see* Network Interface Cards
loadable modules *see* NLMs
memory requirements 75
and other NetWare servers 88
operating system 84-85
and OSI layers 87-88
router *see* Routers, NetWare
runs slowly 80-81
and security 81
shell 85
see NETx, EMSNETx, XMSNETx
SQL server 75
and TCP/IP 50*fig*
troubleshooting 78-81, 88-89
upgrading from NetWare 2.x 89
see User manuals
NetWare Early Warning System 38-39*figs*, 80
see also LAN Directory; NetWare Management
NetWare ELS 87
NetWare Lite 22
see Networks, peer-to-peer
NetWare Loadable Modules *see* NLMs
NetWare Management 38*fig*
see also LAN Directory; NetWare Early Warning System
NetWare operating system *see* NetWare 386
NetWire 32, 78-79, 89
Network Interface Cards
base memory address of 114
addresses of 115
brand new 110
cable used with 107*fig*
choosing 58
configuration options 8-9
definition of 4
diagnostic lights on 130
DIP-switches on, setting 112
and DMA channels 114
drivers for 58-61, 79-80
in file server 58
how they work 106
installing 57, 112-15
in authors' test LAN 8-9
in PS/2 30, 82
see ARCNET; Ethernet; PS/2; T5200 portable; Token Ring
jumpers, setting 9*fig*, 113-14
mixing brands 115-16
and PC 107*fig*
reconfiguration timeout setting 115
software 58-59
speed of, compared to parallel port adapters 116
troubleshooting 109-112
wireless 147
see ARCNET; Ethernet; I/O port address; Interrupt; Node address; Remote boot PROM; Token Ring
Network Layer (Layer 3) 85, 88, 150*tbl*, 155
definition of 47-49
and IPX 86
see OSI network layers
Network printing *see* Printer sharing
Networks
client-server 4, 207
distributed processing 208
documenting, need for 119
and graphics programs 64, 112, 116
peer-to-peer 4, 212
choosing 22
structure of *see* OSI network layers
see LAN; WAN
Network supervisor
and SYSCON 43
Network-to-parallel-port adapters
Ethernet 116*fig*
how it works 117
installing 10*fig*, 117
maker of 203
speed of, compared to Network Interface Card 116
troubleshooting 117
see ARCNET; Ethernet; Token Ring
NETx (and NETx.COM) 80, 84, 86-87
definition of 82

(N continued)
- how it works 87
- versions of 89
- *see* EMSNETx; XMSNETx

NEWS *see* NetWare Early Warning System
NFS 88, 212
NIC *see* Network Interface Card
NLMs 92-93, 212
- troubleshooting 78, 93

NMAGENT
- in authors' test LAN 12, 13

NPRINT 99
Node 3, 212
- address 115
- *see* Workstation

Novell 2, 25, 31
- bulletin board *see* NetWire
- certified file servers 76
- Certified Network Engineers 25
- and dealers 25
- market share 85
- software courses 25
- and technical support 25, 203
- *see* NetWare 3.x; MHS

O

ODI driver 58, 59
Ontrack 203
- data recovery service 78
- *see* Disk Manager-N; NetUtils

Open System Interface *see* OSI
Operating system 212
- *see* DOS; NetWare 3.x

"OSI-compliant" hardware 24
OSI network layers 47-54, 49*fig*, 85*fig*
- and ARCNET, Ethernet, Token Ring 50*fig*
- and SNA 54
- *see* Application, Link, Network, Physical, Presentation, Session, and Transport Layer entries

P

Palindrome's Network Archivist 28, 37, 101
Parallel port adapters *see* Network-to-parallel-port adapters
Paradox 58
Passwords 44
- during upgrade 89

PATH 29
PBX connector 127-28
PCAnywhere 162
PCONSOLE 98, 100
PCTools 28, 101, 201
- *see* CPBackup

Peer-to-peer networks *see* Networks 212
Phone connections *see* Telephone connections
Physical Layer (Layer 1) 85, 87-88, 150*tbl*, 151*fig*
- definition of 49
- *see* OSI network layers

Plenum-grade *see* Cable
Presentation Layer (layer 6) 49, 150*tbl*
- *see* OSI network layers

PRINTCON 64, 99
Printer 4*fig*
- attached to file servers 64, 65*fig*
- and graphics printing 64
- heavy-duty vs. light-duty 64
- PostScript, and banner page 67
- remote *see* Print server
- UPS requirements 97

Printer sharing
- and long jobs 64
- network vs. standalone 64
- types 65-67
- *see* PSC; RPRINTER

Print queues 64-65, 67, 97
- creating 99

Print server 41*fig*, 97*fig*
- and AUTOEXEC.BAT 99
- dedicated 65*fig*
  - *see* NetPort; LANPort; LANPress
- definition of 3, 212-13
- direct connect 62*fig*
  - *see* JetPress
- how it works 65-66, 97
- installing 98-99
- software 97-100, 114
- speed of dedicated workstation 99
- troubleshooting 100

(P continued)
- types of 65-66
- *see* Remote printer

Propagation delay *see* Network Interface Cards, reconfiguration timeout
PS/2
- installing Network Interface Card 82*fig*
- *see* Micro Channel Architecture bus

PSC 100
PSERVER 67, 98, 99, 100
- in authors' test LAN 14-15

PUBLIC *see* Directories

Q

QAPlus/fe 36, 38, 77, 82, 109, 113, 114, 156, 160
- why favored 83
- maker of 202
- and printer port 100

QEMM 61
Queues *see* Print queues

R

RCONSOLE 81, 92
Reconfiguration timeout *see* Network Interface Cards
Remote boot PROM 83, 115
Remote printer 66-67*fig*, 100, 213
- *see* RPRINTER

RENDIR 42
Repeater 150*tbl*, 151-52*figs*
- choosing 51
- definition of 51, 151
- *see* Bridge; FOIRL; Router

Resistor *see* Terminating resistor
RG-11/U 135*tbl*
RG-58 135*tbl*
- *see* Ethernet, thin coax cable

RG-59/U 135*tbl*, 136
RG-62 135*tbl*, 136
- *see* ARCNET, coax cable

RIGHTS 41
Ring cabling *see* Cable, topology
RJ-11 126
RJ-45 105*fig*, 126, 128, 131*fig*, 134*fig*, 142*fig*
Router 150*tbl*
- and ARCNET 54
- NetWare 23, 54-55, 153, 155-56
- definition 51, 53-54, 213
- and Ethernet 53-54, 156
- how it works 157-58
- installing 158
- troubleshooting 156
- *see* Bridge; Repeater

ROUTEGEN 155, 157
RPRINTER 99
- and LOGIN 100

RS-232, RS-422 153

S

SALVAGE 42
SDLC 114
SECURE CONSOLE 92
Security 31, 44, 92
- and printers 64

SERVER.EXE 76, 87, 90
SESSION 43
Session Layer (Layer 5) 150*tbl*
- definition of 49
- *see* OSI network layers

SHELL.CFG 83
- if no local printer 84
- with dedicated workstation print server 99
- with remote printer 100

SHGEN 58, 79, 92, 109, 214
Shielded twisted-pair cable *see* Twisted-pair cable
SLIST 42
SMA connector 145
SNA 159, 214
- gateways 54, 158*fig*
- and OSI 54
- *see* WAN

SNMP 54, 75, 214
Source routing 52
Spanning tree protocol (or algorithm) 52
- *see* Bridge

SPOOL 64, 65, 68, 97
Sprint 159

(S continued)
SPRINT MAIL 72
SPX 88, 99, 100, 214
SQE 126*fig*
ST connector 145*fig*
Star bus cabling *see* Cable, topology
Star ring cabling *see* Cable, topology
STARTUP.NCF 90
STP *see* Twisted-pair cable
Supervisor *see* Network supervisor
SUPERVISOR
  and multiple users 31
"Switched 56" 159, 214
SYS: 86
SYSCON 43, 89
  and passwords 44
SYSTEM *see* Directories
System administrator *see* Network supervisor

T

T-1 53, 159, 215
Tapcis 32
Tape backup units 27-28
  choosing types of 101
  DAT 37
  installing 101
T connectors 9*fig*, 12*fig*, 104*fig*, 121
  quality of 122
TCP/IP 50*fig*, 59, 75, 88
  definition of 76, 215
TDR *see* Test equipment, time domain reflectometer
Telenet 159
Telephone connections *see* FT-1, T-1, X.25
Temporary users 31
Terminiating resistor (terminator) 12*fig*, 13*fig*
Test equipment
  BNC test cap 122, 140
  coax tester 122
  makers of 202
  ohmeter 122
  outlet tester 96-97*fig*
  printer port wrap plug 100
  time domain reflectometer 121, 122, 130, 140
  twisted-pair tester 130, 131*fig*
  see Diagnostic utilities
Test LAN, authors' 7-15
  and interrupts 114
ThickNet *see* Ethernet, thick coax cable
ThinNet *see* Ethernet, thin coax cable
Thomas-Conrad, Network Interface Card 103*fig*
TIA 130
Token Ring 141*fig*, 143*fig*
  access protocol (or access scheme) 109
  addresses 58
  cable
    how it works 142
    IEEE specification (IEEE 802.5) 142-144
    installing 143-44
    overview 107-8
    troubleshooting 142-43
    twisted-pair 143*fig*
  connections 142*fig*
    to IBM mainframes 54
    to other Token Ring LANs 52
  MAU (concentrator/hub) 141*fig*
    connector 142*fig*
  Network Interface Card 106*fig*
  and OSI network layers 50, 51*fig*
  speed of 109, 141
  topology 109
Topology 215
  see ARCNET; Ethernet; Token Ring
Toshiba 5200 portable 116
  installing an Ethernet network card 10*fig*
Transport Layer (Layer 4) 150*tbl*
  definition of 49
  see OSI network layers
Troubleshooting
  and boot disks 84
  with COMCHECK 199-200
  by users 44-45
  see Diagnostic utilities; LAN Directory; NetWare 3.x; NetWare Management; NetWare Early Warning System
  see software and hardware entries
Troubleshooting Flowcharts 163-195
TSR programs 84, 162, 215
Tunneling 76

(T *continued*)
Twisted-pair cable 104
  classifications of 129
  EIA/TIA connections 128, 131
  and electromagnetic interference
  telephone-style connectors 126*fig*
  shielded 104
  Silver Satin 130
  unshielded
  USOC 131*fig*
  see ARCNET; AT&T 258A; RJ-45; Ethernet; Token Ring
TXD 38, 111, 122, 203
Tymenet 159
Type 1, 2, 3, 6, 9 cable 142-43*tbl*

U

Undelete *see* SALVAGE
Uninterruptible Power Supply 27, 94*fig*
  in authors' test LAN 10
  capacity required 97
  choosing 94
  charging routine 96
  ferroresonant transformer 95
  how it works 95
  installing 94, 96-97
  maker of 203
  monitor card 11*fig*, 95*fig*
  troubleshooting 196
  types of 95
Universal 48-bit address format *see* 48-bit universal address format
UNIX 76, 88
  see NFS
UNLOAD 93
Unshielded twisted-pair *see* Twisted-pair cable
UPS *see* Uninterruptible Power Supply
UPS STATUS 96
User groups 32, 78
User manuals, Novell 8, 32, 41, 88, 197-198
Users
  and printing 68-69
  troubleshooting 44-45
USOC *see* Twisted-pair cable
Utilities *see* Diagnostic utilities
UTP *see* Twisted-pair cable

V

VAP 216
  troubleshooting 78
  and NetWare 2.x 98
VOLINFO 68
VolksNet *see* Hubs
VREPAIR 77-78, 79
  and NetWare 2.x 78

W

Wall jack *see* RJ-45
WAN 158
  see SNA
WaveLAN 145, 147, 203
WHOAMI 42
Wide Area Network *see* WAN
Windows (Microsoft) 89, 116, 216
WinSleuth 58
Wireless networks 145-47
WNIM+ communications server 161*fig*
WordPerfect Office 72
Workstation 4*fig*, 82-84
  boot disk for 84, 86
    creating 91-92
  definition of 3, 82, 216
  diskless, with remote boot PROM 83, 86
  how it works 91
  installing 84
  I/O intensive 112
  Network Interface Cards in 82*figs*
  troubleshooting 83
  see SHGEN; WSGEN
WORM drives 37
WSGEN 58, 79, 92, 109, 216

X

X.25 53, 71-72, 159
X.400 71-72, 203
XMSNETx 59, 61, 86-87
  and XMS driver 84, 216
  and TSRs 84
  see NETx